# 5,460 MILES FROM SILICON VALLEY

# HANS PETER BECH

## 5,460 Miles from
# SILICON VALLEY

## The In-depth Case Study of What Became Microsoft's First Billion Dollar Acquisition outside the USA

The story of Brdr. Damgaard Data:
Erik and Preben Damgaard establish their
software company in 1984, embark on a strategic
partnership with IBM in 1994 (only to dissolve
it 4 years later), list their company on
the Copenhagen Stock Exchange in 1999,
merge with Navision Software in 2000 and are
eventually acquired by Microsoft in 2002.

English translation by
## Sinéad Quirke Køngerskov

5,460 Miles from Silicon Valley
The In-depth Case Study of What Became Microsoft's First Billion Dollar Acquisition outside the USA
(Original Danish title: Fra Damgaard til Microsoft)

Copyright © Hans Peter Bech

Published by:
TBK Publishing®
Leerbjerg Lod 11
DK-3400 Hilleröd
Denmark
www.tbkconsult.com

Translator: Sinéad Quirke Køngerskov
Editor: Annie Hagel
Proofing: Emma Crabtree
Layout and design: Mette Schou
Cover: Jesper Frederik Emil Hansen
Cover illustration: Extract of an advertisement from Damgaard A/S from the period 1999-2000 developed by Blue Business A/S (www.bluebusiness.com). The image of the fly in the glass is by photographer Jens Honoré (www.jenshonore.com). The text for the advertisement was: "Finally: an ERP-system that will not stop your e-business plans." The fly in the glass was supposed to represent companies with outdated ERP-systems. In the context of this book the fly in the glass is a metaphor for Damgaard Data's troublesome cooperation with IBM.

ISBN: 978-87-93116-35-1
1st edition, June 2018

To Sue, Maria and Daniel

# Indhold

## Foreword by Preben Damgaard

I have been asked quite often, over the years, whether I would be willing to contribute to a book about the experiences my brother Erik and I had while creating and developing Damgaard Data into an international IT company.

A book about Damgaard Data can hardly avoid focusing on both myself and my brother Erik, which personally I don't think is all that interesting. An attitude that I am sure is shared by my brother. I worked closely with the book's author, Hans Peter Bech, in Damgaard Data for many years and, therefore, I was positive and accommodating when he first told me about his project. And I have to admit, I was also sceptical. However, the more he elaborated on his thoughts, the more positive I became. Scepticism had now been replaced by curiosity. Hans Peter wanted to emphasise the technological, pioneering work so characteristic of the time he wanted to chronicle. Just as he wanted to share the stories of – not just the Damgaard brothers – but also the many talented, committed and witty people who helped create Damgaard Data. Colleagues and partners, many of whom are now life-long friends, and without whom Damgaard Data would never have been as successful as it was. Unlike previous inquiries about book projects, he didn't want to write a book about Preben and Erik alone. He wanted to write a book about a company. He wanted to write about Damgaard Data.

That is a story to which I am happy to contribute. Not for my own or my brother's sake, but for the many colleagues who put so much work and energy into creating something together over the years. And also because Damgaard Data was the first entrepreneurial project in which I was involved. A project that, for me, lasted almost 20 years. Since then, I have been involved in a variety of start-ups, and hopefully Hans Peter's book and the story of Damgaard Data can prevent others from making the same mistakes that we did. This biography may even inspire or motivate others to start their own business.

Thus – just like previous colleagues, partners, customers, suppliers, board members and so on – I have contributed with how I remember my time in Damgaard Data; our victories, defeats, triumphs, challenges, struggles and, not least, the funny moments.

With his impressive research, extensive fact-checking and use of both written and oral sources, Hans Peter relates his story of Damgaard Data.

Some may find the book a little nerdy, but entrepreneurship appeals to a very special kind of person. For me, personally, the book has been a trip and a look down memory lane. Hans Peter's biography has reminded me of many encounters, events and experiences that I still hold dear. In Damgaard Data, we not only learned how to develop, market and sell our software to customers throughout the Western world; we also learned about life, about the satisfaction that comes from creating something and the joy that emanates from achieving results with others. A joy I personally have felt privileged to have been involved in at such an early stage in my life.

I am grateful for all the work that Hans Peter has put into this book. His level of detail has enabled me to relive an amazing time. And it has reminded me of why I enjoy developing businesses and working with young entrepreneurs to this day.

Preben Damgaard
Holte, August 2017

## Author's foreword

The inspiration to write a book about Damgaard Data arose after a conversation with Preben Damgaard in early 2014. In connection with preparing a series of courses held on behalf of Sabanci University in Istanbul for top managers within the Turkish software industry, I wanted to use Damgaard Data as an example of how a company from a small country can achieve huge results in just a few years.

My chat with Preben took a little longer than expected as I could feel both his great desire and need to tell his story. In the weeks that followed, my thoughts continued to return to our conversation. Slowly the idea of writing Damgaard Data's biography was formed.

A biography about the company and not just a portrait of the brothers, Erik[1] and Preben Damgaard. Though, naturally, they would come to play vital roles in the book. I contacted Preben again to see if he and Erik agreed with my idea. They did, and in April 2014 we met to discuss the terms; their involvement as primary sources and access to material that they no doubt had kept from the company. They agreed with those stipulations and the work began in earnest.

As early as the first interview it became clear that the memories of what had happened so many years previously differed greatly. Some could recall in detail events which, it later turned out, they hadn't been part of. Others gave very different accounts of episodes in which they had been instrumental. It quickly became evident that successes have many fathers and mothers, while failures are largely orphans. However, as more and more details were unearthed, the questions I posed to my sources became more and more accurate – I could now relate their inconsisten-

---

1    Erik Damgaard has been somewhat portrayed in Birgitte Erhardsen's two books: *Milliardærklubben* [*The Billionaire's Club*] (Gyldendal, 2009) and *Erik Damgaard – Rigdommens pris* [*Erik Damgaard – The Price of Wealth*] (Gyldendal, 2012).

cies to the other sources. It was a tremendous help for the memories of most, but it didn't eliminate all the situations where there were completely different perceptions of what had passed. I haven't evaluated who told the "true" version. Therefore, I have chosen to refer to the different perceptions in a number of cases. It is difficult for even the best of us to remember the exact times of past events – and with good reason. Fortunately, I had Preben Damgaard's personal notebooks to support me. Moreover, internal staff papers and documents, and newspaper and journal articles covering the entire period helped to determine what took place when. Getting the chronology in place has been instrumental in determining the quality of a large number of statements from the over 100 interviews that were carried out. Many episodes often presuppose each other.

When the project started, I was not aware of the role that the competitor PC&C, who changed its name to Navision Software in 1995, actually contributed to Damgaard Data's view of themselves. Once that became clear, I felt it necessary to dive into their story, too. The two companies merged in December 2000, but they had already meant a lot to each other as early as the 1980s. Thus, this book is also a partial Navision Software biography, despite that not being the original intention.

Damgaard Data was a software company that navigated in an industry where development in the years from 1984 to 2002, which is the period covered in this book, happened at high speed. It is not possible to understand the company's history without having a clear insight into the development that was known as Electronic Data Processing (EDP) in the 1980s, and which later changed its name to Information Technology (IT). The book, therefore, contains a number of professional terms and sections in the hope that it will enable the reader to understand both the technical and industrial reality to which the company was subject. Readers already familiar with this can easily skim over such passages. At the back of the book is a glossary and an index, which the reader can turn to if any doubts regarding the definition and meaning of any professional expressions arise.

The story of Damgaard Data is an attempt at digging deep; going behind the results, illustrating the difficulties, the coincidences, the strokes of genius, the problems and what we so flippantly call the challenges. Some will certainly find the biography of Damgaard Data detailed, and some will also believe that reading it requires a technical prerequisite. But reality is detailed, and there are relationships that cannot be understood without having first comprehended their circumstances. This book about Damgaard Data is for those who would like to delve deeper and gain an understanding of what business success can look like on the inside.

It is also an account of how to create a success without stepping on other people. In my opinion, the founders of both Damgaard Data and Navision Software deserve a great deal of respect for the way in which they ran their businesses. They behaved properly. Despite being businessmen through and through and having to terminate contracts and fire employees, it was done with respect and decency. As the book shows, there were dismissals of both employees and litigation claims for compensation, but that was the exception, not the rule. I myself worked for Damgaard Data in the period from December 1997 to June 2001, when it became Damgaard, NavisionDamgaard and later Navision. I saw first-hand how the company was run. I experienced a management making great strides to behave properly and treat everyone with decency and fairness. A brief summary of my own story can be found after the epilogue.

To finish, let me emphasise that the biography of Damgaard Data is not the recipe for success. Such a recipe doesn't exist. There are certainly elements, which you can take and learn from, but even when two people cook with the same ingredients, they rarely produce the same dish.
Business success requires diligence, talent and luck. Diligence can be present from day one, but talent is relatively unknown until unforeseen challenges have to be faced. Luck is encountered along the way.
    In the case of Damgaard Data, both Erik and Preben were extremely diligent, and their first stroke of luck was Erik discovering his talent for software development so early on. And he probably wouldn't have uncovered that talent had he not taken the initiative to study in the USA.

Preben's talent for management was first discovered many years later, but it was instrumental in bringing the company into the big league. They experienced luck many times along the way, but they experienced misfortune many more times. Business luck is a function of the initiatives taken, combined with the ability to quickly bounce back from mistakes and misfortune. Once you have read the book, I think you will know what I mean.

Happy reading!

Hans Peter Bech
Hillerød, August 2017

# CHAPTER I

# AFTER MICROSOFT

## Preben leaves Microsoft

When Preben Damgaard returns from work on Friday, 20th June 2003, no one is home. He carries the presents he received at his farewell reception at Microsoft in Vedbæk, north of Copenhagen, into the kitchen and takes a deep breath. The silence in the house is almost deafening. It's a nice day, so he brews a cup of coffee, sits out on the terrace, puts his legs up on the fence and looks out over Furesø Lake. The final chapter has now definitely been closed on the story that began when he and his brother, Erik, had the idea to develop a financial management program for micro-computers in 1983. A program that was better than HERA-SOFT, which the master carpenter Helmuth Rasmussen from Gundsømagle, north of Roskilde, had had so much success with. Twenty hectic years that almost cost him his life. From the age of 20 until now, almost age 40, he has been the managing director of his and his brother's business. A myriad of memories, people and experiences are behind him, and only a vast abyss lies ahead. What is he supposed to do now? He takes a sip of coffee as he looks over at the houses on the other side of the lake. They are so far away that he cannot see any signs of life, despite there being people at home on this lovely Friday afternoon.

The twenty amazing years with Damgaard Data were primarily due to working with a lot of inspiring people, particularly his brother, Erik. To work every day with a brother you have always known, and have absolute confidence in, is a gift. They complemented each other nicely. There were, of course, disagreements, but they had a joint project and a common interest. And they respected each other's skills. But Preben is also thinking of all the other people who were just as passionate for the Damgaard project as they themselves were. They translated all the resistance, all the problems and all the regrets into what business jargon calls "challenges". That's how it is. Big solutions require big problems. Big solutions to small problems don't exist. It feels great to do the impossible and give your fellow players a high-five. For Preben, the value of life is found in being together, interacting and cooperating with other people, and he has had all this in abundance every single day for the past twenty years.

He had actually been looking forward to working for Microsoft, where he had been responsible for the marketing of all Business Solutions' products in Europe, the Middle East and Africa after his company had been acquired by the software giant. And he must have been doing something right, because after less than a year, they had offered him the responsibility of an even greater business area. It was only when his wife, Charlotte, asked him why he wanted to spend so much of his energy on a company that wasn't his own that he had actually thought about it. He'd had to admit that although the job title of "Vice President, EMEA[2] operations" sounded nice and included thousands of employees and billions in revenue on paper, it was nothing compared to being the top executive of his own business, despite it being on a smaller scale. The vice presidency didn't include a seat at Microsoft's strategic management table; his job had primarily had an internal focus. Not to mention that having a great love of PowerPoint presentations was necessary for thriving there. As were the insane number of days spent travelling. The new job he had been offered would require even more days on the road, leaving even less time for family and domestic responsibilities.

---

2    Europe, Middle East and Africa.

Upon accepting the job at Microsoft after the acquisition, he'd had to take a 50 per cent cut in salary, but that didn't matter so much when a nice little sum ending in million was deposited into his account in his holding company.

After reviewing his options with Charlotte, he decided to politely decline the new job offer and indeed any other job as an employee in a company that wasn't his own.

While taking his last sip of coffee, his thoughts drift to how privileged he has been and, of course, still is. What would have happened if Erik hadn't gone to the USA to study in 1983? If he hadn't seen the software program from HERA-SOFT immediately after his return, and if they hadn't purchased a stand at the Kontor&Data[3] exhibition at the Bella Center in 1984?

But that's all in the past now. The last shares in Navision have been sold or exchanged for shares in Microsoft. He is, in principle, unemployed. And despite not having to sign on at a job centre, he now has to figure out where he will find new content – workwise – for his life again. Invitations for positions on boards in a few listed companies are already piling up, so maybe he should take a look at them. At any rate, there's more time to spend with family, and what better way to start than with a good, long summer holiday. He'll just have to wait and see what comes along then.

## Erik leaves Microsoft

On 15th April 2004, an SAS flight takes off from Seattle-Tacoma International Airport heading for Copenhagen. In the fore of the cabin sits Erik Damgaard. Looking out of the window, he notes that the pilot is making a right turn over Mercer Island. Soon, he will be able to see Redmond, where Microsoft's headquarters are located, and where he has been endeavouring to get a key role in the development of the company's financial management software products for the past year. It has certainly not gone as hoped. Indeed, the merger with their competitor, Navision

---

3   Kontor&Data [Office&Data] at the Bella Center in Copenhagen was the largest IT fair in Denmark during the 1980s and 1990s.

Software, at the end of 2000 to which he and his brother Preben had agreed, hadn't been his dream scenario. The merger, which had undoubtedly been a major financial success, had been a disappointment for him in all other areas.

When Microsoft bought out the entire shop in May 2002, he knew the days of the Damgaard adventure were finally over. But he had hoped to be able to play a role at the top of the world's largest software company.

He had been delighted that Microsoft had quickly closed Navision's overly-ambitious Jamaica project, which, he knew, once he had become aware of it after the merger, didn't have a chance of survival. But so great was his disappointment when, after arriving at Microsoft's headquarters, he discovered that Great Plains Software, which Microsoft had purchased at the end of 2000 – and which in practice was the company that had bought Navision – had their own answer to a new financial system. He had observed the development of the system for a few months and couldn't see how it could ever get airborne. There were too many technicians and too few practitioners on the project. It would take far too long before specific applications could be identified for the technology. He tried to offer his input, but nobody would listen. When asked to design a report generator for the new product, codenamed Green, he equated it with being asked to design a bathroom for a building without yet knowing whether it was to be a single-family house or a 50-storey hotel.

He then moved on to the Magellan project, to develop a new financial system for very small businesses. He didn't feel at home here either. To have influence in Microsoft meant being a manager with responsibility for a lot of employees. That was the last thing he wanted. Maybe he should have realised that Microsoft was likely to have even more bureaucracy than Navision after the merger of Damgaard and Navision Software. At least he knew it now, so it didn't make sense to linger. Due to the way in which things had developed, he had lost his motivation. In fact, after the merger with Navision Software it had become increasingly difficult to go to the office on a daily basis and more enticing to leave early. If nothing else, the last twelve months had only confirmed what he had experienced over the last few years in Damgaard: he was not designed for large organisations. Politics and bureaucracy didn't suit his nature. Creating vast, complicated software products that required planning, coordination and involved many people didn't suit him either.

Even before the merger with Navision Software, Damgaard had grown too large for him. But Axapta was a sublime product. Had he been able to carve out a niche with a handful of skilled developers, they could undoubtedly have made a new international version of the successful Concorde C5.

That wasn't to be the case. What was he supposed to do now? He hadn't asked himself that question once during the twenty years that had passed since he had returned home from studying in the USA in 1983, having discovered that software development was one of the most fun activities in the world. It had taken him six months to develop Danmax, which he and Preben had then presented at the Kontor&Data expo in autumn 1984. It had been an instant success. And when – just two years later – he presented Concorde, in collaboration with Morten Gregersen and Jens Riis, they had nearly brought the house down. In 1991 came XAL; in 1995, Concorde C5 and in 1998, Axapta. During all those years there had always been a list of possibilities and things to do. A list that grew larger than the time he had available. The question of what he was supposed to do had always been about declining something, so he could have the time to accomplish his own ideas.

When he compared Damgaard to Microsoft, he was proud of what he had achieved working with a handful of skilled software developers. Had Damgaard been in the USA, the opportunities would have looked quite different. With half of the world's market on its doorstep, Damgaard would have been in a position to buy out Great Plains Software, not the other way around.

Since Microsoft bought Navision, their plans for the future had become clear. Plans he was convinced wouldn't amount to anything. There were too many chefs and too few cooks on the projects, but there might just be an opportunity for him among the products that Microsoft didn't want to continue in the long run? He'd have to investigate that once he'd returned home.

His thoughts are interrupted by a stewardess, passing with the drinks cart. The chat begins to flow among the family who, after a year in the USA, are also looking forward to coming home to Denmark again. The past is over and the future can easily wait a few weeks.

# CHAPTER 2

# TWO
# BROTHERS

## The Damgaard Family

The story of Damgaard Data has its seeds in Jutland in the years between World War I and World War II. Knud Damgaard, from Klinkby between Lemvig and Harboøre in northwest Jutland, was the son of a master carpenter, the third in a flock of ten children and was born on 15ᵗʰ February 1927. After taking a lower secondary school leaving exam, Knud trained as a manager with the co-op and subsequently gained a job as a mobile substitute manager. He travelled around Jutland, temping for the local managers when they were ill or suddenly had to stop working at short notice. In the evenings, Knud attended an educational programme to be a state-authorised estate agent. However, he didn't end up buying and selling houses, because in 1951 he gratefully accepted a job as a sales agent with the insurance company Fjerde Sø in Copenhagen.

Kirsten Petersen, born 25ᵗʰ January 1929, grew up in Rørkærgård in Skanderup between Kolding and Lunderskov in southern Jutland. She was the second of five siblings. After leaving school, she studied office administration and bookkeeping. In 1951, she too commenced employment with the insurance company Fjerde Sø and, therefore, moved to Copenhagen.

Knud Damgaard and Kirsten Petersen came from completely ordinary stock, as it was called back then. Their parents got by, but the children's practical involvement in the housekeeping and work was both the norm and necessary.

Knud and Kirsten grew up in a turbulent period of world history. When World War II ended in May 1945, they were 18 and 16, respectively. The war provided them with solid evidence that you have to fight for your values. And you have to fight to get by. There's no food on the table, roof over your head or clothes on your back without you yourself making an effort.

They got married in Skanderup Church, west of Kolding, on Saturday, 15th September 1956. After four years of marriage, came their first child who suffered heart failure and died a few weeks after birth. Fortunately, they got through this traumatic experience. On 15th February 1961, Erik Damgaard entered the world, and on 23rd August 1963, Preben Damgaard was born.

When the boys took their first steps, Denmark had long left the war behind. But the war had sped up technological development, and that, combined with peace, laid the foundation for an economic growth and prosperity that was to form the basis of Erik's and Preben's lives. The Cold War ensured continued development, and when the then President of the United States, John F. Kennedy, promised a manned return trip to the moon by the end of the 1960s, in a speech to Congress on 25th May 1961, it was the final spurt in an initiative that twenty years later made possible an entirely new industry.

## Solbærvænget in Bagsværd

In 1968, the Damgaard family moved into Solbærvænget 23 in Bagsværd, a lower middleclass suburb of Copenhagen. The following year, they watched the televised report of Neil Armstrong setting foot on the surface of the moon.

Erik and Preben grew up in a typical Danish middleclass home. Knud and Kirsten were hard-working people who gave their boys a bourgeois upbringing with equal portions of love, freedom, guidance and admonition. Kirsten worked part-time as a bookkeeper in Fogh & Mørup in Søborg and was able to collect the children early from kindergarten.

When Erik and Preben started school, she was always home when they had finished for the day. They performed well in school and participated in the everyday pranks of boys on an equal footing with their chums. They were actively interested in sports and were good at making friends.

Working-hard, honesty, being organised, taking responsibility and keeping your word were fundamental values in Knud and Kirsten's universe. But freedom, including personal freedom, was also a core value in the Damgaard home. When you attended school (your first priority), and were earning your own money (your second priority), you then deserved the right to decide most of what you got up to (in your own time).

## Erik Damgaard

After the 1968 summer holiday, Erik started in his first year of primary school.[4] Over the years, he developed a great interest in technology. Like so many other boys at that time, he designed, assembled and sold radios, amplifiers and speakers for stereo systems. Not only to save up some money, but because he found it fun. He had a paper round on Wednesdays. Preben, who wasn't yet old enough to have his own round, often helped him by taking "half" and Erik paid Preben ten of the 28 Danish kroner he earned for his round.

When Erik turned 15, he bought a Puch moped, which he later replaced with a Japanese Yamaha. The Yamaha was – unlike most other mopeds – factory-fitted with a fuel injector compliant with Danish legislation. Therefore, it wasn't as easy to tune as the more common brands, where you simply had to coax out the seal. And like so many other boys in the 1970s, Erik believed the moped could be optimised on a number of points. He found a simple solution for the problem: he created a new fuel injector with a larger opening. Now he could keep up with his buddies, whose Puch mopeds were able to handle about 60 km/h.

## School, money, mopeds and girls

As Erik started in secondary school in 1977, the film "Saturday Night Fever" featuring John Travolta was starring in cinemas around the world.

---

4   In Denmark formal primary school starts at age six.

A new sophistication emerged, and the music and style of the film didn't go unnoticed by Danish youth in those years.

Secondary school life had four equal focal points for Erik. He had to keep up at school, or else there'd be trouble at home on Solbærvænget. He had to put his foot down on his moped because just driving it was too boring. There were parties to go to and relationships to explore and not least, money to be earned, otherwise his interest in technology, mopeds, parties and relationships couldn't be realised. And to maintain his talent for wooing girls, Erik spent time weight-lifting in the gym. He was an extrovert, funny, had a large circle of friends and, despite his interest in technology, there was nothing nerdy about him.

The later picture of Erik as an introverted, shy person, living in his own technological-world and struggling with girls could hardly be more different. He was by no means introverted, shy or awkward. On the contrary, he was self-confident, outgoing and sometimes quite reckless.

When Erik received his student cap in 1980, marking his graduation from school, his then classmates characterised him as being a good friend, who was averagely gifted, fun and entertaining to be around. He was very interested in technology, was good with his hands and unusually good with the ladies. However, not one of his chums could have predicted in 1980 that one of the world's most gifted software developers had just left secondary school. He himself had no idea that his life would soon head in that direction.

Erik Damgaard (right) and his classmate, Bob Hansen, regularly lifted weights at the gym. The response from girls when they attended parties only confirmed that it was worth the effort. This picture was taken in 1980 with Bob's Nikon F2 camera on self-timer.

## Studying in the USA

Erik starts on the Machine Programme at Denmark's Engineering Academy, in Lyngby, after the summer holiday of 1980. During a lecture in 1982 he ends up talking to an American from Columbia, South Carolina, who is studying in Denmark. This American had met a Dane, who had been studying at his university in the USA, the previous year.

Erik gets in touch with the American's Danish friend, and after having received the basic details, he writes to the University of South Carolina, requesting additional information about studying there. He tells his classmate, Hans Christian Markvardt Pedersen, of his plans and they agree to go to the USA together for the first semester of 1983.

On 3rd January 1983, Erik and Hans Christian check in on SAS Flight SK 911 bound for New York. Their first stop is North Carolina, where Hans Christian has family. As neither of them have been in the States before, they stay there for a few days, acclimatising themselves to their new, American environment. They also buy a car so they have transportation for their stay: a white Chevrolet Monte Carlo with a V8 engine and a cylinder volume of five litres, is the vehicle of choice.

Though upon their arrival at university they have nowhere to live. They are received by a secretary who provides them with shelter in her own home for the first three days after which they find an apartment that suits their purpose and budget.

## Erik learns about computers

Instead of continuing with subjects only related to mechanical engineering, Erik takes a course in data electronics. He learns how a computer is built, how it works and how to program its basic functions. He then takes a course in high-level programming, where he gets the computer to perform various tasks like simple calculations and typing the results on a printer.

At the Danish Technical University (DTU), programming is done using punch cards, but at the University of South Carolina programming students have direct access to a mini-computer from the Digital Equipment Corporation (DEC) with associated online terminals. The entire administration of the programming course is also done on the DEC computer and Erik quickly begins to write all his assignments – even from the other courses – using electronic word processing.

## Mechanics and business studies

During "spring break", a mid-term break, the two young men drive south in the white Chevrolet Monte Carlo to experience a little more of the USA. Their road trip takes them to Florida, where they visit Fort Lauderdale, Miami, Key Largo and Key West. Back at university, Erik takes a couple of classes in mechanics as well as a course in business studies with basic business economics and organisational theory.

He is primarily fascinated by computers and programming in particular, which comes easily to him. Erik does well at university, making the Dean's Honor List, which names those students who have received the highest marks.

Their study abroad concludes formally at the end of May, but Erik and Hans Christian use the opportunity to see a bit more of the Land of Opportunity. In the white Chevrolet Monte Carlo, they drive to Pittsburgh, Pennsylvania, to visit a college mate from their time in South Carolina. He is not home, but his parents offer them food and lodgings until he appears. When he still hasn't shown up after three days, they continue on to Detroit, Illinois, to visit some other friends.

It so happens that Formula 1 motor racing is taking place on the Detroit street circuit while they are visiting, which suits the two car-mad young men. From here, they head to Toronto, Canada, where a fellow student from Denmark is also studying abroad. As usual the itinerary contains sightseeing and parties for almost a week.

At the end of June, they set course for Denmark. They plan a stop in Baltimore, where some family of Hans Christian take ownership of the car so it can be sold. Erik and Hans Christian get the train to New York and fly, full of new knowledge, new impressions and exciting experiences, back to Denmark, where they land in Kastrup airport, just as the summer holiday of 1983 is beginning.

## Back in Denmark again

After returning home, Erik shares his experiences with his parents, friends and, not least, with Preben. In September 1983, he starts back at the Engineering Academy, where he is about to complete his studies and write his dissertation.

In October 1983, he buys a small apartment in Østerbro and moves away from home. He earns money as a caretaker of a property in the neighbourhood, washing stairs and doing minor repairs and, as he is good with his hands, he finds it easy to solve problems and communicate with the skilled craftsmen when slightly bigger projects are contracted.

## Erik meets Morten Gregersen

Bob Hansen, a good friend of Erik's from secondary school, also hears about Erik's new found knowledge and enthusiasm for computers and programming. He introduces him to a friend, Morten Gregersen, who had been in a parallel class at Gladsaxe Gymnasium, but hadn't been part of the same circles as Erik.

After completing his military service, Morten trains as a datamatician and, in autumn 1982, gets a job at Havidan, which imports computers from Taiwan and resells them in Denmark with a good profit margin. There, Morten works with set-up and customer support, but he'd really like to get into software development. Morten and Erik get together and mess about with any computers and software they can get their hands on. As it's all designed and developed in the USA, the computers and software typically can't type the Danish letters "æ, ø or å" either on screen or with the printer. Erik and Morten hack into the code and correct the programs so that now they can also handle the Danish language.

## Preben Damgaard

Preben was six years-old when he started school after the summer holidays in 1970. He didn't share Erik's interest in technology; he was more into sports and making business deals. When a new law was introduced in 1972, prohibiting the sale and use of fireworks in Denmark, it wasn't received well by the nine-year-old Preben. For him, New Year's Eve was, without comparison, the biggest event of the year, wherein the rules for what you could and could not do, as well as when you were to be at home and in bed, were significantly relaxed. Fireworks and sky rockets played a central role in the games and pranks that he and his friends prepared and carried out in the days either side of New Year's Eve.

But he discovered that New Year's fireworks, which had been banned in Denmark, could be purchased on the other side of the Øresund in Sweden. In December 1973, he went on his first shopping trip to Malmö and returned home with his backpack full of fire crackers. The supplies were received with great enthusiasm among his chums at home in Bagsværd, whom immediately offered to pay a good price for a share of the goods.

In woodworking, Preben built himself a "fireworks locker" and when he went to Malmö for the second time in 1974, he was loaded up with all the empty cardboard boxes that a brave boy aged eleven could carry. The journey home through customs went smoothly, and soon the fireworks locker was bursting at the seams.

News of the sale of real New Year fireworks at Preben's on Solbærvænget quickly spread among his classmates. It wasn't long before he was sold-out and for quite a good profit. Trading in fireworks around New Year's was excellent business and, moreover, his customers were satisfied.

The shopping trip to Malmö quickly became routine. Every year, on a day in December and loaded up with shoe boxes and cigar boxes, Preben left early in the morning heading for Malmö to buy saluting fireworks and fire crackers. After making his purchases, he distributed the goods among the various shoe and cigar boxes and wrapped them up to resemble innocent Christmas presents.

He was well aware that his trips to Malmö weren't completely by the book. But there were no objections from either his own parents or those of his classmates and, thankfully, no one was injured by the not completely harmless fireworks.

The greatest risk was passing through customs, and it was very nearly about to go wrong. Preben used the tactic of placing himself in a group of people, suggesting he was just a boy, in the company of adults, who had been Christmas shopping in Malmö. And, thereby, there was little risk of him being singled out by the authorities.

When he was on his way back through customs, after the big shopping trip of December 1975, he saw, from the corner of his eye, a customs officer spot him and shout: *'You there! Come here.'*

Preben ignored the order. If he made eye contact with the customs officer, he would have to go with him. It was better to act like it was nothing. He moved closer to some adults, consciously keeping a constant pace, so as not to look like he was hurrying, but he could still feel the eyes of the officer on his neck.

Suddenly a large number of people enter the customs area and the customs officer's attention was diverted.

Phew! His tactic had worked. Even in an emergency situation.

The nice profit earned from the annual firework-trip to Sweden ensured that Preben had the best gear for his sports interests. Later, when the clothes worn and physical appearance became important, the fireworks business also funded a rather nice wardrobe. All in all, Preben could afford to buy lemonade and hot dogs whenever it suited him. But he didn't. The money didn't burn a hole in his pocket. It was better to save it for a rainy day. That was a nice feeling.

The shopping trips continued until the Danish ninth grade (UK Year 11), when an interest in other New Year's Eve activities now overshadowed the need for fireworks. Preben started distributing advertisement magazines, so he could earn his own money regularly and not work for Erik. Later, he supplemented the magazine distribution with jobs as a delivery boy for a grocer and a baker.

## Possibly suitable

Preben did well at school, but the teachers thought he showed potential for more. He had a great need to spend a lot of time in class debating and discussing. His teachers' preference was for him to make more of an effort on his actual schoolwork. Just as they believed he didn't always have to be a part of the group in the middle of a prank. In the ninth grade, he was assessed as only "possibly suitable" for upper secondary school as his teachers were unsure whether his level of maturity was enough for the somewhat greater demands of further education. However, at his "final evaluation" he, like many others at that time, got through by the skin of his teeth and was able to start class 1 Z in Gladsaxe Gymnasium in 1979.

## Hitting the books, parties, girls and part-time jobs

Being judged as "possibly suitable" made a big impression on Preben. Therefore, he applied himself much more throughout his time in upper secondary school. The weekly magazine round was replaced with a cleaning job at the Peerless factories, and he only took on a morning paper round during the holiday periods. The jobs were well paid and financed his colourful school activities, including Interrail tours with classmates around Europe during the summer holidays.

Although Preben probably hit the books more than his big brother, there was certainly still time for parties. The years in upper secondary school also had four main elements for Preben. His subjects and school work occupied most of his time, with parties and girls coming next and then the jobs that financed his leisure activities. When Preben was awarded his student cap in 1982, his then classmates characterised him as a good friend who was clever, hard-working and outgoing. He was fun to be around and was unusually good with the girls. He wasn't quite as reckless as his older brother, but he certainly wasn't lacking in the self-confidence or the get-up-and-go departments.

In 1982, nobody in Preben's circle – least of all himself – could have predicted that one of Denmark's future successful businessmen had just left upper secondary school.

When on his summer holidays from secondary school, Preben used the time to go inter-railing through Europe. This picture, taken by Gonzo's girlfriend Anette at a hotel in Italy, shows classmates Preben Damgaard (L), Henrik Klinkvort ("Gonzo"), Henrik Sander and Anders Gerhardt.

## Business school and bookkeeping

After graduating, Preben applies to Electronic Data Processing School, but his school exam results and the result of the entrance examination are 0.1 points below the admission requirement. So instead, after the summer holidays of 1982, he starts a professional bachelor programme at Business School.

As early as his first year of study, Preben gets a part-time job book-keeping at the head-hunting firm Bronee & Selnæs. However, it's a tad ambitious; it's one thing to know about the principle of double book-keeping, assets and liabilities, liquidity management, budgeting and so on, but it's something else entirely to manage the accounts of a real company where there are expenses, cash differences, ongoing work and the like. It results in the firm's chartered accountant taking over the daily bookkeeping. Preben, on the other hand, later sells his and Erik's first financial management system, Danmax, to the company.

Despite having to let go of the daily bookkeeping, Preben gains valu-able, practical experience and respect for real life accounting from the year he spends at Bronee & Selnæs.

Later, during his studies, he gets a job with the company MRK (Mar-keting, Research and Communication), which conducts, for example, market analyses through personal interviews. He is handed lists of com-panies and people to be interviewed as well as the questions they are to be asked. The rest he has to deal with himself.

But he also manages to establish his own little Value Added Tax (VAT)-registered business from which he offers cleaning services and can issue his customers real invoices with VAT and everything.

# CHAPTER 3

# THE RUN-UP

## The Damgaard brothers get to work

After Erik's return from the USA, much of the talk is about computers when he and Preben meet up with their parents on Solbærvænget. Through Morten Gregersen, they become acquainted with the magazine *Asian Sources*, in which products and suppliers from the Far East are described. Together they found the company Brdr. Damgaard Data I/S, which imports and resells floppy disks and printers from Taiwan.

In order for them to afford their own computers, the brothers borrow 12,000 USD[5] from their parents and import six Tatung computers, running the CP/M operating system, from Taiwan. The machines arrive a few weeks later, whereupon four of them are resold and with the resulting profit of exactly 12,000 USD the loan is repaid.

A Tatung Z80-based system was
the first computer Erik and Preben
ordered from Taiwan.

---

5   Amounts converted from Danish Kroner (DKK) to
US Dollars (USD) are using an exchange rate of 1 USD = 5 DKK.

In 1983, Brdr. Damgaard Data I/S is nothing more than a side-job. The brothers concentrate primarily on their studies and everything else you do when you're in your early 20s. Erik, who took a course in business studies during his stay in the USA, would like to learn more about book-keeping and accounting and, therefore, he signs up for a class at the Copenhagen Business College in December 1983.

## HERA-SOFT from HERA-DATA

In spring 1984, Morten Gregersen shows Erik a Danish financial pro-gram, HERA-SOFT, developed for CP/M-based microcomputers by HERA-DATA in southern Zealand, Denmark. Havidan, the company which Morten works for, is going to sell the program at a retail price of approximately 1,600 USD. He tells Erik that HERA-DATA expects to sell 100 programs a month.

They go through the program and Erik can see – thanks to his newly acquired skills in programming, bookkeeping and accounting – that he could develop a far more user-friendly program.

He discusses the idea with Preben and their parents. Preben thinks it's an open-and-shut case. His mother, Kirsten, herself a bookkeeper in a small company, sees the need, and Knud thinks the idea of the boys starting their own business is exciting.

## Erik develops his first financial program

At the end of February, Erik hands in his engineering thesis. Immedi-ately afterwards he reports to Høvelte barracks, north of Copenhagen, where he is required to fulfil his conscripted military service as part of the sanitary corps.

He now puts all his efforts into realising his plans for developing a financial program that is better than the HERA-DATA program. The military duty, being served during the day, doesn't offer any major in-tellectual challenges, but he discusses the developmental aspect of his plans regularly with his mother, who offers many professional insights into a bookkeeper's work in practice. Erik listens to his mother's feed-back and counsel, targeting his program to best suit the way in which she describes how bookkeepers use their daily paper-based daybooks, ledgers and account cards.

During the summer, Erik shows his program to the owner of the company Havidan, who is excited and would like to sell it with his imported computers from Taiwan. Erik promises him a five per cent higher retailer discount than HERA-DATA offers, and they also agree that he and Preben will stop importing hardware.

## Heading for the Bella Center

One day in late summer, Morten is again visiting Erik and this time he tells him that Havidan is going to have a stand at the Kontor&Data fair in the Bella Center that October. It would very much like to introduce Erik's new product, which is to be sold with a computer, printer and software for word processing for a total price of around 10,000 USD. That same evening, Erik and Preben discuss the possibility of exhibiting and introducing the product themselves. They decide to book the smallest stand available: nine square metres. Decision made, they now have a deadline for when the first edition of the Damgaard brothers' new financial program has to be ready for public viewing: 3rd October 1984.

That deadline is the catalyst for Erik now seriously focusing on the program's development, and he goes so far as to announce to friends and acquaintances that there'll be no more nights out and celebrations at the weekends.

As the program is being completed, Erik regularly shows it to people from Havidan. What was to have been a simple bookkeeping system now also includes an invoicing module and when a system is able to invoice, then there has to be a little product catalogue and a customer card, too. And, of course, it all has to be integrated so that the system itself records the VAT on a sales order in a separate account and places the invoiced amount as a receivable amount in the debtor's account. The development work is a tad more extensive than he'd originally imagined.

The small CP/M-based computers from Taiwan can be equipped with two floppy disk drives, but Erik's ambition is for the entire program to fit on one disk. The other floppy disk should only be used for data. That way the bookkeeper doesn't have to constantly switch disks at work, as is so often the case with the competing systems. With the new milestone set and a clear ambition for what the program is to be capable of, there's now only one thing left to resolve: the time investment needed to make it a success. Erik works day and night when not at the barracks in Høvelte or at his job as a caretaker.

## Preben gets more involved

After the summer holidays, Preben gets more involved in the work, writing the user manual and marketing material and, actually, dealing with everything else but the development of the product itself. This means that Preben himself has to know the program inside out, so he can demonstrate it to future dealers and customers at the exhibition. By the end of September 1984, the brothers are ready to move the furniture from Preben's room to the fair in the Bella Center using shelving and woollen carpets. The program is not completely finished, but it is ready enough for the brothers to demonstrate its most important features and give an idea of its user-friendliness and fully-integrated financial program, all designed with the small business bookkeeper in mind.

Erik's time with the sanitary troops is drawing to a close, but he needs time off for the week of the fair. Thankfully, the military is very keen on supporting the conscripts' efforts to get work once their military service has come to an end, and, without any hassle, he is granted a week's leave. And so, on 2nd October 1984, 23-year-old Erik sticks the key into the ignition of his used Sunbeam, and with his 21-year-old brother, Preben, in the passenger seat, they head off for the Bella Center in Copenhagen.

The two brothers have no idea that they are embarking on one of the biggest Danish business adventures in recent history.

# CHAPTER 4

# THE IT INDUSTRY AD 1984

## EDP becomes IT

There is already rapid development within IT by the time the two young Damgaard brothers are preparing their entry into the market. However, the brothers are (fortunately?) totally unaware of this.

Actually, it wasn't even called IT back then. Rather it was known as EDP – Electronic Data Processing. In the 1990s, the term EDP disappears in favour of the term IT for Information Technology.

In the early 1980s, IT equipment and software are divided into three main categories: mainframes, minicomputers and microcomputers.

## Mainframes

IBM, Control Data Corporation (CDC), Sperry, Siemens Computer Systems, General Electric, Honeywell, NCR, ICL, Burroughs and a number of other major businesses develop and produce computer systems called "mainframes".

Mainframes were large computer systems that required rooms, designed specifically with raised floors to both conceal the many cables and maintain a constant temperature. Servicing also required specially trained staff, and work was often done in a three-shift operation so as to optimise the use of the system. The picture shows a Cyber installation from the company Control Data Corporation.

Mainframes are big and – for the time – powerful computers, and with prices from one million dollars and upwards, also ludicrously expensive. The programs (software) for mainframes are typically bespoke for the individual customer and, therefore, also cost millions of dollars. Only the largest businesses with many customers and many transactions or public companies with many routine tasks can justify purchasing and operating mainframe-based IT systems.

Much of the work for mainframes such as batch jobs, which can be run at any time of the day, thus keeping the expensive computer fully occupied, is planned and carried out by specially trained technicians. To service small and medium-sized enterprises with IT services, service centres, which purchase and operate large, mainframe-based systems, are set up whereby customers only pay for the capacity they actually use. Typically, the service works by customers sending in their data on forms, after which the service centre inputs the data and a few days later, the results are returned as lists and pre-printed forms.

The interactive and online use of computers that we know of today, where we each have our own screen, tablet or smartphone with direct access, begin to gain popularity in the early 1980s. Developing, establishing and running interactive programs for mainframes is astonishingly expensive, and the terminals themselves – the screens and keyboards – are costly. In 1984, an IBM 3179G terminal is introduced at a price of about 3,000 USD, which equates to approximately 6,000 USD today (2017). Without a connection to the mainframe, which is facilitated via a separate communications server, the terminal can't do anything and is, therefore, often called a "dumb" terminal.

Service centres lay the early foundation for the development of software to handle tasks that are generally identical in all businesses. For example, almost every business pays its employees, records customer information, sends invoices, tracks inventory, pays suppliers and charges their customers money for not paying on time. Every business also likes to keep an eye on the state of its financial situation at the end of the month.

When the Damgaard brothers enter the market in 1984, German SAP[6] opens its first office abroad, in Biel, Switzerland. SAP, today the world's largest provider of financial systems for large enterprises, had been operating since 1972 and employed 163 employees. The then software, SAP R/2, ran exclusively on IBM mainframes and had no customers outside of the German-speaking countries.

---

6   SAP is an abbreviation for Systems, Applications and Products in data processing.

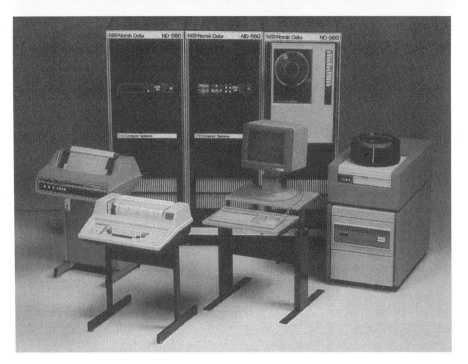

From today's perspective, minicomputers were not exactly mini, but compared to mainframes, they were significantly smaller systems. Moreover, installing a minicomputer was less demanding and whereas many mainframes needed water cooling systems, too, minicomputers were all air-cooled. Shown is a minicomputer system from Norsk Data.

## Minicomputers

Companies such as Regnecentralen, Nixdorf, Norsk Data, Olivetti, Christian Rovsing A/S (which filed for bankruptcy in August 1984), Digital Equipment Corporation, Prime Computers and Data General, developed so-called minicomputers in the 1970s. With prices starting at a couple of hundred thousand dollars, they are far cheaper than the bulky mainframes, but they're not as powerful. Nevertheless, they earn huge success in specialist areas such as technical calculations and financial analyses. Large and medium-sized enterprises are particularly interested in minicomputers and, in the early 1980s, both service bureaus and mainframe manufacturers are threatened by them to the extent that a few years later, most of them have gone out of business or have been bought over.

Minicomputers are, however, still too expensive for very small businesses and there is nonetheless a need for user-friendly and inexpensive software to cope with everyday tasks such as financial and administrative office work.

## Microcomputers

Technological developments within IT are greatly accelerated by the US space programme. High quality, highly reliable and compact computers are needed for sending a man to the moon and back again, all while keeping him alive and in good condition.

For the first time, in the early 1970s, an entire computer was integrated successfully on a small silicon plate (a microprocessor). It is given the

A Commodore microcomputer with the CP/M operating system and a single 5¼" floppy disk drive.

nerdy name 8080 and is developed by Intel. The computer's operating system, known as CP/M, is developed by a small American company, Digital Research. With an Intel 8080, you can build a complete single-user computer system with a keyboard, monitor, two floppy disk drives and a printer for a retail price of around 8,000 USD.

In 1974, one of Intel's development engineers establishes his own company under the name Zilog Inc. It then develops the Z80 microprocessor, which is bit-compatible with the 8080s. Zilog gives other manufacturers of electronics licence to produce their processor, thereby creating a much greater production capacity than Zilog is capable of under its own roof. At the same time, this creates a price war, driving the price down and the quantity up. The Z80 is, in many ways, a better processor than the 8080 and, thus, it is widely distributed. Indeed, both the technology and business models around the Z80 and CP/M are the starting point for another acceleration in the IT industry.

The Intel 8080 and Z80 technology have a critical limitation: an 8-bit processor. In practice, it means that the programs for the computer can't take up too much memory. The programs for the CP/M systems are, therefore, quite primitive but, on the other hand, they are far cheaper than the solutions based on mainframes and minicomputers. And from the beginning of the 1980s, microcomputers also gain ground in Denmark.

An IBM Personal Computer (PC) with two 5¼" diskette drives and the PC-DOS operating system from Microsoft. The first model, launched in August 1981, is named 5150.

## The Personal Computer

IBM is the first to market with a microcomputer that has a 16-bit processor. It dubs the machine "Personal Computer" (PC). IBM wasn't the first to use the moniker Personal Computer, but due to the commercial success of the product concept, the name becomes associated with IBM for the next 30 years. With a 16-bit processor, bigger programs with more functions can be developed.

The operating system doesn't come directly from IBM, but from the completely unknown company, Microsoft. However, the overall system faces two fundamental challenges when it launches in autumn 1981. Firstly, a usable system costs about 20,000 USD and, secondly, there is no application software. A Personal Computer without applications only evokes excitement among a few IT-savvy enthusiasts, and despite the situation changing dramatically later, it will be some years before it really gets going.

Despite IBM's superior technology, Z80 and CP/M-based systems, which cost about half as much and have many available software packages, are allowed to survive for the time being. This is due in part to the fact that it takes IBM a few years to become aware of the potential of the personal computer.

IBM first introduces its new PC in Denmark on 18th January 1983.

# CHAPTER 5

# THE START

## Kontor&Data 1984

When Kontor&Data (Denmark's largest exhibition of office furniture, EDP equipment and software) opens its doors at the Bella Center, in Copenhagen, on 3rd October 1984, Preben and Erik Damgaard are ready in their nine square metre stand. Every bit of furniture, right down to the red woollen rug, comes from Preben's room at their parents' house on Solbærvænget. He has written a few pages about the new financial management system, describing the most important features and benefits, and he has made enough copies for passers-by to take one home. He has also made small cards on which visitors can leave their names and phone numbers to be contacted after the fair.

They each have their computers with them. Erik has set his up with the screen facing out to the aisle where the many visitors walk by. When someone asks for a demonstration, other passers-by become curious, stop and peer over their shoulders. Their product demonstrations often attract a gaggle of people. During the breaks, or when Preben demonstrates on his own, Erik continues programming the system, after which the fresh changes are immediately transferred to the demo-machine.

## Maxisoft has to change its name

At another stand in the Bella Center, their first reseller, Havidan, is also presenting the new Maxisoft, which the easy-to-use financial system for bookkeepers in small businesses has been named. Many visitors are referred from their stand to the Damgaard brothers to hear more.

One of the very early versions of Danmax on 5¼" floppy disks. The program was contained on one disk while user data could be saved onto the other (Photo Bob Hansen).

The competing product from HERA-DATA is represented at the exhibition, too. It is available in two versions, one of which is called Maxi. As some of the visitors at the fair ask Erik and Preben if Maxisoft is based on HERA-DATA's program, they quickly realise they have to find a different name.

The exhibition is an undeniable success. Roughly 40 customers place orders for the system, and two companies, in addition to Havidan, want to resell Maxisoft.

The product is delivered in a number of modules, which can be purchased individually:

- General ledger (800 USD)
- Accounts receivable (600 USD)
- Accounts payable (440 USD)
- Stock control (600 USD)
- Invoicing (500 USD)

40 units of Maxisoft at 2,940 USD is 117,600 USD (corresponding to 240,000 USD at 2017 prices), and less the reseller discount, it leaves about 60,000 USD for the Damgaard brothers. Attending Kontor&Data cost them approximately 2,400 USD, so they have made a nice profit. The figures correspond roughly to the takings they later report as turnover for the whole of 1984. The biggest hurdle that almost all start-up companies struggle long and hard with – convincing and selling to the first customers – is overcome by Brdr. Damgaard Data in only eight days. They now have to deliver what they have promised, so the customers are happy and can spread that happiness via word-of-mouth to other potential customers. They also need more resellers selling the product.

## Maxisoft becomes Danmax

After the show, the brothers discuss their experiences with their parents, particularly the problem of their Maxisoft being confused with Maxi from HERA-DATA. Although the exhibition was a huge success, Brdr. Damgaard Data is still much less well known than HERA-DATA, and it is too great a risk for this confusion to continue. Kirsten proposes the name be changed to Danmax. And so it is. After Kontor&Data, the brothers have a long list of contacts to be processed. Preben prepares an official price list, and together they decide that a business partner can buy the licences for 60 per cent of the recommended retail price. Contacting the visitors on the list is the next step. Even the brothers themselves are surprised at just how fast they're able to start selling. They haven't even considered how to organise the work. However, as resellers begin selling, and ringing in orders on a daily basis, they need to establish a permanently staffed office. Preben moves out of the basement of Solbærvænget, which instead is turned into a work base for the newly minted entrepreneurs.

When work is done, the whole family often gathers for dinner and chats about the day's events in the business based in the basement. Erik (left), who finished his military service at the end of November 1984, is now in the office every day, continuing his work on Danmax. Preben is in the office when not at his other job or at Business School. (This picture is from 1986, when they moved the company to Landemærket in Copenhagen city centre.)

## Eight years before the internet

1984 is still eight years before the internet becomes a reality, so communication is based primarily on landline telephones and the postal service. The fax has been invented, but the cost is still too high for it to have become widely used in business. Therefore, resellers continue to ring in their orders and, in 1984, these are initially follow-up orders stemming from the Kontor&Data exhibition, but soon additional orders start rolling in. Erik puts all his energy into the company, travelling around Denmark and visiting new business partners, while Preben, who still has to study and do his other job, answers the phone, and processes and dispatches orders.

## PCs are still too expensive

When Danmax was presented at the Kontor&Data expo, it ran on a computer with the CP/M operating system. That type of computer had been on the market for more than ten years, and cost around 8,000 USD,[7]

---

7   Unless otherwise stated, all prices in this book are given excluding Value Added Tax.

including word processing and a dot matrix printer. A full installation of Danmax costs 2,940 USD, and a complete package with hardware can be acquired for a price in the region of 11,000 USD.

IBM had launched the more powerful Personal Computer in 1981 and began marketing it on the Danish market in January 1983, so its penetration by October 1984 was relatively modest. Not to mention that an IBM PC cost more than twice as much as a CP/M machine.

Erik and Preben's decision to go to market with a financial system for CP/M machines is certainly not based on any deep market analyses, but it turns out to be the right choice. In autumn 1984, an IBM PC system at a price of about 20,000 USD is still far too expensive for companies with a single user. IBM was just beginning to build its business-oriented reseller network and the business partners it recruited didn't have very small businesses as their primary target group.

## IBM sells most

In early 1985, the analysis institute, Intelligent Electronics, estimates that a total of 16,500 microcomputers were sold in Denmark in the previous year, with IBM accounting for about 33 per cent. The Regnecentralen computer company, whose microcomputers run on CP/M, accounts for just over 20 per cent. Apple, which has its own operating system, accounts for just under ten per cent and the remainder is spread over many other suppliers, most of which run on CP/M. That IBM is able to take a third of the market in just under two years seems to indicate the direction development is going. But at that time it isn't quite so clear cut, partly because IBM sells primarily to its large customers, where word processing and spreadsheets are the primary requirements.

There are also suppliers trying to take the market away from IBM and, moreover, the market develops differently among large companies than it does, small businesses. Furthermore, special attention is paid to companies such as Regnecentralen and Dansk Data Elektronik in the public sector as they represent Danish-produced IT products. Even though there is a strong suggestion as to which direction development will head, the uncertainty is still great.

## Danmax is easier to use

Danmax is a good product. It can't do much more than other similar products, but it's different and, more importantly, considerably easier to use. Erik's ongoing discussions with his mother have ensured that Danmax behaves as a bookkeeper expects it to and as an accountant is used to working. Emphasis has been placed on the daybooks – often a bookkeeper's preferred tool. The order in which data is to be entered accurately matches the paper-based daybooks that all bookkeepers have used before switching to EDP and, therefore, it is completely familiar. For most customers, Danmax is their first introduction to EDP. You can go back and forth in the daybook's fields, insert new lines into the daybook, and even leave it and return to the same place again later. Such flexibility is a given today, but it certainly wasn't in the early 1980s.

There are bugs in all software programs, and they are typically corrected in the order that customers encounter and report them to the manufacturer, but Danmax is stable with only a small number of identifiable bugs. It works consistently, resulting in fewer break downs, which, in turn, reduces the number of start overs required. By this time, Erik has succeeded in his ambition of the program filling only one floppy disk, meaning that the bookkeeper doesn't need to switch floppy disks each time a new feature of the program is required. The price is the same as the other products on the market, so it is unsurprising that Danmax quickly becomes popular among small businesses. It's simply a better product for the same price demanded by its competitors.

## CP/M has its limits

One of the disadvantages of CP/M is the wide diversity of the hardware. Every time a business partner presents a new type of CP/M computer, Erik has to study the technical documentation and develop a new version of Danmax capable of running on that particular machine. But to ensure the widest possible spread of Danmax, Erik takes on the task. It is undoubtedly a contributing factor to Danmax being so successful, but it's an annoying and – for the customers – intangible investment. On the whole, CP/M is limited to what can be developed according to its 8-bit based facilities. Adding new features and making systems user-friendly are major challenges.

A computer screen showing the menu from Damgaard Data's first product, Danmax. Looking at it today, it doesn't seem so ground-breaking, but its simple structure made it one of the first examples of a piece of Danish software for the non-IT-savvy user.

## Anti-theft precautions

As early as 1984, Erik and Preben are aware that software can and is being pirated to a large extent. They also realise that their decision to sell through resellers necessitates they ensure those business partners don't just copy and sell on their software without settling their accounts. Therefore, they consider thoroughly how they can best ensure that they aren't taken advantage of.

The resulting solution is a separate piece of software called the Calc, which Erik himself develops. When a customer orders Danmax through a reseller, Brdr. Damgaard Data must be informed of the customer's name and which modules have been purchased. Those details are then entered into the Calc, which stores the information, and generates an encrypted code specific to the individual customer, which then unlocks the purchased modules. When the customer installs Danmax, the code must be entered, after which the program can be activated and utilised. The code from Calc works with Danmax in such a way that the customer's name is now written directly into their version of the program. If the customer or anyone else passes on the code to others, the origin of the code and an infringement of Brdr. Damgaard Data's copyright can easily be identified. Copyright infringement is, of course, illegal, and the offending party must reimburse the loss of earnings to the holder of the rights. The loss of earnings typically corresponds to the price of the product.

All codes can be broken, but the Calc generates codes that can't be altered by something as simple as mistyping one or two letters. If someone were to attempt to recreate the way in which the Calc generates its codes, it would have to be done with devious intent. And should anyone do so, the information pertaining to the affected customers would, in any case, be missing in Brdr. Damgaard Data's own Calc. The code concept prevents the program from being pirated on a large scale.

The decision to learn the identity of all customers probably complicated logistics a bit more initially, but it will prove to be a huge advantage in the future.

## FK-DATA – a little company in Ringsted

A little company in Ringsted, which leases slot machines to restaurants and hostels, is one of the first to acquire Maxisoft. The proprietor, who does the accounts himself, had already tried some of the competing systems when he got his hands on Erik's program. After working with Maxisoft for a few days, he has an idea, picks up the phone and calls the brothers behind Brdr. Damgaard Data on Solbærvænget in Bagsværd.

*'Damgaard Data, Erik speaking.'*

*'Hello Erik, my name is Finn Kusk. I'd like to meet you,'* says the voice on the other end of the receiver.

Finn drives from Ringsted to Bagsværd to explain his plan to the two brothers. He would like to establish a business selling computer equipment and software to small businesses, but he wants to do it under his own name. Therefore, he would like to enter into a "private label" agreement with Brdr. Damgaard Data. From there, he does everything himself. He also says hello to Knud and Kirsten. 'Nice, clever people,' thinks Finn Kusk on his way back to Ringsted. He has his lawyer draft a proposal for a written agreement and, in mid-December 1984, Brdr. Damgaard Data and FK-DATA, as Finn Kusk is now calling his company, sign a business partner agreement, giving Finn the right to market Maxisoft under his own name. He receives a reseller discount of 40 per cent of the suggested sales price, as well as permission for FK-DATA to create its own nation-wide network of resellers.

Every time he sells a licence, he must submit an order to Brdr. Damgaard Data, which will then generate and send him the program codes for that customer. He is responsible for all production and dispatching of floppy disks and manuals. He must also provide training and support for customers. And, just to be sure, Finn Kusk has a clause written into the agreement stating that should the brothers file for bankruptcy, their father, Knud Damgaard, will be obliged to take over the agreement.

Back home on Bregnebjergvej, in Ringsted, Finn gets going on his new business. He prepares his own design and advertises in local newspapers. Finn Kusk is a good businessman with a vast personal network and he is greatly respected among his business associates, so it isn't long before orders begin rolling ever more quickly into the basement business in Bagsværd.

## The right product at the right time

When Erik and Preben celebrate New Year's Eve on 31st December 1984, they can look back on a year marked by unusual events. At the ages of 23 and 21, respectively, they have got a business up and running and are off to a very good start. Without debt and high costs, and a turnover of approximately 60,000 USD, they can note a good, solid plus in their bank account.

While partying and toasting with friends and wishing them a Happy New Year, the future looks bright and promising. But 1985 brings new challenges. Preben, who until now had a part-time job as well as studying, resigns from MRK so he can spend all his spare time on the Damgaard Data project, while Erik, still the caretaker of a property in Østerbro, quits his job, too. They have hit the market for financial systems aimed at small businesses with absolutely the right product at absolutely the right time. Their decision not to sell directly to end customers will also prove to be very sensible. However, the distribution strategy is not quite in place yet, and the brothers are also a little uncertain as to which products they should actually focus on.

## Mikrodata 1985

At this point in time, Denmark has two annual IT fairs: Mikrodata, early on in the year, and the much larger Kontor&Data, in October. In light of the success of 1984, the brothers now also sign up for the MikroData exhibition, which is set to run between 6th and 12th February, 1985.

The monthly magazine, *Datatid*, which premieres in November 1984, features a review of the participants of the exhibition in its February 1985 issue, including a piece from Brdr. Damgaard Data that describes what they are going to present.

An excerpt reports on a program that can connect a word processing system with an IBM "composer". It's probably quite smart, but doesn't have much to do with financial systems. Damgaard Data was tempted by the business opportunities that were complementary or just plain profitable – and there were plenty of those.

# Administrative program and type systems

Brdr. Damgaard Data have developed the administrative system Danmax, which has attained huge popularity. Though it is only the few who know the name of the program as the company's system is primarily sold under a "private label" – that is, under the retailer's own trademark.

The programs are 100 per cent Danish developed and the entire system is completely integrated. Danmax comprises financial book-keeping, debt management, credit control, invoicing, stock control, an index and word processing.

The programs can run on most personal computers, regardless of them being 8 or 16-bit based systems. Modules can be purchased individually or in combinations as requested – that way you do not pay for features you do not need.

Another program actually connects a word processing system with an IBM composer. The program allows all forms of formatting and lay-outs, and the composer enables access to more than 100 different fonts.

The system can be viewed at Damgaard's stand at the exhibition, number 035 in hall B.

DATATID NR. 2 - FEBRUAR 1985

The article mentions that they mostly sell Danmax under "private labels", which means that the product is sold under names other than Danmax. There is a reference to the agreement with Finn Kusk, because no other private label agreements have been entered into at that time. By formulating it that way, the hope is to give the Brdr. Damgaard Data brand a little boost. The company has, after all, only been on the market for less than half a year.

At the Mikrodata exhibition, the brothers sign another private label deal. This time with the company Max Manus, but the venture never makes any significant revenue. After that – and for strategic reasons – the brothers don't enter into any more agreements whereby their products can be sold under a different name.

With approximately 35,000 visitors, Mikrodata is a small exhibition compared to Kontor&Data. On the other hand, there is more focus on small systems. The exhibition is a success. The brothers make many new contacts, with both potential customers and resellers.

## The brothers get their first salary

Turnover increases steadily. Business is actually so good that the brothers decide the time has come for them to be employed in their own company. By the end of January 1985, they receive a salary from their company for the first time. They each start at 1,200 USD a month. As business continues to go well in the months that follow, they agree that a little extravagance is in order. They both go out and buy a red Toyota Twincam each. Erik's is a brand new model, while Preben's is a slightly used second hand model.

Erik Damgaard (L), Lars Sodemann (R) and Bob Hansen (who took the picture) have set off on a camping holiday to northern Spain in Erik's spanking new, red Toyota Corolla GT Twincam. The little 1.6 litre 16-valve engine and double overhead camshaft provided 124 horsepower and could reach 200 km/h. Judging by the vehicle registration plate, it can be assumed that a number of insects lost their lives on that occasion.

For a 23 and a 21 year-old in 1985, a red Toyota Twincam is probably one of the coolest things you can imagine. The car is a Corolla, but the engine is jazzed up with 16 valves and two overhead camshafts, so that they can whizz around Denmark when searching for new business partners and taking care of the existing ones.

## FK-DATA is a success

In March 1985, when it seems that Finn Kusk is successful in getting resellers to sell his version of Maxisoft, he proposes that the agreement from December 1984 be revised; from now on, he will trade as a "private label" distributor only, no longer selling directly to end customers. In April 1985, a new agreement is entered into with Finn Kusk, confirming his right to distribute Danmax – including all future versions. The reseller discount is increased from 40 to 70 per cent, against a guaranteed minimum turnover of 150,000 USD a year. It is also agreed that Brdr. Damgaard Data will not attempt to recruit his resellers. Finally, the new agreement includes a clause whereby Finn Kusk gets his own version of the Calc so that he can issue program codes himself, in return for submitting an inventory of all licences sold at the beginning of each month. He will then be invoiced accordingly. However, this is also on condition that he will not develop or market similar products.

## An office with a photocopier in the garage

Finn Kusk then sends out a version of Danmax, under the name FK-SOFT Revisor [FK-SOFT for Chartered Accountants], to all chartered accountants in Denmark, with a cover letter. He writes: *"If this isn't for you, then keep the floppy disk – just delete its contents and use it for something else"*.

However, it appears that FK-SOFT Revisor is definitely something for chartered accountants. Moreover, they can use the program in their own business for free. The user-friendly design and the low price suit the chartered accountants' small customers. With Erik, Finn Kusk develops a facility that allows customers to write data onto a floppy disk that the chartered accountant can load into FK-SOFT Revisor, which can then do what is necessary in relation to the year-end reports, saving both time and paper on the annual audit, preparation of the annual accounts and the company's tax return.

Business grows steadily, and Finn turns his garage into an office. He acquires a large photocopier so he can print the many manuals that accompany the deliveries to the customers. Later, he expands with a training department on Søgade in Ringsted, and as business continues to grow, he buys a property on Nørretorvet and moves all his activities there.

## A job-placement scheme

In spring 1985, a man from the municipality rings the doorbell of Solbærvænget in Bagsværd. It is a service visit, which all start-up companies in Gladsaxe Municipality receive.

*"Would Brdr. Damgaard Data not like a few extra hands to help with the work?"* asks the representative. There are some young people in the municipality who have nothing sensible with which to occupy their time and hands. That's not good for anyone. If Brdr. Damgaard Data takes on one or two young people, it comes with a wage subsidy, so it doesn't put pressure on the budget.

In a software company in 1985, there is a lot of practical, manual work. When processing an order, the latest version of the software must be copied onto floppy disks in the relevant format and for the particular computer as ordered by the customer. Manuals have to be printed and inserted into ring binders and codes must be generated, as without them Danmax can't run. Customer-specific codes are printed on labels that are then attached to the floppy disks. Everything must be packaged and taken to the post office. The brothers could easily use a few extra hands, and immediately take on two young people from the municipality's job-placement scheme.

## Damgaard Data ApS

Since its inception in 1983, Erik and Preben's company has been run as a personally-owned entity under the name Brdr. Damgaard Data I/S. However, due to the increasing activity, turnover and earnings, the brothers set up a private limited company under the name Damgaard-Data

ApS[8] on 17<sup>th</sup> April 1985. The company is established with a cash deposit of 16,000 USD, with both brothers on the board of directors and the first financial year covering the period 1<sup>st</sup> January 1985 to 30<sup>th</sup> April 1986.

## FK-DATA improves Danmax

The partnership with FK-DATA is very good business, and Finn Kusk quickly becomes the largest business partner. He meets the brothers frequently to discuss business opportunities, most often at his home in Ringsted. Once the meeting is over, Finn's wife, Ulla, invites everyone to dinner.

Finn's contact with Erik is particularly close. He finds bugs that have to be corrected and he frequently encounters requests for new or changed product features in his sales work. When he is to receive a new version of Danmax, he usually drives north while Erik Damgaard drives west. They meet at the Q8 petrol station in Roskilde, where Køgevej crosses the Holbæk motorway, and here Finn is handed a new floppy disk.

Over time, Finn Kusk builds up a nationwide network with close to 100 resellers. So despite receiving a 70 per cent discount on the recommended retail price, he still accounts for about 20 per cent of the revenue in Damgaard Data.

## Preben decides to take a Higher Diploma

In June 1985, Preben completes his BA studies at the Copenhagen Business School. The plan to take an MSc in Economics and Business Administration is no longer a particularly attractive one. He's more interested in working on their software business, and yet, at the same time, he still thinks he needs to learn more. He decides to take a Higher Diploma in Organisation, which also offers a computer science module. That way he can still do his full-time job as an entrepreneur.

---

8  An ApS is a limited liability company with limited capital requirements and no requirement for a registered board of directors.

## IBM's PC gains ground

During 1985, the IBM PC and its compatible competitors gain ground on the market. Technology is improving, prices are falling and there is a steady stream of new software, which all together provoke the interest of small and medium-sized businesses. Despite Digital Research's CPM-86 being technically a better product than Microsoft's DOS – the standard operating system in IBM's PC – it is IBM's Personal Computer concept that wins customers.

Essentially, customers aren't interested in hardware and operating systems; instead, they demand software that can help them solve everyday tasks. The "platform" that wins the software developers' preference wins everything else, including the market. With IBM's gigantic marketing engine supporting it, and with the ability to operate compatible systems, Microsoft creates a preference for DOS among software developers.

## Previously unseen market forces

Market forces in the IT industry are often self-perpetuating. The more software that exists for a platform, the greater the demand there will be for that particular platform. Greater demand drives unit costs and, thereby, prices down, which, in turn, further stimulates demand. However, this formula only works if all participants can and do compete and that is exactly the case on the PC market. For reasons that still amaze many, IBM didn't assert exclusivity over either hardware or software for their Personal Computer. Others could produce Personal Computers, and Microsoft may freely sell their variant of DOS to the other manufacturers. Due to being a market forerunner and a strong brand, IBM succeeds in generating confidence in its technology among both software developers and customers, and market forces the likes of which have never been seen in any industry are released.

## IBM's PC is a threat

Erik had developed Danmax in the Polypascal language for CP/M. Fortunately, he had refrained from making a lot of program calls directly on the operating system. Therefore, it is quite easy for him to compile Danmax with the other operating systems supported by Polypascal. Thus, Danmax can also run on IBM's PC. But it doesn't take full advantage of the PC's capacity and the many new features of the DOS operating system. The new PC is actually a threat that could pull the rug out from under Damgaard Data's Danmax-based business. Danmax is selling like hot cakes, but the IT industry is unpredictable. It doesn't stand still. Erik and Preben can see both the challenges and opportunities and know they will have to be faced soon.

## Erik develops a new financial system

In summer 1985, Erik begins to consider the opportunities offered by IBM's PC. With the new architecture, he can skip many of the technical leaps necessary in order to get CP/M machines from different suppliers to run Danmax. As the research progresses, many other benefits appear as well.

At IBM's introduction of the AT version of the PC in late 1984, it has a 10 MB hard drive and a floppy drive that can read 5¼" floppy disks with 1.2 MB data. Improvements to DOS also make it possible for the PCs to be connected to networks and share facilities. PC screens are now in colour and simple graphics can be created to make programs even more user-friendly. The increased capacity also makes it possible to develop larger programs with multiple functions. With the PC, Erik now sees an opportunity for developing an even more user-friendly financial system; one that features far more facilities, which can be used by more than one user and which simultaneously requires less technical maintenance than the current CP/M-based Danmax.

But a new system with a greater level of ambition can't be developed in only a few months. Thus, Erik has to estimate how the market will develop over the next 12 months and which developments a new system is likely to make. He also has to continue to develop and correct any bugs in

Danmax. In addition, he is busy helping business partners and recruiting new resellers. So he can't dedicate himself to the development of the new system 100 per cent, and it is still too early to employ staff and commit to paying fixed salaries. He continues to work on Danmax and the specification for the new system alone during all hours of the day and night.

## Kontor&Data 1985

Morten Gregersen still visits Solbærvænget. After work, he often drives over to see Erik, where they spend hours discussing software development. Damgaard Data engages him every so often as a consultant, carrying out tasks related to customer projects or developing little improvements to Danmax.

In October, they participate once again in Kontor&Data at the Bella Center. With Preben and Erik busy manning the stand, Morten keeps an eye on the competitors. A new financial system called PCPLUS, from the start-up company PC&C (Personal Computing & Consulting, which in 1995 becomes Navision Software) particularly captures their attention. The system is designed for the new PC and is extremely user-friendly. PolyData's financial system, PolySoft, which is probably the market leader in Denmark, is also scrutinised.

Danmax is still selling well, but at Kontor&Data 1985, it is clear that IBM's PC and other compatible machines are taking the market by storm. There are new competitors, who have developed their products specifically for the new platform. If they don't make a move, time could run out fast for Danmax.

## A network of PCs

Erik now has to allocate more time to developing the new financial system. Apart from allowing more features and increased user-friendliness, products that enable computers to connect to networks so as to share programs, printers and storage have also emerged. In the first half of the 1980s, mid-market companies with multiple IT users working on the same data were primarily advised to acquire and utilise minicomputers, which had also become popular. With the new network technology, it will be possible to make PC-based solutions for these companies. A network of PCs can solve roughly the same IT tasks as minicomputers, but are much cheaper to acquire.

If the new financial system from Damgaard Data can serve more users simultaneously, the brothers will be able to sell to the slightly larger companies; thereby, achieving a much higher price per sale. However, more competing technologies are on the way, so Erik has to choose the one that is most solid and which is expected to have the greatest market penetration. After some research and testing, he chooses MS-DOS from Microsoft and the network product Netware, from the American company Novell.

## Danmax XT – a new financial system

In late autumn, the design criteria are set, and Erik goes ahead with the programming itself. The project is entitled Danmax XT, taking its inspiration from the IBM PC, which due to its 10 MB hard drive has the term XT in its name. He decides from the outset that the new system won't be backward compatible with Danmax.

It is a brave and unusual decision in the software industry, where programs are usually always backward compatible. On the one hand, backward compatibility is a service for existing customers, who can easily apply the new software without much hassle. On the other hand, it's also a way of protecting a business's customer base; if a new software program is not backward compatible, existing customers might be inclined to consider an alternative solution, such as those offered by competitors. Without compatibility, there is no immediate difference between the inconvenience involved in switching to a new system from the current provider or installing a new system from a competitor.

For Erik there are two reasons for dropping backward compatibility:

1. It removes the limitations and complications that backward compatibility always entails. He can focus on making the new product as good as it could possibly be given the opportunities offered by the new technology. Development is less complex, can be implemented quicker, cheaper and with fewer restrictions
2. The new product is aimed at a slightly different target group than Danmax's existing customers. Therefore, it doesn't make sense to expend resources offering them a technical upgrade. It would be better to offer any Danmax customers, who would like to change, a more attractive price for the new product, and possibly some tools for transferring their data.

## User-friendliness is paramount

In October, the monthly magazine, *Datatid*, features an article with the heading "User-friendliness is paramount", where Danmax is reviewed extremely positively. In the article, Preben talks about a "Danmax Mini" for companies with only a few transactions; whereas the full version costs around 3,200 USD, the Mini can be purchased for just 1,600 USD. He reveals their plans to launch a product for multiple simultaneous users. At the end of the article, it mentions that Danmax can't be purchased directly from Damgaard Data, but "is delivered as a private label via resellers throughout the country; therefore, the product may be called something else by a reseller, despite it being the same product". The article concludes that setting up Danmax probably requires the help of a chartered accountant, but that it is a user-friendly program that meets the needs of most small businesses.

The article makes no mention of competing products – nor does it imply that Danmax doesn't actually take advantage of all the facilities offered by the PC. The differences between the various computer systems haven't really been a factor for the Damgaard brothers' target group; the deciding factors are a chartered accountant's recommendation, how easy it is to get started and whether the price is somewhat competitive. So, although technological advances are overtaking Danmax, the sluggishness of the market is still so great and the transparency so little that demand for the product continues to increase. Thus, during 1986,

*Datatid* publishes a series of "educational articles" describing in detail how Danmax should be used.

## Danmax sells well

At turn of the year (1985/86) business is good. The one-year-old Danmax product is still selling. The financial year ending 19th April 1986, with a turnover of a little less than 1 million USD, has been an acceptable one. It is a very nice improvement on the previous year's turnover of approximately 60,000 USD. As the workforce consists of just Erik and Preben as well as the two youngsters from the Gladsaxe municipality's job-placement scheme, and as the company is being run from their parents' basement, a considerable amount remains on the bottom line once all the overheads have been paid.

## The Albatros takes off

Erik works day and night on supporting and further developing Danmax, at the same time as developing Danmax XT. Preben, who also works full time in the company when not attending to his Higher Diploma studies at Business School in the evenings, looks after the commercial aspects, expanding the reseller network as more and more inquiries come in.

From 16th to 20th February 1986, they exhibit both their Danmax and Danmax Mini at the Mikrodata fair in the Bella Center. At the exhibition, PolySoft A/S presents its new system, Albatros, a multi-user system based on DOS. Albatros takes advantage of all the facilities offered by the PC: it has wider functionality, is more user-friendly and can be used by users simultaneously. PolySoft, which is part of the PolyData group, has chosen to bank on the network system 10-net, which they themselves import and distribute, for connecting the computers and enabling users to share programs, data and printers.

Albatros is not launched as a competitor to Danmax, HERA-SOFT and PCPLUS, but is instead positioned as an alternative to the larger and more expensive solutions based on minicomputers from Norsk Data, Prime, DEC, Nixdorf, NCR, DDE and so on. The price of Albatros starts at 5,400 USD for a complete solution for two users, while a four-user solution costs 6,800 USD and a nine-user solution, 8,000 USD. Additional users cost 400 USD apiece. PolySoft has high hopes for Albatros and already expects to take a third of the 1986/87 market for this type of system.

Concurrent with the announcement of Albatros, PolySoft halves the prices of the product Polysoft Version 4, which competes directly with Danmax. A complete single-user solution now costs only 2,800 USD. With the launch of Albatros, PolySoft has taken the lead in the market for PC-based financial systems for small and medium-sized enterprises in Denmark. Erik and Preben are well aware that something will have to be done soon if they are to enter the market for multi-user systems.

However, developing a multi-user system using the PC's facilities is a much greater task than the development of a single-user system for CP/M. Even PolyData had four developers working on the Albatros project, and PC&C had three developers on its PCPLUS.

## Morten Gregersen comes aboard

If a new product is to be ready for the Kontor&Data exhibition that autumn, then more bodies are needed to work on development. So Erik drafts a job advertisement for the Sunday edition of the oldest Danish newspaper, *Berlingske Tidende*. When Morten Gregersen comes down to the basement of Solbærvnget one afternoon in February, he sees a notepad on Erik's desk on which is written, at the top of the page, "Programmer wanted". While Erik is away from his desk, Morten writes:

*Here I am!*
*Best regards,*
*Morten Gregersen.*

When Erik returns and sees Morten's note, he laughs and calls Preben. An employment contract needs to be drawn up.

Apart from the two employees from the municipality's job-placement scheme, Morten Gregersen is the first employee of Damgaard Data. As early as the first employment agreement, the right that everything developed in the company belonged to the company was emphasised. The starting salary of 2,800 USD is the equivalent of 6,000 USD today (2017).

Apart from the two "youth workers", Morten Gregersen is the first employee of Damgaard Data. However, it's not long until Jens Riis (now Svanholdt) also comes aboard as a programmer. Jens, an assistant to a land surveyor, has a passion for software development. He even bought an RC-Partner computer for around 12,000 USD, on which he learned how to program. After visiting Mikrodata in 1986, he wrote unsolicited applications to all the exhibitors, one of which landed on Erik Damgaard's desk at an opportune moment. Jens is called, invited to an interview and subsequently employed from 1st June. His job is to develop a word-processing system that can be integrated with Danmax XT, so users can send letters to their customers and suppliers directly through the financial system. It is a smaller project that will be offered as an add-on, but which is expected to give customers a great deal of value. Erik estimates that the modest development will create a nice extra income.

## Lack of space in the family home

The greatly increased activity takes up a lot of space in the Damgaard's terraced house in Bagsværd. The young entrepreneurs have now extended their activities into the upper storeys, where they've also made themselves at home in the kitchen, using it as a canteen. What's in the fridge in the morning won't necessarily still be there in the evening. With four employees plus Preben and Erik, there is no longer room for the business in their parents' house at Solbærvænget 23.

From the very early days of 1986, before Damgaard Data had moved to Landemærket in Copenhagen city centre. The picture shows Morten Gregersen (L) and Jens Riis (now Svanholdt), who had just joined the basement on Solbærvænget in Bagsværd. This picture was taken by either Erik or Preben Damgaard.

In spring 1986, Preben is living in Frederiksberg, while Erik is in Østerbro. They agree to move their offices to central Copenhagen, where they'll be close to restaurants, pubs and discos, and the electricity and buzz of the city centre. With their flying start and a very healthy bank balance, the brothers listen to their father's advice and look for a property that they can purchase. The choice is an old house on Landemærket, near the Rosenborg Castle Gardens. The property is vacant and on Monday, 5th May 1986, with the sun shining from a bright blue sky, the six staff members of Damgaard Data move into Landemærket 51. Kirsten and Knud Damgaard finally get their house back and can now thoroughly air the basement.

# CHAPTER 6

# CONCORDE IS LAUNCHED

## The business in Landemærket 51

When Erik and Preben chat about where the company should move to having out-grown Solbærvænget, money isn't the deciding factor. Since their start in October 1984, they have been increasing revenue, keeping costs down and building up a nice little reserve. The ongoing business remains highly profitable and it makes sense to invest some of that profit in property. With the acquisition of Landemærket 51 in Copenhagen's city centre for 600,000 USD, Damgaard Data is now a real company.

For the brothers, the move away from the basement of their childhood home is also a shift in their daily contact with their parents, though Kirsten Damgaard continues to look after the payroll. It gives her an insight into the staff of the company and she works at Landemærket several times a week. Their parents remain supportive from the side-lines and show a great interest in the business. Erik and Preben listen to their parents' advice and concerns, but make their own independent decisions regarding the company's strategies, investments and operations.

The move from
the basement on
Solbærvænget to
their premises at
Landemærket 51 was
announced in the trade
press. The text reveals
that in the mid-
eighties, the formal
form of you in Danish,
*De*, was still in use.

A sign is hung on the door of Landemærket 51, second-hand office furniture is purchased and a reception area is created in the hallway. Preben
gets his own office. Erik, and his newly appointed programmers, Morten
and Jens, establish a development department in a slightly larger room,
while facilities for copying floppy disks, printing labels and manuals,
packing and shipping are set up in the basement.

Later on in the year, a training venue is organised on the first floor.
And as the courses increase in popularity, Preben gets in touch with
Jørgen Holck-Christensen, who had shown an interest in Danmax earli-
er and is now working as a dedicated freelance consultant for Damgaard
Data's customers and business partners.

Although sales are going well and there is a growing demand for
training from both resellers and customers, Preben has difficulty finding
the money to hire yet another full-time employee. He, therefore, makes a

freelancer agreement with Jørgen, whereby he will be paid only for the time he spends on Damgaard tasks. And so, when the oil company Q8 enquires about purchasing Danmax as a PC-based accounting solution for their fifty self-employed oil-tanker drivers, Jørgen immediately takes the bull by the horns. Q8 wants Damgaard Data to provide direct support. The result is that Q8 becomes a reseller with Jørgen providing training and support through his own company, essentially guaranteeing him full-time employment without being on the pay-roll at Damgaard Data.

Erik decides to sell his apartment in Østerbro and moves in on the top floor of Landemærket. However, it's not long before he has to find somewhere else to live as the number of employees greatly increases.

## Caught red-handed

Meanwhile, one of the young employees assigned by Gladsaxe municipality is apparently confused about which bank account the cheques received by the company should be lodged to, and a number of them find their way into her own account. Preben fires her upon discovering the source of the discrepancies in the cash box. He also contacts her parents who, astounded, make sure the misplaced money is paid back immediately. It's a vital lesson for Preben: employing the right people is a critical responsibility of management. Employing the wrong people creates difficulties, unease and extra work. And due to firing her, Preben now finds himself acutely short on resources. But a quick search among friends reveals that an acquaintance, who is in the process of selling her clothing fashion boutique in Hellerup, just north of Copenhagen, can jump aboard at short notice until a permanent replacement is found. A "temp" position it isn't – she stays for nine years.

## A serious competitor

Soon after the Mikrodata exhibition in February 1986, PolySoft starts selling its new financial system, Albatros. Albatros, unlike the other competitors, is a PC-based multi-user system, focusing precisely on the niche Erik had intended for his new Danmax XT. As the associated company, PolyData, handles distribution and already has a well-established network of resellers, it is a serious competitor.

Development needs to be accelerated so that the new product can be launched as soon as possible. Otherwise, they risk losing their market share. Danmax alone won't be able to go the distance competing with systems such as PCPLUS, and Albatros shouldn't be allowed to get too much of a head start on the market on which Danmax XT is to be sold. Erik gets stuck in immediately, fine-tuning Danmax XT according to the strengths and weaknesses of the competing products to ensure it's a stand out program. While Erik, Morten and Jens toil away with development and programming, Preben plans the marketing. Erik and Preben agree that "Danmax XT" is not the best name for the new product. It suggests backward compatibility, and it sounds a tad provincial, too. Preben comes up with the idea of borrowing the Concorde name from the civil aviation industry. The supersonic passenger aeroplane Concorde, set into operation in 1976, represents the best in international aviation in the 1980s. It signals advanced technology, ultra-high speed, quality and comfort. Compared to PolySoft's choice of Albatros, Preben believes that Concorde alludes to something more modern, more streamlined, faster and more agile. An albatross can almost certainly endure, but it has difficulty getting airborne and its landings aren't particularly elegant.

Whether customers perceived the suggested connection is doubtful, but for the brothers the choice of the name Concorde was far from random and was greatly inspired by their competitor.

## Finn Kusk further develops Danmax

In mid-1986, when Erik and Preben's attention and focus are aimed at getting the new Concorde product on the market, Finn Kusk continues to sell his versions of FK-SOFT in large quantities and he is still submitting a steady stream of suggestions for improvements. As Erik has decided to put his new developers on the Concorde project, only he can make the changes and fix the bugs in Danmax. Something he's not particularly motivated to spend his time doing. Therefore, an agreement is made in which Finn Kusk receives a copy of the source code for Danmax. If he hires a programmer, he can have any bugs repaired and make any changes requested by his customers. Finn thinks it's a good idea, and from that date on, he further develops Danmax for his customers. The rights to the source code still belong to Damgaard Data, but Finn is entitled to make changes to the program.

## Erik invents the grid menu

Based on his knowledge of HERA-DATA, PCPLUS and Albatros, Erik knows exactly which points to improve on Concorde so it's even better. PCPLUS is an easy-to-use program, but it has limited functionality and is only developed for a single user, so it doesn't pose any real risk in the competition for Concorde's customers. Albatros is a multi-user system that also has many features, and it will be difficult to develop something similar if the product is to come quickly to market. Albatros' weaknesses are a combination of its dependence on the relatively primitive network 10-net, which PolyData itself imports and distributes, and the many features that make the product somewhat complicated.

While working on designing the Concorde user interface, Erik invents the grid menu – which later becomes well renowned – and gives the user access to the features supported by the system. The grid menu enables users to get a complete overview of the application's facilities at a glance and to then choose directly which application to activate.

When Erik Damgaard presented his grid menu for the forthcoming Concorde to Morten Gregersen, the latter recognised it as a breakthrough in user-friendliness. Via the grid menu, the user had easy access to 35 options.

With his two developers, Erik decides that Concorde must be ready for launch at the Kontor&Data exhibition taking place from 1st to 8th October, 1986.

In September, Preben takes out a number of full page advertisements in newspapers and trade magazines. The ads contain neither text nor logo; rather they depict a single floppy disk with white contrails in a blue sky. For those in the know, it's a nudge and a wink to Albatros whose ads show just the eponymous bird on a blue sky background.

Damgaard Data's first advertisement for Concorde was completely devoid of text and logo. It was to create interest and curiosity among the potential retailers and customers.

## Concorde at Kontor&Data 1986

As the brothers themselves wish to focus on the financial-side of Concorde at the upcoming Kontor&Data fair, there is a need for someone to demonstrate Concorde Text, its word processing program. One of Eric's acquaintances, Henrik Steen Petersen, who after a short career as a UN soldier is now working as a porter at Hvidovre Hospital, attends pre-drinks for a night at the Annabel disco, in inner Copenhagen, one Saturday evening in September. During the celebrations, Erik asks if Henrik could help out at the Kontor&Data exhibition by demonstrating Concorde Text. A week later, Henrik receives an Olivetti M24 PC at home so he can now become familiar with the program.

Their participation in Kontor&Data 1986 is based on the same concept as that of the previous years. Preben brings some furniture from home and establishes a little interim office environment in their stand. But this time the shelves, desks and woollen rug form the backdrop for launching something that later turns out to be one of Denmark's greatest box office hits within the field of software.

While Erik and Preben demonstrate Concorde Økonomi [Concorde Finance], Henrik demonstrates Concorde Text. Instead of taking the days off work, Henrik has decided to pull a few sick days. When his boss from Hvidovre Hospital suddenly turns up not only at the fair, but at their stand wanting to look at the new Concorde system, the end of Henrik's career as a porter in the Danish hospital system flashes before his very eyes. His boss asks him to drop by after the exhibition to deal with the practicalities.

The interest in Concorde at the Kontor&Data expo is good, with many appreciative words from visitors. But the competition is tough. PCPLUS, distributed by Berendsen Computer Products A/S, and Albatros, distributed by PolyData A/S, are both represented by large, professional stands at the exhibition. And prior to the fair, they both ran major marketing campaigns.

With the launch of Concorde, any further development of Danmax comes to an end. Customers can, of course, continue to buy and use the program, but Damgaard Data will no longer commit itself to correcting or making improvements. Customers, who would like more, can purchase the brand new Concorde. Formally, Danmax has had a life of only two years, which is a short one for a software product. But rapid technological developments meant it no longer made sense to continue using resources on the product.

Today, such a decision would raise an outcry among customers, but it didn't cause any major problems in 1986. And, although the program is not being further developed, it is still bought in the years that follow.

## Employee number five

When the exhibition is over, Erik and Henrik drive back to the office together. Henrik says that his days as a porter at Hvidovre Hospital are over. He has to find a new job. Erik wouldn't like to let a friend down, so he has a chat with Preben. They agree to offer Henrik backdated permanent employment. They just need to figure out what he's going to do. Henrik officially starts as employee number five on 1st October.

## An impressive advertisement

The launch of Concorde at Kontor&Data in 1986 went well enough, but it didn't leave such a big impression on media outlets. When the magazine *Datatid* features two overview articles about the exhibition in its November 1986 issue, neither Damgaard Data nor Concorde are mentioned at all. In general, the Danish software industry isn't really on the media's radar. In those days, the trade press was heavily dominated by foreign hardware suppliers. Only on the very last pages of the magazine do you find something about Damgaard Data – where Preben himself has taken out an impressive two-page advertisement entitled:

## Concorde – a product in the DANMAX series.

CONCORDE *is an administrative program in a class of its own.*

CONCORDE *is multi-user capable right down to bit-level – an unlimited number of users can work in the same program at the same time.*

CONCORDE *gives you a complete overview and is far ahead of anything else. The latest technology within programming is employed for the benefit of the user. Years of experience from programs such as the DANMAX series have formed the basis for a future-proof multi-user program that leaves its competitors behind. The result of close collaboration between professionals with many years of experience.*

CONCORDE *contains the general ledger, accounts receivable, accounts payable, invoicing, order and stock management, item listing and a report*

The text of the advertisement doesn't hide the product's features under a bushel.

generator. CONCORDE can later be expanded with payroll, purchase and lease management as well as time/case management and word processing.

CONCORDE can be acquired in to your specifications. All subprograms are fully integrated so you can jump from point to point – between print and queries and even between programs. While invoicing, you can hop directly to stock and create a new item number, return to invoicing at the push of a button and invoice the new item.

No matter where you are in CONCORDE, you can scroll through all of the information on the screen without interrupting the current job.

CONCORDE is user-friendly right down to your fingertips with a built-in manual and help texts for each program. Confidential information is secured with a password.

Training is offered to both partners and users at our own course centre.

Please refer to your nearest reseller.

DAMGAARD DATA ApS

Landemærket 51, 1119 Copenhagen K, Telephone 01 32 25 26

The text of the advertisement testifies to the challenges that the contemporary programmers faced when offering user-friendliness, including the ability to jump around between the various functions. As the underlying operating systems were simple, any user-friendliness had to be incorporated into the program itself. Exactly the area to which Erik had invested considerable amounts of energy during development. Customers welcome Concorde as a complete and user-friendly financial system for small and medium-sized businesses. But the product's later success and market penetration is also helped along by an unexpected source.

## Gold-digging in the IT industry

That period, when microcomputers enter into the market in the mid-80s, is characterised by a sense of gold-digging. Prices and gross margins are sky high. Good money can be earned selling even a limited number of units. Indeed, one of the companies that throws itself into the microcomputer market is AudioScan; a company that, during previous years, had annoyed its competitors in the hi-fi industry when it set up its own imports, thereby by-passing wholesalers, and passing-on the savings to customers. But like so many others who tried their luck in the IT industry, they had to throw in the towel relatively early. AudioScan, which sells Danmax and Concorde, lays off its employees, including sales manager Henrik Rose, who immediately requests a meeting with Preben Damgaard.

Damgaard Data isn't exactly lacking employees at the moment, so Preben isn't so interested in looking at CVs from the now available employees. However, he sees an opportunity in Henrik Rose himself. Henrik has an idea to start importing and distributing IBM compatible PCs from the Far East. As Damgaard Data already distributes its own products, the earnings per business partner could certainly be improved by also delivering the computers themselves. Preben isn't very interested in that, but he could use a hand recruiting and managing the resellers of the new Concorde, so he offers Henrik a job as a manager – though without employees – of retailer sales. Henrik Rose accepts the offer and starts as the first salesman in the company on 1st November.

## Professional marketing

With increasing revenue and earnings, there is room in the budget to invest more in marketing. In this context, advertising in daily newspapers plays a major role. But it's expensive and the money spent is only reimbursed much later, when – and if – the product is successful.

At a private dinner party held by one of Preben's schoolmates, the host's older brother, Michael Sander-Jensen, is also in attendance. Michael, having received his MSc. (Business), is now working at a well-known advertising agency. He knows how to navigate the world of advertising, so Preben asks him to help Damgaard Data's marketing efforts on a consultancy basis. It turns out to be a good move for the company. Michael gets discounts on advertisements that exceed his consulting fee and, therefore, he is soon affiliated as a permanent marketing freelancer.

With their check trousers, white socks, boat shoes and moustaches, Erik (L) and Preben Damgaard were completely in vogue in the mid-1980s.

75

## Damgaard Udvikling ApS
## [Damgaard Development Ltd]

On 27th October 1986, Erik and Preben set up Damgaard Udvikling ApS, [Damgaard Development Ltd], which is 100 per cent owned by Damgaard Data ApS. It is a remarkable move for a small company to divide its activities into separate companies at this early stage – the brothers have hardly had time to think about the company's future structure. However, through a girlfriend who worked at a law firm, Preben is introduced to lawyer Jesper Guldbrandsen whom he likes and appoints as the company's affiliated legal advisor. Preben often asks Jesper Guldbrandsen for his counsel when making strategic and fundamental decisions, and the inspiration for establishing Damgaard Udvikling ApS comes after just such a consultation with the lawyer. Its establishment has no practical significance at the time, but it will have later.

Preben, who is 23 years-old and hasn't yet completed his HD studies, compensates for his lack of business experience and expertise by gathering a group of external experts around both himself and the company. The ability to recognise limitations and to reach out to and draw upon the experience and skills of such a network is a crucial contributing factor to the company's development and success.

## FK-DATA gets better terms

In December 1986, Finn Kusk, who is now also selling the new Concorde under his own name, proposes that they change how his account is settled, so that he pays a fixed monthly sum of 100,000 USD in return for the right to sell an unlimited number of licences instead. Erik likes the idea, but Preben sees no reason to change the way in which FK-DATA pays for licences sold. He believes the only reason Finn Kusk is suggesting the new settlement method is to pay less in licence fees in the long run and that might not be in their best interest. Instead, they agree to raise the distributor discount from 70 to 75 per cent.

Preben's gut feeling was spot on – in early 1987, FK-DATA buys products for more than 100,000 USD a month.

## Competing in the Big League

By the end of 1986, Damgaard Data has really stuck their neck out with the new Concorde. The product, which is far more extensive and complex than Danmax, has to compete with minicomputer-based systems offered by larger companies such as Prime Computers, DDE, Nixdorf, IBM, HP, Digital, Norsk Data, Olivetti and so on.

Distribution capacity was a key factor for success in the IT industry. It's not enough to have a good product if you can't get the message out to the market and get resellers to sell the product. Once a partner has chosen which financial system to sell, it's not always so attractive for them to jump ship if the product is working and selling well. Damgaard Data came to market more than half a year later than PolySoft's competing system Albatros, which has the support of PolyData. PolyData, founded in 1978, is a well-consolidated company with a turnover of 28 million USD and extensive experience in distributing IT products throughout Denmark and Sweden. Albatros has received good reviews and already has many customers when Concorde sets its sights on winning over resellers and customers. PCPLUS, a big competitor of Danmax, is distributed by Berendsen Computer Products, which is also a large and well-established IT distribution company.

Erik and Preben have chosen to manage the distribution themselves, and they can hardly claim to have had much experience – let alone to have a large organisation supporting them. On the other hand, they are young, full of confidence supported by their success with Danmax and don't possess the burden of doubt. But as in business as in war: they who come first and have the most soldiers, usually win the battle – unless mistakes are made. When, according to tradition, the brothers don their funny hats on New Year's Eve, hardly any worries dampen their party spirit, despite the odds of the market for financial systems in Denmark being objectively not in their favour.

# CHAPTER 7

# NATIONWIDE EXPANSION

## Damgaard Data Distribution ApS

Erik and Preben choose to sell their financial systems through partners. And given they recruit and see to their business partners themselves, unlike, for example, PC&C, it isn't surprising that they establish the subsidiary company, Damgaard Distribution ApS, in January 1987. Yet again, it is unusual for such a small company to be so aware of the huge differences between the various aspects of business within the company that they actually separate them into independent, legal entities. In most software companies, the various disciplines: development, marketing, distribution, sales, support and so on are well and truly mixed together until the company reaches a certain size and maturity where they are then gradually divided into internal departments. And only rarely into separate companies.

The legal structure of Erik and Preben's going concern reflects a high level of business maturity, which comes to play a decisive role in the company's development during the coming years – for good and bad! PolyData, which supports PolySoft and Albatros, and which operated a similar business structure, is probably a good source of inspiration.

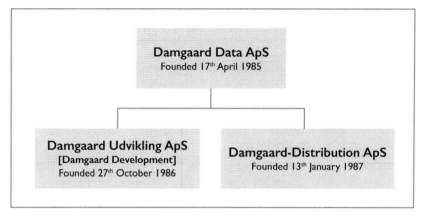

As early as 1986, Erik and Preben Damgaard divide their activities up into separate legal entities. The creation of a holding company and two operational subsidiaries was quite an unusual step at such an early stage in the company's development.

## 100 per cent growth rate

That there is a considerable amount of money to be earned via distribution during these early years is due to a combination of several factors. There was a latent demand for IT-based solutions, which could potentially increase productivity in business. The greatest hindrance to that demand was the high cost of solutions based on mainframes and minicomputers. However, once microcomputers became more powerful, coupled with a fall in price and can be linked into networks that share programs, data and printers, and when user-friendly software in Danish is made available by companies such as Damgaard Data, PC&C, DSI and PolySoft, demand explodes.

Annual growth rates in sales of over 100 per cent are seen, and even the growth margins on the products are quite satisfactory. Such paradisiac conditions rarely last but in 1985-86 it seems attractive to be on the distribution wagon.

With the establishment of the separate Damgaard Distribution ApS company, Preben gains legitimacy for contacting other manufacturers in order to obtain distribution rights for products that complement Danmax and Concorde, which then increases sales, earnings and loyalty among partners.

## The need for support and training explodes

As the number of resellers and customers escalates, there is a corresponding increase in the range of telephone inquiries regarding the products. Partners have questions that need to be clarified before a customer can decide to buy. And even after purchasing, technical or operational issues often arise that must be answered before customers can use the products as intended. They are primarily advised to contact a reseller, but anyone needing urgent help is never refused. And so as to enable business partners to independently sell and provide support for the products, a permanent training facility is organised on the first floor of Landemærket in autumn 1986.

Initially, Erik and Preben themselves are responsible for the training, but as demand grows, greater capacity is needed. In spring 1987, when the increase in demand proves to be stable, they ask Jørgen Holck-Christensen to be responsible for all training and support activities, which requires, in turn, that he winds up his own customer projects. As new employees are continuously being recruited for training and support, he will be the one to lead them. Jørgen, born in 1937, and thus the doyen of the company, has no ambition for a career as a manager and boss. But his background in teaching and his practical insight into how the products are used means he becomes the one responsible for building the training and support department.

With the introduction of the multi-user system Concorde, which is a great success from the very start, the need for support also increases. Customers, mainly bookkeepers and chartered accountants in small and medium-sized enterprises, are basically indifferent to all the technical details of an IT solution. When the financial system doesn't work, they can't immediately identify where the problem lies. Many of the technologies on which the Concorde multi-user solution is based are so new that even the resellers have very little experience with all the details, so they themselves need help when customers ask questions or have operational issues.

Essentially, there are two ways to handle such challenges: reject all questions relating to the products, which you yourself didn't supply, thereby passing all responsibility onto business partners. This is the choice that the company PC&C consciously makes by handing over distribution and support to Berendsen Computer Products, a professional organisation capable of handling such a task. Damgaard Data, in contrast, chooses the direct opposite: accepting responsibility for the overall solution, so that their partners can, in principle, get answers to all questions, no matter where a problem arises.

Typically, fees are charged for courses and training for customers and resellers, but the tradition of paying for support didn't exist in the 1980s. PolyData advertised its FriService concept directly, whereby customers could ring for free and get help with any product sold by PolyData. It goes without saying that providing support for products, which you yourself haven't supplied and thus have no growth margin on, can quickly become bad for business. However, Preben and Erik take a deeper look at the problem, choosing to give customer and reseller satisfaction highest priority. The business then just has to be organised accordingly.

## OS/2 is announced

While launching a new series of PCs called Personal System/2 (PS/2) in April 1987, IBM also announces that it's developing a new operating system entitled OS/2 in collaboration with Microsoft. It will be available later in the year. The introduction of the PC and DOS in 1981 was a major advance compared to CP/M, and a significant market for both hardware and software for the platform quickly emerged. The development of software, in particular, sped up. Customers proved more than ready to buy the many new ideas for how to automate and streamline manual processes with software-based systems on PCs. The inventiveness is enormous, and despite development on the hardware-side constantly increasing capacity, software developers are always a few steps ahead, and can use even more capacity.

The original PC and DOS design had a number of limitations that really only begin to surface as the market explodes, and the imagination and creativity of software developers unfold. Moreover, IBM had probably predicted that the strategy of making the design open to all other manufacturers would create a larger market than if it kept it solely for itself, but it underestimated the enormous competitive pressure that it would be exposed to at the same time. The advertisement of OS/2 is, on the one hand, a relevant wish to have an operating system that better meets the needs of software developers wanting to develop advanced and user-friendly software. On the other hand, there is also a desire to gain more control over the market by banking on the development of the operating system and obtaining licence fees from manufacturers taking advantage of IBM's innovations.

IBM was known for consciously exploiting its strong position to create uncertainty among its customers. When the company needed to come up for air to catch up in an area where they had lost ground, they would announce products still on the drawing board. The strategy was called spreading "FUD", which stands for Fear, Uncertainty and Doubt. The many large companies using IBM as a supplier now preferred to wait and see what the company would come up with and, therefore, often postponed investing in new technology rather than choosing innovative solutions from a competitor.

The announcement of OS/2, which happens a good while before the product is actually delivered, also creates significant uncertainty in the market. For Erik Damgaard, who has just launched Concorde based on DOS, the question of the market's reaction to IBM's announcement is crucial. Should he now invest in developing Concorde for OS/2 and will there still be a market for DOS-based systems? However, IBM has released a monster it no longer has any control over. It quickly becomes clear that customers are continuing to ask for DOS-based solutions on PCs – and not only those delivered by IBM.

The M24 PC from the Italian company, Olivetti, was immensely popular in Denmark. However, the M24 turned out to have problems with networks based on Novell, which Damgaard recommended for multi-user environments. The problem could be solved by replacing the keyboard(!). When customers asked what they should use the original keyboard for, Damgaard Data's support department suggested they throw it in the harbour! A good example of dark IT humour.

Erik is technically excited about the design specifications of OS/2 and he's convinced that IBM will return strong. But he chooses to just keep an eye on development and not invest any development resources into getting an OS/2 dedicated system early to market.

## An office in Jutland

In summer 1986, Preben is contacted by Jesper Carl Hansen, who works as a salesman at a Danmax reseller in Esbjerg. He proposes that Preben hire him to open and run an office in Jutland. But Preben has plenty to see to in Zealand and isn't mad about the idea of setting up an office on the other side of the Great Belt. Initially, Jesper Carl's offer is politely declined.

With the release of Concorde in October 1986 and the subsequent positive market response, the time for expansion in Jutland seems right, and Preben contacts Jesper Carl in spring 1987 to hear if he is still interested in opening and running that office in Jutland. He is, and with effect from 1st June 1987, Jesper Carl starts preparing for the establishment of a branch in west Denmark. Preben asks Michael Sander to help him get started as soon as possible. Together they look at the geography of Jutland to identify the most suitable location. As Preben and Erik already have family near Kolding, it's agreed that the triangle of Vejle-Kolding-Fredericia is most appropriate. On 7th August, the office at Pakhustorvet in Kolding opens with Jesper Carl Hansen as head of activities in Jutland and Funen. The increased effort in west Denmark quickly proves to be a great success.

Henrik Pedersen, who in early spring 1987 moves from working on packaging and shipping to taking care of business partners, returns home with Jesper Carl from visiting the business partners in Jutland at the end of June. He reports that Damgaard Data is close to unknown west of the Little Belt and that there is great confusion about the relationship between Damgaard Data and FK-DATA. Some resellers believe that FK-DATA is responsible for the development of Danmax and Concorde, and that it is Damgaard Data, which distributes an OEM (Original Equipment Manufacturer) version of their software. Furthermore, many partners are extremely dissatisfied with having to compete with FK-DATA, which offers exactly the same product and allegedly often at a reduced price so as to win customers.

FK-DATA's activities are quite profitable for Damgaard Data, but their success is apparently turning into a problem.

## Damgaard produces a network card and sets up Connect A/S

When multiple users in a company all need to use the same Concorde as well as share data and printers, the PCs need to be connected in a network. Unlike today, delivering PCs with networking facilities wasn't standard, and wireless networks hadn't yet been invented. To get a PC network up and running, you first had to purchase network cards that were mounted on each PC and connected with a cable. Thereafter, you had to acquire a piece of networking software capable of handling the shared resources. In the 1980s, the network market was characterised by a lack of common standards. Network cards from different manufacturers use different types of cables and can't communicate with each other. Getting a PC network to function isn't something that small businesses can immediately do for themselves. Therefore, they need their EDP provider to deal with the technicalities on their behalf.

Many small partners don't have a great deal of technical competence. Often, both resellers and their customers struggle to get the network to work properly. Preben and Erik discuss how to handle the many problems and queries regarding networks that, technically, have nothing to do with Danmax or Concorde. They agree that Damgaard Data will have to come up with technical solutions in regard to their business partners and will now have to start distributing the network products in order to get the growth margin needed to finance the extended support.

In the mid-1980s, when PC networking technology is still young, both prices and growth margins on hardware and software are quite high. At the cheap end are products like 10-net, which costs around 1,600 USD per work station and can handle the connection of up to ten such stations. However, Erik has chosen to go with Novell Netware, which is significantly more expensive, but also much more robust and scalable. In principle, Danmax and Concorde can run on any type of network, but supporting them all is an insurmountable task, which is why it makes sense to standardise.

When Søren Kristensen, an acquaintance of Erik Damgaard, suggests that they get together and develop and produce network cards for PCs, it seems like the exact commercial solution they've been looking for. If they produce the cards themselves, they can skip the import step, thereby attaining a significantly higher growth margin. And as a manufacturer of network cards, they can go directly to Novell and get an OEM agreement, which also allows them to bypass the distributor, thereby further increasing the gross margin. Erik and Preben want to maintain their primary focus on software development, but there is an urgent need to get the other parts under control, too.

As the production and distribution of network cards doesn't have to be limited to Concorde partners, they decide to place that activity in a separate company, under the name Connect A/S, owned jointly with Søren Kristensen and Erik Carlsen, the latter being responsible for its day-to-day management.

At the same time, they take over the neighbouring building at Landemærket 49, where the basement is converted for the production of network cards. With the subsidiary company, Connect, Erik and Preben have taken a step into a market in which they have little insight and experience. What at first glance looks like good business quickly turns out to be much more challenging and difficult.

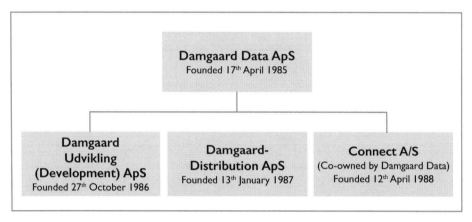

With the establishment of Connect A/S in spring 1988, Damgaard Data entered into the development and production of hardware for connecting PCs. Such products came with high prices and attractive contribution margins, but the situation changed significantly in only a few years.

## Conflicts with FK-DATA

Danmax and Concorde are popular, sought after products. Both Damgaard Data and FK-DATA have been successful in building up their reseller networks, and so they begin to cross paths more and more just as happened in Jutland; they are often trying to recruit the same partners, and often their business partners are competing for the same customers. The success of FK-DATA also means that many customers and resellers are under the impression that Danmax and Concorde are products developed by FK-DATA, for which Damgaard Data has been granted distribution rights.

From the latter half of 1986, Damgaard Data starts recruiting more and more employees to handle the many resellers. But it's still primarily Preben and Erik who have a relationship with Finn Kusk. Due to the informal management structure, strategic issues are regularly discussed at lunch on Fridays in Preben's office, and despite the fact that FK-DATA adds a lot of money to the coffers, there is widespread dissatisfaction with the confusion that working with FK-DATA creates. As Damgaard

Data gradually grows its distribution capacity to serve the entire market, most employees believe that FK-DATA is becoming more and more unnecessary.

## A rumour is born and dies

At the end of spring 1987, Damgaard Data employees frequently encounter a rumour that questions whether or not Concorde is a genuine multi-user system. A real multi-user system must be able to handle a situation whereby many employees need to access and change the same data at the same time. Erik has worked a lot on precisely that issue, and has even designed the system to take into account a situation wherein the connection between the user's PC and the shared data server is interrupted in the middle of updating the books. The rumour has no base in reality. But as neither resellers nor customers, in particular, possess the necessary technical insight to assess the validity of the rumour, Henrik Rose proposes that they send Concorde to the Danish Technological Institute for testing. A number of very specific questions on which Concorde is to be tested is then compiled.

The report from the Danish Technological Institute describes in detail the results of the tests carried out and can confirm that Concorde operates and behaves as it should. It is also robust in terms of network crashes and can handle conflicts that may occur when many users carry out simultaneous updates.

Based on the report, Damgaard Data takes out a number of advertisements in newspapers and magazines, after which the rumour dies. Those who contributed to its spread are left red-faced. Concorde is now the only system on the market that has received the blue stamp from the Danish Technological Institute. A threat has been turned into a marketing asset.

## Irregularities at FK-DATA

In August 1987, a suspicion that FK-DATA isn't settling its account for all licences sold arises. The suspicion is the result of unsettled licences for a number of customers listed on FK-DATA's own official reference list. Henrik Pedersen gets an FK-DATA employee to send a complete list of licences from FK-DATA's Calc so that he can compare them with the reports from the company. A careful review and comparison reveals that FK-DATA has neither reported nor paid for a large number of licences.

Preben raises the problem with Finn Kusk when they meet at the Herning Fair in late summer, informing him that due to the circumstances, FK-DATA's distribution of Concorde must cease. Finn Kusk is definitely not happy about that. It will pull the rug out from under his business in one fell swoop. He argues that any irregularities must be due to banal mistakes and simply forgetting to record correctly, but, after consulting with his lawyer, he agrees to discontinue the sale of Concorde as of 1st October.

FK-DATA, founded and operated by Finn Kusk, played a major role in the period 1984 to 1986 and contributed to Damgaard Data's rapid take-off. When FK-DATA had to cease selling Concorde Finance in October 1987, it essentially pulled the rug out from under the company, and Finn Kusk had to hastily complete the development of a replacement product, which came to market in 1988 under the name System 2.

## Internationalisation and an OEM agreement with Novell

The rumours of Damgaard Data's success spread rapidly throughout the industry, and soon unsolicited applications and phone calls from people wanting to jump on the bandwagon start pouring in. One of the requests comes from Morten Vedel Nielsen, who after a short career in a Danish

IT import company dreams of working abroad. And as, in principle, Connect's network card for PCs can cross national borders far easier than a financial system such as Concorde, Morten is hired to get international sales up and running. The global market for network cards is gigantic and growing rapidly. There is certainly no lack of marketing potential for a company such as Connect. But whereas the slightly more cautious approach to expanding a new business would probably be to focus on the home market first and then on neighbouring markets, Morten immediately takes a huge leap, setting course directly for the USA. He organises a sales trip to California and Utah, where Novell has its headquarters. Preben is part of the sales contingent, but when Morten pleads for a posting in the USA at the expense of Damgaard Data, the former puts on the brakes and says no. Morten resigns and moves to the USA to try his luck on his own.

Nevertheless, the visit to Novell in Provo, Utah, proves to be not a complete waste of time. When later, in autumn 1987, a need to acquire distribution rights for Novell's Netware emerges, in order to circumvent Danish importers, Preben gets out the business cards and builds on existing relationships. After some correspondence via fax and telephone, he is able to contact the responsible party in Novell in the USA, who replies that they would like to visit Connect and Damgaard Data in Copenhagen before entering an agreement.

## A white Mercedes for the guests

Sealing that deal is crucial for Erik and Preben's business. Every effort must be made to create the best possible impression. Novell is informed that representatives from Connect will be at the airport to greet them upon their arrival. And so as not to seem cheap, they plan on renting a large Mercedes for chauffeuring their guests during their stay. But there's a snag – neither of them is old enough to rent such a large car, so they have to ask one of the older employees to sign the lease. With an eye on detail, Erik removes all signs that the car is a rental for the occasion the night before the guests are due to arrive. The visit goes well and the people from Novell are suitably impressed by both the business and the vision. They send an OEM agreement for signing under which Damgaard

Data becomes a manufacturer and distributor of network cards as well as Novell networking software.

## The network department

Now there is even more pressure on the support phones. Therefore, a networking department is established to help business partners and customers get the systems set up and operational, to keep an eye on the market and to help build up distribution outside of the original reseller channel.

In the late summer, Preben places a job advertisement in *Berlingske Tidende* and starts selecting candidates for interview. Choosing the right employees is every leader's first but also most difficult task. In large companies, hiring the wrong person can be tolerated from time to time. But for Damgaard Data, which grows from 6 to 24 employees in the period 1987-88, every employee plays a crucial role.

The choice of new staff for the network department falls on Allan Mathiassen, who had worked with Novell Netware for a couple of years. He is ridiculously technically competent, able to convey his knowledge to others who don't share the same technical know-how and possesses a kind of responsiveness and patience that makes others feel safe in approaching him. Allan, completely devoid of traditional career aspirations, has a major impact on the success of Concorde and the expansion of the reseller network. Essentially, he removes any uncertainty and insecurity from the entire network problem, which is a prerequisite for the systems being able to function, but which in itself is often pure technical anarchy.

The strategy of providing technical support to their customers and business partners as well as finding, employing and retaining employees such as Allan Mathiassen represents a major part of the recipe for the success that the company experiences in the years to come.

## PolySoft shuffles and Albatros sniffles

During 1987, rumours that Albatros from PolySoft is extremely faulty, that the company has difficulty fixing the bugs quickly and that, overall, it doesn't provide satisfactory support are rife in the industry. Erik, Preben and Michael Sander, who now constitute the top management team, perceive Albatros, PolySoft and PolyData as their biggest competitor. They put their heads together to figure out how they can wrestle customers, business partners and thus market share away from them.

In late summer, an appreciated helping hand comes from outside the business in the form of an independent report from the analysis company, Information Technology Management (ITM). ITM makes a comparison of the financial systems on the Danish market, placing Concorde at the top. Similarly, a report from the audit company, Price Waterhouse, also has nothing but praise for Concorde. Taken together with the network report from the Danish Technological Institute, it is a powerful cocktail of external recognition, which they waste no time in exploiting.

In full-page advertisements in newspapers and magazines, Damgaard Data draws attention to the independent reports, which readers can receive for free by submitting a coupon. Coupons are soon flowing in from new, potential customers and business partners.

Every customer knows that suppliers praise their own products to the hilt so, therefore, they don't take much heed of that kind of propaganda. In 1987, when Damgaard Data distinguished itself with no less than three external, independent reports from recognised institutions, all stamping Concorde with the seal of approval, they wasted no time in exploiting the situation and including it in their overall marketing strategy. We know from contemporary social media that independent recommendations are one of the strongest marketing tools available. The very same mechanisms worked for Damgaard Data in the 1980s.

In November, the firm Marketing Expansion publishes the first half of a satisfaction survey carried out by 330 Danish PC and software resellers, where PolySoft is expected to lose additional market shares to Concorde. PolyData's 10-net is also expected to be pushed out of the market. When the second half of the report is published, just before Denmark takes its Christmas holidays, Albatros once again receives a negative review and is judged not worth the money. Damgaard Data and Concorde are once more placed at the top when it comes to satisfaction and positive expectations from resellers.

In light of this, Preben, Erik and Michael put a long-term strategy in place aimed at making life even rougher for PolyData.

## Preben makes Jesper Balser an offer

PC&C, which came to market with PCPLUS for single-user financial systems in 1985, is now looking into the possibilities of entering the multi-user system market, too. It had assigned Berendsen Computer Products to distribute their first product but, in autumn 1987, it announces that its new Navigator will be distributed by none other than IBM. Despite the announcement giving rise to a few furrowed brows, the market in Denmark is so divided that IBM's business partners comprise a category all on their own and, therefore, are not immediately considered to be a threat to Concorde.

Preben learns that the management of Berendsen Computer Products feels insulted by PC&C not giving them the business of distributing Navigator and, therefore, it no longer wishes to continue distributing PCPLUS. He gets an idea and calls Jesper Balser with an unusual offer: he will assume distribution of PCPLUS. Jesper, who can see where the idea is going, immediately invites Preben to coffee.

PCPLUS and Danmax are in what is known as an aftermarket or secondary market. That is, the companies behind the products don't want to invest any more in development, but they still want to be able to take advantage of the remaining market potential. Damgaard Data has over 250 resellers for financial systems for small and medium-sized businesses, and as there is a continued demand for single-use solutions, it's hard to imagine a better retirement home for PCPLUS. Jesper, of course, needs

# Nyt dansk adm.program sælges gennem IBM

PC&C, som har udviklet PC Plus, der sælges gennem Berendsens Computer Products, er nu ved at være klar med næste skud, Navigator. Denne gang er samarbejdspartneren dog IBM, som står for salg og markedsføring.

Jesper Balser fra PC&C oplyser, at der ikke blot er tale om en udbygget version af PC Plus, men at man er startet helt fra bunden og har udviklet et helt nyt administrativt program.

Man har satset på at gøre det nye system så fleksibelt som overhovedet muligt, således at programmet direkte kan anvendes i sammenhænge, hvor man tidligere har måttet ty til dyre specialtilpassede programmer. Dertil kommer en stor brugervenlighed bl.a. gennem opbygning i vinduer.

14

*Både Carl Chr. Ægidius, IBM, og Jesper Balser, PC&C, er glade for samarbejdet omkring det nye administrative program Navigator.*

IBM-Navigator vil fra midten af november findes hos de autoriserede IBM-forhandlere i tre versioner: N1, der udelukkende består af finans-bogholderi, til kr. 6.500. N5, der endvidere omfatter debitorstyring, salgsordrestyring, fakturering og lager-styring, koster kr. 15.500. Endelig N10, der indeholder det hele, til kr. 25.000. Dertil kommer en net-mulighed til kr. 7.500.

Det er ikke første gang, IBM har indledt samarbejde med et mindre dansk softwarefirma om markedsføring af deres produkter, oplyser Carl Chr. Ægidius IBM Danmark og henviser bl.a. til Aura Analyse, Prolog og Comal. Fra IBM Danmarks side ser man ligefrem en mission i at udbrede danske programmer.                    KE

DATATID NR. 10 - OKTOBER 1987

When PC&C announced the choice of IBM for distributing their new Navigator, the partnership had been on-going for some time. The founders of PC&C were primarily IT nerds capable of developing modern software and they didn't have much experience with or insight into the user requirements of the companies to which Navigator was to be sold. Thus, René Stockner from IBM helped PC&C specify precisely which user features Navigator was to include. When PC&C chose IBM, their previous distributor, Berendsen Computer Products, was offended and took the young entrepreneurs to court on claims of being entitled to compensation. That episode brought Jesper Balser and Preben Damgaard together for the first time.

to be convinced that Preben isn't taking over the distribution right to kill a competitor to Danmax, so there is good reason to chat over a cup of coffee or two.

When the two meet at PC&C's office at Hans Knudsens Plads in northern Copenhagen, the chemistry is good. They see each other as reliable and rational business people. Jesper would prefer Preben to purchase the rights to PCPLUS for a lump sum, after which he can freely maximise his profit through his distribution business. Preben isn't against this in principle, and he discusses the possibilities with Erik. They are uncertain as to how fast the market will dry up and would prefer to pay a running royalty to PC&C instead. The negotiations achieve a positive result, and Damgaard Data is now responsible for distributing PCPLUS.

Preben's sole motive for the unusual initiative is to collect the millions that Berendsen Computer Products has now thrown onto the streets. Moreover, now they won't end up in the pocket of someone who could use them to hurt his own project. With Damgaard Data's partner channels and organisation, only a modest investment is required to wring the last hundreds of thousands out of PCPLUS. The project, which meets both Preben and Jesper's expectations, doesn't take up too much space in the accounts of the two companies, but it helps to create a relationship and mutual respect, which will be worth a lot of money many years later.

Berendsen Computer Products is so upset that PC&C has changed distributor that it brings proceedings against the company for breach of their distribution agreement, claiming that Navigator is a copy of PCPLUS and requires a reimbursement of 600,000 USD. When the case is settled in the Danish Maritime and Commercial Court in 1993, PC&C is released completely from any contractual burden. Berendsen, on the other hand, has to cough up 56,000 USD to cover the other party's legal expenses.

## Damgaard Data becomes a limited company

With the many initiatives aimed at establishing relationships with other companies, including particularly large companies such as Novell, lawyer Jesper Guldbrandsen recommends that Damgaard Data ApS be transformed into a limited company. Thus, on 20th November 1987, the company increases its share capital from 16,000 to 60,000 USD by transferring from the reserves and converting to Damgaard Data A/S [Ltd]. Erik and Preben continue to form the Executive Board, while their parents, Kirsten and Knud, and Jesper Guldbrandsen, become the board of directors.

As 1987 rings out, expectations for revenue in the going concern are around 4.8 million USD, and there are 24 employees on the payroll. It doesn't take any great mental arithmetic to see that business is good. However, focus isn't on profits and pay-outs to the owners but on investment and growth.

# CHAPTER 8

# THE CONFLICT WITH FK-DATA COMES TO A HEAD

## The partnership with FK-DATA comes to an end

The missing information in the reports submitted by FK-DATA regarding the sale of Concorde at the end of 1987 now provides an opportunity to investigate account settlements pertaining to the sale of Danmax. Yet again, irregularities are found. Moreover, Finn Kusk is apparently in the process of developing a competing product, which is an infringement of their 1985 distribution agreement. The situation comes to a head. What began as a positive and promising collaboration in 1984, is now developing into a combination of a hot potato and an irritating stone in a shoe.

Therefore, Damgaard Data demands that the collaboration cease completely, and on 24th March 1988, the parties sign an agreement to terminate all partnership and trade. Licences have not been settled since the end of 1987, but both parties agree that if FK-DATA immediately ends all activities related to Damgaard Data's products and deletes or returns all programs and documentation, they won't owe each other anything. FK-DATA is offered an ordinary reseller agreement for Danmax if they would like to continue in this type of business. Thus concludes the collaboration. But the last word has yet to be heard.

Finn Kusk writes an emotionally-charged letter to all his resellers, criticising Preben and Erik for how they do business. In the letter, he calls the brothers "the Toyota boys" and Preben is referred to as "the zero director". Michael Sander also writes a letter to the resellers, briefly informing them of the cessation of the partnership and offering them the opportunity to deal directly with Damgaard Data instead.

## A flood of telephone calls from resellers

Since the launch of Concorde in October 1986, licences have been sold to over a thousand companies and the number of Danmax and Concorde resellers has grown to around 250. The September issue of the magazine *Datatid* features a portrait article of the company and an interview with Preben entitled: "Danish programmers make the world's best software". The October issue contains an article dubbed: "Concorde PC Management System: a heavy-weight program". Similar, other press media prints positive reviews of the products; in other words, the aircraft is thrusting onwards and upwards when FK-DATA's right to distribute Concorde ceases.

The consequence is a flood of telephone calls from FK-DATA's resellers, who are trying to secure their business and, therefore, would like to sign partnership agreements with Damgaard Data, which now has a relaxed policy towards new partners; if they can provide the necessary technical customer support, they will be granted reselling rights to the products. A minimum purchase isn't required, so only time will tell whether the new resellers are capable of marketing and selling the product as well as retaining customers. If they can't, the damage will be no greater than customers finding a new home with another reseller.

Furthermore, Erik and Preben adhere categorically to selling exclusively through business partners, thus avoiding the detested channel conflict among resellers: partners accept completely that they compete with each other, but they can't abide having to compete with their suppliers. Many software manufacturers sell both directly to customers and through partners. Resellers are naturally suspicious of such trade, where the manufacturer will always – whether they do it or not – be able to undercut in price. Damgaard Data starts to serenade their resellers on both points.

## Injunction proceedings against FK-DATA

In April, employees learn that FK-DATA is continuing to sell licences for Damgaard's version of Danmax. Such activity is both detrimental to Damgaard Data's business partners and contrary to the agreement just entered into. Preben discusses the issue with the company's lawyer and also asks the Danish Association of Software Providers (SUS) to take a look at the case. SUS concludes that there is justified suspicion of a violation of copyright. On 26th April, a complaint is filed at the District Court in Ringsted, and at a hearing held on 5th May, the judge confirms that based on the documents presented by Preben and his lawyer, there is evidence to substantiate the granting of an injunction. A security of 34,000 USD must be given by Damgaard Data within 14 days and, furthermore, Damgaard has to file a petition against FK-DATA, claiming grounds for piracy by 12th May. On 19th May, the Court confirms the money has been deposited and that Damgaard Data has summoned its business partner of many years before the District Court in Ringsted. The Court then informs Finn Kusk that an injunction has been imposed on the continued distribution of software based on Danmax.

## An enquiry from Norway

Despite a wave of Danish software firms popping up in the 1980s, Denmark is still a major importer of software, primarily from the USA. However, Damgaard Data has no immediate plans to enter the export markets with Concorde as there is still much untapped potential in the Danish home market.

When Morten Vedel Nielsen moves to California off his own bat, he is given permission to start exporting Concorde Text to the USA, where his ambition is to compete with WordPerfect, the top market leader in word processing for PCs. The project turns to dust, partly because Morten doesn't have the budget to take on a behemoth like Word-Perfect, and partly because word processing isn't a core business activity for Damgaard Data.

Elsewhere, business goes slightly better when an unsolicited enquiry comes from Norway, where Sigurd Flydal has read of Concorde's success. In spring 1988, he contacts Erik with the aim of becoming a distributor in Norway. Together, they define what changes should be made. To ensure Concorde matches Norwegian market requirements and as that level of development is affordable, the project goes ahead. Nevertheless, it is once again realised that having a good product isn't enough, and Flydal isn't able to achieve anywhere near the same success in Norway as there has been in Denmark. However, as Flydal is responsible for all distribution activities, the partnership needs only small investments from Damgaard Data's end.

## Erik embarks on Concorde Version 4

Concorde sells extremely well in Denmark. The growing number of resellers and customers generates an increasing flow of suggestions and ideas regarding additional capabilities for the product. Similarly, the expanding businesses of the customers create demand for new facilities. For many customers, Concorde is the first step into the Age of EDP. Parallel to them becoming familiar with the basic functions of bookkeeping, stock control, invoicing, accounts receivable and accounts payable, requests for changes and extensions emerge so the system better suits their individual situations and new needs. Some requests are specific to individual customers, while others apply to an entire industry. And some are features that every customer in every industry would benefit from.

In autumn 1987, Erik embarks on developing Concorde Version 4, which is going to accommodate some of the many requests. He also wants to change the file system so that partners and customers themselves can customise and extend the product. Erik has seen that as soon as he gives resellers and customers the possibility of changing something in the system, they do it in a flash. The changes to the file system make it possible to meet special requests from existing and new users faster, and resellers can now expand their consulting businesses by offering to undertake such changes. Essentially, resellers do better business when they can both sell products and offer consulting. At the same time, Damgaard Data doesn't have to take care of every request for an extension, but can focus on developing only the most general improvements.

Concorde Version 4 is the first step on the way to a paradigm shift for the business. The product can be used without setting up anything other than the chart of accounts and standard reports. But now customers can also add new data fields and functions to deal with tasks that the standard product doesn't immediately support. In addition to making Concorde more flexible for each customer, resellers use the enhanced flexibility of Version 4 to develop features that serve brand new customer groups. In other words, business partners can now serve customers about whom Damgaard Data has no particular knowledge and therefore can't develop products for.

## Damgaard Data politely declines Apple

In spring 1988, an enquiry comes in from Apple Computers in Denmark. Would Damgaard be interested in making Concorde available for Macintosh?

In 1986 Apple had the Borland Software Corporation move from TurboPascal to Macintosh, and as Concorde has been developed in PolyPascal, a porting may be possible with little effort. With Concorde's unprecedented popularity in Denmark, Apple spots an opportunity to gain market share for the underlying hardware. After exploring what it would take to get Concorde to run on an Apple Macintosh, Erik and Preben consider the task too great in relation to the size of the market they would reach. Moreover, compared to the return on the same investment in a further improvement of the product for DOS, the decision isn't a difficult one. Damgaard Data politely declines the offer to move Concorde to Apple Macintosh.

## Concorde Version 4 is a success,
## Concorde 5 is on the way

During the development of Concorde Version 4, it becomes clear to Erik that the product's technological platform can't accommodate the many requests of customers and resellers. There are many limitations on how comprehensive he can make the toolbox with which partners and customers can further develop the product. He, therefore, decides to embark on Version 5, even before Version 4 is ready for launching.

In light of the positive press attention, unsolicited applications from jobseekers are continuously pouring in. One such application is from Poul-Jørgen Brinck, a young, yet experienced developer from Computer Resources International (now Terma). He is seeking a job at a company with vision and potential, which he realises is precisely what Damgaard has after reading an article about Erik and Preben. His application lands on Erik's desk in early summer 1988 – just when the company has decided to take on more employees. Erik invites Poul-Jørgen to an interview and hires him as the first developer for Concorde Version 5.

As Erik and Poul-Jørgen discuss the design specifications, it becomes clear that more developers are needed for the project. After another tour around the internal network, they land at Mads Westermann.

## A police search at FK-DATA

Yet again, Preben hears reports that FK-DATA is still not respecting their termination agreement and the injunction. He returns to the Court in Ringsted, this time seeking access to FK-DATA's offices in Ringsted and Vejle with the help of the police. All programs and documents that can be used to continue the illegal operation must be deleted and destroyed.

Despite the Court issuing a search warrant, the police are not particularly cooperative. They find it difficult to understand the issues at stake and how to deal with the actual search. Preben has to go through the Ministry of Justice to ensure the police show up and secure access to FK-DATA's offices.

Entering the premises of a former business partner, accompanied by the police, is not an everyday occurrence for many – not even for seasoned business people. But it is exactly what Preben gets to experience when, at the age of 25, he arrives at FK-DATA in Ringsted on 9th August to ensure that the contract-breaching activities involving Danmax and Concorde definitely cease.

What happens then is unclear. Representatives from Damgaard Data claim that they find copies of the source code for both Concorde and Danmax as well as the Calc, which is used to produce the program codes.

Finn Kusk claims that they don't find anything. However, this doesn't match his later testimony in court. Nevertheless, there is now a definite end to FK-DATA's activities involving Danmax and Concorde, though the case is only settled many years later.

## Connect moves to Herlev and files for bankruptcy

After Connect is up and running and has developed a network card for IBM's new PS/2, disagreements arise regarding strategy and management issues in spring 1988. Erik Carlsen leaves the company, and Preben is appointed CEO effective from 12th April.

Connect A/S, which grows in step with the rest of the business, can no longer have its premises at Landemærket and, therefore, in November it moves to Hørkær 7-9 in Herlev. However, the growth is far from being adequate to maintain competitiveness. In order to ensure sufficiently low production costs, sales both outside of Damgaard Data's own reseller channel and outside Denmark's borders need to be increased. Preben, whose plate is full of the core business, doesn't have time to take on Connect. Thus, in November, he hands over his directorship to a sales manager who had been employed by Damgaard Data a few months before, but hadn't really found his feet.

With the standardisation of the network area, the ownership of Connect gradually becomes less strategically important, and the main shareholders, Preben and Erik are reluctant to make the necessary investments that a commitment to international growth would require. And as the company is neither doing well nor growing organically, they decide to spin off the activities in spring 1989. They negotiate with potential buyers, which results in an agreement to sell the company. However, the completion of the agreement papers drags out and, as the operation has a deficit and can't finance its own operations, they choose to let it go bankrupt in September 1989. The buyer then has to attend bankruptcy court to buy out the activities.

# CHAPTER 9

# A BREAK WITH A FUNDAMENTAL PRINCIPLE

## Damgaard Data turns five

In April 1989, Damgaard Data turns five. The accounts, ending on 30th April, show a turnover of about 12 million USD, a profit of well over 200,000 USD and a net worth of 1.2 million USD. The staff consist of 36 full-time employees. Erik and Preben pay themselves 100,000 USD each in annual salary, but they don't pay out any dividends; rather they invest heavily in the growth of the company. Preben has earned the nickname "Scrooge" from among the employees, because he's very careful with the money, but when it comes to marking the five-year anniversary, he doesn't hold back. Indeed, the party planning committee is given free rein to ensure that employees and their partners have an unforgettable evening at an event held at the Odd Fellow Palace in Copenhagen as thanks for all their hard work for and contribution to the undisputed success of the company.

## On the way to the software industry's first division

In spring 1989, Poul-Jørgen Brinck and Mads Westermann suggest dividing the development project of Concorde Version 5 into two, each with its own team. One team will develop the foundation and general development tools, which the second team can then use to develop application functionality: finance, accounts payable, accounts receivable, stock, invoicing, project, production and so on.

Erik Damgaard agrees with the idea in principle, but it would significantly delay the project. Team two can't start before team one has the foundation in place. The prime catalyst for the suggestion is the fact that neither Poul-Jørgen nor Mads has any background and insight into financial systems and neither are they motivated to work directly with application functionality. On the other hand, a project developing a new foundation and set of development tools is a much more challenging and interesting assignment computer scientifically-speaking. Furthermore, rumours that PC&C are developing a new system based on roughly the same principles are circling. And apart from causing a delay, the new division would require recruiting additional developers, thereby making the project significantly more expensive.

The new architecture would give the company a major boost and would enable Concorde to be further developed so as to cover more industries, serve larger customers and launch internationally. On the downside is a need for greater investment, prolonged development time for a market that is extremely difficult to predict as well as having to establish a development department with many more employees in need of management and coordination.

After weighing up the pros and cons, Erik and Preben decide it is worth investing further and accept a delay.

## Praise for Concorde Version 4

In May, Concorde Version 4 is ready. Employees from the 250 resellers are invited to full-day seminars at Hotel 3 Falke in Copenhagen and at Hotel Scanticon in Kolding, where the new functions and abilities are presented. The improved version of Concorde receives many words of praise along the way. In a comparative test of financial systems in the magazine *PC World*, the Concorde system is given the following review:

*Within the framework of standard systems, Concorde has gradually become such a flexible system that it can be adapted to many different requirements. This is mainly due to the new database structure, which enables the user to create custom fields, screenshots and batch-runs.*

*Apart from being a standard financial system, Concorde can also be considered a form of development tool for special administrative applications.*

*However, there is a fear of individual users (and PC resellers) being able to understand the possibilities in the new system, thus, having external assistance during the implementation process is recommended.*

*PC World January 1989*

Erik had made it possible to change the names and lengths of the fields, and with the ability to define algorithms in a field, Concorde was now also enabled to calculate gross margins and other key ratios directly from the current data. The report generator was also conclusively improved. As *PC World* writes, Concorde is not just a financial system but a development tool, which partners and customers alike can use to develop new functions. Resellers are quick to take that flexibility to heart, and through their own development and adaptation of the system, they are able to reach even more small and medium-sized businesses throughout Denmark.

Erik and Preben Damgaard posing for the photographer when pictures are needed for new marketing material.

## Subscribing for updates

Prior to the launch of Concorde Version 4, Damgaard Data introduces a subscription service whereby customers will automatically receive a new version of the product in return for paying an annual fee. The fee is calculated as a percentage of the current valid licence price. Previously, customers who wished to switch to a new version had to pay the full list price. The subscription service is attractive to customers and simultaneously ensures Damgaard Data a fixed, predictable and prepaid income. In order to stimulate sales, resellers are offered a profit on selling the update subscription to customers.

This subscription service turns out to be a gold mine and helps to fund new, better and even more competitive products.

## Competition in Great Britain is too hard

Despite the market for small and medium-sized financial systems being decidedly local in the 1980s, Preben and Erik are aware of the very large potential outside of Denmark's borders. The partnership with Sigurd Flydal in Norway is going reasonably well, even though it doesn't have the explosive growth that has been experienced in the domestic market.

In late summer 1989, Morten Vedel Nielsen proposes to Preben that they try to break into the British market. It's more a fresh idea than a plan, but seeing as the brothers would like to test the waters abroad, they give the project the green light. In October 1989, the subsidiary Damgaard Corporation Ltd is established with Damgaard Data owning 99 per cent of the company, and Morten Vedel Nielsen owning 1 per cent. They hire a couple of supporters and Morten starts recruiting resellers.

The project isn't successful for many reasons: Concorde Version 4 not being prepared for internationalisation is one of them. Erik has a version made with English text, so the product can be demonstrated to business partners and customers, but nothing more comes of it.

Moreover, the competitive situation in Great Britain turns out to be completely different and much harder than in Denmark. The market situation hadn't been investigated in advance, so the product has to be adapted *after* customers have presented their requirements and wishes.

The British division is not geared up to enter into a dialogue with the development team in Denmark, and Erik is not too excited about investing too much in Version 4 as it won't be the foundation for the future of the company.

Despite the technical difficulties, a few partners have come on board and they succeed in selling Concorde to a few customers. When it is decided to tackle the development of Version 5 in a completely different manner in 1989, the prospect of an English version is pushed even further into the future. Thus, it makes absolutely no sense to continue investing in the British market. The employees are offered the opportunity to acquire all the activities for a symbolic sum and Damgaard Corporation Ltd will cease their activities. Morten Vedel Nielsen travels to Singapore to start selling there. This time without financial support from Damgaard Data.

The ambition regarding activities outside of Denmark has certainly not been set on the back burner, but the brothers realise that international activities need to be based on Concorde Version 5, just as they understand that they need to find a strong distributor before they can move into a new country. Preben tries to get in touch with potential distributors in Sweden and in a few other European countries, but it's hard to find the right companies and people. His initiative is received coolly and hesitantly.

In a major series of articles in *PC World* in spring 1989, featuring a number of experts testing and comparing a large number of Danish financial management systems, the closing article chronicles the following conclusion:

*At PriceWaterhouse, we have analysed similar systems not only from Denmark but also from other European countries as well as from the USA. It is our clear understanding that at this point in time, Danish PC-based financial packages are of high – even very high – quality. A number of the financial packages we have analysed are several generations ahead of similar packages from other countries due to their user-friendliness, flexibility, functionality and capacity.*

*As we are continually assisting in the choice of financial systems in relation to client-oriented tasks, we have an in-depth knowledge of major systems for both minicomputers and mainframes. It is our opinion that a number of the analysed systems are of such high quality that they could compare themselves to much larger systems.*

*Therefore, we would recommend that every company includes one or more PC-based system in their selection when faced with choosing a financial system.*

*PC World July 1989*


One would think that such a recommendation would give both Damgaard Data and PC&C cause to straighten up and invest more energy in the international project. But it doesn't happen, probably due to a mixture of the great success in the domestic market and the lack of a clear path to foreign markets. Erik and Preben quickly lose their appetite for taking the direct route, establishing subsidiaries and recruiting their own employees after their experience in Great Britain. At PC&C, it's the combination of excellent experiences with the establishment of a joint venture in Germany in 1990 and the positive experience of the establishment of a subsidiary in the USA that same year that drives their internationalisation.

## An advanced and robust system

Concorde Version 4 is undoubtedly the most advanced and robust financial system for small and medium-sized enterprises in Denmark. Navigator from PC&C is a good product, too, but it doesn't have the same flexibility as Concorde. Furthermore, PC&C is limited by having chosen a hardware supplier as their exclusive distributor. IBM, with its 35 per cent market share, is the largest supplier of PCs in Denmark, but that still leaves 65 per cent of the market for Damgaard Data. A fact they don't waste time exploiting. With the release of Concorde Version 4, Damgaard Data takes the leader's position in the Danish market. Despite Concorde 4 not playing a role in the subsequent internationalisation, it's instrumental in creating the economic foundation that makes financing global growth possible.

## Damgaard Data collaborates
## with Dansk System Industri

Alongside Damgaard's success, first with Danmax and then with Concorde, another Danish software business has great success with its integrated word processing and database system, DSI-TEKST. Dansk System Industri (DSI), founded by Anne Grethe Pind, who later gets Thomas Hejlsberg (now a senior software architect at Microsoft) on board, uses primarily the same business partners as Damgaard Data. It is from here that the desire to connect the two products originates. When DSI releases a completely new version under the name of DSI-SYSTEM in spring 1989, Anne Grethe, who already knows Preben through the Danish ITC Industry Association [IT-Branchen], contacts him to explore the possibilities and interest in a partnership.

When Erik hears about the proposal to connect Concorde and DSI-SYSTEM, he is immediately in favour of the idea. Such an integration could accommodate a wide range of the requests and requirements asked of Concorde, which – as it stands – would only be available in the upcoming Version 5 that is to be completed in 1990 at the earliest.

At the preliminary meeting, Anne Grethe tells Preben that DSI would also like to change distributor. Indeed, a collaboration seems to offer so many potential benefits that it makes sense for Thomas Hejlsberg and Erik Damgaard to investigate whether an integration of the two products could be achieved with modest effort. They both give the thumbs up and work commences. The connection between Concorde Version 4 and DSI-SYSTEM, which can also exchange data with the spreadsheet product SuperCalc5, is released on 3rd September and is a major success.

DSI's products had been distributed by PolyData, which has now lost out on an important product for its portfolio. Instead, DSI chooses to let Damgaard Distribution and Esselte share distribution of the product in Denmark. Damgaard Data is fully aware that they have killed two birds with the one stone. Losing the distribution of DSI will hurt PolyData, thereby weakening the competitiveness of Albatros, while Damgaard

Data will receive an increased gross margin that can be used to strengthen the competitive power of the Concorde products.

The connection makes it possible for Concorde to read from and write to DSI-SYSTEM and vice versa. Moreover, it enables customers and resellers to make further extensions and adjustments themselves. The connector, which becomes an integral part of DSI-SYSTEM, is well received and also gets very positive reviews in the trade press, which even goes so far as to say that with Concorde, DSI-SYSTEM and SuperCalc5 all the IT needs of small and medium-sized businesses are covered. Both Preben and Erik actively support the partnership as it helps maintain sales of Concorde Version 4, while internal development resources can be applied to the forthcoming Version 5.

In conjunction with integrating DSI-SYSTEM, Erik develops features that enable other external programs to communicate with Concorde's file system. The same functionality can now be achieved without customers having to purchase DSI-SYSTEM. When Preben hears about this, he suggests that the component be made into an independent product and sold as an extension to the main Concorde product. The module is named Toolbox.

## Toolbox generates a turnover of millions

Toolbox is released later in the year, generating a turnover of around 2-2.4 million USD over the next couple of years. A freelance consultant immediately sees the possibilities in the Toolbox module and builds up a profitable business around a wide range of extensions for Concorde Version 4, which he later expands to include new Concorde products. Other resellers are also using the Toolbox and broaden their consultancy and programming activities.

In 1990, Damgaard Data enters into an additional partnership with Dantekst, the Jutlandic counterpart to DSI, further expanding the market for Concorde.

Integrating with DSI-SYSTEM and Dantekst and launching the Toolbox contribute to the value that customers and partners can glean from Concorde, which has a wide distribution and a loyal reseller-base. In turn, this enables the continued sale of new licences and, at the very least, it ensures that customers continue paying for the extremely profitable update subscription. In fact, the subscriptions are so lucrative that Preben jests of having that item number engraved on his tombstone.

## PolySoft goes bankrupt

PolySoft Albatros gets off to a bad start. The product had a lot of bugs, but it is the combination of a number of other issues that is the final deciding factor that leads the company to file for bankruptcy in 1990.

PolySoft is a company within the PolyData Group, which, parallel to developing the Albatros financial system, started a retail chain selling PCs in Denmark, Norway and Sweden. The venture is a complete failure, and in 1989/90 all the companies within the group file for bankruptcy, under which Albatros comes under the hammer at the Insolvency Court in Hillerød.

Preben Damgaard contacts Jesper Balser at PC&C to find out if he would like to share the cost of buying the trademark and source code. That would enable them to offer customers a conversion to Concorde or PCPLUS. And if that isn't technically possible, they can at least ensure that the product is well and truly buried. Jesper isn't particularly interested, but he would be happy to put up to 10,000 USD if they can acquire the rights for around 20,000 USD.

Preben attends Insolvency Court, where the product rights are up for auction. Several people bid, and Preben goes every step of the way, eventually submitting the winning bid of 35,000 USD. However, to his great surprise, the former owner, Flemming Østergaard, has an option to make a final bid. He offers a tiny bit more, and thus he is able to continue developing and marketing the product. Unfortunately for Flemming Østergaard, the train has already left the station. Damgaard Data and PC&C have a good grip on the Danish market and have built up powerful organisations and nicely-cushioned marketing budgets that he can't compete with. Albatross never threatens the two market leaders again.

## Damgaard Data expands distribution of third-party products

Sale and support of the data network necessary for Concorde to serve multiple users simultaneously, thereby making the product relevant for small and medium-sized enterprises, began in 1987 as a kind of necessary emergency measure. But it would prove to be crucial to the success that Damgaard Data experiences with both customers and resellers. When, in 1987, Preben surprises the industry somewhat by taking over PCPLUS's distribution from competitor PC&C, the great value of the large network of business partners becomes clear. Therefore, it makes complete sense that the distribution of DSI-SYSTEM also be taken over and that an agreement be reached with Computer Associates regarding the distribution of a number of their Concorde-complementary products. The gross margin on the distribution activity is roughly 30 per cent, and as the focus is primarily on the Concorde resellers, the work can be done with relatively few employees.

Allan Mathiasen resigns in the beginning of 1989 to start his own business, after which Carsten Kaae, product manager in the network department, assumes the managerial position. Carsten has a technical background and is passionate about both the commercial and managerial aspects. He introduces an expansive style, which increases both turnover and earnings.

## Damgaard Data Large Account is established

Demand for PCs and the network technology that connects them explodes, while prices – due to mass production and increasing competition – plummet. IT solutions based on PC technology and software are, therefore, becoming increasingly attractive as replacements for expensive solutions based on mainframes and minicomputers. Damgaard Data becomes more and more involved in projects concerning solutions for multiple users and more complex requirements.

Many of the 250 resellers have difficulty keeping up with the technological developments and acquiring the necessary skills for advising customers and delivering more complex solutions. In many instances, customers come straight to Damgaard Data and ask about direct delivery and support without reseller involvement.

The new Concorde Version 4 makes it possible to develop comprehensive custom solutions for companies with special requests. But it requires technical skills – skills that many resellers simply don't have. Damgaard employees feel the increase in customer pressure for direct sales, delivery and technical support, and over the summer of 1989, Bo Nielsson thinks about how the situation could be better handled. He had been employed a few months previously to support the sale of Concorde to resellers. His suggestion is simply to create a department for handling large customers.

Erik and Preben agree to direct products and marketing towards larger companies in the future. Many resellers can't or won't employ staff with the particular skills required to serve those types of customers and that is a problem.

Despite being well aware that the establishment of a division serving customers directly won't sit well with the business partners, Erik and Preben choose to support the idea nevertheless. In August 1989, Damgaard Data Large Account ApS is founded with Bo Nielsson as manager and director.

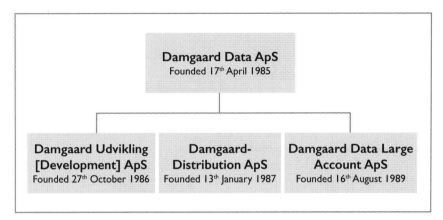

After establishing Damgaard Data Large Account, the concern comprised of four companies.

This decision can hardly be pointed at retrospectively for breaking with the principle of serving customers exclusively through resellers, but it shakes up the market and the organisation. On the other hand, they get direct contact to customers, which will play a crucial role for the speed with which new products can be rolled out and gain a foothold.

# CHAPTER 10

# A NEW DECADE AND TURNOVER OF MORE THAN 20 MILLION USD

## From hardware to software

At the beginning of the 1990s, the IT industry is turned upside down and inside out. Digital Equipment Corporation (DEC), which broke into the market at the end of the 1970s and during the 1980s with its PDP and VAX minicomputers, making life difficult for large companies such as IBM, Control Data, Honeywell, Burroughs and Sperry to name but a few, records a loss of 256 million USD in the first half of 1990. Regnecentralen, Norsk Data, Nixdorf, Data General, Prime Computer, Wang Laboratories and many, many more – who all enjoyed great success in the 1980s – follow in the aftermath of DEC as the 1990s are proven to be very difficult times. Most of them go bankrupt or are bought for next to nothing, after which their activities are closed down. Minicomputers, which exerted hard pressure on mainframe producers in the 1980s, were in reality only small and slightly cheaper mainframes that enabled medium-sized enterprises and departments of large companies to acquire their own EDP facilities. The concept was to choose the hardware first and then search for or develop software for the machines afterwards. As the software couldn't be transferred between the various manufacturers' machines, customers were well and truly bound to their hardware supplier. This monopoly-like situation hindered innovation and evoked arrogance among the suppliers. When PC manufacturers, who are subject to competition and have a completely different cost structure, business model and corporate culture, storm and penetrate the market at the end of the 1980s, almost all mainframe and minicomputer manufacturers are caught napping.

The capacity of the PCs, supplied by many of the manufacturers, is increased; they become cheaper and start to make inroads into businesses, organisations and even private homes; thereby, making the PC the preferred platform for software developers, who can now reach millions of customers around the world. Parallel to this, network technology to connect PCs also becomes more efficient, robust and cheaper to acquire. With the PC platform, customers are not bound to a single supplier, but can shop around and switch hardware according to whom has the best deal. Customers don't love PCs because of the technology or because the DOS operating system from Microsoft is comprehensive and user-friendly – something it certainly isn't – but rather because the fierce competition, technological innovation and penetration make IT both more cost efficient and more accessible, allowing customers more freedom of choice. The 1990s is the decade in which the IT industry switches from being hardware-driven to being software-driven. Even IBM receives a slap in the face in the form of a loss of no less than eight billion dollars at the beginning of the 1990s – the biggest deficit ever recorded in an American company at that time.

## IBM or Microsoft

It is still unclear whether the market will choose OS/2 from IBM or stick to DOS from Microsoft. UNIX is gaining a good foothold on the mini-computer side, and a number of manufacturers such as Sun Computer Systems, Silicon Graphics, NCR, Data General, Olivetti and DDE bet exclusively on that operating system.

Apple's introduction of Macintosh featuring a graphic user-interface in the mid-1980s is the catalyst for a wave of innovation within the software industry. One aimed at making it much easier to use computers. Microsoft launches the first versions of Windows in the 1980s, but it was only in the 1990s that the serious development really began.

PC platforms being cheaper create a sharp demand for software that can help improve and make the thousands of slow, expensive and faulty manual processes in businesses more efficient and effective. However, software development is in itself a costly discipline that requires employees with specific qualifications. Many program elements have to perform the same tasks, regardless of the ultimate aim of the software. Therefore, a new industry that develops software to help software developers do their job emerges during the 1980s. The aim of these tools is to assume some of the routine tasks to help quicken development and ensure higher quality (fewer bugs) and better performance. DSI-SYSTEM from Dansk System Industri is a good example of such development, but giants like Microsoft, Oracle and many others are developing productivity tools for their colleagues in the software industry, too.

## An appraisal in the FK-DATA case

The case against Finn Kusk, which the brothers filed in May 1988, has been handed over to the lawyers. Nevertheless, it appears on Preben's desk from time to time, demanding his attention. At the beginning of January 1990, the results of a legal appraisal to determine whether or not Finn Kusk violated Damgaard Data's copyright are available. The conclusion is definite. It is estimated that FK Soft Finance Version 5 is 90 per cent identical to Danmax Version 4.01 and thus must, in essence, be considered a copy. Finn Kusk has violated Damgaard Data's copyright, which he acknowledges. The final allegation against Finn Kusk is now formulated and the case sent to the High Court of Eastern Denmark. But the cogs of justice turn slowly. A preliminary decision is first reached in 1991.

## Erik and Preben have to demonstrate leadership

At the beginning of the 1990s, turnover exceeds 20 million USD, and the 100th employee is hired. 80 work in Zealand, and 20 are affiliated to the office in Jutland. While Erik and his ten employees work on technological innovation, Preben works on everything else.

Nowhere is it written that those who are good at starting a business are also good at running it. When it comes to Erik and Preben, however, there is not the slightest doubt in their own minds. They are extremely successful and proficient in their respective job roles. Their individual interests and driving forces ensure that the entire spectrum of leadership is covered without any major overlapping between them. Their mutual relationship and trust in each other ensures that conflicts are quickly identified, handled and resolved so that they can move on.

However, the 1990s is the decade in which Erik and Preben have to prove in all seriousness that together they can develop not only a company with global potential but also one that can operate in every way in a turbulent market. They have to demonstrate whether they can attract, retain, develop and motivate skilled employees. Despite the core roles that Erik and Preben play in the company, it is increasingly the staff who get the everyday cogs and gears to run smoothly and at a constant level of acceleration. From the moment the company started employing staff in 1986, the management philosophy has been clear. Erik and Preben seek employees who are more skilled than themselves in their respective fields and who will take the initiative and responsibility for developing their areas. Neither of them wants to micro-manage their employees. As owners of the business, they are never challenged by political pressure from above and don't need to make themselves look good in front of a board of directors. Therefore, they have no reason not to hire only the best and most skilled employees they can find.

Preben, who has the top and most comprehensive management position, has – apart from this Higher Diploma in Organisation – no management concepts or experience from previous jobs. He and Erik have to deal with challenges as they arise.

## Erik focuses on development

For Erik, leadership as a professional discipline is not interesting in itself. His focus is on developing innovative and competitive products, which retailers can refine and extend and customers will buy. He operates from a completely flat team structure where everyone can contribute and everyone can partake in the decision-making. Due to the nature of the work, he has to know the details of the development work, but that doesn't equate to him deciding everything. Not that he wouldn't like to – but a good argument can win him over and change his opinion. Since the beginning, in 1983, Erik has always spent a lot of time and energy on being in close contact with retailers and customers. The development of both Danmax and Concorde took place in close interplay between his own ideas regarding the design of user-friendly software and an open and welcoming attitude to input and feedback from those selling and using the product. He focuses all of his energy on the product, ensuring both new versions of current products and new thinking for the years ahead. He deliberately chooses to entrust development of the rest of the organisation to Preben and only expresses his opinion when and if he is asked directly.

## Concrete ambitions

For Preben, leadership as a professional discipline holds great interest and passion. And being responsible for 80 employees means that there is a need for a certain amount of structure and a team of middle managers. From the start, Preben is aware of not always being the driving force and the sole initiative-taker. He lays out and maintains the overall strategy together with Erik, and is the one developing and running the organisation, the one executing the strategy. After experiencing success first with Danmax and then with Concorde, there is a now more concrete ambition: to be the leading supplier of user-friendly software for financial management in small and medium-sized companies. The strategy to ensure that goal is based on customers being served by retailers, and that goal is to be achieved in Denmark before international penetration gets underway in earnest.

Both brothers want to pursue an aggressive growth strategy. They know the market is changing rapidly, and that the software company that takes the lead will find it easier to maintain its leadership position. That aggressiveness is clearly visible in the accounts, where there is heavy investment in product development, organisation and marketing while the brothers refrain from withdrawing money for themselves. All initiatives from employees and managers are compared to the strategy and are only escalated if they clearly support the overall objectives.

There has to be room for all employees to do their work based on a thorough understanding of the company's strategy and values. In particular, managers taking ownership of their respective business areas and pursuing the strategy without having to run it past Preben has to be accommodated.

A formal management team is established, which holds weekly meetings where decisions are maintained and documented in minutes. Erik Damgaard is responsible for all product development and the related technical documentation. Claus Winblad, who has taken over from Henrik Rose as sales manager, is responsible for the sale of Danmax, Concorde and later Concorde XAL to retailers as well as for distributing the products from DSI and Computer Associates, including logistics and shipping. Support and training are Jørgen Holck's remit. Michael Sander is responsible for marketing and PR, while Jesper Carl Hansen is responsible for Jutland, but not for sales and marketing, which falls under Claus Winblad and Michael Sander, respectively. Bo Nielsson is responsible for Large Accounts, which is legally located in a separate company, but is managerially a department on an equal footing with all the others. Carsten Kaae is responsible for the sale and support of network products for the entire country. Each of them must focus on optimising the business within their respective areas, and they have free rein to do so.

Some of those employees, who came aboard in Landemærket during the very first year, where everyone worked as a single team, find it difficult to accept that there is now an intermediary between them and the brothers. So they find their way to Preben's office from time to time to express their dissatisfaction with the situation, but Preben backs up his managers and asks them to try working together.

## Carsten runs his own course

Each of the mid-level managers handles their areas satisfactorily, but there are difficulties with collaborating across the company. As the business grows and new employees are recruited and trained, it becomes a mounting challenge. The network department under Carsten Kaae, in particular, runs its own course. The department, originally a technical support function for the sale of Concorde, develops a new vision under Carsten: it now targets the entire Danish market. The demand for network products and expertise is not limited to retailers who sell Concorde. Everyone needs these types of products and services, so Carsten's philosophy is why not serve the whole market. Networking is Carsten's home field, and he does it well. Turnover and earnings are significant and deliver a welcome contribution to the entire business. But both Carsten's management style and activities outside of Damgaard Data's core market are often met with raised eyebrows from his colleagues in the management team.

## Damgaard Data moves to Birkerød

The company can no longer be accommodated in the premises on Landemærket with adjacent rented offices on Gothersgade. The big question is whether to stay in the centre of Copenhagen with the distinct atmosphere associated with being close to the city's heart and nightlife, or to move to the suburbs? Erik and Preben are both starting families, so proximity to Copenhagen is less urgent. Plus it's difficult for many visitors to find parking spaces when attending courses or going to meetings at the office in Copenhagen city centre.

After a few searches and viewings, the choice falls on a residential building on Bregnerødvej in Birkerød, where rent prices are reasonable, there are good transportation links and the surrounding buildings offer opportunities for expansion.

## The Volkswagen Passat principle

The choice of Bregnerødvej and the subsequent interior layout is characteristic of the management culture of Damgaard Data, which is later entitled "the Passat principle" (after the Volkswagen Passat). The company earns good money and could easily have moved into a marble palace in the city centre – that would have been the Rolls-Royce solution – and the company certainly had the finances for it. Erik and Preben could also have chosen some inexpensive warehouses in southern Copenhagen, have lowered their outgoings, increased earnings and paid themselves a bigger dividend. That would have been the Lada solution, which the employees would probably have accepted but not been too excited about.

The brothers choose an upper middle class solution, thereby signalling a certain level that shows that they are neither extravagant nor stingy. Decisions have to be made daily in every business in matters where it is difficult to determine the correlation between investment or cost on the one hand, and customer satisfaction, employee well-being as well as the company's results on the other. The Passat principle makes it easier for everyone with budget responsibility to make sound decisions that agree with that stage of development at which the company finds itself. In June 1990, they move into premises at Bregnerødvej 133, 3460 Birkerød, which become the background for the business until the merger with Navision Software in 2000.

Later in the month, Preben's girlfriend, Charlotte, gives birth to their daughter Katrine.

Bregnerødvej 133, to where Damgaard Data moves on 1st June 1990, becomes synonymous with the company in the 1990s. With the major investments in the development of Concorde Version 5, cash flow is a bit tight in 1990/91 and savings have to be made where possible. The move from Landemærket in central Copenhagen to Birkerød in North Zealand is done by the employees themselves. The picture shows Michael Sander (L), Erik Damgaard and Preben Damgaard (Photo: Morten Gregersen).

The move and refurbishing of the new premises, which is in addition to the ordinary day-to-day operations, pulls hard on the company's liquidity and, at a rather late stage, Preben realises there will be difficulties paying salaries and creditors at the turn of the next month. He contacts Handelsbanken, the company's standing bank, explains the situation and asks for a temporary overdraft on the bank account. Surprisingly, the bank refuses to grant such credit. Preben won't allow the problem to affect the company's creditors by delaying payment and risking the good name of the company, so via Jesper Carl Hansen at the Jutland office, he contacts a senior director of Sydbank. Within a few days Preben has paid a flying visit to Aabenraa and established an overdraft facility, after which all accounts in Handelsbanken are moved to southern Jutland. Handelsbanken later comes with their tail between their legs to apologise and try to put right the damage done, but Preben won't waste time talking to them. After a brief chat with some employees from the finance department, the bankers have to go home empty-handed and minus a customer.

The liquidity squeeze of 1990 teaches Preben and others in the management team that from now on they need to have more focus on the terms of payment negotiated with customers, retailers and suppliers. The sale of foreign products, in particular, which now accounts for half the revenue, includes significant sales costs with payment terms and inventory levels, which could be crucial for total liquidity. Work dedicated to increasing the credit period is commenced, especially on products bought abroad for which it is necessary to maintain a certain level of stock in order to sustain short delivery times. The credit period is successfully extended to 90 days and more. With 15 days credit on the debtor side and an average inventory level of less than 30 days, the increasing sales of foreign products suddenly creates liquidity. Where suppliers have warehouses in Denmark, they operate with small buffer stocks as the products can be reordered and delivered within a few days.

The sale of the properties on Landemærket brings in approx. 720,000 USD, which greatly warms up the accounts for 1990/91. Due to the major investments in Concorde XAL, the profit is only around 160,000 USD. The margin on the properties rescues the situation and gives a final result of plus 460,000 USD. This equates to approx. three per cent of the turnover, which under normal circumstances would be completely unsatisfactory for a software company. As the revenue isn't publically disclosed, nobody notices the "bad" accounts, and it's not even worth mentioning for the owners. The business is still extremely well-cushioned with a net worth of close to two million USD, of which more than half is liquid cash.

## Making software industry world history

After deciding to divide the development of Concorde Version 5 into a core group and an application group, additional staff are recruited for both development and documentation. The completed core group consists of Erik Damgaard, Poul Jørgen Brink, Mads Westermann, Keld Jørgensen and Jesper Theil Hansen. When, in the middle of 1989, Jesper Theil Hansen demonstrates a tool he has developed for generating screen displays, Erik realises the potential of the new system. He intensifies the ambitions and decides to design a brand new development environment that will make retailers into software developers, thereby enabling them to develop their own industry and customer solutions as extensions of Concorde Version 5. The inspiration for this move comes first and foremost from Erik's experience of the market potential of a product that resellers and customers themselves can work further on. But it is also supported by the technological development within the software industry, where the term "fourth generation tools" is the contemporary catchphrase and where expertise has been infused with new employees.

During spring 1990, Erik and the team have come so far with the core system that they can begin developing the basic functions of the actual financial system. Erik deals with the key financial programs and co-opts employees from other departments to assist in the development of the other modules. Additional employees from the support departments in Copenhagen and Jutland are brought in for drawing up documentation and everyone tests the modules as they are ready.

## The start of a new chapter

At the end of 1990, PC&C launches Version 3 of their Navigator. It has an architecture and some facilities that resemble those, which Damgaard Data is in the process of developing – including a development environment, which they call AL (Application Language). PC&C coming first to market doesn't arouse excitement; instead it's the catalyst for a discussion about what can be done to catch up on such a head start. As no-one has the time to or needs to look into Navigator's nooks and crannies in order to identify differences, a quick thinker suggests calling Concorde's new development environment XAL (eXtended Application Language), which signals that the product is a class above PC&C's.

To support Concorde XAL's position in the market, large amounts of money are invested in design, packaging and marketing. A recognised professional designer is affiliated to the product's launch. Indeed, the profiling of XAL gets a significant boost on the whole compared to previous products to signify precisely that something new is on its way. As development work progresses, it's acknowledged that Concorde XAL will make great demands on the technical capabilities of the retailers. Therefore, a certification program is designed, which requires resellers to participate in training over the course of many days before they are allowed to resell the product. And to further emphasise the seriousness and exclusivity of the new XAL retailer channel, each course participant receives a TimeSystem® calendar in leather with their name printed in gold on the cover.

With Concorde XAL, Damgaard Data takes a giant leap in terms of both the market and technology, but also regarding its original starting point of developing user-friendly financial systems for small businesses. Concorde XAL is the start of a brand new chapter in the company's history and the introduction of a whole new world.

## Digital Equipment Corporation

One of the world's largest IT companies, Digital Equipment Corporation (DEC), is experiencing hard times. Sales of their previously successful products, VAX and PDP minicomputers, plummet, leaving large gaps in the accounts. As demand for UNIX-based minicomputers is growing, the company decides to make an effort to earn revenue from their variant, called Ultrix. At DEC in Denmark, this task is assigned to Steen Bindslev, Director of Sales and Marketing. He is convinced that such a venture must be taken using software already requested by customers and where solutions aren't already available for UNIX. DEC holds a good market position for technical software, but it lacks financial and administrative solutions. As Concorde is popular in Denmark and operates only on PCs, Steen Bindslev contacts Preben Damgaard to hear about possible interest in a collaboration. At a meeting at Damgaard Data in Birkerød, Preben and Erik unveil the new version of Concorde and express their interest in a partnership based on that product. Not only will the new Concorde XAL appeal to larger customers and therefore suit UNIX systems, but the porting to UNIX will be considerably easier than if it were Concorde Version 4.

As all parties agree that the collaboration will be based on the new Concorde XAL, discussing the terms can now go ahead. Steen would like DEC to have unlimited exclusivity to market Concorde XAL. But despite DEC being more than a thousand times bigger and having subsidiaries worldwide, Preben isn't interested in placing his most promising egg in one basket, no matter how big and impressive that basket is. The negotiations end with DEC Denmark getting a 12-month lead on Concorde XAL for DEC's version of UNIX. Thus, Damgaard Data is still free to distribute the product to the PC market and enter into agreements with other suppliers of UNIX machines. DEC will build up a new retailer network in Denmark, which will sell the systems and service the customers. In other words, they become the distributor of Concorde XAL for their own future Ultrix retailers.

Despite DEC's financial difficulties, it is still a well-known and recognised brand within the industry, and the agreement with DEC regarding the marketing of Concorde XAL supports the intended position of the new product. Actually, it's difficult to see a better starting point regarding market strategy for the new Concorde XAL than such a partnership with DEC, which in terms of reputation ranks just below giant IBM.

The partnership with Damgaard Data was a breath of fresh air for DEC, which was fighting falling sales and major deficits at this time. The director of the Danish subsidiary, Niels Birkemose Møller, formed close ties with Preben Damgaard and later joined Damgaard Data's board. This picture was taken in conjunction with the signing of the distribution agreement. From the left is Preben Damgaard, Niels Birkemose Møller and Erik Damgaard.

Steen Bindslev decides that the leader of the XAL project is to be found outside of the company and, therefore, he instigates an external recruitment process that ends with the appointment of Per Steen Pedersen. He comes to play a major role in Damgaard Data's later development.

# CHAPTER II

# CONCORDE XAL IS LAUNCHED

## Danotherm becomes a guinea pig for XAL

The date is set. So spring 1991 is hectic. After all the delays, Concorde XAL *has* to come to market. Employees set their daily jobs aside so as to help write documentation, prepare training material and test the program modules. But the final test will come when the product is installed for real customers. Unlike Danmax and Concorde, XAL will also facilitate production and material management, and Erik Damgaard himself is responsible for the development of the first version of the modules.

Preben has agreed with Michael Laursen, director of the company Danotherm, that its employees will carry out a so-called beta test of XAL before it's launched. The company, which uses a Nixdorf 8870 minicomputer with the Comet financial system, is in need of thoroughly modernising its business processes, including increasing productivity and gross margins with the help of EDP in production. Danotherm must buy the necessary hardware, but it can get XAL at a favourable price and be supported directly by Damgaard Data free of charge. In addition, the company will have some influence on the development of the product, particularly on the parts concerning production and material management.

Testing begins in January 1991, and Michael Laursen quickly decides to implement the system with all 25 users and at the same time turn off the Nixdorf system. This means that the business's safety net is gone, but as production is manual, users can easily live with some temporary inconvenience, which will be remedied later. All agreements regarding the terms of the "beta test" are entered into as verbal "gentlemen's agreements". Danotherm experiences that help from Damgaard Data always shows up whenever there are problems and helps resolve them. No matter what weekday it is or what time of day is best to fix them.

For Danotherm there are unexpected benefits from being a guinea pig. Firstly, they get the opportunity to scrutinise every detail of all business processes within the company, thereby shedding light on their own internal inexpediencies, which can subsequently be rectified. Secondly, their staff become expert users of the XAL system, excelling at systematically recording data, which, in turn, ensures a high degree of dependability in the costings and key figures calculated by the system. Thirdly, the company gets the opportunity to discuss its business processes and needs directly with Erik and his colleagues, which gives rise to further optimisations. Finally, most of the users' wishes are incorporated into the standard edition of XAL. Taken together, Concorde XAL contributes to a significant improvement in productivity at Danotherm and creates such transparency that piecework can be abolished and performance-based pay introduced instead in production to the benefit of both employees and the company. The partnership with Damgaard Data and the implementation of XAL help create the foundation for an economic turnaround that supports growth and profitability in the years to come.

There were similar benefits for Damgaard Data in relation to developing the production and material management modules based on real customer needs. Moreover, they were able to use Danotherm as a testimonial – one which potential customers could visit and learn from.

## Chartered accountants give
## Concorde XAL the stamp of approval

The Danish Institute of Chartered Accountants (FRR) carries out a comprehensive trial run of Concorde XAL and approves the program as a financial system that complies with all formal rules and good practice for financial management in Danish companies. The approval means that XAL can be marketed as compliant with System FRR Version 91. It is a stamp of approval that helps XAL to the position as Denmark's most popular financial management system for small and medium-sized enterprises.

## Pre-release and a birth

On 11th April, a couple of weeks before the official launch, a number of resellers are invited to a little pre-release of XAL in the company's canteen in Birkerød. The plan was for Erik to demonstrate the new system and answer questions, but that morning a call comes in from Gentofte Hospital: Erik's pregnant girlfriend, Signe, has been hospitalised. Her water has broken and the contractions have started. Erik tells Bo Nielsson about the situation, hands him his notes and asks him to make the presentation that afternoon. Bo looks at the notes, laughs and sends Erik off to the hospital. They aren't of much use and land in the bin. But Bo, who helped develop the applications for XAL, accomplishes the task at hand, and there is great enthusiasm among the resellers. Signe and Erik have a girl.

## Concorde XAL is launched
## with a trip into space

Concorde XAL is officially presented at a large-scale seminar at the end of April in DEC's new premises in Hørsholm. The resellers from Jutland and Funen have been collected by bus and driven to Zealand. Everyone is sitting close together in the large, impressive auditorium when the lights dim and a video is switched on. The short film tells the story of the product's creation and purpose accompanied by loud music and special effects. The audience is taken on a journey into outer space that finishes with a safe landing in the auditorium where the presentation is taking place as Erik and Preben Damgaard come on stage.

A lot of time and money have been invested in elevating the overall impression and supporting the understanding that XAL is a major product for larger customers than those who have been served so far and, therefore, the projects are also in a completely different price range. The marketing plays on the Concorde theme of space, speed and advanced technology – not least because PC&C with Navigator 3.0 has chosen a more subdued theme of ships and the sea.

The launch goes well, but the business partners are divided into two camps. There are over 300 resellers of Concorde Version 4, and many of the smaller resellers are reluctant to invest in the skills required to work with XAL. They also feel uncertain about potentially servicing the size of company for which the product is intended. The thresholds for reselling XAL are quite high and demand that employees participate in the comprehensive and expensive training program. About two thirds of resellers politely decline and continue only with Concorde Version 4, which is still selling well and continues to be upgraded with new facilities.

The other group, consisting of approximately 100 resellers, shows interest in the product and the strategy it represents. The market for minicomputers, which XAL is about to pull the rug out from under, is already free falling at this time, and software companies are no longer investing in solutions for the ailing market. Many medium-sized customers are, therefore, left with old financial solutions, which are no longer supported. The alternative: choosing a PC platform, which is what small businesses do, isn't so clear-cut for large companies. They find it safer to continue with a central minicomputer and terminals for those users who have regular, routine tasks. For them, the combination of DEC's Ultrix and XAL is absolutely perfect – in theory.

With the resellers having the possibility of customising XAL and developing new modules, project prices range from 3-4,000 USD all the way into the millions. In such projects, XAL accounts for about only 25 per cent of the price. The rest are adjustments, project management, training and additional modules, which the business partners develop and, therefore, have the entire gross margin on.

## DEC are left with egg on their face

DEC initiates a major marketing campaign, which is launched with a road show where, together with some of Damgaard Data's people, they travel around Denmark presenting the combination of XAL and Ultrix machines to potential resellers and customers. The interest is great and the events are well-attended. DEC succeeds in recruiting a number of resellers, but it doesn't lead to many sales of Ultrix machines.

The reseller universe in Denmark is concentrated on the PC platform and its associated software, printers, networks, backup systems and so on. Mainframes had always been bought directly from manufacturers, and minicomputers were, to a large extent, also bought directly from manufacturers in collaboration with software suppliers. With its AS/400 minicomputers, IBM had a well-developed business partner concept. Other suppliers had more mixed or rather diffuse sales concepts, where they sold primarily directly and only sporadically indirectly. Therefore, there was no established minicomputer reseller channel for DEC to plunder. And neither did they have a well-established network of PC resellers, which they could motivate to take on the reselling of their Ultrix machines. Instead, DEC tries to recruit new PC resellers who see the opportunities in serving larger companies or would just like an alternative to the PC platform. The strategy succeeds, but in the end, business partners choose to offer customers a solution based on the PC platform with which they are already familiar. This results in Damgaard Data getting licence sales, but as DEC doesn't have the distribution rights to the PC platform, they are left with only egg on their face.

## XAL for Ultrix encounters technical problems

Due to its good reputation, however, DEC manages to sell a few Ultrix-based solutions to a couple of larger companies, but these customers are now encountering technical problems. The customers experience long response times. Damgaard Data's development department doesn't immediately recognise the problems and the cases remain pending.

Only when Erik Damgaard and Mads Westermann visit a customer does it become clear that there is a basic design flaw that isn't easy to fix. The way in which Ultrix organises and handles data on the computer will, by definition, make XAL run slower and slower as the volume of data, the number of transactions and the number of users increase. Erik makes some modifications to XAL's file system, which can alleviate some of the problem. But a proper solution will require either the development of a new file system specifically for Ultrix or that DEC's development department in the USA reworks their data management system. Such a level of investment in development doesn't make sense for either Damgaard Data or DEC.

The solution is to utilise the Oracle database system, which circumvents Ultrix's data management system completely and, therefore, doesn't run into the same bottleneck. Moreover, a version of XAL that uses Oracle as an alternative to the built-in file system, which will be recommended to customers with many users and many transactions, is already in the pipeline. But nearly two years pass before that is available: it took time to acknowledge the problem; time to identify the root of the problem and time to ascertain that no quick fix could be found. The solution is just to wait for Version 2, which will support Oracle. In the meantime, customers affected by the problems grow more and more impatient.

Damgaard Data and DEC hold regular status meetings with customers who let their frustration be known in capital letters. Those unfortunate enough to have a combination of DEC's Ultrix machines and XAL with a Native file system are helped by more powerful computers and faster hard drives. Likewise, resellers gradually learn to use the development tools to keep an eye on and continuously modify the routines that are slowing down the system.

The episodes with the unfortunate customers illustrate to Erik and Preben that they have now moved into a brand new market segment, where customers are far more sensitive to the availability of their core financial system. And they shout out loud if problems, which threaten the operation of their businesses, arise. Despite Damgaard Data not, or at least only rarely, having a formal legal responsibility that could lead to lengthy and costly litigations, there is a risk that such problems may adversely affect the company and its products.

But that doesn't happen. Luckily, the massive performance problems experienced by some customers don't seem to make it to the press. But rumours run rife among resellers, and many opt out of selling DEC's Ultrix platform in favour of other platforms, where such problems don't occur to the same extent.

## Damgaard Data enters the big league

The development of Concorde XAL was more expensive than Erik and Preben had anticipated. They employed only a handful of actual developers, but the project drew on many resources from other areas of the organisation. The investments in marketing were also more expensive compared to earlier products. Revenue from Concorde Version 4 and from the sale of network products, DSI and other third party products continue to rise, covering the vast majority of the XAL investments.

The sale of third party products is good business. The products are sold to the same customers, via the same resellers, who purchase Danmax and Concorde products. Therefore, there is no need for a large, separate sales and marketing unit. Most of the gross margin on third-party products land directly on the bottom line, thereby contributing positively to financing investments in their own products. The contribution from the third party products makes it possible to invest in the development and launch of Concorde XAL directly without having to eat into the net worth. An additional benefit is a strengthening of business relations with the resellers, which makes it harder for competitors to get a foot in the door.

In 1990, Damgaard Data expands its range of third party products with tape-backup solutions from Emerald Systems. In January 1991, a general distribution agreement is entered into with Novell, which also allows for sales outside of the reseller network for their own products. In March comes a distribution agreement with Computer Associates, followed in June by an agreement for the distribution of Lotus products, which are immensely popular. Later, Damgaard also receives distribution rights to WordPerfect and the Microsoft Office suite.

When the sales of third party products are at their highest, they include the products DSI-SYSTEM, Lotus 1-2-3, Lotus Ami Pro, Lotus Freelance Graphics, Lotus Organizer, Lotus Approach, WordPerfect and Microsoft Word, Excel, PowerPoint and Mail. The products are grouped in a range of "Concorde Business" packages, together with Concorde Version 4, and are sold for extremely attractive prices. During this time, many small and medium-sized enterprises start introducing EDP and the aggressively priced packages undoubtedly contribute to the gain in market share.

Due to selling third party products, knowledge of Damgaard Data becomes much more widespread in Denmark than if they had been selling only their own financial systems. Thus, the company is one of the largest exhibitors – with two stands – at the Mikrodata exhibition in October 1991.

### Damgaard Data A/S enters the big league of exhibitors at Mikrodata '91 in the Bella Center.

*With two stands totalling 396 m2, Damgaard Data A/S is among the major exhibitors at Mikrodata '91 in the Bella Center.*

*Damgaard Data has always been excited about participating in the EDP exhibitions held at the Bella Center – the company was essentially founded at Kontor&Data in 1984. It was here that the brothers, Preben and Erik Damgaard, presented the Danmax financial system for the first time.*

*Damgaard Data has a lot of exciting news to present at Mikrodata '91, including the new Concorde XAL financial management system and exciting news from Lotus, for whom Damgaard Data was appointed main distributor in June. The new 1-2-3 for Windows, Ami Pro Version 2.0, Lotus cc:Mail, Lotus Notes and Lotus Freelance Graphics can be seen at the stand.*

*An "Idea and Service Centre" has been established at Damgaard Data's special reseller stand, where visitors can come with any questions they may have regarding Damgaard Data's products.*

*At the company's own stand, there is focus on the new Concorde XAL financial system, which combines a powerful development tool with advanced financial management facilities. Concorde XAL covers a wide range of operating system platforms, including DOS, OS/2 and UNIX as well as providing almost unlimited options for easily and efficiently developing customised versions.*

The Danish news agency, *Dagbladenes Bureau*, 13th September 1991

## A money-making machine

With XAL, a brand new market segment has been entered, in which the scale of delivery enables higher prices. To make XAL competitive – among the smaller companies – a price structure with a basic package that can only handle a small number of transactions is designed. If customers need to carry out a greater number of transactions, they can buy "database space" concurrent with growth and demand. The starting price is between 6,800 USD and 24,600 USD, depending on which modules are chosen, to which is added 600 USD per additional user. The limited database space is introduced to keep the starting price attractive to smaller customers, but it quickly turns out to be a real money-making machine. On the whole, every customer exceeds the limit over time and continuously orders more and more database space. The release of more database space requires nothing more than a new code from Damgaard Data.

## Should a payment for support be introduced?

With the launch of XAL, the quantity of telephone enquiries to the support department rockets. The increased pressure on the phones results in long waiting times, and often the person with whom the resellers speak can't answer the question. Resellers are extremely dissatisfied.

Dispatchers are introduced to alleviate the pressure; people who receive the calls and note what it is regarding. After which, the task is assessed and escalated to the appropriate specialist who will call the reseller back. It is revealed that over half of the enquiries are now resolved before the support staff return the calls.

Despite the extensive training program, many unforeseen situations, which cause business partners to contact Damgaard Data, still arise. Resellers can often find the answers to the questions themselves, but it is easier and faster to call Damgaard Data than it is to look it up in the manual or ask a colleague within their own company. Even after the introduction of dispatchers, there is still concern about the situation. To entice the resellers to try to find the answer themselves first, introducing a payment for support is considered. Meanwhile, some of the enquiries report bugs and inconveniences in the product, and similarly the documentation may not always be perfect. Paying for support continues to pop up for consideration, but for now it's just talk.

## The case against FK-DATA comes to an end

In the case against FK-DATA, which comes before the High Court in spring 1991 and ends on 11th June that year, the judges uphold the justification of the District Court's injunction. FK-DATA had violated the agreement of 24th March 1988 and is, therefore, ordered to pay compensation as well as all incurred legal fees. The partnership with FK-DATA, active from December 1984 to March 1988, has a time-consuming, judicial fallout that lasts for three years.

## FK-DATA goes bankrupt but lives on

The agreement with FK-DATA was important in those first fragile years, but it became less attractive as Damgaard Data expanded its own organisation and reseller network. At the end of 1987, the agreement is an irritation, and with the irregularities regarding the payments for licences, Damgaard Data gets a "get-out-of-jail" card to dissolve the deal faster than the nine month termination period originally agreed. When the conflict arose, FK-DATA was buying over one hundred thousand dollars' worth of products every month, corresponding to an external turnover of 320,000 USD. The gross margin earned by FK-DATA amounted to approximately one hundred thousand dollars. Despite FK-DATA retaining the full revenue for a period, they lost a gross margin of approx. one million dollars in one blow, which they could have realised if the agreement had been terminated according to the originally agreed terms.

After the verdict is reached, neither an auditor's report of FK-DATA's accounts to determine the actual extent of the inadequate reporting nor the payment of royalties for the unregistered licences is requested. Thus, Finn Kusk's real losses are somewhat less than the one million dollars, but as he has no other product to sell, his business runs into liquidity problems over time and he has to declare himself bankrupt.

However, some suggest it is a technical bankruptcy, because immediately afterwards Finn Kusk's son sets up a company that continues the development of the financial program, which was started earlier, and launched in 1990 under the name "2001". In 1994, Finn Kusk purchases a copy of the source code for the product Visual Business, developed by a few dissenters from Damgaard Data, and launches WinKompas. In August 2005, Norwegian Visma buys WinKompas for one million US dollars.

## Resellers continue with Danmax and Concorde

For Damgaard Data, the end of the partnership had a somewhat different and more positive consequence. FK-DATA's business partners choose, to a large extent, to continue selling Danmax and Concorde, and on the whole the immediate gain is, therefore, roughly equal to the loss from FK-DATA.

After all, under the circumstances, the agreement with FK-DATA would have been terminated, and if Finn Kusk had been more meticulous in dealing with the Calc and the licences, the consequences wouldn't have been so devastating for him. With this case, Preben demonstrates that he can play hardball if needs be.

The extent of the payment irregularities for licences makes it difficult to perceive the issue as just the result of sloppy business conduct. And as it is simultaneously of strategic and financial advantage to make short shrift of the situation, it isn't difficult to understand why Preben chooses to put on the brakes.

Finn Kusk chooses to appeal the High Court's ruling in the Supreme Court, but when FK-DATA petitions for bankruptcy in spring 1992, the official receiver decides not to pursue the case.

## Finn Kusk won't cry many tears

The termination of the collaboration completely pulled the rug out from under Finn Kusk's business at a time when activities, turnover and profits were showing strong growth. Finn Kusk perceived the entire aftermath with the injunction, search warrant and court case as a mockery of the contribution he had made to Damgaard Data's success. When he receives the verdict in the District Court and has to pay both compensation and legal fees, he feels completely crushed. He is a bitter man and he directs his anger towards Preben Damgaard, whom he suspects of having carefully orchestrated the campaign against his business. Ingratitude is the way of the world. If Preben Damgaard were to be knocked down on a quiet residential street after dark, Finn Kusk wouldn't cry many tears.

## A professional board

The formal requirement to have a board, which accompanied the conversion to an Aktieselskab[9] in 1987 was fulfilled with a team consisting of lawyer Jesper Guldbrandsen and Erik and Preben's parents, Knud and Kirsten Damgaard. In October 1991, Damgaard Data Distribution also converts to an Aktieselskab with the same board. Michael Sander, now a small shareholder (two per cent), pushes, in particular, for a more professional board, and in December 1991, Niels Birkemose Møller, country manager of DEC Denmark, and Henning Kruse Petersen, who shortly before had left the top post as Chief Executive Officer of the then Unibank, come aboard. Recruiting Henning Kruse Petersen proves, not least, to be of great importance to the company's development.

## Dropping disguises

The flying start in 1984 and the subsequent success means Preben never really needed to create detailed budgets and follow up on them. With the constant increase in turnover and earnings, he makes decisions about costs and investments along the way. However, in the early 1990s, and not least after the high costs of developing and launching Concorde XAL, there is a need for more structure regarding plans, activities and finances. With help from Niels Birkemose Møller, Preben draws up a system of activity-based budgets to ensure that the benefits of the many investments are reaped. During 1992, budgeting and following-up are incorporated into the organisation for the first time.

---

9  An Aktieselskab (A/S) is a private limited liability company with higher capital requirements than the Anpartsselskab (ApS) and a requirement for a registered board of directors.

As remuneration principles that are closely linked to the achievement of the budgeted goals are introduced at the same time, Preben runs right into a – for him – unknown but classic issue. Those with responsibility for results quickly learn that their chances of achieving the goals, and thereby earning their bonuses, are greater if they can get their turnover budgets to be as low as possible and their cost budgets to be as high as possible. Preben and Erik have ambitions of winning market share. They push to have turnover targets as high as possible as well as ensuring a profit, which allows for both a high level of continued investment and the building of a buffer for bad times at the same time. However, Preben is particularly aware that employees don't necessarily feel obliged to reach goals, which they themselves haven't helped to determine, and that it can greatly demotivate staff if they have targets they don't believe in.

From the many budget discussions held, a culture of "dropping disguises" gradually develops. This means that instead of sitting across from each other and negotiating as counterparts, they sit on the same side of the table and try to reach agreement on what is necessary for the business to fulfil its ambitions.

Budget negotiations are normally quite political, but Preben succeeds in creating a culture that avoids the worst suboptimisation, helped along naturally by the constant forward motion of the company.

# CHAPTER 12

# LEADERSHIP PROBLEMS

## The Calc for XAL becomes the Licence Generator

In the late 1980s and the early 1990s, significant improvements were made in data communication technology. Not only is it now possible to connect PCs internally in businesses, but data communication with the outside world via telephone lines becomes both faster and cheaper. Many companies were already using the technology to connect their own departments in different locations, enabling their computers to exchange data. It is becoming more and more common to call another computer – outside of a company – to gain access to different information services. Naturally, this development emerges among IT nerds, who set up so-called "bulletin boards", where they can exchange information about and discuss technical subjects. Mads Westermann, responsible for the development and maintenance of the UNIX versions of Concorde XAL, makes extensive use of the knowledge available via bulletin boards, thereby, identifying a range of options that would make it easier for resellers to obtain licence codes for new customers and download new versions of the software.

In 1992, the logistics department of Damgaard employs several people. When a customer orders Concorde Version 4 or Concorde XAL, the logistics department adds a sequential serial number and the customer's name to the licence generator, which then generates codes for all modules in the product. Codes for the modules, which the customer has ordered, are delivered in a "code letter", while the additional codes remain ready for when and if the customer returns to purchase them. With the introduction of XAL for UNIX and later for OS/2, the complexity of this logistical work is also significantly increased, and as there are regular updates, logistics is not only costly but often a source of both mistakes and bottlenecks.

With the beginnings of internationalisation in the early 1990s, where customers come from countries such as Norway, the UK and Singapore, the manual logistic procedure involving postal deliveries is unbearably cumbersome and slow. Therefore, Mads Westermann proposes that he set up a computer, which resellers can call and from which they can download the relevant versions of the programs as well as retrieving patches and updates error recoveries as they become available. Given the contemporary speed of the data lines, downloading Concorde XAL takes a couple of hours, but it's significantly faster than waiting several days to get a large stack of floppy disks by post. As many of the resellers have neither the experience nor the facilities to make this kind of electronic transfer, a computer, called an FTP server, is the primary modus operandi of the international resellers only. Maintenance of the server starts as a side project for Mads Westermann.

## Leadership problems continue

The launch of Concorde XAL the year before caused an intensified level of activity throughout the organisation, but cooperation in management did not improve, rather the reverse. There are continuous discussions regarding the remit of duties and complaints about lack of efficiency and professionalism in "the others'" departments within the company. Internal collaboration problems land more and more often on Preben's desk, and he then has to spend time and energy on understanding and mediating between the conflicting parties. The expanding business entails the constant recruitment of new employees throughout the organisation and their onboarding is impeded by the many controversies of middle management.

Damgaard Data is still considered an excellent place to work by the employees, but cracks start to show in several places. After the somewhat lean result for the 1990/91 financial year, there is, naturally, full focus on reaping the rewards of the major investments, particularly of XAL. That increase in activity and the many new jobs that follow in the aftermath of XAL and the many third-party products places great demands on management and internal collaboration, which the organisation struggles to deliver.

At the end of 1992, the number of employees has passed the 100 mark and so as to have something to work further on, Preben commissions an external consultant to be in charge of the company's first internal employee satisfaction survey at the beginning of 1993.

## Damgaard Data at the world's biggest IT exhibition

Once XAL launches, international marketing activities increase significantly. Despite the product not being ready for internationalisation in the first version, there is nothing preventing it from being presented abroad in an English-language version.

After entering into the partnership with DEC in April 1991, a handful of employees, led by Erik and Preben, attend a major international event in Orlando, Florida, and in March 1992, Damgaard Data participates in the world's largest IT exhibition, CeBIT, in Hanover, Germany, for the first time. There is a lot of interest in the product from all quarters, but nothing concrete comes from it. There is still a little bit of activity in the UK as a result of the original investments, and likewise Morten Vedel's activities in Singapore bring in a few projects, but none of these ventures are at a level that seems to be growing or of crucial importance for the markets concerned.

After the CeBIT fair, Preben gives a statement to *Berlingske Tidende* on 11th March 1992: *"We have to acknowledge that our distribution network is not built for it [internationalisation]. The penetration time for financial systems is long and difficult, so it is about finding the right partner abroad".*

When you have a home market that accounts for less than half a per cent of the world market, there are limitations on how much growth can be reached. Finding the right distributors abroad proves to be crucial for who will succeed in global growth in the market for financial systems.

## The world awaits

Some of the Danish subsidiaries of the major – primarily American – IT companies, which have become resellers of Concorde products in Denmark, make a pitch to replicate that success in other countries. However, it repeatedly turns out that getting the attention of the sister companies is difficult. There is rarely interest in what has been successful in Denmark outside of its borders.

Despite both Erik and Preben wanting internationalisation, they don't have the recipe for how it should be done. Simply investing in building up their own subsidiaries seems far too uncertain and risky at a time when they are spending a lot of energy on getting the Danish organisation back on track.

At the end of 1992, Motorola Denmark is on the lookout for a new financial system for its European activities. They are interested in looking at XAL and so Peter Wagner, a system analyst in the Large Account Department, is put on the case. The contract, which entails rolling out to all of Motorola's branches in Europe, is won. Just a few months later, a contract with the Singapore Foreign Ministry is won via DEC's subsidiary there in conjunction with Morten Vedel. In summer 1993, it is decided that from now on all international activities will be the remit of the Large Account department and Peter Wagner is appointed international sales manager. Via Sigurd Flydal in Norway, a request is received from the tyre company, Continental, in autumn 1993, and it is again Peter Wagner who responds, though this time with backup from Erik Damgaard and Bo Nielsson. After a few visits to the IT Director at Continental's headquarters in Hanover, Germany, Damgaard Data is awarded the project, and another major international company can be added to their list of customers.

Motorola, Continental and the project in Singapore demonstrate clearly that, as a product, Concorde XAL can easily handle itself in an international context, but the model for how to systematically open the markets is still lacking. Norway is doing well with Sigurd Flydal at the helm. A request also comes in from a Dutch reseller with whom an agreement is subsequently reached. Nothing comes of it. The reseller Hugur gains good ground in Iceland, where the market is shared equally with PC&C. But it is difficult to make headway in large markets such as Sweden, Germany and the UK. At some point, there are also negotiations with a Swedish software company that is considering replacing an older self-developed financial system with XAL, but again negotiations end without a deal.

The desire for international expansion is strong, but the strategy isn't working. Any requests that come in and the opportunities that arise are responded to, but still the right distributors can't be found. One reason may be that the task sits primarily on Preben's shoulders, and he has enough on his plate with ensuring growth on the domestic market.

## Internationalisation is hard

The challenge wasn't unique to Damgaard Data. Every software business had – and still has – difficulty when it comes to internationalisation. American software companies though, in particular, enjoyed a number of clear benefits. This is partly due to the huge home market where they could grow big and strong before tackling any international activities. And partly due to a significant spillover effect via English-language specialist media. American software companies that were successful in the domestic market were quickly sought after by third-party distributors and resellers who recognised an import opportunity with low risk. And despite being successful in Denmark, that success wasn't especially worth mentioning in the international markets. Starting your own subsidiaries and employing your own crew to carry out the task would require enormous investments, and even though it would give full control, it was by no means risk free. If Damgaard Data had chosen that strategy they would quickly have burned up funds, which is actually what happened to a number of their Swedish competitors. The strategy of seeking out distributors, who would build up a market at their own expense and risk, is popular within the software industry, but Erik and Preben can't get it started.

## Concorde XAL is a success with problems

Both customers and resellers are excited about XAL, but the more they engage with the product, the more they discover that Damgaard Data is unable to provide adequate support. XAL is a much more comprehensive product that takes longer to learn than previous products. It generates several unforeseen situations and has more bugs and inconveniences in its first version than previous products. With XAL, Damgaard Data has moved into completely new territory and has underestimated the need for systematic quality assurance both prior to main releases of the product and in connection with updates, including the fixing of bugs and improvements. Furthermore, the need for clear support processes once the product has come to market has also been underestimated. Therefore, when customers and resellers experience slow and bad support, it is due to internal difficulties in getting the cases properly registered, documented, prioritised and submitted for fixing in the development department.

Just how great the dissatisfaction really is only becomes clear when Preben Damgaard and Michael Sander's girlfriends are employed to sell courses in and subscriptions for updates to Concorde XAL. They systematically call every reseller and customer, thereby getting a first-hand impression of the widespread discontent.

The number of employees working in training and support increases steadily, so it's not a shortage of resources that's creating the problems. Jørgen Holck-Christensen, Head of Support, asked as early as late summer 1991, to be released from his management responsibilities, so maybe the time has come to find a new leader better able to manage the work at hand.

Preben employs Hanne Haubert to establish the internal support processes and increase customer and reseller satisfaction. It's a big undertaking that will take a long time to address. Hanne often finds herself in the firing line when customers and business partners point out the bad support they have experienced, which is largely due to a learning process Damgaard Data is undergoing as the business expands.

Despite the difficulties with support, performance and product bugs, Concorde XAL gains a good foothold in the Danish market during 1992 and 1993. The product, which can be fully customised, requires that resellers have a good deal of experience. They have to go through the first projects before they know the routine for correctly estimating project costs and can deliver with a positive gross margin. When the first business partners emerge from the introductory phase, other resellers see how XAL allows for an extremely profitable business. New partners now continuously approach Damgaard. The many resellers can develop their own solutions, which reduce the competitive pressure from other business partners. They can sell their extensions without having to pay licence fees to Damgaard Data, and they can also provide ongoing consultancy services to their customers. Consultants, who understand both business and IT, can set attractive hourly rates and are often fully booked with work. All in all, an attractive business model.

When Concorde XAL is released to also run on Oracle's database system in spring 1992, the market expands even further. Partly due to the performance problems being remedied, and partly due to Oracle being a well-established name among larger companies.

## C5 – a difficult birth

Every aspect of the activities around XAL are valued internally as well, motivating developers and sales and marketing people. Customers are often blue-chip companies that are recognised and respected within the industry, with project prices in the million-class bracket. However, despite all the good signals, vibrations and results, Erik Damgaard notes in autumn 1992 that with XAL they have betrayed their original core market: those small companies that wanted a simple product without the need for an army of consultants. That market is still being served by Concorde Version 4. Whereas Version 5 should have resulted in a replacement, XAL has landed them in a completely different market segment. Version 4 needs to be revised and there are two options.

One option is to continue using Pascal as a development platform. Developers such as Morten Gregersen are well-versed in Pascal and argue for staying on that track. The new turbo version has removed some of the limitations that were one of the reasons for starting the Version 5 project, which ended up being XAL. However, continuing with TurboPascal would necessitate the development department using two different technical platforms in the future. XAL is based on the C-platform. A financial system for very small businesses requires only a small development team. If it has its own technical platform, it would be too vulnerable. Erik Damgaard is also unsure whether or not it is a good idea to keep new versions of Concorde Version 4 backward compatible forever just as he finds the dependence on TurboPascal's development unfortunate.

The increasing market popularity enjoyed by Microsoft's Windows certainly can't be ignored either. Version 3.1, released by Microsoft in March 1992, gains widespread popularity, and it is clear to Erik that in time XAL must also be migrated to Windows. Indeed, in 1991, versions of TurboPascal, which support Windows come out, but as many are in support of rewriting the entire code rather than continuing with a product that originated in 1985, Erik is more in favour of recycling the work they have to do for XAL anyway.

After the discussion has gone back and forth for some time, and the supporters of the TurboPascal route try to get Preben on their side by arguing that it would enable them to come to market faster, Erik Damgaard takes charge. He decides that the new version of Concorde Finance, again called Version 5, will be based on the same technical platform as XAL. Morten Gregersen is certainly not happy about that decision and after receiving an offer to join the XAL team, he decides instead to resign.

Erik and the core team now get started on making a new version of XAL, which is to form the foundation for Concorde Økonomi [Concorde Finance] Version 5. After Morten's resignation, Erik asks another developer to take over as team leader on the new project. Immediately afterwards, the team is supplemented with an employee to write documentation and assist Damgaard Data's grand old man, Jørgen Holck, with the testing. Development, which is to be close to Concorde Økonomi in functionality, is now underway at full speed. And to ensure the product also meets the needs and requests of the market, a structured beta testing program is established for the first time for selected resellers and customers.

The project is affected by problems again in the autumn. The development department suddenly has to part with some programmers who had begun developing a competing product. However, in April 1993, the first beta version is sent for testing with 11 selected resellers across the country. The feedback is generally positive. The product is installed on 18th June 1993 at Bodum, the first beta customer, handled directly by Large Accounts, and production starts as early as 28th June.

## IBM Denmark is doing well

In spite of a somewhat higher price level than its competitors, IBM enjoys a share of approximately 35 per cent of the PC market in the early 1990s, putting it in undisputed first place in Denmark. That also gives it a top ranking within the group worldwide, where market share never exceeds 25 per cent. On the whole, IBM Denmark is a very well run and successful company, which, given the market size, performs significantly better than its sister companies around the globe. The concept of the IBM Business Center, a Danish invention, where PC solutions are sold based on, for instance, Navigator from PC&C, works well. The company is extremely selective about who is allowed to be appointed as an IBM Business Center. High demands regarding training and revenue must be met and IBM is absolutely adamant that resellers not sell products from their competitors.

The remaining 65 per cent of the Danish market is served by a range of other PC brands, which, in turn, lean primarily on Damgaard Data. When XAL arrives at UNIX, DEC hops on the bandwagon first. Later, a large number of other major companies follow: Unisys, Control Data, Olivetti, NCR, HP, ICL and Sun. The market expands significantly with XAL. IBM's choice to distribute Navigator, thereby blocking 35 per cent of the PC market, isn't really an issue, despite a desire to get a hold of that share, too. But it is an issue for PC&C, who have to passively watch its products reaching only the 35 per cent covered by IBM, and it certainly isn't satisfied with that.

Thanks to its outstanding results and impressive market share, IBM Denmark enjoys great respect at its European headquarters at the end of the 1980s and early 1990s. At meetings of the management of European subsidiaries, Denmark is highlighted as a role model, and the central role played by the Business Centers with Navigator from PC&C is highlighted. The good example is believed to be a motivating factor, which the other subsidiaries could copy, but it is quite the opposite. The managers from the other countries are irritated by both the constant emphasising of Denmark and that the European leadership doesn't seem to understand that conditions in the individual countries are completely different. The Danish concept can't be copied just like that. Despite all IBM's subsidiaries being made familiar with the Danish Business Center concept, including with PC&C's Navigator, it is only IBM in Spain, Austria and Iceland that take the product for a short period of time. Everyone else politely decline.

## PC&C say no to IBM

PC&C learns early on that although IBM is probably the most well-known and recognised brand within the IT industry, the company isn't organised internally with an eye to exploit the global benefits of good ideas arising in the individual countries. To get anywhere near IBM's global marketing muscle, you have to go through the headquarters in Armonk, New York and have your products recognised as a core product that is subsequently rolled out to the various countries via the established hierarchy of the organisation. Pursuing such a strategy requires an internal sponsor – one high up in the hierarchy – and the patience to work through a bureaucracy of officials, most of whom are keener on avoiding mistakes and minimising risks than they are on exploiting obvious market opportunities.

When, in 1992 and 1993, the company is pressed hard on all fronts and has to file one of the world's greatest deficits, the situation only worsens. The company's contemporary management team was characterised by turmoil as a result of the collapse of their core business: mainframes for the world's largest companies. A small business like PC&C would drown in such vast bureaucracy.

Actually, IBM Denmark, which is dependent upon Navigator in their PC business, tries to gain an equity share in PC&C in the early 1990s. But Jesper Balser and his two co-founders, Torben Wind and Peter Bang, politely decline. PC&C can't see an advantage in having the giant as a co-owner in Denmark, just as they don't see a partnership with IBM as a road to international expansion.

# CHAPTER 13

# TWO AMERICAN COMPANIES PROPOSE

## Criticism and crisis

While the business breaks records in turnover and earnings, the challenges within the management team become more and more pronounced. At the same time, the results of the external satisfaction survey completed by resellers are not particularly positive. Concorde products are still popular and receive positive reviews, but the company is criticised for being less responsive and service-minded than before. Some of this dissatisfaction can be attributed to the company becoming stricter regarding whom it allows into its reseller circle. Increasing demands for training and certification are imposed, and a deliberate policy of treating all business partners the same is followed. Some partners perceive this as a lack of flexibility.

But that doesn't explain everything. The internal collaboration problems seem to bring about challenges on the outside. After a meeting of the management team in January 1993, during which the discussions are endless and fraught with conflict, Erik says to Preben: *"You have to fix this now. If you can't play the hand, new cards have to be dealt"*. Preben returns home and contemplates the situation. Via his personal network, he gets in touch with Kåre Fjalland, a consultant specialising in organisational relationships. Together they implement an organisational development project.

## Staff start their own newsletter

That spring a group of employees takes the initiative to release an informal staff newsletter *DDE* (Damgaard Data Exchange), which premieres on 17th March 1993. The initiative is typified by coming from employees and not from management. It is further characterised by being a newsletter completely independent of management and, for the first few years, it is produced on a voluntary basis with Anna Eskelund as the driving force, but with the full support of both Erik and Preben. It epitomises the informal culture, which empowers employees to take initiatives that can solve the problems they encounter and seize the opportunities that arise. When a number of employees realise that an informal employee newsletter could contribute positively to the company's development, they immediately get the green light to launch such a project alongside their other tasks. The DDE project is run by those employees who are motivated, and only time will tell how it will evolve.

As early as the second issue, published 23rd March, Preben has an editorial on the front page entitled "Embrace changes or die," where he writes:

*If a frog is thrown into a pot of boiling water, it will instantly jump out of the pot unharmed. If, on the other hand, the frog is put in a pot of cold water and the pot is slowly warmed up until it boils, the frog will not notice the change and will be boiled alive.*

*I use this example as it can be applied to Damgaard Data and the EDP industry.*

*We are in a market that constantly and rapidly changes. Today's EDP industry doesn't resemble the EDP industry of 1988, and it almost certainly won't resemble the IT industry to come in 1998.*

*If we are to ensure the survival of Damgaard Data as a healthy company, we need to adapt to the constant changes.*

*The problem for Damgaard Data might actually be that things are going as well as they are. Unless we remain vigilant, we risk the great years we're experiencing now lulling us into a false sense of security, so we won't notice* the changes and we will slowly let ourselves be boiled alive. There is no crisis now, but a crisis could occur if we don't adapt on a regular basis.

Being a member of a company such as Damgaard Data, in a changing industry, places great demands on each individual employee. But change doesn't mean that we adjust everything overnight. It's about all employees, through the way we think and work, continually adjusting and gradually adapting the business to the changing market conditions.

In other words, Damgaard Data is dependent upon all employees helping the company adapt. To make this possible, we will launch an organisational development project (see elsewhere in the newsletter), which will include all employees.

I have various suggestions as to what changes we will experience in the years to come. The price of EDP programs will fall because end-users will know more about IT, and competition will become tougher and harder. We have experienced how the prices of products such as, Lotus and WordPerfect have fallen sharply over the past year, and that, too, will happen to products such as CONCORDE Økonomi [Version 4]. Instead, Damgaard Data and similar companies will increasingly earn their living selling training, support, consulting and other forms of services.

Moreover, an increasing proportion of the programs will be sold via mail order companies and in large IT supermarkets like Metro, Fona, Merlin, etc., where the programs sit on shelves, like in SuperBrugsen. This will also apply to programs such as CONCORDE Økonomi.

End-users want branded goods. Therefore, CONCORDE has to be a name for financial management, just as Levi is for jeans. Standards for almost everything in a program will be a requirement. If a program doesn't meet the standards for keyboard layout, menu structure, data saving and downloading, screen display, etc., the program won't sell. Thus, programs are resembling each other more and more.

The message is this: learn to embrace change. If you don't adapt you'll die.

Preben Damgaard

## Out of the teenage years

In four years, the number of employees has grown from 40 to 140 – an expansion that is difficult to manage for any business. As Preben writes in the editorial, the financial results are excellent, but they must not be lulled into a false sense of security that prevents the company from adapting to the ever-changing conditions of the market. Giant companies, such as DEC and IBM, have received some mighty beatings as a result of arrogance and smugness, so it's certainly not without reason that Preben is vigilant and careful. The article in the staff newsletter is intended to illustrate and create an external pressure for adaptation, which managers and employees are perhaps not feeling so acutely in their everyday lives. The situation is this: too much energy is being used on internal disputes and the quality of both the products and the support offered to business partners and customers is suffering as a result. Efforts to create a functioning and respected brand on the market demand that the organisation moves out of its teenage phase, professionalises and grows up.

The organisational development project, OUP, which has the overall goals of job satisfaction, better quality and higher productivity, is to include the entire organisation, but it doesn't yet have the answers for how to achieve those improvements. The project is organised around a number of meetings for the management team, for the individual departments and for all employees. Everyone is involved in the work of discussing and formulating strategy, culture and collaboration guidelines, which will then be presented and discussed at the planned meetings. A future set meeting structure for the departments and for the company as a whole is announced. This is intended to ensure a continuous and consistent flow of information. It is also expected that concrete initiatives will wait until everyone has had the opportunity to say their piece. However, a joint induction programme is announced for all new employees, and an HR department is established as of 1st April.

OUP, which has the overall slogan "User-friendly software – for everyone" clearly illustrates Preben's management style. He is aware that there is a need for change, but he chooses not to dictate it himself. Nor does he restrict the work to the management team, but rather involves the entire company. It goes without saying that such work requires many hours of effort in addition to the usual daily workload, but the expectation is that the process will produce better results as it will be thoroughly anchored throughout the organisation. The aim with the OUP is, first and foremost, that Damgaard Data should become a better place to work, and one from which a strong common culture will develop, and finally, that the organisation can deliver effectively and profitably to the market. Many senior executives would probably choose the latter first, but Preben is convinced that everything starts with the employees. An effective organisation has enlightened, happy, engaged, enterprising and self-leading employees. Such an organisation requires a broad framework, and under no circumstances can it be created from the top down.

Work commences and from mid-March all managers are interviewed. They have to work with their employees on formulating a mission statement for their area, on articulating their dissatisfaction with their colleagues and on addressing any criticism coming in the opposite direction.

The project receives a mixed response from the employees. Some find it hard to understand what it's really all about, what exactly is to be achieved and how they're supposed to measure progress and results. No one in the organisation has tried or done anything like this before. But as the project progresses, the employees throw themselves into the debate, clarifying their areas and explaining their expectations to colleagues.

## Business partners need project management skills

In 1992, a version of Concorde XAL is launched with a serious bug which, in some situations, destroys the customer's database. When the bug occurs, a great deal of effort has to be invested in rebuilding the system. Therefore, Bo Nielsson takes the initiative to start a quality development project in the development department. The project is to ensure that, from now on, fatal bugs are found and fixed before a product is released to market. During this work, it becomes clear to Bo that there is also a need to improve the way in which his own department, Large Account, implements customer projects. The ability to customise software according to the specific needs of the customer makes XAL attractive to large customers, just as the modules for production and material management attract businesses with much more complex business processes than those known in Concorde *Økonomi*. XAL is just the core of the solution and rarely represents more than 25 per cent of the total price. The rest of the project price comprises consultant assistance in defining business processes, customisations, project management, training and support. If projects aren't carefully defined and managed, there will be inevitable discussions with customers about what delivery actually includes and, not least, how requests for changes are managed along the way. In fact, more and more large customers are now asking Damgaard Data to describe their project method. It is now necessary to have something concrete and relevant to present.

It's not only Large Account that has difficulty estimating and making their projects profitable. Moreover, partners, who have their roots in Concorde *Økonomi* and other standard products, struggle to manage their projects in the beginning, too. This leads to unsatisfied customers, increased pressure on the support organisation and sometimes chips away at the perception of XAL as an advanced, but somewhat buggy product. Preben suggests aiming the development of the project management methodology to include resellers, too, so as to better equip them to handle projects. Three employees and an external consultant are assigned to develop and document a project management method.

After the summer holidays of 1993, Damgaard Data is ready to start training the partners in the project management methodology, but despite the stated need and the prospect of improved gross margins, only a few sign up. Preben now has the idea to bestow a special status on those resellers, who complete the training, which can further benefit their marketing. The programme is entitled ProjectPartner, and those business partners who finish the programme can call themselves Certified. From now on, large customers will primarily be referred to these business partners. The incentive increases interest somewhat, but still only a handful of resellers sign up for the training.

In July 1994, the project is re-evaluated. Perhaps a methodology that includes 800 pages of documentation has become too ambitious. If it could be reduced to 100 pages, more resellers will probably sign up. If they can't get more than half of the XAL business partners through the certification program, it could backfire. Customers could be left with the impression that only a few resellers can handle large projects.

In December 1995, the new reduced edition of ProjectPartner is launched at a partner meeting at the Hotel Eremitage in Lyngby, north of Copenhagen. And even though Santa Claus distributes the method manuals, wrapped in red paper, with Christmas elves and gold ribbons, they are obviously not something very high on the business partners' wish lists.

In January 1996, a status check is carried out and it confirms once again that ProjectPartner is not a success. With four people on the payroll, cost is exceeding turnover, and there is no likelihood of this changing. A large number of resellers learned an expensive lesson from their first projects and have themselves figured out how to handle their customers. Despite the ProjectPartner certification being a stamp of approval that can add some market value, the same effect can be achieved with a long list of satisfied customers. The department suggests a redesign of the program, but Preben comes to the conclusion that time has run out for Project-Partner, and the activity is closed in February 1996.

ProjectPartner undoubtedly addressed a real and serious problem. With the introduction of XAL, both Damgaard Data and the resellers ended up with jobs they were not prepared for. Whereas very large customers explicitly asked for project management skills and would not sign any agreements without these being documented, medium-sized customers often landed in a quagmire, where the desire to reach the goal was great, but the ability to find the way there was not so. Projects often failed on all four main elements: time, price, specifications and quality. It was painful for both customers who didn't get what they expected and for resellers who had to record losses on deliveries that were more extensive and took longer than estimated. Despite ProjectPartner not being a success when seen in isolation, the initiative did address the problem. Resellers, who participated in the programme benefited greatly from it, while those who didn't had to seek out other ways to achieve the same result.

Nevertheless, in spring 1996, and with or without ProjectPartner, Damgaard Data has a strong business partner channel, skilled in projects in Denmark and it can now put every effort into the area that will determine whether or not the company can be called a success: internationalisation.

## The great re-organisation (D-Day)

As the organisational development project progresses, Preben reaches the conclusion that he can't continue with the current management structure. Partly due to how much of his time is spent resolving the conflicts in the management team. And partly because the management layer itself is contributing to the problem that the OUP is trying to solve. He feels a need to act quickly and, therefore, he decides to construct a new management team based on the people already in the organisation, knowing that only few will be completely satisfied and many will be either dissatisfied or, at best, merely mollified. Most urgent is getting a new manager in place in sales and marketing.

Preben wants one person responsible for the sale of all products, and can choose between Claus Winblad, responsible for the company's own and third party products, and Carsten Kaae, responsible for network products. They present two completely different profiles. Claus is calm, structured and cautious. Carsten is a wild card. According to Preben's perception, neither of the two candidates is total-sales-and-marketing-responsibility material, but he assesses the risk of finding an external candidate to be even greater. The choice comes down to whom he can best do without. Knowing that Carsten would resign if overlooked, probably taking the entire network business with him, letting Claus Winblad go seems the path of least risk. Preben decides to offer Carsten total responsibility for sales and marketing, with the consequence that he has to dismiss Claus.

Once revealed an organisational change should ideally cause as few surprises as possible. Therefore, the unveiling has to happen at a certain pace, so that those employees most affected are informed first. The OUP hasn't been completed yet, so it is crucial that changes in the management team and the subsequent adjustments in the organisation quickly fall into place so that work can carry on. As this reorganisation is the biggest one Preben has made to date, he contacts Freddie Jørgensen, HR Director of DEC Denmark, who he has got to know through the XAL partnership. On 15th June 1993, they meet at Preben's office and together they review the changes in the organisation and the roadmap to be followed for announcing it, including how the new roles and placements should be presented to the employees, who, Preben knows, will have to swallow some bitter pills. The outcome of the meeting is a detailed screenplay with precise times for the individual meetings and what should be said to each person. Preben knows that some people will be upset and that as there is a tradition and acceptance of protest when there are disagreements, Freddie advises him not to engage in long explanations but instead to state "that was the old way, now help make this work". Changes to management and organisation are Preben's responsibility and once the decisions have been made, they must be carried out, not discussed. Wednesday, 18th August goes down in the history of the company as the day the new organisational structure is announced.

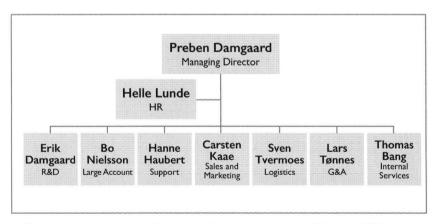

The management group after the major reorganisation of August 1993.

In the internal staff newsletter, Preben writes:

*...Thus, I hope, that much of the energy previously spent on internal con-
flicts, coordination, power struggles and duplication of work, will from now
on be directed out towards the market and utilised as an asset, both in terms
of the well-being of employees, but also in terms of our customers and their
perception of Damgaard Data in the future...Therefore, I hope that all employees will help make the new structure successful and that any criticism
can be dealt with in all openness.*

On paper the organisation looks fine, but it soon proves not to be
long-lasting. Every organisation consists of a structure as well as the
people operating within that structure. In this case, the structure is acceptable, but making it work will require a few key replacements.

## Power shifts over to the customers

In 1993, the financial statements are published in a four-colour printed
version for the first time with an expanded report, retrospective and outlook for the future. The accounts serve as a company profile brochure. It
makes use of the undeniable success that the company has had and documents an extremely well-consolidated balance sheet. The story of the
company's development is used to paint a picture that isn't quite in line
with the historical facts, but which cleverly plays on the changes within
the IT industry that are putting the customers in the driver's seat (and
also benefits Damgaard Data). This is described in the report as follows:

*"Today, the major hardware manufacturers are shaken to their core. Power
is shifting to the customers because software producers take pride in making their systems user-friendly, open and flexible".*

The analysis is correct. During this period, everything within the IT industry is turned upside down. It's about developing software that the
not so IT-savvy users can understand, will purchase and, not least, retain. The open PC and network standards enabled this development, and
Damgaard Data was at the right time and right place with the right prod-

ucts with a solid sales and marketing strategy. The combination of Erik Damgaard's professional skills and ambitions and Preben Damgaard's commercial and, not least, organisational skills, got the company off to a good start and through the first difficult phases. Impressive growth can now be presented, with heavy investment in the development of new products, in marketing and in the expansion of the organisation. This explains the relatively low earnings rate for a software company, which at the end of the 1992/93 financial year accounts for nine per cent of a revenue of almost 28 million USD produced by a staff of 140. The future is described in glowing terms and it is expected that the low export of only five per cent of total turnover will grow:

*"That percentage should be relatively easy to grow. Concorde products are already available in various different languages today – and the systems are, due to their flexibility, easy to adapt to the demands of the various export markets".*

It is an optimistic prediction that is not proven correct. In fact, that percentage proves to be even more difficult to change; likewise adapting the products to the national markets demands much more effort than first imagined. Indeed, the statement from the chairman of the board, Henning Kruse Petersen, to the *Berlinske Tidende* newspaper on 10th September 1993, after the publication of the financial statements, highlights a vast distance between expectation and reality:

*"We have high expectations for export orders in the next financial year and for two software packages purchased by international companies in the USA and the Far East".*

## User-friendly software for everyone

In the annual reports, the public is introduced to the phrase "user-friendly software for everyone", which is now designated as the company's philosophy. This motto is linked to five principles:

- Openness
- Partnership
- Survivability
- Freedom of choice
- Standards

"Openness" is used to characterise the products where the source code of Concorde XAL can be customised by partners and customers. It is a new phenomenon, which has also been successful for PC&C's Navigator 3.0.

"Partnership" covers primarily going to market through resellers known as business partners.

"Survivability" refers to Damgaard Data as a solid company, capable of surviving. This element has gained increased significance as the company has targeted larger customers and well-established resellers with Concorde XAL.

## Freedom of choice

As most businesses, over a certain size, have experienced being in the pocket of an IT provider in the 1970s and 1980s, the concept of "standards" is key for customers wishing to maintain their "freedom of choice" and take advantage of the improvements that both technology and competition offer from the end of the 1980s. Despite customers being largely locked into Damgaard Data's products, flexibility to choose the underlying hardware and operating systems as well as which business partner customers wish to be served by, is cleverly incorporated.

In 1993, the "family board" of the first few years was replaced by a professional team consisting of (from left) Vagn Thorup, Henning Kruse Petersen, Preben Damgaard, Erik Damgaard and Michael Sander. This picture is from the 1992/93 annual report, which was published as a colour profile brochure for the first time.

## Ten-year anniversary party at the D'Angleterre Hotel

When all of the employees and their respective spouses and partners gather to celebrate the company's 10th anniversary at the D'Angleterre Hotel on Kongens Nytorv (the King's New Square) in central Copenhagen on 4th September 1993, the purse strings have once again been loosened to deliver a great experience and thank you for their work and effort. The dress code is black tie, which is definitely not everyday wear, but it helps create the framework for celebrating an outstanding success within the Danish IT industry. In the internal staff newsletter, Anna Eskelund writes:

*...The brothers received standing ovations. Despite them sometimes making decisions that are difficult to agree with, I'm sure that the rounds of applause expressed both respect for them and love for our common workplace. Was I really the only sentimental fool whose eyes were watering a tiny little bit?*

After dinner, the Danish comedy band, De Nattergale, provide entertainment, and when dancing and relaxing in the free bar follow, the first ten years are celebrated without worry, one success replacing the other – without any suspicion of the coming upheavals, which will change the company significantly over the next few months.

## Control Data want to acquire Damgaard Data

Control Data Corporation (CDC) with its headquarters in Minneapolis, in the USA, is a leader within mainframe systems for computation-heavy purposes. As the market for such systems is quite small in Denmark, the Danish subsidiary builds up a large department of software developers and system consultants in the 1970s, which can instead help customers to develop and service administrative solutions. This strategy enables CDC to succeed in winning large customers such as Postgiro, the post office's package sorting service; Jydsk Telefon; the Magasin du Nord department store; Rigshospital and the then Ministry of Fisheries. And the accounting centres of the universities of Aarhus and Aalborg, too. In the mid-1980s, in order to serve medium-sized companies, CDC establishes a service bureau in Copenhagen, based on the company's own mainframes, where customers such as FTF's A-kasse [unemployment fund], Bonnier Magazines and the Danish Civil Aviation Administration are served.

When the PC wave hits the market in earnest in the second half of the 1980s, and IBM increases the competitive pressure on the mainframe area, CDC also comes under pressure. In the late 1980s, some customers decide to move their data processing to minicomputers from Norsk Data and IBM, and when Postgiro, the most prominent customer, decides to switch to IBM mainframes in the early 1990s, the future of CDC on Søndre Boulevard in Copenhagen's city centre looks bleak.

To obtain a share of the growing market for minicomputers in 1991, CDC launches a new series of products that run on a variant of the UNIX operating system, which is somewhat more affordable than the company's expensive mainframes. At the end of 1991, the Danish subsidiary enjoys a good position with a turnover of approximately 60 million USD, a nice profit, a sensible net worth and 150 employees. However, the market has already changed in the meantime. UNIX machines are sold chiefly as platforms for standard applications tailored to customers' needs and not as mainframes for which customers primarily develop their own software systems.

When a potential customer requests a financial management solution with a range of special features, a CDC employee suggests looking into the new Concorde XAL. Following a demonstration of the product, it is decided in autumn 1991 to build a business based on XAL and, therefore, to enter into a reseller agreement with Damgaard Data. Normally, the staff of new resellers are required to attend a one week course, but in light of CDC's Danish consultants having many years of experience in administrative solutions, it is agreed to hold a compressed course over a weekend for the eight employees due to start up the activity.

XAL, which is aimed at larger companies with individual require-ments and necessitates consultancy assistance for its implementation, suits CDC extremely well as they are both used to complex system sales and it has consultants for project management, training, data conversion, customisation, integration, system technology and so on. During 1992, CDC's XAL business grows strongly and the company starts – via its sis-ter companies – to work on the Norwegian market, as well as contacting potential customers in Germany, Great Britain and Singapore. At the beginning of 1993, CDC – with more than 50 employees working on XAL activities – is not only the largest XAL reseller, but is also a role model for a system partner, who can successfully serve the very large customers.

There's just one little snag. CDC arrives late to the UNIX market and is up against virtually all the established minicomputer suppliers, who are flocking to get a stake in the growing market. Hardware from CDC is powerful, but it's also expensive, and as CDC is not a well-known brand, they have to discount so deeply that it's a direct loss for them. However, the vast majority of customers are opting for a PC-based solution and as CDC doesn't produce PCs themselves, they enter into a reseller agree-ment with the Dutch company Tulip Computers. In cases where UNIX is chosen, it is often the customers themselves who acquire the hardware, and CDC is not the preference here either. Nobody at Damgaard Data can recollect having ported XAL to CDC's UNIX hardware. Indeed, there is much to indicate that they have never actually sold a single CDC computer with XAL, despite that being the strategic objective.

## Customers choose software before hardware

CDC was far from being alone – many hardware suppliers suffered likewise during the period. Whereas in the 1970s and 1980s, customers chose hardware first and software afterwards, this behaviour changes completely in the 1990s. Many hardware suppliers start developing software or enter into agreements with software companies in an attempt to adapt themselves to the customers' behaviour, but it's a misjudgement of the situation. When customers choose software first, they want the freedom to choose hardware later. They don't want to be forced into choosing the software supplier's hardware. Once hardware suppliers establish software solutions and build up organisations to market, sell and service the solutions, employee loyalty to the hardware platform disappears. Software professionals quickly identify the huge advantage of their software being able to run on all types of hardware and don't care for losing a project due to the customer – for political reasons – not wanting the software supplier's hardware. This is exactly what happens to CDC. The consultancy department, which is responsible for software delivery, is eager to meet customers' hardware preferences and doesn't make any great effort to include a CDC computer in the package. Had they done that, they would have lost many potential customers, too, just as they would have had to accept major losses on the customers they could win. Instead, they position themselves as a provider of hardware-independent solutions, achieving huge success with this approach.

The positive experience with XAL causes CDC's Danish management to consider whether or not the business concept could be rolled out in the 147 sister companies worldwide. At the beginning of 1993, the heads of the Northern European subsidiaries meet at Rungsted harbour. Here, Benny Michelsen, Managing Director of the Danish subsidiary, presents the XAL Business unit, which has attracted many new customers in Denmark and has generated a highly acceptable gross margin. The business potential is clearly visible to the participants, but they are somewhat concerned that no products from the parent company in the USA are included. One solution to the problem could be CDC buying into Damgaard Data. Benny Michelsen approaches Preben Damgaard to test the waters.

Preben takes the enquiry seriously and gets the company's lawyers on the case. Sources close to the negotiations say that the parties actually sign a letter of intent, under which CDC has to pay between 8 and 14 million USD in cash for a stake in the company. As early as the first query, Preben Damgaard emphasises that there is no desire to sell shares to Control Data A/S, but that there may be an interest in a strategic partnership with CDC's headquarters, thereby ensuring a partnership happens with a global roll-out as the objective. Benny Michelsen assures him that the approach has full approval from the parent company and that it is precisely the global potential, which is driving the project. The shares being held by the Danish subsidiary is just a formality.

Preben wonders at the lack of representation from the parent company at the negotiations and asks for the names and contact information of the people in Minneapolis involved in the decision making process. Benny Michelsen promises to provide a list with the information, but it never materialises, because a few weeks later he is no longer with the company. As it turns out, the acquisition initiative isn't popular with the parent company, which, on the contrary, wants to put an end to the project. CDC's headquarters in the USA wants its subsidiaries to focus on the company's core business and not to invest further in local business areas that are unrelated to the company's own products.

Instead, the parent company replaces Benny Michelsen with the director of the Norwegian subsidiary, Omar Lien, whose task is to reduce the organisation in Denmark by approximately 100 employees by spinning off local activities and, thereby, generating cash for the destitute parent company. However, CDC's Danish XAL activities are allowed to continue, though they dwindle somewhat. Many of the employees seek jobs with other resellers, and by the end of 1993, CDC is no longer the largest XAL business partner.

## Concorde XAL Version 2 with significant improvements

Concorde XAL Version 2 is released in October 1993 with a whole range of improvements. A review in *PC World* in April 1994 concludes that the production and materials management functions, in particular, have significantly improved and that the product can now be utilised by even larger companies than before. The report generator has also been enhanced and Concorde XAL can now transfer data to other systems, including Lotus 1-2-3, Quattro, WordPerfect and Excel. Concorde XAL is available for DOS, OS/2 as well as several UNIX systems and, apparently, there is also a plan to offer the product under OSF/1. The article mentions neither the many bugs that have been fixed in the program nor the improvement of the link to the Oracle database system.

When Expansion Marketing publishes the latest satisfaction survey from IT suppliers within the Danish market in December 1993, Damgaard Data's position has improved on product quality and technical support, while overall the company has dropped from seventh to fifteenth place with regard to reliability, collaboration, flexibility, speed of service, the range of needs covered by products, stability, viability and marketing.

It's difficult to put a finger on the specific reason for the drop in reseller satisfaction, but there is hardly any doubt that XAL has challenged both the company and its business partners considerably. Nevertheless, there was probably a significant long term advantage in getting to market early, rather than waiting for all the support functions to be in place and product quality to be improved. Firstly, XAL was a brand new type of product and no one could have predicted which support features would be needed. Secondly, coming to market early and closing it off to any competitors was attractive. XAL Version 1 catches on conceptually speaking and any resulting negativity is contained and addressed along the way. When the highly improved Version 2 is released, both reference customers and experienced resellers are already in place.

## Improved logistics efficiency

Distributing the many third-party products is an extensive activity employing 12 employees and contributing to half the gross margin. At this point in time, software for PCs are physical products, purchased and stocked for delivery at short notice. When new versions of the products are released, the old versions in the warehouse become obsolete and worthless. The prices of third-party products continue to fall and as the investment in the marketing of Concorde Business increases, the quantities to be handled grow steadily. At its peak, the third-party business serves around 800 resellers and fulfils an average of 275 orders every single day.

Therefore, in June 1993, an optimisation project is started so as to increase delivery assurance to 95 per cent, increase stock turnover rate from six to ten times a year, reduce tied-up capital, enable the inclusion of new distribution partners without increasing costs and evaluate the options for introducing new technology, which could optimise customer experience and further improve the other logistical parameters. The consultancy firm, Sant+Bendix, experts within the field, are engaged to support the project and impart additional skills.

## New pressure on IT distribution

Parallel with a massively increased supply of hardware and software products for the PC platform, competition in the market intensifies, putting additional pressure on prices. With falling prices, demand increases for an escalation in volume on the sales side, placing further pressure on prices. The developments that are highly advantageous for customers cause problems throughout the IT industry. It becomes harder and harder to maintain gross margins and thus, profits come under pressure. Manufacturers seek out new ways of getting products to customers without costly intermediaries, and new types of distributors, capable of operating on lower gross margins, emerge.

Dell Computer Corporation, which had succeeded in selling directly to customers without either distributors or resellers in the USA at the end of the 1980s, enters the major European markets. It gets a good grip of the German market, after which Norway and Sweden follow en route to Denmark. Here, DEC and NCR have begun selling directly to customers via mail order, and the company Ravenholm even specialises in direct mail order sales of standard products to customers without any support, but in return for low prices. Life becomes more and more difficult for traditional resellers such as Multi-inform, DanaData and BFC Data. Denmark's third-largest reseller, Formula Micro, goes bankrupt as early as December 1991. PolyData, which seemed to be a tough competitor with PolySoft in the late 1980s, gets burned by its distribution and business partner activities, taking it completely out of the picture in the 1990s.

In the first half of the 1993/94 financial year, Damgaard Data's turnover hits 14.84 million USD of which network products account for 25 per cent, other third-party software products represent 25 per cent and the company's own products, roughly 30 per cent. 15 per cent of revenue is divided across services, while exports amount to around five per cent of total turnover. Earnings fall short of the budget, amounting to only 20,000 USD. Falling prices on third-party products and an extraordinary draw on internal resources in order to complete Concorde XAL Version 2 puts pressure on the company's finances. In other words, as the target for the entire financial year is a turnover of 34 million USD and a profit of 2.3 million USD, the following six months have to be strong. That the different product areas no longer target the same market segment and don't have the same business model doesn't make things any easier. In the Concorde *Økonomi* and third-party products market, the recipe is called "increased volume". Competition is tough here, and falling prices and decreased gross margins are to be expected. The XAL business necessitates better earnings per project, which are to be supported by the improvement in quality that a new Version 2 is supposed to represent. On top of the challenges of changing market conditions, a demand for products based on Microsoft Windows starts to come from the bottom of the market, while a battle between UNIX and OS/2 still rages at the upper end.

## Buy your Concorde in the supermarket

To support the sales volume of Concorde *Økonomi*, Damgaard Data enters into reseller agreements with FDB's OBS department stores [the Danish co-operative], Metro stores, CPU Hyperstore, EDP supermarkets and a number of mail order companies in autumn 1993. The aim is to reach all corners of the market and obtain even more small customers who, in line with the constant fall in PC prices, are choosing to introduce IT into their businesses. After buying the product in these "supermarkets", customers can then purchase consultancy assistance and get support via the resellers. Similarly they can subscribe to updates, thereby ensuring they receive new versions. A special edition is launched under the name Concorde Light at a wholesale price of 299 USD for resellers for one, 279 USD apiece when purchasing five and 259 USD per unit when purchasing 50 or more. Buying 500 units includes an advertising subsidy of 10,000 USD, and as the suggested retail price is 399 USD, it is a very interesting product for retail businesses. Sales exceed all expectations, and in mid-1994 Microsoft Works 3.0 for Windows is added to the package, which is sold to resellers for 319 USD. This means that there is no gross margin on the Microsoft component, but as it stimulates sales of Concorde Light, it remains a profitable business. In 1994, more than 10,000 Concorde Light packages are sold. Certainly not all customers expand and buy more modules, but many do. The huge marketing effort and visibility in shops, where every Dane does their regular shopping, means that Damgaard Data achieves an exceptionally high level of brand awareness. Despite Concorde Light only being sold via retail, the company has an effect on the entire market, because decision makers in large companies as well as private individuals make regular trips to major supermarkets.

## Partners complain about Large Account

Due to Concorde XAL, activities within Large Account increase significantly, causing it to grow rapidly. Bo Nielsson, who is quite passionate
about working directly with customers, makes sure that his department
contributes to the development of XAL, thereby obtaining a head start
in comparison to the business partners. Danotherm, now a test customer
for XAL, is served directly by Large Account, enabling valuable experience to be gained, which is then channelled back to the development
department. And when performance and quality problems with XAL
surface at a later point, it is again Large Account that steps in and helps
to solve the issues. Large Account also wins a number of major foreign
customers.

Over time, several resellers, such as Dolberg Data, Columbus IT Partner, Thy Data Center, CDC, Erik Mainz and PC Systemgruppen, build up
the same range of skills as Large Account. This leads to a good deal of
friction due to the competition, which they feel Damgaard Data imposes
on them. They also find it unreasonable that the smaller resellers, who
haven't invested in building their own organisation around XAL, can offer larger projects with the support of Large Account. Finally, business
partners express the need to have better insight into future plans so they
don't end up developing the same extensions as Damgaard Data, which
will – at some point – be included in the standard package. Insight is also
needed if resellers are to support their customers with their IT planning.

On 4th October 1993, representatives from a large number of resellers
meet in Preben's office to complain about Large Account and discuss
how collaboration can be improved in general. Resellers petition hard
for Large Account to cease selling directly in competition to them and
to become a resource, which authorised business partners can draw on
instead. Actually, they would like to see the entire department scrapped
given that most skilled XAL consultants feel compelled to work directly
for Damgaard Data. Many customers also prefer being served directly
by the manufacturer. Finally, they point out an understandable, but unfortunate, clash of loyalty between Large Account and the development

department that is blurring the performance and quality problems that have marred XAL in its first version.

Preben listens, takes diligent notes and thoroughly understands the objections. But he doesn't feel that the time is right to end Large Account's activities. There is still a need for the department when it comes to maintaining a high level of skill regarding the implementation and customisation of the product and to stepping in when major and, not least, international customers present themselves or when there are serious product issues that need to be resolved quickly. Large Account persists, thereby continuing to be a major source of irritation for both the many Danish XAL business partners and the internal departments of Damgaard Data that work directly with the resellers.

## IBM wants to acquire Damgaard Data

On 3rd August 1993, Peter Perregaard from IBM comes to Preben Damgaard's office to gauge interest in a distribution agreement with IBM for Concorde XAL. Peter was the former sales manager of the successful Business Centres in Denmark and after a secondment at the European headquarters in Paris, he is now the head of the entire software business within the Nordic region. He wishes to expand the Business Centre concept throughout the region and needs a financial software package to support the initiative.

Since IBM received the cold shoulder from PC&C, Peter Perregaard has been interested in getting Concorde products on the agenda – especially the version running on the OS/2 operating system. What Preben doesn't know is that IBM's highest ranking executives have decided to invest massively in the marketing of OS/2. The company wants to secure a share of the growing market for software for PCs and to prevent Microsoft from having it all. In Scandinavia, where IBM enjoys significant success with PC sales and OS/2 also performs decently, they are convinced that the battle of the PC market doesn't depend on the operating system's technical superiority, but on which useful applications can be offered to small and medium-sized enterprises, in particular. IBM's subsidiaries in each country have the authority to take any steps necessary to ensure their OS/2 business, including making acquisitions when deemed appropriate.

Preben expresses interest and shortly after the initial meeting, a new delegation turns up, now headed by Country Manager Henrik E. Nyegaard. IBM would like to acquire all the shares in Damgaard Data. Although IBM was a competitor with Navigator from PC&C, Preben and Erik haven't had much contact with the company before, and this takes them completely by surprise. Naturally, such an announcement from the world's largest IT company is quite flattering. After consulting Henning Kruse Pedersen, the chairman of the board, they decide to pursue the opportunity. The two brothers have absolutely no intention to sell, but it could be interesting to get the company valued. And if the price is high enough, it might also be worth considering whether the future could be different to what they had otherwise imagined.

When you say "yes, thank you" to entering into a process that enables a potential buyer to make a bid, you also need to be prepared to invest a lot of time in that process. First, there is the preparatory information work, which gives the buyer insight into the business. Next, a long-term scenario has to be drawn up to assess where the business could go if you were to continue operating it yourself. That type of exploration and negotiation are extremely time consuming; they have to be carried out in the utmost secrecy, and the activity must not affect the daily operations of the company. Only a few employees are involved in the process and so that Erik and Preben can see to their everyday work, the meetings take place primarily at the weekends, at IBM's offices in Paris or at their Danish headquarters in Lyngby, north of Copenhagen.

The bidding process is formally run by Carsten Jørring from IBM Denmark, but – due to the size of the transaction – the actual negotiations are carried out by the M&A department in Paris. They end with IBM offering to pay 44 million USD in cash for all shares. But as Preben and Erik's own calculations result in a desired price of 60 million USD with a threshold of 53 million USD, there is no overlap between the two valuations. Intense negotiations ensue over several weekends, but IBM's M&A can't improve on the business case of their first bid, so Erik and Preben politely decline the offer. They are both convinced that they can run the business to a much higher value than the one offered. They are also unsure what selling to IBM would mean for their own future roles. Henning Kruse, who participates from the side-lines during the entire process, supports the brothers in making a thoroughly considered decision. Money alone shouldn't dictate the outcome.

The disagreement lies primarily in the assessment of how fast international scaling can occur. As of yet, Damgaard Data hasn't demonstrated any convincing results in that area. IBM, as the owner, could make a huge difference, but they are, of course, not ready to pay a high price for a contribution they themselves would make.

It takes a not insignificant amount of self-confidence to say no to 44 million USD in cold cash at a time when they don't have other liquidity opportunities and can barely spell "Initial Public Offering". But both Erik and Preben feel satisfied with the decision. Throughout the process, they have been on full par with the people from IBM, and thanks to their professional backing, they have had a continual solid foundation on which to assess their opportunities. Preben, in particular, leaves the negotiations richer for the experience and learns, not least, that in critical negotiation situations, it's preferable to have one or two alternatives in your back pocket. In no way did Erik and Preben have their backs against the wall during the negotiations, but it would have been nice if one or more of IBM's competitors had been waiting in the wings for similar negotiations. When talks break down, and Erik and Preben let it be known that they can't accept the offer, IBM's chief negotiator says the two brothers can obviously see something that IBM can't see.

He's right.

## Why do Preben and Erik say "no, thank you"?

In 1993, IBM is the world's biggest IT company with a turnover of over 14 billion USD and more than 300,000 employees. Despite the company recording some gigantic deficits, which for the 1991-93 period amount to a total of 3.2 billion USD, it is a heavyweight whose name is known and largely admired by business people worldwide. IBM in Denmark has managed to do especially well, enjoying a much larger market share there than anywhere else in the world. They have been successful with their Business Centre concept and, therefore, have a visible profile on the very market in which Damgaard Data operates. The contemporary equivalent (2017) would be an approach from Google, Apple or Microsoft, and then saying no to what would be 70 million USD in cash in today's money. The rejection indicates not only that the price is too low, but perhaps also a desire to remain independent and self-determining. The idea of standing up in front of all the employees in Birkerød and Kolding and telling them that the company had been sold didn't sit well. Erik, age 32, and Preben, age 30, have demonstrated to the outside world and to themselves that they know how to run a business and they aren't finished sitting at the head of the table where the direction is to be decided. Nothing in the negotiations – apart from the many millions placed on the table in front of them – catches their interest or whets their appetite. The growth that IBM might add would belong to IBM, and Erik and Preben would receive their salary as employed directors.

## IBM returns with a new proposal

Everyday life carries on back in Birkerød. The experience of the Paris negotiations fades quickly into the background, but not many weeks pass before IBM comes back with a new proposal. People within the Nordic organisation are keen on having some form of ownership of a financial management software package, which can form the foundation of a Nordic, and thereafter global, sales effort targeted towards small and medium-sized businesses. They would like to repeat the success of the Business Centres, thereby improving IBM's market shares in the national markets around the world. This was also the starting point for the original discussions regarding a complete take-over. As those discussions didn't result in agreement, IBM is now interested in acquiring an equity share of the product rights and using them primarily for activities outside of Denmark. Future collaboration would focus exclusively on global scaling and would not affect the Danish activities.

The proposal is sweet music to Preben and Erik's ears and would solve the challenges of international expansion, including the head start already gained by competitor PC&C, in one fell swoop. Having such an agreement in place would mean Concorde XAL would have IBM as a global distributor with well-established subsidiaries in all countries around the globe.

It's hard to imagine a company better suited than IBM for getting Damgaard Data out to every market. And against that background, negotiations move quickly, with the outcome being that IBM will buy 50 per cent of Damgaard Udvikling ApS [Damgaard Development], which holds the rights to the products, but they won't acquire an equity share of Damgaard Data Holding A/S, Damgaard Data Distribution A/S or Damgaard Data Large Account ApS, which will all continue to serve the Danish market. The small, newly-started German subsidiary, XAL Software Vertrieb GmbH, is also to be transferred to the jointly-owned company. During January, a purchase agreement and a shareholders' agreement are drafted, and on 21st January the new partnership is announced after which negotiations regarding the practical implementation can commence. The price for the 50 per cent share of Damgaard Udvikling ApS is agreed at 1 million USD plus half the net worth, which amounts to less than 40,000 USD. A whole range of follow-up agreements now have to be negotiated, pertaining to the organisation of trade and logistics, agreements regarding Damgaard Data Holding's administrative servicing of the joint venture, new articles of association for the joint enterprise and a new contract for Erik Damgaard. This process entails comprehensive, complex agreements, and the invoice for legal assistance runs to over 200,000 USD before everything is in place.

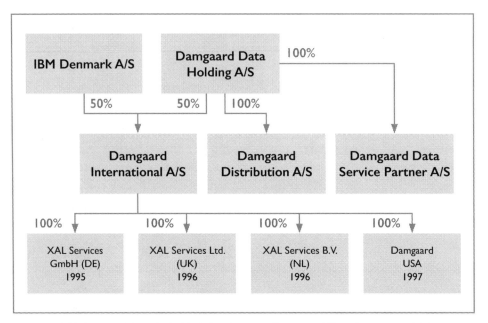

IBM Denmark bought half of the shares in Damgaard Development, which thereafter changed its name to Damgaard International A/S (commonly known as DIAS).

The agreement means IBM actually gets exclusive distribution of Concorde products outside of Denmark. According to the purchase agreement, IBM will initially launch the products in Norway, Sweden and Finland, "after which IBM will also commit to making the greatest of efforts to launch the products in other countries". Maintaining this exclusivity necessitates IBM buying for a minimum of 8 million USD during the period from when the agreement starts until 1st May 1997. If this minimum is met, exclusivity can be sustained as long as buying from the joint venture amounts to a minimum of 30 per cent of the company's annual total royalty and licence income. If the minimum conditions are not fulfilled, Damgaard Data Holding may buy back the shares for the prices agreed in the shareholders' agreement. Both the purchase agreement and the shareholders' agreement explicitly state that the purpose of the collaboration is to "develop Damgaard International into a high-quality, internationally competitive software company by employing the existing and future sales and distribution channels of the IBM Corporation". The price paid by IBM Denmark lies just within the limit of what they have at their disposal without having to involve the European headquarters. Therefore, not only can the contracts be drawn up in Danish, but there is also more licence to write what is deemed fit for the situation. This context may explain how the agreements could describe vast global visions and expectations for the partnership that have not the slightest backing from IBM's international organisation.

## Competitors – not enemies

The collaboration with IBM comes as a huge surprise to the employees, to the public and, not least, to PC&C, who knew nothing of the negotiations between their main competitor and their exclusive distributor and close business partner. And despite Jesper Balser from PC&C not predicting an agreement between IBM and Damgaard Data as a future competitive scenario, his experience tells him that partnering with IBM is a two-edged sword. When he had politely declined a similar collaboration, it hadn't been without thorough and mature consideration. When journalists request a comment, he is positive and offers his congratulations on the engagement, but inside he knows that getting involved with the world's largest IT company is by no means a bed of roses. He is later proven more than correct in his reservations than he himself could have imagined at this time, when he is also somewhat shaken by the sudden loss of his biggest distributor and by having learned from people at IBM that they will deliberately target his business.

In a double interview in the trade journal *Datatid* in March 1994, Preben and Jesper respond to questions about the new competitive situation. It is evident from the interview that Jesper Balser is surprised – bordering on shaken – and also significantly disappointed by IBM's engagement to the competitor. On the other hand, there is no hint of jealousy, and PC&C's decision not to sell to IBM is still completely supported. Damgaard Data has an annual turnover of 34 million USD, employs 160 members of staff and has an export share of just five per cent of the total revenue. Corresponding figures for PC&C reveal a turnover of around 8 million USD, 45 employees and an export share of 30 per cent due, in part, to having landed the large German market, but also due to them breaking into Spain, Austria and the USA. Both Preben Damgaard and Jesper Balser are fully aware that the key to great success isn't to be found in the relatively small Danish market, where it is difficult to move market shares that don't yield very much either. Success is to be found in the international markets, where both Concorde XAL and Navigator have proven to be extraordinarily competitive. PC&C has a really nice head start in precisely that area. Neither of the two directors is dismissive regarding the question of whether they can envisage a closer collaboration in the future. Jesper Balser says: "We may be competitors, but we're not enemies", and he refers to the positive experience from their distribution partnership of PC&C's PCPLUS. There is no love lost between the two companies, but Jesper's remark is clever and it strikes a chord with something in both his and Preben's personalities: only business opportunities can determine what is conceivable for the future and nothing is sacred.

CHAPTER 14

# A NEW SALES DIRECTOR

## IBM wants to sell both "Tuborg and Carlsberg"

At the beginning of January 1994, IBM petitions PC&C to get an extension of the 1994 distribution agreement prepared as soon as possible. The European headquarters has announced an internal audit of the Danish subsidiary; therefore, all formalities have to be in place. Jesper Balser senses the need for haste and proposes the minimum purchase requirement be raised to 5.8 million USD. This is accepted and the agreement is signed. A few days later, IBM announces publically its purchase of 50 per cent of Damgaard Data's development company. When resellers and journalists inquire about what is going to happen to the partnership with PC&C, the answer is that IBM wants to sell both Tuborg and Carlsberg.

The collaboration between PC&C and IBM Denmark is actually closer than ever in 1993-94. Staff at IBM are deeply involved in helping to devise the functional requirement specifications for a new product to be launched the following year, and which is to be fully compatible with the forthcoming version of Microsoft Windows. IBM's management have possibly overestimated the negotiating position given to them by the close partnership, or they have underestimated Balser and Damgaard's commercial skills.

The attempt to buy PC&C the previous year was amateurish at best. IBM's negotiators showed up with a ready-made purchase contract and a price they could neither account for nor negotiate. When they then tried to obtain exclusive distribution rights for the Nordic region, they were unable to formulate credible plans for how they would ensure a high market share for the product. PC&C sensed that IBM's size and position had gone to the heads of some of the leading employees, giving them the idea they could dictate the terms of partnership to their business partners. With PC&C, they had underestimated their host. And so, when IBM chooses to buy into the competitor, they simultaneously force PC&C to stand on their own two feet. It is not going to turn out well.

## We're going airborne

Damgaard Data organises conferences twice a year for its resellers. The day-long seminars are held in both Jutland and Copenhagen, always drawing full houses with 200-300 participants attending at each location. Much effort goes into preparing the conferences and providing the business partners with a good experience, including the opportunity to personally meet the company's top management team. As many resellers are small businesses with only a few employees, these meetings mean a lot to the resellers' self-worth.

Under the heading "Concorde Takes Off – we're going airborne", resellers gather for conferences in February, in Copenhagen on the 21st and Kolding on the 24th. Here, they hear about upcoming news in Concorde Økonomi, about the plans for Version 5, about Concorde XAL, about ProjectPartner, plans to get the products onto the Microsoft Windows platform, the market positioning of the product, about the marketing campaigns for 1994, about pricing and reseller policies and about the new partnership with IBM. A marketing campaign for Concorde Business is presented, which is to be launched in May that same year. It includes a new brochure, addressless customer letters, adverts in national and local media and bus ads as well as exhibition material for the resellers' showrooms. Partners are invited to join the campaign as "senders", meaning they get to promote their individual brands and subsequently obtain the addresses of potential customers generated by the campaign within their area. Resellers receive the concept free of charge and pay for only half the production and insertion costs.

A nationwide advertising campaign for XAL runs in April. It is followed up with letters to all Danish companies with ten or more employees and with telemarketing offers to participate in seminars on the product. It is the resellers, now called XAL Systemcentre, who are to run the seminars. Damgaard Data develops and pays the campaign concept, while partners pay half the ad insertion and production costs.

Getting resellers to co-finance the costs means the campaign has twice the range. Partners get "free" access to professional material and can purchase promotional activities for half of what they would have to pay should they be responsible for everything themselves. There are close to 500 Concorde resellers competing with each other, so most of them choose to sign up.

Damgaard Data participates with a stand of over 100 square metres at the Network '94 exhibition, taking place from 3$^{rd}$ to 5$^{th}$ May at the Bella Center. This activity is also supported by an ad campaign and letters to 2,500 decision makers and opinion formers in major Danish companies, including all XAL customers.

Whereas the campaigns for Concorde Business and XAL clearly support the image of the company as a supplier of financial management systems to the Danish business world, the campaigns for the networking products have a more transverse target group, because the range of products has been expanded to include backup and general network monitoring capabilities.

The Concorde Cup '94, which is announced as the world's first Concorde Indoor Football Cup, was a good example of the many social events held for business partners. 14 teams were involved in the competition. Damgaard Data's own team won the cup with a victory of 4-2 over Computerland Systemforum. From the left, in the back row, is Morten Jensen, Jan Vinjebo, Ole Jakobsen, Jesper Theil Hansen, John Holdt, Rene Vernon and Bo Nielsson, and in front row is Michael Beisner, Michael Graves, Casper Guldbrandsen, Jacob Michelsen, Per Nielsson and Carsten Tesgaard (Photo: Kenneth Estrup).

The social arrangements facilitate close ties and friendships. Damgaard showed great respect for its resellers and tried to cultivate a culture in which they felt a part of the Damgaard Data "family". Of course, it's about business and even direct conflicts of interest in many situations, but the shared interests and culture are to ensure support of the vision and help amicably solve those problems that inevitably arise between a supplier and its resellers.

## The IBM model

The practicalities of the partnership are discussed in the months leading up to 1st May; the date the agreements with IBM become effective. IBM might be one legal entity when it comes to the joint ownership of Damgaard International, but not when it comes to trade. Each subsidiary operates independently, making decisions about which products they will introduce in addition to IBM's own core products. It is agreed that the terms of logistics and trade must be mutual and that IBM and Damgaard Data Distribution are to be on an equal-footing.

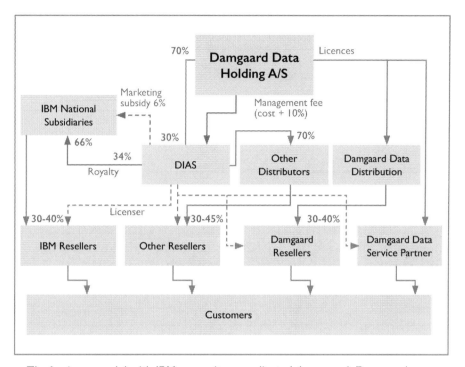

The business model with IBM was quite complicated. In general, Damgaard Data Distribution and IBM could purchase licences for 30 per cent of the list price. Resellers are expected to buy for 60 per cent of the list price, which gave IBM and Damgaard Data Distribution a 30 per cent gross margin to cover all the costs of the distribution activities. Initially, IBM paid 66 per cent, but it received a marketing contribution from Damgaard International of 6 percent.

Both IBM and Damgaard Data Holding agree to each purchase licences for 30 per cent of the recommended list price, which is determined by Damgaard International based on an assessment of the competition. Logistically-speaking it is clear that the distribution of data media and manuals will be both cumbersome and costly given it is to happen across national borders. Moreover, IBM's global software distribution, which operates from a centre in Allerød, in North Zealand, proves unsuitable for handling such distribution. Instead, interest grows in the FTP server that Mads Westermann established back in 1992, and which is primarily used by resellers in Norway, Singapore and the UK.

## Digital logistics

Someone gets the bright idea to connect the physical delivery to paying for the licences so that the resellers pay in advance. Practically speaking, partners are to buy so-called "point certificates" at their local IBM company. IBM forwards the order on the point certificate to Damgaard International, which sends an order confirmation to the reseller. The reseller connects to their account on the licence server at Damgaard International in Birkerød, where they enter or scan their order code, after which the number of points purchased is activated in the account. They can now pull licences for their customers. When the reseller inputs the customer's name and the modules to be used, the licence server generates unique codes, which the dealer can download and load into the client's program, after which the purchased modules are active.

Licence codes were originally sent by mail and later, by fax, after which they had to be entered manually into the customer's program. It was awkward and often simple typing errors were the cause of problems and misunderstandings. Delivering the codes electronically enabled Damgaard International to develop a facility whereby the code file can be pointed to in Concorde products, after which it automatically loads and activates the number of users and those modules purchased by the customer. Once the reseller has received the licences, their account on the licence server is adjusted accordingly. If the account is empty, they must order new point certificates before obtaining licences again. The dealer can also download the documentation and either deliver it digitally to the customer or print it out. Should the reseller prefer to deliver the software or the documentation on physical media, it can be done at extra cost. At the beginning of each month, Damgaard International sends an invoice to individual IBM companies for the number of point certificates delivered in the previous month.

For Damgaard International, the advantage is the simplification and significant savings on logistics, which are now digital, and that the debt risk is passed entirely to IBM. Whether they would like to wait to release the points paid to the reseller or whether they are willing to give advantageous credit terms is of no concern to Damgaard International. But what is almost missed is that this model involves a complete separation of invoicing, licence purchasing and payment. The model, which sounds beneficial to all parties at first, later creates a few problems.

As Damgaard International is housed in the same buildings as Damgaard Data Holding, it is further agreed to deduct administrative facilities in the holding company and pay for them according to consumption with an additional ten per cent. The holding company supplies Damgaard International with offices and canteens as well as HR, finance and legal services.

Damgaard Data Distribution and IBM are each responsible for market penetration, recruitment, training and management of resellers on top of providing ongoing support. Damgaard Data Distribution in Denmark has been built up over the last ten years and doesn't run into any problems following the new setup, but IBM is only getting started. Seen from the outside, one might think that the large company has the resources and means to deal with these tasks, but it soon becomes clear that a misjudgement has been made. When the collaboration commences in January 1994, it's on the cards for IBM's Nordic organisation to be made ready to launch Concorde XAL, while Damgaard International will deal with the necessary modifications regarding language and country specific functionality.

## IBM is to internationalise Damgaard Data

The agreement with IBM completely alters the market situation and is perceived internally within the company and externally among the resellers as well as in the press as the solution to the challenges of international expansion. In an interview in the March edition of *Datatid*, Preben Damgaard expresses an expectation that IBM will account for 80-90 per cent of worldwide revenue over the course of "some years".

The partial ownership construction of Damgaard International doesn't initially affect the activities in Denmark and, therefore, neither does it directly affect the majority of employees in the company. Erik Damgaard is formally appointed Managing Director of the company, while Peter Wagner is offered the position of Sales Director. Preben continues as Managing Director of Damgaard Data A/S and Damgaard Data Distribution A/S.

A new board is appointed at Damgaard International in that Per Hald-bo (chairman) and Peter Perregaard come aboard as IBM representatives, while Henning Kruse Pedersen and Preben Damgaard represent Damgaard Data Holding. For their part, IBM appoints a dedicated Nordic Concorde sales manager, who is tasked with getting the project on track for the Nordic markets.

The expectation is for IBM to drive marketing, recruiting and management of partners as well as supporting direct sales in the same way as they have with Navigator in Denmark. Damgaard International is primarily to be a development organisation that doesn't need commercial management or its own marketing and sales organisation other than the few people dealing with IBM.

Under the new setup, Damgaard International is no longer part of the Damgaard Data group. As managing director, Erik Damgaard reports solely to the board – not to Preben Damgaard. The two talk often, but Preben can't set the daily agenda for Damgaard International like he can in the other companies. Likewise, the ownership structure implies that the financial results will no longer be consolidated into Damgaard Data Holding, which won't contain export revenue. The joy over collaborating with the world's largest IT company is great, so no one is fully aware of what challenges this company and managerial structure will bring about.

## What do the employees think of Damgaard Data?

The results of the latest staff satisfaction survey are made available in January 1994. An overwhelming majority of the answers indicate that *"Damgaard Data is (in general) a place of work of which you can be proud and happy". "Within the company, it is distinctly accepted that it is possible to solve tasks in different ways"* and *"the implemented organisational change contains the right elements"*. Only 44 per cent of the employees participated in the survey, but most of them are satisfied and feel that they are listened to and receive any necessary information. However, they would like the motto "user-friendly software – for everyone" to be concretised; they believe that too many projects are begun and left unfinished, and they also feel insecure about the way in which employees are dismissed.

The need for better collaboration between the departments so the duplication of work can be avoided and work doesn't fall between the cracks and be perceived as poor service by resellers and customers is also expressed in the comments. A follow-up to the organisational development project is also called for as it is perceived as running on a side track. Finally, a more visible and consistent management team that keeps its promises is called for.

The results of the survey are described in the internal staff newsletter, which summarises the conditions that need to be worked on further:

- Making visible a common understanding of "user-friendly software – for everyone"
- Creation of action plans within the departments
- Structured flow of information
- Teamwork and cross-organisational collaboration
- A visible and competent-at-transacting-business management team
- Service and quality in relation to customers

One area that had been thoroughly debated before was the need for formalised and written policies, which – it was now concluded – is not part of the distinctive Damgaard Data culture. The individual person's freedom to deal with their work as they deem appropriate is highly valued. As it says in the conclusion: *"a little chaos does little harm; on the contrary – it can be constructive"*. The employee survey comes almost six months after the major organisational change and testifies to a strong backing for the company, but also to the continued organisational and managerial challenges.

## A non-breakthrough on the German market

One of the dilemmas of collaborating with IBM is clearly expressed when it comes to participating in the CeBIT exhibition in Hanover. Damgaard International is not represented at IBM's stand, which is run by IBM in Germany, but instead is included in the pool of exhibitors presenting at the Danish IT Industry Association's pavilion.

In light of the great international ambitions, participation in a Danish pavilion doesn't send a strong signal. However, getting excellent press coverage at home in Denmark does. On 23rd March, *Computerworld* features a rose-tinted story about breaking into the German market: *"IBM Denmark has bought into a gold mine through the Concorde deal with Damgaard International. Damgaard has sold for almost 8 million USD"*. However, that's not the case. The sale to Continental to which the article refers is certainly big business, but it doesn't represent a "breakthrough" into the German market. IBM Germany hasn't – as is claimed later in the article – committed to selling Damgaard's products. In autumn 1993, Damgaard Data itself sets up a little office with three technicians in Hamburg. An entire year passes before IBM in Germany starts to stir, and even with IBM's name on the product, it demands a lot more than a single order to break into the vast German market.

## Internet in the service department

Nowadays, it's hard to imagine a time without the internet, but it didn't exist during the first ten years of Damgaard Data. In spring 1994, the support department introduces a so-called Bulletin Board Server (BBS), where descriptions of bugs reported by customers and resellers are posted weekly. The purpose is to help partners, so they don't need to spend time on reporting bugs already reported. The BBS service is a temporary internet-based support system with better search capabilities, and where the status of individual errors can be seen is already being developed. Moreover, the new system will allow for suggestions for improvements and additions, which can then be included in the development plans.

## 200 USD an hour consultants

A new support concept is introduced for those resellers who would like to sell Concorde XAL with the Oracle database, which is exclusively for large customers or customers with large volumes of transactions. Business partners can purchase expert assistance at Damgaard Data – fixed content at fixed prices – which they can then sell on to customers. It really helps those resellers who are going to start offering the XAL/Oracle combination but haven't yet built up the required expertise and experience. As partners get more customers with Oracle, they can justify employing their own experts; thereby recovering the entire gross margin on the rather expensive consultancy hours that as early as the mid-1990s already cost around 200 USD an hour.

The Oracle support concept is a good example of how Damgaard Data supports the resellers. XAL/Oracle is technically complicated, but absolutely necessary for the large customers. Leaving the resellers to sink or swim would only result in dissatisfied customers who would experience XAL as a bad product. It would demotivate partners and give Damgaard Data and its products a bad reputation. Providing free support to resellers means they would have no incentive to build up their own organisation. But offering expertise through partners – at full real market prices – ensures that customers are cared for and that resellers can easily see the potential earnings.

## Focus on the company's own products

To best realise the potential of the IBM agreement, Preben decides that in future focus will be exclusively on the company's own products. The distribution and support of network products that played a crucial role in the enormous success of Concorde in the 1980s as well as the distribution of third-party complementary software packages are no longer strategically important. Network technologies have significantly improved and no longer demand the same level of technical skills in order to be used. Furthermore, the market for network products as well as standard PC software has changed drastically. There is no longer the same synergy as just a few years earlier. Whereas the extra gross margin was enjoyed in the 1980s, third-party products are used primarily to subsidise and support the sale of Concorde Økonomi in the 1990s.

While an extensive campaign for Concorde Business is running in spring 1994 with bus advertisements, in-store promotions and full-page advertisements in daily newspapers, Preben – without the involvement of his management team – plans to phase out all activities with third-party products.

As PC prices fall sharply, standard software prices are almost free falling, too, so the "bundling effect" becomes less and less important. Plus the sale of Concorde products and the sale of third-party products are two completely different types of businesses that become a lot less compatible in the mid-90s. But the last push to stop distributing third-party products comes from the partnership with IBM; partly because the bundling strategy has to be executed at distribution level, and thus will be outside of Denmark if IBM, who is to take on the task, finds it meaningful. But Preben would also like to concentrate all management resources on Damgaard Data's own products, which have now become the de facto standard of financial systems – at least in the Danish market – with IBM's stamp of approval.

However, the network department and the distribution of third-party products still represent a business potential, and the stock of third-party products will be difficult to shift if you just stop selling from one day to the next. Therefore, Preben tries to find new owners to take over the activities. In March 1994, the internal telesales department for third-party products is wound up; in April, the Computer Associates activity comes to an end; in June, the distribution agreements with DSI, Lotus and WordPerfect are terminated, and in that same month, the entire network division is sold to the British company Azlan.

The sale of the network and third-party products activities leads, naturally, to a decrease in the company's revenue and earnings. But the reduction in staff and the increased focus on the company's own products are to compensate for the consequences. Revenue falls from 34.2 million USD in 1993/94 to 30.4 million in 1994/95. But net earnings grows from 2.4 to 4 million USD during the same period. The operation has been a success and the patient is alive and kicking.

With a profit margin of almost 14 per cent, Damgaard Data is heading towards the level needed for survival in the software industry. Now it's about getting the growth in revenue in order, too.

## Becoming global

When compared to the accounts for 1992/93, those for the period 1 May 1993 to 31 April 1994 show a growth in revenue of almost 25 per cent, with the resulting profit of 2.42 million USD being 460,000 USD worse than the previous year. The agreement with IBM has cost just over 200,000 USD on lawyers and consultants, while the wound-down third-party products has cost a depreciation of 220,000 USD. Lawyer and consultant expenses for the spinning off of the network department to Azlan are included in the accounts, while the sales price of 2 million USD is included in the following year's accounts. The main culprits in the declining profit on an increasing revenue are increased development costs of 1.3 million USD and a decreasing gross margin on third-party products. With a net worth of 31 million, a solvency ratio of 36 per cent and a liquidity ratio of 175 per cent, the group continues to be a very healthy and well-cushioned company. With IBM as a partner in the international markets, the spin-off of third-party products, complete focus on its own products and a new and well-trimmed organisation, Damgaard Data seems to be stronger than ever to meet the ambitions of becoming a global brand for financial software for small and medium-sized enterprises.

A single column addresses the collaboration with IBM in the official 1994/95 financial report, where it is referred to as an export activity only:

*The aim of Damgaard International A/S is not only to strengthen Concorde products internationally but also nationally. Internationally, the company benefits from IBM's worldwide distribution network and brand recognition. And nationally, Damgaard Data can now expend all forces on the Danish market.*

## Employees get a share of the profit

At the beginning of the 1990s, the American principle of stock options comes to Denmark. In the IT industry, in particular, where key employees can make a significant difference, these options gain ground. A stock option is an option to buy shares at a predefined share price after a certain point of time in the future. The predefined share price is expected to be less than the share price at the time of purchase. If the employee takes advantage of the option, buys and then sells the shares immediately afterwards, the difference will be paid out without the employee having to put their hand in their pocket. The scheme often means that employees regularly receive additional stock options which expire if they leave the company. The options are to motivate employees to stay with the company and are, therefore, called "golden handcuffs".

Erik and Preben are aware that both the ambitions and opportunities for growth, not least in light of the partnership with IBM, bring about huge changes for the staff. Damgaard Data isn't a company where employees work robotically in line with written guidelines or under the close supervision of their managers. Rather there is an expectation that individuals take the initiative when it comes to improvements within their respective areas of expertise, while relating to the external challenges and opportunities. This culture, held in high regard by the vast majority of the employees, ensures the organisation can handle the constant changes and the accompanying workload.

Erik and Preben discuss whether they can and should do anything to ensure that the most important employees are retained and become more difficult to entice away. But the company isn't listed, so stock options won't work. Instead, they decide to introduce a form of profit sharing, whereby 30 per cent of the profit between 10 and 15 per cent of revenue, and 50 per cent of profit exceeding 15 per cent of revenue is distributed among employees as a special bonus in August 1995. 90 per cent of the bonus pool is distributed in proportion to the employees' wages, while the remaining 10 per cent is distributed by department heads according to individual criteria. The scheme is introduced as a two-year trial. Damgaard International, 50 per cent of which is owned by IBM, enters a joint arrangement in the first year, but in the following year is measured on its own results alone. Other salary adjustments are suspended as long as the trial scheme runs.

The scheme is well received by employees and helps to reinforce the perception of Damgaard Data as a company where employees come first.

## A new director of sales

With IBM as a new international partner and with the spin-off of network and third-party products, Preben feels the need for new energy at the top of the Danish sales and marketing organisation. And he already has a candidate in mind.

Preben met Per Pedersen through the collaboration with DEC, where Per was responsible for operations. Preben likes Per's stable, direct and no-nonsense manner. Preben sees Per as a coach, who plays ball and shares Damgaard Data's leadership values of freedom under responsibility, and as a person who is exceptionally true to his word, doesn't push people and works so systematically and structured that even a German field marshal would turn green with envy. Moreover, Per already knows the products, the market, the resellers and many of the employees in Damgaard Data. After mulling over the idea with Erik and getting his consent, Preben and Per meet for lunch in February 1994, but to Preben's great surprise, Per politely declines the offer.

In 1990, Per Steen Pedersen is hired by the Danish Department of Digital Equipment Corporation to head up the sale of Concorde XAL for the company's UNIX machines. In autumn 1993, he is appointed divisional director for the company's PC business, gets a seat on the company's top management and no longer has anything to do with Damgaard Data. Preben Damgaard tried to recruit Per in spring 1994 for the role of sales director, but to his great surprise, Per initially politely declined. As fate would have it, Per subsequently had a falling out with a chief executive at DEC's European headquarters, after which he changed his mind and said yes to Preben. Had Per originally said yes, he could have received a transfer bonus of 10,000 USD, which Preben had offered him as an enticement. This picture is from the Digitalks company magazine, dated 15th October 1993, where Per explains to the readers that he will increase DEC's market share of the PC market from 2 to 15 per cent within two years.

Immediately after lunch with Preben, Per travels to meet his European DEC colleagues and their joint manager, where they each have to present their businesses. When Per shows examples of an ad campaign run in Danish newspapers, which is a little on the sexual side, the European boss hits the roof and gives Per a public scolding right in front of his colleagues. Per tries to explain that the campaign has been well received in Denmark; that it fits in with Danish culture and is fully funded via local budgets. But the German boss is furious about the design of the advertisements. Per receives the subsequent support of his Danish manager, who, however, advises him to go "hide" for a while until the European manager moves on to another job or a new case turns up to draw his attention. Per doesn't care for either a public telling-off or for hiding for an indefinite amount of time, so instead he calls Preben, who doesn't need to know why Per changed his mind. He and Per just agree on how the change to the sales and marketing director post is to happen. Preben has to carry out the obvious redundancies and organisational changes before Per starts, after which Per can begin to rebuild and develop Damgaard Data. Preben is excited to have Per on board. He is relieved not to have to recruit through the open market of candidates he doesn't know and who don't know Damgaard Data. He knows from experience that the number of potential candidates is modest. The risk of making the wrong choice is great and could have serious consequences for the operation of the business unit, which is the nucleus of the company's future – at least in the short term. The position of sales and marketing director for the Danish activities, which account for 95 per cent of revenue and close to 100 per cent of the profits, is critical for the company.

## Per Pedersen rolls up his sleeves

With Per in the post as sales and marketing director from 1st June 1994, a key piece in the puzzle for the future of the organisation has fallen into place. Preben can now work on the other parts of the organisation, ensuring the potential of the collaboration with IBM is fully utilised.

Per starts very traditionally by going around the business partners and employees to hear their assessment of the situation and problems. But as early as mid-August, he announces four major internal challenges that need to be addressed immediately:

1. The support department is too slow in responding to enquiries.
2. Damgaard Data doesn't deliver on its own announcements regarding the release of new products.
3. Damgaard Data utilises its strong position to unilaterally deteriorate the terms of the resellers.
4. The larger business partners feel threatened by Damgaard Data's Large Account Department.

He emphasises that the sales strategy for the future is built on 100 per cent sales via resellers; that resellers should in fact be considered business partners and that Damgaard Data's partner account managers should be business-oriented rather than product-specialists. Working with resellers needs to be strategic so their businesses can grow and be profitable, thereby ensuring that Concorde products reach every corner of the market. The development and training of employees will be invested in to support these changes. The value-based management philosophy, which Damgaard Data has always strived for, will continue to be the foundation of a positive and motivating work environment. Finally, he underscores that there is no longer open access to Preben, who can only be called in for extraordinary situations and even then only in prior agreement with Per.

Following the announcements and after reorganising the sales and marketing department, he invites the entire staff to a seminar at Gilleleje Feriecenter on 18th-19th August. The new initiatives need to be discussed and the team, shaken up. Per gives employees free rein on the social part of the event. Dinner on the evening of 18th August, followed by a mock wedding. Every participant receives a predetermined role: speeches have to be given, songs invented and other wedding "traditions" participated in during the party. The role play has built-in intrigues and assigns participants completely different characters and profiles than those they have. Participants throw themselves into the mock wedding, which helps break the ice, gets the laughing muscles working and contributes to the unrestrained, open and informal style that Per wants to nurture and has become widespread in the company.

After the wedding, real work begins. Changes to improve results in turnover, earnings, and reseller and customer satisfaction must be made. In *Forhandlernyt* [Reseller News] magazine, sent via post to all business partners, Per repeats his observations and his strategy with virtually the same words he used in his internal communication. He explains the division of resellers into three segments:

- The small business segment: serving small customers with a budget of less than 2,000 USD
- The mid-market segment: serving the medium-sized customers with a need for adjustments in their financial system, and where the budget is up to 20,000 USD
- The enterprise segment: serving the large and demanding customers, where the budget typically exceeds 20,000 USD.

Partner account managers are then divided into three corresponding teams, with marketing activities tailored to the specific purchasing patterns applicable to each market segment. As early as September, Per takes stock of the results and reports clearly in *Forhandlernyt* what has happened and what has yet to happen.

Large Account changes its name to ServicePartner and is restricted to doing business directly with only 20 named customers to whom they are already contractually obligated. Furthermore, the department will no longer sell directly and, thus, not compete with resellers. Courses and consultancy services can still be sold directly, but at a price level that gives partners the opportunity to compete. Resellers must also be offered a reduction if they wish to arrange courses or buy consultants for their own projects. A more transparent policy for managing sales leads received by Damgaard Data and to be forwarded to business partners is introduced. From now on, resellers will be involved in all marketing concepts; thereby, achieving profiling on attractive terms. Last but not least, Per repeats several fundamental conditions they must strive to maintain:

- Keeping promises: delivery of information and release of programs must be on time. Answering telephone messages and other inquiries must be done without unnecessary delays.
- Quality: external consultants are going to measure reseller satisfaction with Damgaard Data every six months and the performance-related pay of the sales and marketing organisation will depend on how that satisfaction is developing.
- Consistent behaviour: no resellers will be allowed to sell products or modules before they have the necessary authorisation.

- Open and honest communication: Damgaard Data promises to be 100 per cent transparent in its communication with resellers. All business partners will receive exactly the same information and any changes to plans will be communicated immediately.

With his no-nonsense and consistent statements, Per has addressed those problems and challenges that have long been discussed by all the resellers and which have led to the growing frustration reported regularly in the market surveys from Marketing Expansion. He quickly scores points among the partners and as his position is more powerful than his predecessor's, initiatives can be implemented to ensure that the stated promises deliver results.

Per Pedersen's no-nonsense style would probably have encountered resistance in many other companies because it more than suggested that the previous course was wrong. That doesn't happen because Preben knows very well what Per stands for, and they agreed on the strategy and direction in advance. Per gets a free rein for the operational implementation. When Preben sees that the implementation fits in with the spirit of the strategy, he supports Per when hitches crop up and when another department head feels that it's too much too soon. With Per responsible for marketing and sales in the home market, Preben can tick that off his list and focus his energy on other areas.

## User-friendly software – for everyone

The organisational development project (OUP), which led to major re-organisation in August 1993, was restarted in August 1994. In an editorial of the internal staff magazine, *DDE*, Preben explains why time and effort are again to be spent on identifying and removing problems and inconveniences. The overall motto is still "User-friendly software – for everyone". Preben writes:

*The starting point for the OUP… was, as some remember, that what we do for a living is our way of doing things: we give the customer a positive experience. What we are selling is our culture and, therefore, it must be strong and clear.*

*The culture of Damgaard Data is strong and clear. It is based on an incredible employee commitment and a belief that what we are doing is the best. There may still be minor strifes in and between departments, but it is also clear that there is great tolerance and generosity – not just towards the company but also between the employees.*

*I hope you want to use your commitment and lifeblood – not just for toiling in everyday life, not just on serving the bottom line, not just on keeping the wheels running, but also for showing who you are – as individuals and as departments. Hold your managers to the project. They are your guarantee for OUP becoming a priority.*

Preben then explains that Damgaard International isn't going to participate in the OUP due to a heavy workload preparing new products for release.

## BFC Data becomes a business partner

After several preliminary meetings, BFC Data, a major IBM Business Centre, decides to enter into a reseller agreement in August 1994 for the Concorde XAL products and the forthcoming C5. It's a huge feather in Damgaard Data's cap. BFC is PC&C's largest reseller in Denmark. As per the agreement, BFC Data will convert nine industry solutions and launch a program so their 2,500 customers can move to XAL and C5. IBM Denmark, which has close connections to the management of BFC Data due to its work as a distributor of PC&C, has assisted with the negotiations and even contributed to a joint marketing fund. To ensure a successful start to the collaboration, a working group is established, comprised of representatives from BFC Data, Damgaard Data and IBM Denmark. As part of the efforts to get existing Navigator customers to switch to Concorde products, BFC is offered some extraordinarily favourable terms, which in practice mean that current customers can get Concorde free of charge, but new customers can get a Concorde- solution for a very reasonable price, too.

The only problem for IBM is that the more success they have getting Navigator resellers to switch to Concorde, the more difficulty they will have covering the guarantee for the purchase of licences, which they made to PC&C when they extended the distribution agreement in January. The revenue lost by IBM due to them knocking PC&C out of the market is – thanks to the favourable arrangements offered – only converted to a much lower revenue at Damgaard Data Distribution, which is again recorded as an even smaller business of Damgaard International and of which IBM Denmark owns only 50 per cent. IBM, therefore, applies to PC&C to be released from the guarantee obligation, without specifying the underlying causes. PC&C is not dismissive but would like some kind of *quid pro quo*, such as a marketing campaign for Navigator, which would also confirm IBM's official line of supporting both "Tuborg" and "Carlsberg". IBM accepts. However, the agreement releasing it from the guarantee obligation isn't signed before the campaign kicks off. Later, when the parties are about to sign the papers, PC&C claims to have experienced IBM employees voicing negative opinions about PC&C's future in the Danish market. Thus, PC&C finds that the terms of the agreement have been changed and the papers aren't signed. The management at IBM Denmark is furious, but can't do anything and must resign itself to being saddled with the guarantee obligation. Fortunately for IBM, not many PC&C resellers swap over to Concorde products, and the sale of Navigator continues to increase; thereby covering the guarantee obligation. When *Computerworld* carries out a survey of all PC&C resellers in late 1995, it appears that nobody has stopped reselling Navigator, and only a few are supplementing with Concorde products.

## Dolberg Data becomes Columbus IT Partner

In August 1994, Michael Gaardboe and Lars Andersen from Dolberg Data meet with Preben Damgaard to discuss a number of issues bothering the two gentlemen. Also in attendance is sales director, Per Pedersen, and the sales manager in daily contact with Dolberg Data. The guests present their criticism:

- Damgaard Data doesn't treat business partners alike.
- They have to compete with ServicePartner, which – by the way – doesn't have the top specialists they claim to have.
- Major resellers, who invest heavily in Concorde products, don't receive the recognition they deserve.
- Not enough is done with shared customer references from which all partners could benefit.
- DEC has better discounts than other resellers.
- Beta customers on the C5 program are given far too poor terms.
- Finally, the notice of termination on the business partner agreements is far too short.

That Preben and his people listen carefully and patiently to the many criticisms is due to the fact that Gaardboe and Andersen also have something attractive up their sleeves. They have decided to become Damgaard Data's largest business partner in the Danish market and, moreover, Denmark's largest provider of financial systems in general, too. This position is to be built around Concorde Økonomi and Concorde XAL; similarly, they will be 100 per cent behind the new C5 when it's released. They don't want to offer PC&C's Navigator and neither do they want to work with IBM. To support these ambitions, Dolberg Data plans to establish offices in Odense, Esbjerg, Aalborg and Herning.

Per Pedersen and Lars Andersen already know each other well from their time together in DEC and there is good chemistry between the two. Per nods his acknowledgement to most of the criticisms, so when they all take their leave it's with the best of intentions to improve conditions; thereby supporting Dolberg Data's ambitions for growth. In September that same year, Dolberg Data becomes Columbus IT Partner. As it turns out that Michael Gaardboe and Lars Andersen are actually capable of fulfilling their own ambitions and implementing their plans.

## Sven Tvermoes becomes HR Manager

The company has now grown to 170 employees. Preben needs to be both released from several internal operational tasks and to ensure that initiatives are still being taken for improvements – without them necessarily coming from him. Development of the organisation is an area that takes up much of his time; in particular he would like to plug the gap between himself and the management team when it comes to questions regarding the staff. Sven Tvermoes, who was employed as a logistics manager in 1991 and was once a naval officer, is already one of Preben's closest advisors. Sven has a great interest in people and actively helps drug addicts and people with challenging behaviour problems to get their lives back together. He willingly shares his honest opinion of the conflicts and inconveniences within the organisation with Preben and isn't afraid to criticise Preben's own decisions. Everything is looked at with two pairs of eyes and he is loyal to any decisions made. In September 1994, Preben asks Sven to assume the position of Human Resources Manager, covering all personnel-related issues including training, and organisational and cultural development. He is to be the sounding board for management concerning all things organisational, so Preben is free to exercise his overall leadership role and implement the long-term market strategy. Sven, who already has several motivated people in his own division, accepts the job of HR in addition to his job as Head of Logistics.

## An image campaign for Erik and Preben

Per Pedersen wants a fresh take on marketing. In the middle of the summer, he contacts his former colleague, Dorrit Overgaard, from DEC Denmark, to see if she would like the job of Head of Marketing. She accepts and starts in September, while Michael Sander moves to a newly created position as Head of Public Relations.

The company runs its own internal advertising agency. After reviewing her new department and talking to the "customers", Dorrit decides it needs to be revamped. To increase capacity and quality, most of the work is to be subcontracted to external agencies. From now on, the marketing department will be responsible for strategy, coordination and execution only. Dorrit wants a smaller department that draws on external resources, including a creative advertising agency. The concept isn't well received by the employees who are sceptical of the changes. But Dorrit has carte blanche from both Per and Preben and lays off all employees with the exception of Casper Guldbrandsen, who has been there since Landemærket.

Whereas marketing activities were product-focused during the first ten years, Dorrit implements an image campaign with Preben and Erik at its core at the turn of 1995.

Given the many products, the marketing budget was rapidly diluted as each product was marketed separately. Therefore, at the turn of 1994/95, the new marketing manager, Dorrit Overgaard implements an image and company-centric ad campaign focused on the photogenic Damgaard brothers.

"Samspil er en betingelse for vækst"

DAMGAARD DATA

## 15 sub-agreements with IBM

Starting-up with IBM is complicated by the fact that Damgaard Data already has a distributor in Norway – Sigurd Flydal – and, therefore, IBM has to try to negotiate an agreement with him first. In Sweden and Finland, the local organisations need to first consider how to tackle the new assignment. Enquiries do, however, come in from countries where Damgaard Data itself is already working on something; even IBM in Australia and South Africa show interest. As early as February 1994, Damgaard International participates in a four-day IT exhibition with IBM in Norway, but as it's at short notice, there is no time to brief the Norwegian press. Neither is there room to show Concorde XAL, but Damgaard Data employees get the opportunity to meet their Norwegian IBM colleagues.

By May 1994, the flow of logistics and the invoicing process is defined. The original partnership agreement has now resulted in 15 sub-agreements, which lawyers have helped review to ensure quality and clarity. In Denmark, Damgaard Data Distribution A/S has exclusivity. IBM can get a sub-distribution agreement if it can be agreed upon, but there is no immediate need for any changes. Individual IBM subsidiaries around the rest of the world can, in principle, buy directly from Damgaard International – but the signed agreements are explicitly valid for Norway, Sweden and Finland only.

In May, Damgaard International announces that beta-testing on Concorde XAL Version 2.1 (which is already released on the Danish market) will be conducted over the summer with language versions in German, English, Swedish and Norwegian. Version 1.31 is available in Dutch, and later in the year this language is transferred to Version 2.1. Moreover, negotiations are underway with Columbus IT Partner for Russian and Czech versions. Damgaard can finally tell resellers it is also working intensively on getting Concorde XAL onto the Microsoft Windows platform, and to that end new employees with expertise in graphic user interfaces have been hired. However, it isn't possible to set a release date.

The plan is to release Concorde C5 for DOS first, then for OS/2 and for Windows in 1995. IBM's representative on Damgaard International's board, Peter Perregaard, asks for a meeting with Preben Damgaard to discuss this plan. He is annoyed the first release is to be on DOS and the OS/2 version can't, at least, be released at the same time. Unfortunately, it signals that OS/2 is less important; not least internally in IBM, where there are enough challenges motivating the sister companies to take on Concorde. Preben explains that demand for Concorde on OS/2 is very limited and, therefore, it's difficult to prioritise that platform at the expense of other platforms. But he promises to check whether it's possible to change the plans so the two versions can be released simultaneously.

This episode documents the objective differences of the partners' interests. OS/2 is a strategic product for IBM in the battle against Microsoft. Damgaard Data's interest is to ensure the availability of its products on those platforms currently demanded by the market regardless of them coming from IBM, Microsoft or another provider. It won't be the last time, the lack of common interests and goals frustrates the partnership.

When the results are checked in October that same year, the agreement with IBM has generated less than 20,000 USD in revenue – a far cry from the target of 2 million USD, but Rome wasn't built in a day, so confidence and optimism prevail. With trust in IBM's intentions and abilities, there is no Plan B. Preben remarks in his notebook as early as the end of September that there is a lack of reciprocity in the partnership and that PC&C still seems to be running at full speed both inside and outside of Denmark.

## PC&C embark on a close partnership with Mærsk Data

For IBM Denmark, the break with PC&C is a catastrophe. After overcoming the shock of IBM's engagement to the competitor, Jesper Balser considers whether there are other alliance possibilities within the Danish market that, on the one hand, can carry on the stamp of approval – which the partnership with IBM brought with it – and, on the other hand, can help prevent IBM from using its power to crush PC&C given that they are no longer bound by a minimum purchase requirement. From sources within his personal network, Jesper hears that things have turned cold between IBM Denmark and Mærsk Data. The A.P. Moller Group, to which

Mærsk Data belongs, had been a major customer of IBM for many years, and the owner, Mærsk McKinney-Møller, had even been on IBM's top board from 1970 to 1984. IBM is displeased with Mærsk Data's behaviour, which includes purchasing used mainframes (though not from IBM); close collaboration with other suppliers, outsourcing IT operations to other parts of the world as well as not following IBM's recommendations in general. High-ranking IBM people have even complained to top management in the A.P. Møller Group about Mærsk Data's dispositions.

Despite there being a close bond between IBM and A.P. Møller, business in Mærsk Data is not characterised by camaraderie. IBM wasn't the exclusive supplier of IT to A.P. Møller, just as A.P. Møller wasn't IBM's exclusive carrier. Mærsk Data receives full support from its head office. Perhaps PC&C can exploit this tense situation to its advantage? Jesper Balser contacts Mærsk Data's director, Steen Hundevad Knudsen, briefs him and asks if they would be interested in collaborating on distribution in Denmark. The proposal is well-received and in November 1994, PC&C announces in partnership with Mærsk Data the establishment of PC&C Denmark.

After IBM bought into Damgaard Data, it only renewed the agreement with PC&C for a single year, and from 1st January 1995, IBM loses distribution of Navigator and must wave goodbye to a handsome revenue of millions. The opportunities for targeting PC&C are impaired up front as that would be a thorn in the side of the A.P. Møller/Mærsk Group as well. IBM's resellers continue selling Navigator, but are now served directly by the new distribution company, and as IBM never gets a share in the distribution of Concorde products in Denmark, there is nothing to compensate for the loss. By the beginning of 1995, IBM is completely out of the market for financial systems for PCs in Denmark and, thereby, loses a very important pawn for controlling its Business Centres. Resellers and customers who would like to use PC&C products are no longer bound to purchasing the hardware from IBM. When the competitive pressure prompts a simultaneous constant fall in prices and the related gross margin on hardware products, IBM is on its way to losing the foundation of its entire sales concept for the PC market in Denmark.

## Sales continue to increase

In July, it is finally announced to business partners that the date for releasing Concorde C5 has been set: 15th November that year. Concorde Version 5 was supposed to have been on the market in 1991, but became XAL instead – a completely different product. XAL enabled access to blue chip customers such as Royal Copenhagen, B&O, Motorola, Continental, Bodum and many more, but it didn't facilitate the revival intended for the many small – and original core – business customers. Fortunately, Concorde Økonomi – strongly supplemented by DSI and Business editions – held the fort, preventing resellers and customers from fleeing to the competition, which there was plenty of technically-speaking. It doesn't happen, first and foremost, because Concorde Økonomi in Business versions was actually an excellent solution for customers, but also due to how well partners were treated. And lastly, none of the competitors – apart from PC&C – had a marketing muscle to match Damgaard Data's.

Customers who subscribe to Concorde Økonomi updates can get Concorde C5 free of charge by simply putting themselves down for the upgrade by a certain deadline. After that date, there is an option to upgrade from Concorde Økonomi to Concorde C5 at a favourable price. This is to make it difficult for competitors to get their hands on customers wanting to change. As Concorde C5 is more comprehensive than Concorde Økonomi, the training and certification requirements are intensified, requiring new resellers to invest in 12 course days, while Concorde Økonomi partners have to invest ten course days and XAL resellers, two course days. Course costs are between 1,200 USD and 3,600 USD plus the time the employees are out of production. Resellers are promised that the release of Concorde C5 will be followed by massive advertising campaigns in the days after Kontor&Data and in the first half of 1995. However, it isn't hard to convince resellers to jump onto the C5 bandwagon.

Concorde C5 hits the market on 15th November and everything is in place for the largest product launch to date. Each reseller receives a copy of the marketing and sales materials containing individual PR activities for the 15 largest newspapers and trade journals, while information packs and trial versions are sent to the editors of 80 other trade publications and newspapers. The product costs the same as Concorde Økonomi, though for the first time, a special licence is introduced for PC laptops. Vocational schools can purchase Concorde C5 for educational use for an unlimited amount of users for a fixed subscription price of 1,000 USD per year.

C5 is welcomed by the market and sales climb every day. A set of tools is launched to make it easy for customers on Concorde Økonomi to convert their data to XAL and C5, respectively.

When the half-yearly accounts are done for May to October 1994, in November of the same year and compared with the same period in 1993, revenue hasn't decreased despite spinning off network products and closing down third-party products. With an increase of 45 per cent, sales of Concorde products have filled the potential gap. XAL now stands for 66 per cent and Concorde Økonomi accounts for 33 per cent of revenue, while the number of employees is 171, of which 26 are employed in Damgaard International. 1994 was an exceptionally hectic year of major changes. First, the grand partnership with IBM, then the winding-up of network and third-party products, followed by a major organisational change with new people in the top positions of marketing and sales and, finally, the launching of a brand new product. Indeed, 1994 bears witness to Preben's motto: "the only constant is change".

## C4 lives on

Concorde Økonomi, which after the launch of the Concorde C5 in September 1994 changes its name to Concorde C4, has a wide penetration in Denmark. Given the possibilities of integrating with DSI and being able to develop individual customisation later via the Toolbox, many customers choose to remain with the product for many years. Despite the explosive penetration of Microsoft Windows from 1995 onwards, those customers using Damgaard Data's products aren't the first ones to adopt Windows-based programs. The graphic user interface, which uses a mouse for on-screen navigation, makes programs more intuitive and easier to use for the occasional user, but for a user who does the same tasks several times over the course of a day, it affects productivity. As Windows progresses in the mid-1990s, the imagination and inventiveness of the programmers once again surpasses the capacity offered by the underlying hardware, and Windows-based programs are typically significantly slower than text-based ones. Users of Damgaard Data's software are primarily employees with routine administrative functions. They don't fall for Windows in the same way that their colleagues in the design, sales and marketing departments do. Both Erik and Preben are quite aware of this, which explains why they are not at all at the front of the queue when it comes to introducing graphic user interfaces for Concorde products.

# CHAPTER 15

# LEARNING TO LEARN

## Strategy seminar January 1995

To kick-off the New Year, a strategy seminar for all managers of departments dealing with activities in Denmark is held on 11th and 12th January 1995. An external consultant helps to organise a format where participants can formulate their vision for how the company should look in Denmark in 1998. After which the participants define what is needed to fulfil that vision, and finally, the entire plan is revised so that what was to take three years can be achieved in a single year instead.

They work primarily on issues related to recruiting and managing resellers as well as support, sales, marketing and stimulating continued growth in the Danish market in general. With a strategy to exclusively serve the market via business partners, two major issues arise: how to increase the number of resellers and how to ensure the growth of each reseller.

An analysis of the questions identifies the most obvious bottlenecks in both their own organisation and with the resellers. Partners have a shortage of qualified labour within almost all disciplines. Recruiting more resellers, who simply steal employees from each other, is not productive. Efforts need to be made to both increase the supply of qualified labour and better use the existing resources. As a result of the strategy meeting, a number of initiatives are implemented, which, when taken together, are to increase the capacity of the reseller channel.

Business partners earn most of their living selling consultancy services to customers, making adjustments to and developing additional products for Concorde. The work is uncoordinated, which is why resellers – to some extent – can expect to develop exactly the same thing. If the many program extensions were made visible, partners could buy them from each other, just as customers could see if what they need has already been developed. The initial solution is a directory of resellers' extensions for XAL.

It sounds like a simple task, but it is not. There is a big difference between customising a program for just one or a few customers, which the reseller themselves is responsible for, and then documenting and maturing that program customisation as an independent product, which can be priced and sold to another reseller, who will independently resell it to and service it for their customers.

The establishment of a software factory under ServicePartner, where resellers can order smaller development tasks of up to 250 hours for Concorde XAL and C5, is also intended to compensate for the lack of capacity in the business partner channel. The software factory is to help new resellers get started, in particular. But it is also to get the established resellers to take on more projects given they can handle peak demand by using the factory. As more tasks are solved by the factory for partners, they can hire their own employees and take over the work themselves over time. In this way, the factory becomes both a buffer during peak load periods and a midwife for the expansion of staff with resellers.

Finally, an initiative is taken to retrain engineers. In collaboration with the Job Centre in Copenhagen and a handful of business partners, a number of unemployed engineers, considered suitable to be XAL software developers, are selected. They are offered training in XAL programming and an internship. The individual participants are pre-assigned to a reseller, who is prepared to hire them after the completion of the programme. All 20 engineers, who complete the retraining, receive permanent employment.

## Every customer is Damgaard Data's customer

The customer relationship in Damgaard Data's business model is that customers formally enter into a direct licence agreement with Damgaard Data, while the invoicing relationship – payments for both the use of the software and the related services – is with the reseller. Damgaard Data regards all customers as its customers, formally and informally, despite it being the resellers who are in daily contact and have responsibility for all invoicing.

Every company needs close contact with its customers in order to continue developing products and services, which those customers can benefit from and that maintain the company's competitiveness. It's a challenge for Damgaard Data that customer contact is via the resellers, which is also why the ServicePartner business is retained. But ServicePartner's possibilities for serving customers directly is significantly limited after Per Pedersen steps in as sales and marketing director, and states clearly that from now on it's exclusive selling via business partners only. After this, ServicePartner works primarily on major international projects or for the resellers as a subcontractor. So as to maintain and strengthen market contact, XAL customers are invited to participate in a number of user clubs and experience groups in 1995. Members of user clubs receive a magazine with practical tips for using the products, as well as invitations to events where general trends and challenges are presented along with how to solve them using XAL. Membership of a user club costs 100 USD per quarter and covers four employees from the customer's company. The experience groups are arranged according to company type, geography and function, and go right down to the individual company's use of XAL. Membership of an experience group costs 300 USD per quarter per person and membership of a user club is a pre-requisite. Experience groups are established initially in the areas of retail, service, production, projects and salary management.

## The reseller panel

To strengthen relationships to the business partner channel, a panel of representatives, comprising of the most important resellers, is established. Its purpose is to improve the joint business, but also to provide room for dealing with the ever-smouldering dissatisfaction within the reseller channel. Damgaard Data and the partners have a wide range of shared interests, but also a lot of conflicts.

Whereas Damgaard Data and its resellers agree on stimulating market demand and improving product competitiveness, the practical allocation of work is an endless discussion. Damgaard Data's motivation is to support the reseller's long-term growth and not just increase its short-term earnings. Partner are, by nature, fundamentally more short-sighted.

A software company invests in the development of products that are to earn their keep for at least five to ten years. When development costs are initially paid, product-related marginal costs are quite small. The reseller is a trade and service company that makes money on the individual project here and now and their marginal costs are relatively high. In other words, two vastly different business models are at play.

Damgaard Data works closely with the resellers, supporting individual activities with subsidies for marketing, sales, training and management development. Business partners have an interest in optimising their earnings by getting Damgaard Data to co-finance costs they themselves have already taken on. But Damgaard Data wants to stimulate extra efforts not already planned. Damgaard Data often accepts a reduction in the licence price of the core product so as to be competitive in a specific situation. Despite it being difficult to determine whether or not that is necessary.

As the number of resellers grows, so does their individual interest in impeding others from getting better terms than them. Whereas individual resellers may think more favourable terms are necessary, they are, naturally, unhappy if their competitors get even better terms. All parties wish for the Concorde brand to be known on the market, and the number of business partners is crucial for ensuring that. But existing partners aren't so excited about the many new resellers. If a customer gets quotes from, for example, five suppliers, the Concorde reseller would prefer to be the only one, while Damgaard Data would like to see all five offers contain a Concorde product. Every reseller asks for help with their sales and needs testimonials about customers' use of Concorde. And preferably, the name of the reseller, who actually served the customer, should not be mentioned in the testimonial as it might cause potential customers to contact them instead. Business partners who are to contribute reference stories aren't so motivated to participate in the work if their names aren't going to be mentioned.

Manoeuvring in a universe where you want to increase your market share, increase the number of resellers and stimulate the growth and earnings of each individual reseller, while ensuring fairly equal terms to all, is a constant balancing act.

## Partnerships can be addictive

In a business model such as Damgaard Data's, resellers are dependent on their core supplier. Despite Concorde products not representing the largest item in a customer project, they are the foundation. A reseller can't just switch to another product. If they choose to do so, they have to explain it to their existing customers, make major investments in getting to know the new product and build up a customer base in competition to the already established – and more experienced – resellers of the product concerned. If a business partner chooses to supplement their business with another product, such as Navigator, they have to consider whether or not the same investment in the current Concorde business would provide a better and more secure return. The costings are almost always in favour of the status quo. Therefore, the best option for resellers is to ensure a close relationship with the supplier and, thereby, get the best possible conditions for growing under its umbrella.

## Product planning and product quality

Particular critical areas are product planning and product quality. For their own internal planning purposes and for advising customers, resellers need to be familiar with Damgaard Data's development plans; it doesn't make sense for a reseller to invest in the development of a new module that is then released by Damgaard Data as part of the standard product three months later.

Like all other software companies, Damgaard Data has difficulty with development plans. If you are to keep a release date for a new version, then the pressure is on what to include in the product. If, on the other hand, you must guarantee to maintain the promise of the content of a new version, then the pressure is on the date of release. Software development differs from digging trenches in that you can't, for instance, develop more software any faster by assigning more people to the task. (This dilemma was described by Frederick Brooks in the book *The Mythical Man-Month* from 1975.)

Moreover, product planning costs resources that don't directly result in better products. Adhering to a product plan entails that the content be frozen in good time before the release date in order to carry out testing, complete documentation and prepare marketing. Erik Damgaard is still at the head of the table when it comes to product development and he will bypass all plans in case there is something he considers important for the product or market. The advantage of Erik's approach is his quick response to input from customers and resellers, but it creates conflicts as Damgaard Data expands, and more and more become dependent on the company's dispositions. Consequently, product plans and their reliability become recurring themes at internal meetings – and also in talks with distributors IBM and Columbus and with the many business partners in more and more countries.

## Who should pay?

Product quality goes to the top of the agenda for meetings with both distributors and resellers. If an unexpected bug occurs in the product, it must be identified, described and reported. Once the bug is rectified, it has to be implemented for the customer. That work can take a long time and who should pay for it?

Damgaard Data has clearly renounced responsibility in business partner agreements, and it would also be impossible to run a commercial software company if you were to finance that work. Resellers must, therefore, ensure that their customer agreements either exempt them from costs associated with handling bugs in the standard product or ensure a gross margin that leaves room for fixing bugs. Not all resellers are equally skilled in dealing with this quite common issue in their contracts with customers. And, at the same time, the quality level of products fluctuates greatly depending on how many new features a version contains. In the end, there is always a discussion about whether something is a bug, an inconvenience or an intended function. When PC&C and Damgaard Data are compared, the former seems more particular about quality, while Damgaard Data seems the most product-innovative and flexible in relation to business partners. But it isn't possible to be innovative and expand while keeping everyone satisfied and as there is no desire to compromise on innovation, challenges have to be tackled as they occur. The many interests require constant balancing. Preben, Erik and the other members of management are fully aware of this delicate balance, and the many initiatives taken in 1995, not least the user groups and the reseller panel, are to ensure that problems are handled as quickly as possible and in the order of importance dictated by the business.

## PC&C launches Navigator Financials

In January 1995, PC&C announces that depending on when Microsoft releases Windows 95, it is going to launch Navigator Financials later in the year, which will run exclusively on the new Microsoft platform. The emphasis is on it being a brand new product and not an adaptation of the character-based Navigator. Whether it's a broad hint is unknown, but the fact is that the work of making XAL and Concorde C5 ready for Windows doesn't include rewriting the code from scratch. So Concorde products can't get the coveted "Certified for Windows 95" label, which PC&C is consciously targeting. This doesn't mean so much for the Danish market, where both PC&C and Damgaard Data are well-established and well-known brands, but it's crucial for developing export markets.

When *Computerworld* magazine carries out a survey of Danish software companies in February 1995, it seems Damgaard Data is the only one relying on IBM's OS/2. Everyone else is betting on Windows. Erik Damgaard explains to the magazine:

*When we started looking at Windows three years ago, we were uncertain whether it would be the future. Therefore, we ensured the possibility of writing programs for multiple graphic platforms. The solution was a class library for C++. It enables writing programs not bound to one specific graphic user interface. For example, the programmer can write a line of code asking it to draw a window on the screen. When he compiles the code, the class library provides the appropriate commands in either Windows or Presentation Manager [OS/2] – or Macintosh or OSF/Motif for that matter.*

Erik Damgaard admits that more planning is required for that kind of development. Staff-wise it means there is a need for a few extra hands on each supported platform, too. Thus, there are two people in the UNIX group and one and a half persons working on the development of OS/2. Undoubtedly, the close collaboration with IBM affects the company's assessment of the strengths between OS/2 and Windows, but not many months pass before the market's definitive choice manifests itself in a way that is evident to everyone.

## Damgaard International gets a new director

It is clear as early as the latter half of 1994 that the expectations for the partnership with IBM are far from being met. The joint expectation of a turnover of two million USD in the Nordic markets in 1994 was miles away from the 20,000 USD actually made. At the same time, PC&C wasn't suffering in any way from the break with IBM. When the board discusses the situation, it is difficult to point to anything other than everything taking longer than expected. IBM has taken longer than expected to staff the distribution in Norway and Sweden, and Damgaard International has taken longer than expected getting the products ready for the national markets. There is no suspicion of weakness in the collaboration's foundation, and the conclusion of the discussions is to strengthen the management of Damgaard International. As Damgaard Data Distribution is running impeccably under Per Pedersen's management, it seems most urgent to strengthen the partnership with IBM. Henrik E. Nyegaard recommends talking to Jens Haugaard, operations manager for IBM's software activities in the Nordic region. The talks result in Jens being offered the job as managing director of Damgaard International. He takes up the position on 1st February 1995. As managing director, Jens reports to the board of Damgaard International and, in particular, to the chairman, Per Haldbo from IBM.

Jens Haugaard, who worked primarily with administration and wasn't directly involved in sales, sees his primary job as getting the product development plans under control so Damgaard International can ensure IBM quality products in the promised time. He knows IBM's way of working inside out and realises that a successful partnership requires more planning and, thus, more predictability in releasing new versions of the products; similarly, IBM expects products to be more complete than Damgaard Data has either a tradition or reputation for delivering.

## XAL and C5 for Windows and OS/2

Windows 3.1, launched in April 1992, quickly becomes quite popular; the Windows 3.1 version for workgroups, in particular, released at the end of 1993, which enables the sharing of data, applications and hardware, gains Microsoft serious market share. When the company unveils its development plans in January 1994, interest and press coverage is solid. The plan is to release a new 32-bit version of the server product Windows NT (code name *Cairo*), but of more interest are the plans for the project code named *Chicago* or Windows 4.0, which is the operating system for the individual user's PC. Microsoft expects to release Windows 4.0 at the end of 1994, with the development tools for programming the operating system being released in the first quarter of 1994.

At the same time as Microsoft gains market share with Windows, Damgaard Data enters into the partnership with IBM, which pumps billions of dollars into their OS/2 counter-strategy. Concorde Business, which includes a number of other DOS-based software packages is already immensely successful and Concorde XAL is growing at lightning speed. In May 1994, a highly improved XAL Version 2, operating on DOS, OS/2, Ultrix, OSF1 and SCO/UNIX is released, and is available with Damgaard Data's own file system or with the Oracle database system. Preparations are also busily underway for the launch of Concorde C5, which is initially planned for DOS and OS/2. The Windows platform also features in Damgaard International's plans, but as many different operating systems are being supported, the careful considerations focus more on how to easily separate program logic and data management from the user interface itself. Developing a brand new product or moving C5 or XAL over to Windows is not on the cards. Efforts won't be spent on offering Concorde Økonomi in a Windows version, but it would be logical to develop a Windows client for XAL and C5. In February 1994, Damgaard International announces that XAL Version 2.5 will come in versions for DOS, OS/2, Windows 3.1, Windows NT and UNIX, while C5 Version 1.5 will be available for DOS, OS/2 and Windows 3.1. Only the user component comes in Windows versions. Development tools aren't ported. This means the products can be offered in mixed environments, where some users run the DOS version, while others use the new Windows client. As Windows requires new hardware, the option is seen as an advantage to customers. However, XAL and C5 aren't particularly stable on Windows 3.1, and it is only when Windows 95 is released in autumn 1995 that Damgaard Data begins to actively promote the Windows client.

## Its own stand at CeBIT '95

In March 1995, Damgaard International exhibits independently at the CeBIT fair. Despite there being explorations with IBM in Germany regarding the distribution of XAL, Damgaard International has learned that you have to participate independently at the international fairs. IBM's participation at the CeBIT exhibition is gigantic, but is run by the German subsidiary, which focuses exclusively on the German market. Damgaard International has a global focus and wishes to utilise CeBIT's international position to come into contact with potential distributors, resellers and customers from all around the world.

The CeBIT fair allows yet another comparison to PC&C. Their stand is significantly larger and comes with an internationally-oriented image, emphasised by the company's forthcoming product Navigator Financials, which becomes the world's first fully certified financial system for Microsoft's Windows 95.

## The internet is an expensive experience

In January 1995, *Computerworld* carries out a survey to uncover Danish IT companies' use of the internet for commercial purposes and, therefore, contacts Damgaard Data, too. Mads Westermann states:

*It started as an experiment in the development department, where we wanted to see if it [the internet] could be used for marketing, but those "surfing" the web aren't our typical target audience... We would like to put documentation and help files onto the server. We already have an internal WWW server with documentation for Concorde XAL, and some of that will be posted. In Denmark, the internet is a scarily expensive pleasure, but it is extremely valuable when it comes to contacting our foreign resellers.*

At the end of 1994, Microsoft decides to include its new web browser, Internet Explorer, in the forthcoming Windows 95, and simultaneously launch Microsoft Network with services such as chat, discussion groups and electronic mail in 35 countries and in 20 languages. An investment of 100 million USD in marketing ensures rapid penetration of the new facilities. Thus, the heat is turned well up on a development that gives the internet a penetration rate never before demonstrated by any technology. With connection possibilities via modem, bottlenecks still have to be overcome, but with the launch of Windows 95, the internet becomes a phenomenon affecting the IT industry on all fronts.

## IBM's Azanta initiative is a fiasco

Global sales of OS/2 are slow and can in no way keep up with the spread of Microsoft Windows. IBM's Nordic management believes the problem is a lack of applications. If a supply of usable applications can be immediately secured for the OS/2 platform, customers will also buy OS/2 based systems relying on IBM's good name. Therefore, the idea of combining a variety of applications such as wordprocessing, spreadsheets, presentation and database with a financial program in one package is formed. In spring 1995, IBM launches the Azanta product range in Denmark, Norway and Sweden, which is a combination of IBM hardware, Lotus SmartSuite and the new Concorde C5, now translated into Norwegian and Swedish, and adapted to national market conditions. The entire package is based on OS/2 and is meant to be a Microsoft Windows killer.

Azanta is a giant fiasco, and demonstrates that small and medium-sized businesses simply don't want products based on OS/2. After a few months, the product suite is placed on the shelf and receives no further attention. That IBM overestimates its influence on the PC market can be read in *Computerworld* as early as February 1995. Here, it emerges that Damgaard Data is the only Danish software company expressing interest in OS/2. The main argument from the other suppliers is the lack of demand, and the fact that Windows' programs can run on OS/2 is mentioned, but not vice versa.

## Norwegian drama

Since 1988, Sigurd Flydal's company, WAI, has been responsible for localising and distributing Concorde Økonomi in Norway and, since the beginning of 1992, for the distribution of XAL. By the end of 1993, he had a significant number of large resellers on board and was now looking forward to reaping the fruits of his labour. On Monday, 24th January 1994, at half-past three in the afternoon, a fax comes in from Damgaard Data, saying that IBM has taken over distribution in Norway, Sweden and Finland.

Sigurd immediately rings Preben Damgaard, who confirms it. WAI can continue as a distributor, but IBM intends to establish its own distribution as well. Sigurd could also choose to become a reseller if that is considered more attractive. He chooses to continue as a distributor.

One by one, IBM convinces Sigurd's business partners to change, and after a year he has to give up. He lets his company go bankrupt; establishes a new joint venture company and continues as an XAL reseller.

With WAI's resellers on board, IBM has a good base for expanding its position in the Norwegian market, but more people are needed on the project. Therefore, at the beginning of 1995, it engages a headhunting company, which finds Jan-Elling Skaugerum, who was a sales manager at PC Systemer. Jan-Elling, who becomes head of Concorde activities, subsequently finds and recruits Tommy Ødegaard and another employee. Upon appointment Jan-Elling is told that within the next three years he is expected to make XAL the leading financial system in Norway.

Despite IBM Norway operating a major training activity, it is unable to train resellers and customers in XAL. Jan-Elling contacts a private acquaintance who would like to take on the task of developing and being responsible for training, which is then marketed and managed by IBM, and similarly the courses themselves take place at IBM's premises. To further boost sales, Jan-Elling gets IBM Finance, a leasing company, to include XAL and the resellers' implementation services in its financing agreements. Customers can, thereby, pay the relatively large licence costs and consultant fees over a number of years.

From existing and new resellers comes feedback that XAL suddenly lacks a wide range of features that Norwegian customers perceive as standard, and which are already found in other similar software products. WAI had developed the necessary Norwegian functionality as well as corrected many bugs in the standard product received from Damgaard Data. Thus, WAI's XAL version was on a par with the competing products. The version now delivered by IBM has neither fixes for the bugs nor Norwegian functionality. The resellers are extremely dissatisfied with this. Instead of entering into an agreement with WAI for buying the extensions, IBM chooses to develop it all over again with Damgaard International.

## Germany comes aboard

After Norway gets started in 1995, Peter Perregaard contacts his colleagues around Europe to check the interest in starting distribution of Concorde XAL. Positive indications come from the UK, Germany and the Netherlands. During the initial discussions, conducted by Damgaard International, it becomes clear that the situations within the individual markets differ vastly from each other; markedly so compared to the situation in the Nordic region and, not least, to the situation in Denmark. PC distribution outside of the Nordic region covers primarily hardware and IBM's own software. There is little involvement, in general, in distributing software from other suppliers. Therefore, IBM doesn't have an organisation to perform such tasks outside of Denmark and neither do they have channels, which are immediately ready to sell and implement a product such as XAL. As a result, IBM also has much smaller shares of the PC market than in the Nordic region.

However, the European head of the OS/2 business sees an opportunity for winning terrain and asks his colleague in Germany, Thomas Dittus, to look into it. After assessing the potential, the feedback to Damgaard International is positive as far as general marketing and setting up a sales channel is concerned, but IBM Germany can't allocate resources to providing support and training to either resellers or customers. Damgaard International itself has to establish the necessary organisation to deliver those services. In fact, it goes against the partnership agreement and causes considerable additional costs for Damgaard International, but as the agreement is with IBM Denmark, the subsidiaries in other countries aren't bound by it. To get started in the large German market, where PC&C has already had considerable success with over one hundred established resellers, Damgaard International decides to take on the additional costs and establish a German subsidiary.

Thomas Dittus sets up a single position for the project and puts it in the hands of his colleague, Günter Sabeck, who is already working on a similar arrangement with a small software company in southern Germany. Günther, who is the only man on the job of recruiting XAL resellers for the enormous German market, can draw on resources in IBM's organisation to help with PR, marketing and events. He decides to call the product "IBM Concorde XAL" so as to use the company's solid name to create trust and decides to recruit initially only from the existing PC reseller channel. The product represents a new opportunity for increasing earnings here. As a consequence of the XAL initiative, the project with the German software company is shelved.

The German market for financial software for small and medium-sized businesses was extremely fragmented in the mid-1990s with hundreds of small software companies, each operating in a limited geographical area, with focus on a particular type of business. The concept of offering a product with a toolbox, which a reseller can then customise for an industry and individual customer, is largely unknown. PC&C started in Germany in 1990 using the same concept and is well on its way, but still has a market share hardly exceeding one per cent. Günther now has to both recruit resellers and make them understand that this model is completely different from the traditional German model, where the software supplier develops all functionality, and where the reseller alone is responsible for reselling, training and support. With the IBM name behind the product, around 50 business partners are recruited across Germany within 12 months, but Günther doesn't have the time to work with them individually and can't ensure that they really understand and implement the concept, and employ staff with the skills required to serve the customers.

To be responsible for the task of establishing the support company in Germany, Damgaard International reassigns Lars Balle Andersen from ServicePartner in spring 1995. The new office is located in a modern and futuristic office building in Böblingen, approximately ten minutes' drive from IBM's offices in Vaihingen, south of Stuttgart. Several IT companies are already located here, so a sufficient supply of qualified labour can be assumed.

Hanns Klemm Straße 5 in Böblingen, south of Stuttgart, where Damgaard International established an office in 1995. During the time of the partnership with IBM, the location was given the nickname "Europe's asshole" by the employees in Denmark.

Before the German organisation is in place, Damgaard International arranges courses for the first resellers with Danish instructors. The teaching is in English and is a fiasco. Angry complaints pour in from the participants. They struggle with the English language, and are simultaneously dissatisfied with the instructors being completely unaware of the inner workings of a German company and the demands made on financial systems. From now on, all teaching has to be in German, and the instructors must have insight into the local market conditions.

Initially, four employees are hired, and Lars Balle himself moves to Stuttgart to take care of the daily management and help with the work. A three-month training programme is developed where the German resellers are taught by German-speaking employees from Damgaard in Birkerød. The new German employees sit in, clarifying any linguistic or German market issues. Thereafter, the new German employees teach the course with the Danish instructors sitting in, and eventually, they run the courses completely independently. When these employees aren't running courses, they are to man the phones, providing support or reaching out to resellers to help with specific problems.

As resellers make their first sales, a number of challenges again emerge. Firstly, the German version of XAL is not adapted to the general local market conditions and can't even print a regular VAT report; and secondly, many of the partners haven't fully understood the Concorde concept, which is designed so that they themselves develop industry and customer-specific functionality. Resellers report a steady stream of bugs: actual errors and a lack of both general functionality and customer-specific conditions, which resellers themselves can and should be developing. XAL Services in Böblingen handles the incoming reports, communicating with the business partners in German. At Damgaard International, communication takes place in English, and as XAL Services is busy training new resellers at the same time, the situation is sometimes chaotic. The sale of IBM Concorde XAL starts off well enough, and customers seem to have confidence in the IBM logo, and be excited about the product's usability and flexibility. But they are disappointed when they discover that it can't cope with the completely banal everyday tasks in practice. It turns out that the German market reacts quite differently than the Nordic one. Whereas the resellers in the Nordic region quickly get used to taking care of problems themselves until a solution comes from Damgaard Data, the German partners stop, pause the activities and shout out loud. Over time, XAL Services and Damgaard International prioritise which parts of the product are to be improved; similarly, some resellers learn that they have to proactively sell customisations and extensions and, at times, they themselves have to correct bugs and add any lacking functionality. Later, the problems with IBM Concorde XAL reach the ears of the press, and at the end of 1997, a media storm is brewing around the product.

## The existing distributors

Prior to the partnership with IBM, distribution was established in the Netherlands, Russia, the Czech Republic, the UK and Singapore, but they generated little revenue and were all hybrids, which sold directly to their own customers at the same time. Such a set up involves constant conflicts of interest. New potential resellers are reluctant to come aboard when they realise they have to compete with distributors, who are both closer to the manufacturer and enjoy a much better gross margin. Conflicts of interest also occur internally at distributors, who are often encouraged to serve customers themselves rather than pass them on to resellers and not miss out on both the gross margin on the licence and all the earnings from services. Hybrid businesses were allowed to emerge in a time prior to the partnership with IBM, when little attention was paid to international activities and resources weren't allocated to ongoing contact and support. However, it was also due to the international distributors not being the strongest players on the market and, therefore, took the easy path to fast revenue. Instead of spending money and effort on building a channel of resellers, which could take a long time, they took on customer projects that would provide revenue and earnings here and now. With the IBM agreement, Damgaard International spots an opportunity to take advantage of the foundation, which was, after all, created, to stimulate growth.

New difficulties surface following a trip to the UK, the Netherlands, Belgium, the Czech Republic and Russia, the purpose of which was contacting local IBM companies and discussing the situation with current business partners as well as motivating them to collaborate. IBM in the UK and the Netherlands are immediately positive, while IBM in Russia and the Czech Republic are hesitant. However, the agreements with existing distributors need to be changed first, as the difficulties in Norway have taught Damgaard International that parallel distribution is not ideal.

After some negotiations, they manage to change the local distributors in the UK and Holland to resellers. This was possible because they were already primarily working as such and because none of them had reached sales targets that could ensure them continued exclusivity. Formally, the agreements could have been terminated but the desire was for the agreements to be entered into voluntarily to ensure the resources would be retained in the channel, working for the Concorde XAL business, rather than distributors running into the arms of a competitor. Nothing happens in this regard in the other countries.

## IBM tries to buy Damgaard Data in its entirety again

In June 1995, comes a surprising enquiry from IBM Denmark – they would like to buy the entire company again. Preben contacts Henning Kruse Pedersen, who now recommends getting a professional M&A consultant on the case and he points to Lennart Jönsson from the company, Alfred Berg. With Lennart, Erik and Preben travel to Paris once again, to negotiate the sale of the entire Damgaard Group. After four days of negotiations, agreement is reached on a package wherein IBM will pay approximately 60 million USD in cash and both Preben and Erik continue as managing director and development director, respectively. They sign a letter of intent, after which the Danish negotiating delegation returns to their hotel. The atmosphere in the taxi is not great. Not even when Erik, Preben and Lennart have dinner together later that evening in Paris. 60 million dollars is a lot of money, but managing a company that's not their own and that they can't run as they would like is a bitter pill to swallow.

The partnership with IBM has far from fulfilled their expectations, and can they be certain a change in ownership would make that much of a difference? What would working for IBM be like? It has a completely different culture, where the employees, based on the company's dominant position in the market, often behave arrogantly. With very mixed feelings, Erik and Preben return to Copenhagen.

Preben is to start the extensive paperwork that follows in the wake of the letter of intent the week after, but a message is received from Paris that, for tax reasons, a special distribution of the purchase price for the four companies in the group would be preferred. When Preben checks this with his own advisor, it appears to pose a risk of an unexpected and larger tax payment for both him and Erik. They fly to Paris again to negotiate. Now based on the changed terms. It would require a cash payment of approximately 70 million USD to compensate for the increased tax payment. However, IBM's negotiators aren't prepared to increase the offer, and once the lack of compromise becomes clear, Erik and Preben decide, after a brief consultation, to politely decline. They gather up their papers, take their leave from the IBM negotiators and, clearly relieved, return to Copenhagen.

## What went wrong?

In the early 1990s, IBM companies in the individual countries enjoyed a certain independence, which also enabled them to make decisions regarding acquisitions for under a million dollars without having to go through regional offices or headquarters. However, this independence was subjected to an internal audit, which didn't show uplifting results. Partly because the acquired companies largely lost their ability to grow under IBM's ownership, and partly because they bought companies that were direct competitors. The audit also documented that IBM's national companies didn't have the management skills to support the acquisitions, regardless of it being full integration in local IBM companies or management at board level with the acquired company continuing as an independent entity. In light of the disappointing results, the entire acquisition policy came under review; therefore, IBM's M&A department was much more cautious in 1995 than it was in 1993 when it tried to buy Damgaard Data the first time. IBM in Paris was also directly opposed to a new acquisition attempt. It already owned 50 per cent of the rights to the company's products! It was also hard to understand why IBM Denmark should buy a company with no significant growth potential in its domestic market given that its market share was already sky-high. IBM in Paris had difficulty seeing the sense in IBM Denmark purchasing a Danish software company to make it international. The desire for a full acquisition was driven solely by IBM's ambitions in Denmark and wasn't supported by the European headquarters. And as Erik and Preben weren't convinced that a sale of their business was right for their personal future, there was – needless to say – no great drive to achieve a result.

## An extra month's salary for employees

As early as December 1994, Preben can see from the first half-year results that the profit for the entire financial year will be large enough for the agreement on profit sharing to bear fruit. He tells the employees they can look forward to an extra month's salary in August 1995 if that tempo continues.

The spinning off of all third-party products caused a fall in revenue from 34 million USD the year before to 30.4 million USD now. On the other hand, the bottom line, as a consequence of cost reductions and better gross margins on their own products, improved from 1.4 million USD to 4.6 million USD. With a profit ratio of 15 per cent after the employees being paid the extra month's salary, the company must be said to be – in every way – on Easy Street. The spinning off and unwinding of third-party products also resulted in reductions in staff, but in 1995, the number of employees has already passed the two hundred mark. This is due, in particular, to the many hires in Damgaard International. For the first time, the 1994/95 financial statements express the ambition of becoming a European market leader. The company is now twice as big as the number two (PC&C) in the Danish market. It will be used to become one of the three largest software companies in Europe over the next three years. It is estimated that this ambition could be met by a growth in revenue of 25 per cent per year in the years that follow. That growth is to be created with financial systems that can help customers cope with the challenges they now face.

It is actually a significant shift in the rhetoric, which was previously directed at products and resellers. The customers are at the core now and the company is defined strategically in relation to their challenges and is aimed broadly at businesses of all sizes and in all industries. The goal is to win over the hearts of the customers and the reseller channel is just a means to reaching that goal. It is expressed very accurately with the following statement:

*"Damgaard Data's marketing is, therefore, primarily aimed at strengthening Concorde as a branded product as well as generating enquiries from companies directly to the resellers."*

Damgaard Data is no longer a company that works the market through its business partners. The goal is to become a global market leader, and they realise that isn't an objective they can leave to the resellers to fulfil. Resellers are an important cog in the machine, but there are many other cogs, too, and they would like to be in control of the machine's speed and direction.

Astonishingly, given that they started the financial year by embarking on a strategic partnership with the world's largest IT company based on international expansion, it is hardly mentioned in the annual report. The relationship with IBM is described as follows:

*"The partnership is developing extremely well. More than 60 German resellers will sell Concorde XAL this year."*

The playing down of the partnership may be due to it not going as well as planned, and far from the expectations they had when the deal was launched in January 1994.

## A slow start in the Netherlands

Prior to the agreement with IBM, a distributor/reseller has been appointed in the Netherlands, but it had no measurable outcome. In autumn 1995, distribution was placed in the hands of IBM, who chooses to appoint a single part-time employee to the project. Again, it is Lars Balle Andersen, who creates a local XAL Services company. This time in Utrecht. And yet again, PC&C has a head start given they already established distribution in Holland in 1992 and now have 12 active resellers. Sales Director Peter Wagner from Damgaard International reveals to *Computerworld* in October that having IBM as a distributor means there are 20 resellers in the Netherlands and they expect to recruit another 50. It sounds good, but it doesn't reflect the actual circumstances. These expectations certainly don't hold sway in the Dutch market.

## EDAN's solo effort in Belgium

At the end of 1993, in Belgium, a company named EDAN, which resold the Movex financial management system from the Swedish company, Intentia, on AS/400 machines, lost an order to a Dutch reseller. When EDAN's owner, Jacques van Branteghem, later talks with customers, he discovers their choice was down to wanting a PC platform rather than the proprietor's AS/400, but also because the offered software could be better adapted to the customer's specific needs. That software was Concorde XAL from the Danish software company Damgaard Data. Jacques now contacts the distributor in the Netherlands, who sends him a demo package so he can personally check what the product can do. Once EDAN's technical staff purchase a few PCs and install XAL, the feedback is positive. Jacques decides to enter into a reseller agreement with the Dutch distributor.

In the meantime, distribution has been taken over by IBM. IBM in Belgium doesn't show any interest in the case, so EDAN enters into a reseller agreement with IBM in the Netherlands instead. When they are about to start selling, neither IBM in Holland nor Damgaard International show any particular interest. EDAN decides to develop the country-specific functions for the Belgian market. Jacques' rapid initiative gains him a unique position as the only reseller in Belgium, and as he also owns the rights to the country-specific functions, it's difficult for new resellers to break into the market.

EDAN does well, selling on average a few new licences a month, which is far more than most resellers outside of Denmark. As Belgium is divided into two submarkets, each with its own language, it is perceived as a bit difficult by Damgaard International in Birkerød. IBM in Belgium doesn't show any significant interest in marketing a financial management system for PCs, so Jacques receives permission to keep his enjoyable position as sole reseller in Belgium.

In 1995, IBM launches a new model in the AS/400 series especially for the smaller companies, which is to be a "PC killer". Belgium and Italy, which have large bases of AS/400 customers, are designated to be the first markets for the new hardware to be delivered with a pre-installed version of Concorde XAL. Suddenly, IBM in Belgium shows interest in and is very keen on EDAN being in charge of the reselling. However, when Jacques' people check the system, many technical problems come to light. IBM Belgium contacts Damgaard International in Denmark, which doesn't seem to take the AS/400 project seriously. As sales of Concorde XAL for the PC platform are booming, there is no major pressure on EDAN to help resolve the issues. After the initial enthusiasm for the opportunity to sell Concorde XAL for AS/400 has passed, EDAN's consultants are moved back to the PC platform, where customers are ready and willing to buy and pay.

## An ambitious and expensive project
## for all employees

The organisational development project culminates with an employee conference at Hotel Marienlyst on 21st-22nd October 1994. It becomes evident at the conference that each department is still working on its own challenges and that the organisational initiatives are characterised by individual managers' interests and ambitions. Bo Nielsson, head of ServicePartner, is very interested in modern organisational development principles and works with a "second to none" concept. Employees are to set ambitious goals, are not to be limited by the fear of failing, but rather constantly learn from the mistakes they will inevitably make.

Some regard Bo Nielsson's "second to none" as an attempt to create competition between the various departments and as his desire to be seen as the leader of the best department. In a long article in the December issue of the internal employee newsletter, Bo Nielsson explains the principles behind "second to none": it's about finding, developing and retaining employees, who regard their jobs as a vocation and take pride in being involved in both their colleagues and the rest of the company's vitality and viability. Bo succeeds in formulating some principles for management that are in line with Preben Damgaard's own views. He articulates a management philosophy, which can answer how they empower employees to handle the frequent changes imposed on the company from the outside and arising from within.

With the growth of both the organisation and the size of the projects being handled, Bo also sees the need for professionalising the project work, and he initiates the development of a project management method, parallel to the quality work in the development department, in spring 1993. The purpose is to create a common model for implementing customer projects, so deliveries can always be made, according to specifications, within budget and on time.

## The learning organisation

Inspired by contemporary literature and debate on personal development and productivity, Bo Nielsson is aware that a project model consisting of a process description and a number of document templates is not
in itself enough to increase quality and ensure delivery. If high quality is
to be expected, you have to work with the sense of responsibility of the
individual employee and with their ability to work together in a project
team. Having participated in courses on self-empowerment and spiritu-
ality and having read *The Fifth Discipline* by Peter Senge, who introduced
the notion of "the learning organisation", a picture forms for Bo of how to
lift the individual employee and, thereby, the entire organisation's ability to make a much greater effort, and release innovational energy into
every nook and cranny of the company while simultaneously creating
more job satisfaction and, consequently, increasing growth and improving results. After successfully testing some of the principles in his own
department, he presents to Preben the idea of putting the entire organisation through a course of development that will free up the potential of
the individual employee and create a solid culture, which can assimilate
and influence new employees and, generally, make the company more
self-driven without the need for top down management or a growing layer of middle managers. Preben is very receptive and as Bo can document
results from his own organisation, he supports the initiative.

Bo gets carte blanche to develop the programme and travels to Sydney
in spring 1995, where he and Australian Martin J. Wetherill decide all the
details, including estimating what the course will end up costing.

He returns home with plans for a great and ambitious organisational
development project, entitled "Learning-to-Learn" (LAL) based on the
principles in Peter Senge's *The Fifth Discipline*. Essentially, employees
will be taken through an 11-day training camp divided into three modules, where they are to find common values, visions and rules of conduct,
learn to develop and gain support for a business idea and learn how to
utilise their own and the group's potential. In a substantial article about
the project in *Berlingske Tidende* in December 1995, Bo Nielsson is quoted as follows:

*Module 1 aims to introduce employees to the theory of "the learning or-ganisation": building common visions and rules of conduct and practising teamwork.*

*Module 2 aims at cultivating focus, concentration and creativity through an understanding of how stress can be positively controlled. In addition, emphasis will be placed on the importance of work-life balance. The course shows the individual that creativity prompts commitment and adds energy.*

*Module 3 aims to create friendships and solidarity within the workplace. The individual needs to understand that it is about seeing, listening, speak-ing and feeling.*

*"This is what we're going to work on. It may sound trivial, and it is. But why are most of us so bad at it?" asks Bo Nielsson, Director of Attitudes and Behaviour. He is the man behind the courses, and he emphasises that the goal is to achieve "an integrated organisation". "Integration is when the left and right hemisphere of the brain or the logician and the artist work together. That is the goal for the individual and, thus, also for the company," says Bo Nielsson.*

The learning-to-learn project, which is carried out in inter-departmen-tal teams and represents an investment of around 2.5 million USD, is unusual. The return on investment is impossible to calculate, and it is difficult to predict what effect the project will have in practice on the individual employees and on collaboration within the company.

Preben gives the project the green light due to two factors. Firstly, Pre-ben believes that management is something that is driven and happens across and throughout the entire organisation. Secondly, the develop-ment of competitive products, as well as finding and developing produc-tive resellers, and engaging customers in an unpredictable market with strong growth demands that all employees exercise leadership in their daily lives with each other and with their work.

The strategic framework is set by the owners and senior management, but filling in that framework has to be done in accordance with the ev-eryday work. Preben is convinced he doesn't hold the answers to all the questions, but believes that by giving his employees room to manoeuvre, to take responsibility and respect each other's principles, he can drive the business forward faster than if every problem is to constantly go through the formal organisational hierarchy.

The culture in Damgaard Data is quite action-oriented and not very academic. In this light, the Learning-to-Learn project fits in well with Preben's worldview. Moreover, the partnership with and the sale of half of Damgaard International to IBM created a "them" and "us" attitude in relation to the rest of the company. If Damgaard International signs up to the Learning-to-Learn project, an organisation working together to become a global market leader can be created.

Jens Hougaard, Managing Director of Damgaard International, facing one of the many practical and challenging exercises that Learning-to-Learn was built around.

The project becomes popular among the employees. A few turn their noses up at the practical and sometimes boundary-pushing exercises, but the vast majority throw themselves into it, actively participating in the groups. For some employees, it even becomes a process of self-awareness that causes them to resign from their jobs and start their own businesses while others go home and end their relationships. The Learning-to-Learn project confirms the company's values and culture for all participants. It confirms that management is sincerely concerned with the individual's well-being and growth, and that management's philosophy of the path to competitive products and satisfied resellers and customers starting with happy, courageous and enterprising employees isn't just a lot of hot air and nice words at official speeches.

The Learning-to-Learn project becomes the glue helping to keep the organisation together and drive growth in the hardest time in the history of the company. It is a time when expectations for international expansion as a result of the partnership with IBM are sky-high as are the disappointments over the lack of results.

## PC&C becomes Navision Software

At the Comdex Exhibition in Las Vegas in November 1995, PC&C announces the international versions of their new Windows product under the name of Navision Financials (and not Navigator Financials as is initially announced). The company changes its name at the same time to Navision Software. The product, which is marketed as "Certified for Microsoft 95", evokes enormous interest and draws full houses to the exhibition. The company has dedicated distributors with established reseller channels in 14 countries, including Germany and the USA and is, therefore, able to take full advantage of the attention and demand that follow in the aftermath of Microsoft's success with Windows 95. The decision to change the name to Navision Software and, thereby, align with the product name will also prove to be appropriate.

## The first TV ad for an
## IT product in Denmark

In 1994, the sale of Concorde Light was around 10,000 units, but when Windows gains popularity in 1995, it is difficult to maintain the sale of a purely character-based product. In order to maintain those sales figures and the positive effects of having a product to offer small businesses, Erik decides that a version of C5 should be cut to replace Concorde Light. It has to be similar price-wise to other software products for Microsoft Windows. That way seeds can still be planted with small businesses, which grow over time, become customers of the resellers and buy more. In autumn 1995, plans are made for the preparation and marketing of Concorde C5 Light for Windows, which is priced at under 400 USD. The product will continue to be sold only through retailers.

One cold autumn morning at eight o'clock Dorrit Overgaard and Per Pedersen arrive at Preben's office to present three possible marketing campaigns for C5 Light. After reviewing the first two campaign options that include traditional newspaper adverts and customer letters all within the existing budget, Dorrit presents a campaign with television advertising as the central communication channel. After consulting an advertising agency and station TV2's advertising department, the conclusion is that C5 Light, which is aimed at all small, self-employed business owners, is well-suited to promotion via TV commercials. The message is simple: the product can be presented as a physical box and rounded off with a concrete call for action: buy it at your supermarket.

There are two challenges. As this marketing channel hasn't been used for software products in Denmark before, no one really knows if the medium of TV is suitable. Moreover, the budget needs to be at least 200,000 USD to have any effect. Based on its viewer analyses, TV2 recommends the adverts be broadcast later in the evening. Self-employed business owners typically come home later than wage earners, and are, therefore, best represented around the time of the late evening news – when advertising spots are also somewhat cheaper. The channel is very keen on broadcasting Damgaard Data's advertising spots because they represent a new product group for a new target audience, and so TV2 offers several advertising spots for the same price. The other challenge is that Dorrit only has 60,000 USD of her marketing budget left.

Preben asks Per if he can find 60,000 USD in the sales budget, and when that seems possible, Preben promises to find the last 80,000 USD. The decision to use TV commercials to market an IT product for the first time in the history of Denmark is made. Preben stops Dorrit on her way out the door, and praises her for the proposal. He adds that if it doesn't work, they will have to find something else. They made the decision to try TV commercials together, and should they flop, her job will not be at risk for that reason. Innovative suggestions are always welcome.

On Monday, 4th December 1995, the first of 20 TV spots on the Concorde C5 Light financial system for business owners are broadcast, and by the end of the week, retailers are placing new orders. The campaign is a success. But on Monday, 11th December 1995, Damgaard Data is exposed to a veritable phone storm that causes the switchboard to collapse. Concorde C5 Light for Windows is just a tad more complicated than Concorde Light. Sales of the product exceed all expectations, but many of the customers can't get it to work. As retail stores don't provide support, the frustrated customers call the supplier. Customers are supposed to be able to setup and use the product themselves, and with a retail price of 400 USD, a flood of phone calls to the support department isn't budgeted for in the price tag.

Better user guides for the installation, setup and application of C5 Light are now developed and educational companies and publishers are encouraged to produce product-related courses and books. The strategy succeeds and the work of helping customers itself becomes good business. Damgaard Data can now concentrate on product development, marketing and sales, while training and support are provided by other companies.

You may ask why Damgaard Data doesn't take on the business of training and support itself, but it is with good reason. Over the years, management has learned what an ecosystem can mean for growth, and by no means do they want to do everything themselves. On the contrary, they are excited when someone identifies a business opportunity that helps to either increase sales of the products or eliminate the costs of serving the customers. Concorde C5 Light for Windows isn't a core product, and despite selling over 14,000 copies in 1996, Erik and Preben wish to outsource as many non-product-related tasks as possible. The resellers deal with serving the customers when it comes to the other products, but retailers don't traditionally fulfil that task and neither is there a sufficient gross margin on the product to offer service and support. The pressure on the phones on Bregnerødvej gradually decreases, while the sales figures increase. Yet another success from Damgaard Data is launched.

## Paid support is unpopular

Due to the markedly increasing pressure on the phones, it is decided to introduce payment for support. The payment claim is to help nudge customers back to the resellers, but is also to finance support for those customers who bought a product from a retailer and aren't linked to a reseller. Customers, who would like support, can choose between signing up to a subscription and buying a coupon with a certain number of calls. The two options are marketed via customer magazines and direct mailing. When customers ring the support department, they must give their customer number. If they don't have a subscription or a coupon, they are asked to arrange for one of those first.

Both resellers and customers perceive the request for payment for support as unfair. Partners believe many customers would prefer to call the manufacturer directly and feel that they are yet again being subjected to unfair competition. Customers find it unreasonable that they have to pay for the product to work. And Damgaard Data's employees certainly don't like rejecting customers who have a concrete problem or having to sell them a coupon or subscription before they can answer what is perhaps a quite simple question. Paid support never becomes a success, and they cease trying to uphold the principle.

## Great dissatisfaction with the IBM partnership

The partnership with IBM is continually plagued by challenges. Not only due to the very different goals and ways of dealing with things at the two companies, but also because the business expectations are not lived up to at all. The collaboration in Denmark is affected by the fact that Damgaard Data is already a market leader with a solid grip on both customers and the reseller channel. And despite Sales and Marketing Director Per Pedersen making things more systematic and uniform, particularly in relation to how business partners are treated, individual partner account managers have ample room for making ad hoc agreements that can promote sales. Whereas IBM is run by general policies and programs, Damgaard Data manoeuvres far more agilely on a case-by-case basis, and as Damgaard Data is far greater than IBM in the market for financial systems in Denmark, IBM's employees – to their great frustration – have trouble being taken seriously.

The fiasco with Azanta, in which IBM gets Damgaard International to develop OS/2 versions of Concorde C5 for Denmark, Norway and Sweden, but is unable to generate demand for the products, doesn't lend itself to respect for IBM's capabilities. The Danish part of Damgaard Data can't see what they should use IBM for. They perceive the partnership as an unnecessary bind.

There is no satisfaction with the IBM partnership on the international field either. It's going well in Norway, where IBM took over the solid foundation built up by Sigurd Flydal, while Sweden is still in the preparatory phase. And no initiatives have been taken at all in Finland. Starts have been made in Germany, the UK and the Netherlands, but only a single person has been assigned to the task in each country. Similarly, major discussions are underway regarding what functionality is needed to be able to penetrate the markets in question. At the same time, it is clear that being released from its IBM partnership hasn't damaged PC&C on the domestic market and it's taking the export markets by storm.

IBM's representatives on Damgaard International's board aren't satisfied with the results either, but are struggling to do anything about it. Decisions regarding the allocation of resources are sovereign in the individual countries. Reports of a lack of maturity in the products – which is also the case – come in from the different countries. But whereas Damgaard Data's culture is to continue market penetration, while fixing any product problems in the order reported, IBM's culture is to wait for a finished product before launching any marketing at all. Whether or not a more thorough preparation of the products would have made any significant difference is doubtful. Concorde XAL is a small fish in IBM's aquarium, and as the air completely deflates from the OS/2 balloon in 1995, there isn't much IBM content left in the partnership. The parties don't see the situation that way; rather they continue to look for a way to meet the same growth rates shown by PC&C.

# CHAPTER 16

# THE PARTNER-SHIP WITH IBM FALTERS

## Damgaard Data in the press

An article in *Berlingske Tidende* at the end of December 1995 entitled "Honesty as a Management Tool" describes the ongoing Learning-to-Learn project. It causes former employee, Morten Vedel Nielsen, to contact a journalist at *Computerworld* in January 1996 and tell of his ongoing conflict with the company. Morten is now co-owner of competitor, The Software Company, and hears that Damgaard Data's employees are speaking badly about his activities. Moreover, Damgaard Data has asked The Software Company to stop running an ad in which the company compares their product, Visual Business, to Concorde products. Morten manages to get the journalist to write two full articles about his quarrel with Damgaard Data, including a capsized project in Singapore, for which he claims Preben Damgaard should have offered him 80,000 USD in compensation. Head of PR, Michael Sander, talks to the journalist, but the many details means it's difficult for readers to grasp the ins and outs of the story. The same issue of *Computerworld* features an article by the same journalist about foul play at IBM – the promotion of Damgaard Data's interests in Sweden at the expense of Navision Software. Damgaard Data isn't a direct player here, but is placed in a bad light due to the partnership with IBM. After the articles, the stories die and nothing more emerges in the wake of the claims, but it demonstrates clearly that

Damgaard Data has become a well-known name in Denmark and that even relatively small and isolated events can give substance to sudden exposure in the media.

Michael Sander publishes press releases and talks with journalists from both the press and trade journals regularly. The effort bears fruit, and he consistently receives fine editorial mentions in all the printed magazines. The activity is supported by Damgaard Data being Danish, being personified by Erik and Preben Damgaard and being an undoubtedly huge success. As the company simultaneously becomes a well-known public name via broad marketing campaigns, including television commercials, it stimulates journalists' desire and motivation to write about the company.

The not quite so nice articles in *Computerworld* in January 1996 underline the golden rule that applies in all work with the press: *"if you invite journalists to your wedding, they'll also show up at your divorce"*. Journalists know that the content of press releases and of a company's own communication on the whole is a one-sided beautification of the circumstances and never represents the full truth. The more known a company becomes, the more journalists themselves will start looking for holes. Not many months pass before it is Navision Software's turn in the press, when a former employee files a lawsuit against the company claiming several million USD in compensation as a result of an alleged breach of contract. Generally though, both Damgaard Data and Navision Software do well in the media due to their good behaviour and as they are Danish growth comets, they represent something that many Danes admire and feel proud of.

## Starting up in Sweden

In spring 1996, IBM Sweden gently launches its small distribution activities by appointing an internal employee to run the project. However, competition in Sweden differs significantly from the situation in both Denmark and Norway in that it features a number of large, local players who already have a good grip on the market and who have also begun to internationalise. Once Nordic management sees that development in Norway is moving significantly faster than in Sweden, a decision is made to extend Jan-Elling's responsibility to include the business in Sweden. External recruitment works well, so the same model is followed in Sweden. While a head-hunter seeks out suitable talents, Tommy Ødegaard starts recruiting resellers in Sweden from his base in Oslo.

When the head-hunter presents the candidates for the post of head of Swedish activities – the two top candidates are from the same company. They even insist on being employed as a team. But as the budget only allows for a single employee, IBM faces a dilemma. Either they have to move to candidate numbers three or four or increase the budget and hire the two top candidates. They find the money and hire both Thomas Laine and Michael Uhman, who come from the Swedish department of the Norwegian company, Ergosoft. Thomas starts in May 1996, while Michael has to wait until September 1996 due to a competition clause in his Ergosoft contract. At the time of their appointment, IBM doesn't duplicate the Norwegian ambition of becoming a market leader within three years. Instead, it endeavours to ensure that distribution in Sweden be greater than Navision Software's Swedish activities.

## A Concorde for every business

With the launch of C5 Light for Windows via retailers, Damgaard Data in Denmark has a product portfolio aimed at virtually every type of business in all industries. Per Pedersen, who joined as marketing and sales director in July 1994, introduced a breakdown of resellers into three categories as early as August that same year, corresponding to the three market segments. The breakdown affects all of the company's activities in the years that follow given that products, messages and resellers differ to a large extent in each segment. This strategy contrasts starkly with that of competitor Navision Software, where there is only one product and focus is exclusively on small and medium-sized businesses.

The strategy ensures access to a larger market, but also means more products, different market segments and more competitors; thereby enabling the spread of marketing and sales resources across many more areas. Navision Software, on the other hand, is able to focus all efforts on one product in one market segment, which they estimate is large enough to be able to support their aggressive growth ambitions.

As early as 1996, the financial statements of the two companies show that the Navision Software model has generated the greatest growth in revenue, while the Damgaard Data model has achieved the best return on the bottom line. Navision Software's strong growth and rocketing figures are especially due to the German market and the fact that distribution in Denmark was taken over from IBM. However, the following years show that Damgaard Data's broad strategy isn't as growth-stimulating as Navision Software's. It's possible that working closely with IBM played a part – Navision Software stands on its own two feet.

## Country specific versions and Concorde XAL 3.0

Apart from the linguistic variations, the demands for financial management systems vary considerably from country to country. There are various legislative requirements to be fulfilled; conditions and customs that involve different expectations of what a system should be capable of and, finally, the competitive situation determines which requirements must be met. Damgaard International observes that the individual IBM subsidiaries don't want to assume the task of localising Concorde XAL for their respective markets. They expect Damgaard International to understand national market requirements and develop the respective functionality in order to competitively serve the market. Therefore, a Country Specific Engineering (CSE) team is set up in the development department in Birkerød. CSE is to establish contacts with individuals and business partners in each country, who can help plot the details and participate in trials prior to the final release of new products.

Information regarding the regulatory requirements for key accounting functions can usually be purchased from the major local auditing firms, whereas information about customs and practices, as well as what the competitors are offering, is spread across many sources. Given that both the legislation and the competitive situations are constantly evolving and developing in the individual markets, there is a need to continually monitor the situation and include any observations in product planning. In its early editions, Concorde XAL wasn't prepared to handle multiple languages and country-specific features, which is why special versions had to be developed for each country as they became relevant during the early years. The task was hindered by each country version also having to be available on the many different operating systems that were supported, making the amount of possible variants extensive. With version 2.11, launched in late 1994, all country-specific customisations were gathered in one product, and the user interface was translated into English, German, Dutch and Norwegian, while the actual program code used by resellers and customers for customisation is only available in Danish, English and Norwegian. If customers ordered a version other than the Danish one, they had to reckon with a certain amount of time before the system was ready for delivery. Significant investment in localisation, including a necessary change to the core code so it could better handle the many variants followed the plans to expand into even more countries. As it isn't possible to wait for the perfect solution, the individual country versions are released as they are translated, despite knowing it will create some problems on the market. The product is rectified as customers and resellers report bugs, deficiencies and inconveniences.

You would think that this course of action would give the product a bad reputation. And perhaps it does internally, among the resellers, but it doesn't seem to significantly affect sales. Partly as the Concorde XAL concept fits in well with the wishes of many customers, and partly because the resellers are good at establishing a service business around the product, but also because it's very difficult for both customers and partners to stop a project and change to another product once the implementation process has begun.

The concept of gathering all the country versions in one product has the advantage of customers with international activities being able to run on the same Concorde XAL. They can use the local language and local functions of each country, while headquarters gain direct insight into what is happening across the company and can – relatively easily – consolidate the figures for the entire group. Damgaard Data market these facilities quite consciously given that Navision Software's separate, local versions don't offer the same opportunities, and a number of international customers are won on that account.

## Concorde XAL 3.0

Damgaard International is aware of the need to develop a new version of XAL, which is better able to handle the increasing number of national versions. The project name of the new version is Concorde XAL 3.0.

Methods and tools for software development have changed considerably since the start of XAL development in 1989. The elimination race between operating systems also provides a clear picture of what customers prefer. And, finally, Microsoft's entry into the database system market means there is no longer any incentive to continue developing a proprietary file management system.

Once again, Erik Damgaard is the one who understands the possibilities of the new technologies and takes stock of where the market will be in one to two years when version 3.0 is due to be launched. In March 1996, *Computerworld* writes about the plans for Concorde XAL 3.0:

*"There are many international customers, who have a need for a pan-European version – a version that accommodates the rules of all countries," says Director of Development, Erik Damgaard, of Damgaard International. So far, the firm has developed separate country versions.*

*"The problem today is that if a British firm, for example, establishes a subsidiary in Germany, then the English-language version doesn't contain the German rules," says Erik Damgaard. According to the Director of Development, the desire to be eligible for a Windows 95 logo also involves major changes to the program. "We could have chosen to change a little here and there, but we wanted to thoroughly prepare the system with a view to Windows 95," says Erik Damgaard. He adds that the same approach applies regarding internet functionality".*

Erik expects the new version of XAL to be ready in spring 1997.

All resellers and customers now know that Version 3.0 is going to be launched. Due to experience with Danmax and Concorde Økonomi, resellers regularly ask for confirmation that the product will be backward compatible with the current version, which Erik promises it will be. At least, it is until he realises it will make development unreasonably complex and place far too many restrictions on what a new product would be able to offer.

In early summer 1996, he announces that project Royal Oaks covers a new product, which is incompatible with Concorde XAL, but that development of the latter will continue. After which, the entire development department will be re-trained, so they can master the new development's principles and tools. Over the summer, project Royal Oaks changes its name to Atlanta.

A contributing factor for freeing Atlanta from Concorde XAL is the decision to prepare for penetration into the North American market. There are no ties to the past there, but rather a great need to be at the forefront of technology and to ensure unique and explicit sales arguments against the established competitors.

## U.S. Marketing Plan for Concorde

In February 1996, IBM invites the former director of Navision, Erik Seifert, to a meeting at its European Headquarters in Paris to hear his assessment of how to introduce Concorde XAL to the North American market. The meeting ends with Seifert being engaged as a consultant and in May 1996 he delivers his report entitled "U.S. Marketing Plan for Concorde".

The report opens by stating that the name "Concorde" can't be used in the USA. There are already numerous products of that name, so there is a risk of several lawsuits even before getting started. Or worse – when they are well underway.

The report then describes the American market as being fiercely fragmented with over 1,000 software companies offering financial management software. The competition is extreme. The market is dominated by local suppliers; only a few foreign software companies have dared enter it, and, from among them, only the German SAP has noted any visible success.

According to the report, growth will mainly take place within the "small" segment comprising businesses of 20 to 100 IT users as well as in the "medium" segment covering businesses of 100 to 1,000 IT users. Growth in the "large" segment, which encompasses businesses of over 1,000 IT users, is close to zero, while the SOHO (small office/home office) segment, with less than 10 IT users, indicates only modest growth. The "small" and "middle" market segments are expected to double their demand for the type of software developed by Damgaard Data in the period 1996-2000. That market will represent purchases in the order of 200 billion dollars.

The report concludes that technically-speaking, Concorde XAL's architecture of a database foundation, a range of standard functionality modules as well as a development environment for customer-specific adaptation and the development of extra functionality would be competitive in the American market, but it simultaneously documents a weakness in the marketing. The product will be compared to competitors who, from the start, offer significantly more fully developed functionality, and the proprietary development environment will be met with some scepticism. At the technical level, the report notes that the product should be fully certified for Windows 95; that it should be able to be run in a true client/server format; that it must support local American market requirements; that it must be aligned with American terminology and that the entire help function must be accessible via the internet. The report mentions the advance of the internet in several places and predicts that it will greatly affect customer requirements and wishes for future financial systems.

When it comes to sales, the report draws a rather gloomy image of American resellers, who base their sales primarily on leads provided by the software companies. They carry out only a modest amount of independent sales and marketing work. IBM's ambition of Concorde XAL being in a leading position on the US market means massive marketing efforts must be made parallel to recruiting resellers so as to ensure that the newly minted partners get leads to work on.

The report recommends positioning Concorde XAL as "The Son of SAP" and targeting the marketing machine primarily at large companies where the product is to become the default solution for their subsidiaries as well as at small and medium-sized production companies and in an OEM version to the hundreds of software companies looking to change their technological platform.

Finally, the report describes what organisational initiatives IBM should take to make the project succeed. It is recommended that an independent organisation, focusing exclusively on the task at hand, be established, outside of IBM, and that product marketing, product management and product development for the US market be placed within the USA.

Erik Seifert's report makes it clear that the current Concorde XAL can't be successfully marketed in the USA. On the other hand, there is nothing to prevent them announcing their intentions with the Atlanta project at the Comdex Exhibition in Las Vegas from 13th to 17th November that same year.

## Backlash from broken promises

The broken promise of backward compatibility in the Atlanta project causes some backlash among customers and resellers, but as a commitment was made to continue developing XAL and the conversion tools, so customers can port to the new product with only moderate effort, the criticism dies down fairly quickly. It is replaced by curiosity about how the new product will look and what it will be able to do.

It is quickly decided that Atlanta will only run on third-party products such as Microsoft SQL and Oracle. Furthermore, it is decided that the product will be based solely on Microsoft Windows. Despite expecting IBM to protest over the omitting of support for OS/2, it doesn't happen. Even it has recognised that the battle for the operating system for the PC platform is now lost. When talking about a possible version for AS/400 and support for DB/2, it looks like IBM's interests may nevertheless be met.

## Damgaard International
## gets a new board

At a board meeting in April 1996, the director, Jens Haugaard, presents some very positive revenue figures from the international markets. The partnership with IBM can finally be seen in the results. There is relief all around. Things take time, but now the ball is rolling.

In the months that follow, changes are made to IBM's organisation that require some replacements on the board. Peter Perregaard, who has been appointed to another position, is replaced by Henrik E. Nyegaard in January 1996, and at the end of July, Per Haldbo is replaced by American Larry Sheffield, who also takes over as chairman. Larry, who had successfully built up IBM's direct sales to small and medium sized enterprises in the Mid-Western part of the USA, is being relocated to the European headquarters in Paris, where he takes over global responsibility for selling software to the very same customer segment with the exception of Eastern Europe. He reports straight to the top director of EMEA with a so-called "dotted line" to the head of General Business division in the New York headquarters. It seems that the co-ownership of Damgaard International is moving up several floors in IBM's global management hierarchy.

Larry is excited about Concorde XAL. With his experience from the American market, he sees great potential for precisely small and medium-sized enterprises. His ambition is to roll out the product in those areas for which he is responsible. The markets in France, Italy, Brazil and Hong Kong are now on the drawing board. With a view to the Atlanta project coming out on AS/400 and for DB/2, there is a clear synergy with some of IBM's core products and, therefore, better arguments for the national subsidiaries spotting and exploiting the potential.

The agreement, which was signed in 1994, doesn't cover the establishment of distribution networks outside of the Nordic region. In July 1996, agreements are negotiated to cover the new markets, take the experience gained from the start into account and deal with some of the demands IBM has for investing in the global rollout. Despite it being easier and faster to make country adjustments with the Atlanta project, an aggressive international expansion will require significant continuous investments. There is also a need to get those countries jumping on the bandwagon to allocate sufficient resources to marketing and reseller recruitment. Experience from the Nordic and Central European activities has shown that concrete plans and commitments are required from the national IBM subsidiaries; similarly, a firm financial obligation that can justify investment in translation and localisation is a must. In turn, so as to protect its investment in market penetration, IBM insists on exclusivity in the individual markets, and Damgaard International insists on an assurance that IBM will market and sell the products for all software and hardware platforms, including the platforms of its competitors.

## The figures disappoint again

During the preparation of the contract negotiations, new figures are shown for the financial situation of Damgaard International, which reveal that the positive figures from spring weren't quite correct. The figures contained earnings from a large pool of prepaid maintenance subscriptions, the majority of which should have been accrued in subsequent financial years. It's back to square one and it has to be acknowledged that the partnership is still not functioning as expected. Questions as to whether or not IBM even has the skills necessary to recruit and operate a reseller channel for financial management software are now asked. The suspicion arises because Damgaard Data in Denmark experiences unconditional success, whereas the markets in which IBM operates are far from delivering the expected and planned results.

The announcement doesn't fit in with the mindset of IBM's employees, who believe they are highly qualified to do the work, but it is hard to get around the lack of success.

## Who are we making agreements with?

Management now question who they are actually entering into agreements with and how binding these agreements actually are for IBM. Damgaard Data puts all of its eggs in IBM's basket, but it isn't really obliged to do anything. Market opportunities risk being lost while IBM sits on its hands.

Formally, the agreements are signed with IBM's European Headquarters, but they aren't in a position to impose obligations on the subsidiaries unless they pertain to the company's own core products. IBM's global construction means that an agreement with the European headquarters is a non-binding framework agreement that the subsidiaries can, but don't have to, use. Therefore, individual countries must voluntarily take on the task of distributing Concorde products, and they also have to find the funds themselves. Building up a reseller channel takes between three and five years, which is why IBM's subsidiaries that work within annual budgets and goals have difficulty allocating the necessary resources.

Nevertheless, it is decided to continue with the partnership. There is no Plan B, and despite the difficulties, putting an end to the agreement seems inconceivable. Moreover, having Larry Sheffield on the board has placed Damgaard International significantly higher in IBM's organisation, and despite everything, it gives – as does his optimism – renewed hope. Though the most important motives are probably IBM's promise to help Damgaard Data into the North American market and that it is still contributing with half the financing for Damgaard International's activities, which, given the major investments during these years, is a loss-making company. Erik and Preben can absolutely see the advantage of getting a substantial contribution to the development of the new product as well as the value of the platform that IBM creates within the individual markets in the long run.

In June 1996, Damgaard International's board of directors decides to develop a standard model for starting up in a new country, including what investments and minimum obligations IBM has to undertake. A proposal to transfer sales skills from Damgaard Data Distribution to IBM isn't met with great enthusiasm. It is agreed that the USA is a top priority, but new markets, such as Spain, Italy, France, Brazil and Hong Kong are also named. The concept of Damgaard International establishing its own support companies in countries where IBM is launching marketing penetration carries on, and the board agrees that IBM has to assume concrete sales-related obligations so there is no risk of the support companies being left without revenue and, thus, without financing. And, likewise, it is agreed that the current countries be handled by Damgaard International's organisation, while Larry Sheffield works on getting commitments from new markets.

## Damgaard Data gets a legal department

At the beginning of 1995, Preben Damgaard feels the need to add legal expertise to his managerial secretariat and, in August 1995, Marianne Nyegaard, a newly hatched jurist from the University of Copenhagen comes aboard. During a review of all external contracts, Marianne discovers that around 1.4 million USD had been spent on legal fees in the previous financial year. She suggests to Preben that an internal lawyer be employed to take on such work. Dealing with legal work in-house will not only save the company a lot of money, it will also ensure a closer link between business and legal relationships. The law firm Kromann Reumert will still be engaged for special assignments and as legal consultants.

Preben supports the idea and, on 1st June 1996, Mette Berning, who has run her own independent law firm for several years, joins the company. The creation of a legal department brings with it a significant reduction in the cost of external legal assistance and ensures comprehensive and quality assured agreements with both customers and suppliers.

## Profit-sharing plan comes to an end

In 1994/95, the profit-sharing plan gave an additional month's salary to each employee, but it isn't continued in the 1996/97 financial year. In 1995/96, when Damgaard International's employees were to be measured on their own profit there was nothing to pay out. The company reported a loss of around 1.8 million USD.

However, both revenue and profits grew considerably in Damgaard Data Distribution, and with a profit of 20 per cent of revenue gave the best result ever. Nevertheless, Erik and Preben conclude that the profit-sharing plan is unlikely to have any major impact on employee motivation and that the problem of Damgaard International's deficit may risk leading to internal tensions. They might be two separate legal entities, but they aren't two independent activities.

At a staff meeting, Preben explains the decision to cease the profit-sharing plan, explaining that individual salary adjustments will be made instead. Management expects to invest heavily in internationalisation and in the Atlanta project. Despite both being located in Damgaard International and co-financed by IBM, the disappointing international results mean having to make significant investments in order to break through on export markets. From now on, the surplus will be kept for that purpose.

Surprisingly, not many questions are asked about this decision. The vast majority of employees already earn high salaries. Apparently, after paying tax in the highest tax band, an extra month's salary isn't an amount that makes a great difference. In addition, it is conditions other than salary that make the company an attractive place to work for the vast majority of employees; the culture, the success, the influence and recognition in the form of anything but money play a much greater role. The Learning-to-Learn project continues to roll out through the organisation, providing most employees with a personal experience, which is valued far more than an additional month's salary.

## DITEC in Germany

Recruiting DITEC as a distributor of XAL in Germany succeeds in September 1996. It's a huge win. DITEC is a well-known name and one of the few nationwide IT companies. Germany has a fragmented IT market and, apart from the very large IT companies such as Microsoft, IBM, HP, SAP and Oracle, have little nationwide representation. XAL reaches every corner of Germany with DITEC and, at the same time, both potential customers and resellers become aware of XAL as a serious financial management system contender for "Der Middelstand", which is the backbone of the German business world.

## IBM downsizes in Germany

Despite the many business partners recruited in Germany, sales remain sluggish. IBM isn't satisfied with either the quality of Concorde XAL or the German translation or the accompanying documentation and repeatedly demands that the entire manual be reprinted. Apart from DITEC, resellers are small businesses without any great sales forces or a tradition of providing the consulting services essential for the product being sold and implemented. There are indeed bugs and inconveniences in the product, but whereas Danish partners are experienced in handling problems themselves, German resellers expect IBM, as the distributor, to deliver a flawless product suitable for the German market. It can't do that, so it has to pass the ball onto XAL Service, which, in turn, tries to get Damgaard International in Birkerød to help.

In the aftermath of defeat to Microsoft, those resources allocated to becoming the market leader in operating systems for PCs a few years earlier have to be reduced. Positions in the OS/2 area in Germany are also cut, which means that Günther Sabeck's boss, Thomas Dittus, ends up without a job in 1996. He offers Günther an attractive severance package on the basis of the disappointing sales results, and assumes Günther's job himself. Only a few weeks later, Thomas Dittus is hit by a stroke and dies. IBM's XAL business in Germany is suddenly without management.

The job is advertised internally, but as the position of XAL business manager lies outside of IBM's core business, it's not seen as an attractive career move. No one volunteers. After some searching, a very young and inexperienced employee, who isn't suitable for managing the business, but who can at least manage it in the short term, is found.

## Further professionalising in Denmark

While IBM battles fiercely to get distribution to work outside of the Nordic region, Denmark further professionalises both its marketing and reseller care. People with solid experience in sales and marketing as well as insight into and interest in business development are employed as partner account managers. Emphasis is placed on the candidates understanding the resellers' business model. They have to be able to conduct a conversation with the partners' management team about the development of the business on both a strategic and operational level. Internal courses are held in business development and formal strategy meetings are organised with the largest resellers and those showing initiative and growth potential. Once the clear connection between a business approach to reseller care and measurable results in terms of profit and customer success stories is established, the role of partner account managers develops more in the direction of management consultants, who deal solely with strategy, management, marketing and sales. Technical aspects of the products become the remit of the support department and ServicePartner. It explains why the many technical issues – despite everything – with Concorde products, especially after the initial release of new versions, never affect the effort and, therefore, the results on the sales side. Business development and technology are separated and assigned to different people. Technical problems for both customers and resellers are handled by technical staff, which is why the sales people can put all their energy into getting new customers.

## Damgaard Data sponsors sailing trips for adolescents

In autumn 1996, *Berlingske Tidende* writes about Damgaard Data's commitment to helping troubled adolescents. They take smaller groups of young people out sailing for long voyages where none of them can slip away and where they have to do necessary, practical tasks regarding provisions and help steer the ship safely into harbour. The scheme, sponsored by Damgaard Data, is the initiative of HR manager Svend Tvermoes, who has been working with young people on the edge of society for many years. Apart from the PR value of the press coverage, there is no immediate business interest in the project; it is supported because Svend Tvermoes recommends it. The project is a huge success for the participants, but subsequently provides inspiration for the internal team building project, Blue Vision.

## Employees draw up the rules of play

Under the heading, "Employees draw up the rules of play", the financial report for the 1995/96 financial year describes the importance of the company's development and success for the employees. The entire group, including Damgaard International, is in the middle of the Learning-to-Learn project, which probably inspires this passage:

*At training and workshop days, employees drew up four life and team rules all stemming from the company's founding cultural values of mutual respect and trust, willingness to change, creativity and professionalism. The code of practice can be briefly summarised in these concepts: vision, quality, balance and commitment. The philosophy behind them is that just like musicians in an orchestra playing many different instruments form a harmonious whole, Damgaard Data is made up of numerous people, whose efforts and special abilities contribute to the common goals.*

Under Learning-to-Learn, the employees themselves draw up the company's values, and despite seeming banal on paper and hardly any different from what most contemporary businesses write on their posters hanging in the canteen, this type of exercise was far from common in the mid-1990s. These values were born of and chosen by the employees over a long period where they, both individually and in groups, were exposed to considerable pressure. Learning-to-Learn wasn't the kind of course where you go home, put the folder on a shelf, tell your colleagues about the good food and then continue on as though nothing happened. The project, which ends in 1997, alters virtually every employee's perception of themselves and each other. And as they realise that they can and have to live up to those values in their everyday work, a rather special culture emerges from the employees, one that is deeply rooted in the company. In an article in *Ingeniøren* on 31st May, Bo Nielsson is quoted as follows:

*"In our industry, we are in constant crisis, because the industry changes all the time. So we are forced to be creative, innovative and flexible to survive. We have to listen to the employees, because good ideas can come from the canteen lady just as they can the managing director".*

In the mid-1990s, Damgaard Data develops to become every business owner's dream. The products are competitive, the market is in strong growth and the employees take responsibility like never before and are prepared to operate in a state of constant change. Erik and Preben couldn't have predicted this, but by accommodating enthusiasts such as Bo Nielsson, the belief that everything is possible; that anyone who wishes to take an initiative can do so, grows. There is no knife in the back if something goes wrong. The problems with IBM actually strengthen the camaraderie among the employees. They can see with their own eyes that even the world's largest IT company can't accomplish the job like little Damgaard Data can. If you don't need to have respect for IBM, you don't need to respect anyone. Damgaard Data is on its way to evolving into an organisation with a quite unusual self-confidence and a quite unusual ability to fill those big shoes completely. To emphasise that belief in themselves, the entire management group completes the New York Marathon in July 1995.

## Damgaard International gets extra capital

With American Larry Sheffield as the new chairman of the board and with a new international distribution agreement, new life is breathed into the hope that IBM will finally take action. Meanwhile, Damgaard International's cash box is about to run out and, as further investment has to be made in product development for the new markets, notably North American, a new injection of capital is needed. Anyone can spot the challenges in the accounts, so it's important that a capital injection isn't just perceived as pouring money into a black hole. The capital injection amounts to 6 million USD, which is paid equally by Damgaard Data Holding and IBM Denmark, but the official announcement packs the capital increase into a positive message that IBM will invest 20 million USD a year in the coming years in an effort to spread Concorde XAL internationally. On 10th January 1997, Larry Sheffield is quoted in *Computerworld*:

*'"We have chosen Concorde as the only product for companies with less than 1,000 employees, and we expect revenue from resellers to reach 300 million in 2000," says Larry P. Sheffield, Director of Software World Wide, IBM's General Business'.*

When the resellers sell licences for 300 million USD, IBM makes a profit of approximately 200 million USD and Damgaard International a profit of 100 million USD. Damgaard International has an annual turnover of around 18 million, so it's quite the boost needed.

Under the heading "Danish software will create success for IBM", the daily newspaper *Børsen* features Larry, Preben and Erik with big smiles on their faces on 10th January. The 20 million USD is a guesstimate of the cost of operating Damgaard International, paying salaries to those employees who currently and from now on will work with Concorde XAL in IBM, and the funds used for marketing. These are not funds at the command of the three men in the picture, and the largest share of the amount depends on the extent to which individual IBM subsidiaries can be convinced to enter into the activities, and not least how quickly and how much they can get IBM in the USA to contribute. Preben and Erik know it's a media stunt, but they would rather report aggressively on this than be caught up in a story about IBM pouring more money into a destitute company. The press doesn't see through the ruse and writes nice articles about the partnership.

*For anden gang på få måneder har IBM valgt et dansk softwarehus i en global satsning: Her er det fra venstre Larry Sheffield, IBM, og de to ejere og grundlæggere af Damgaard Data: Brødrene Preben og Erik Damgaard.*

# Dansk software skal skaffe IBM succes

For anden gang på tre måneder vælger verdens største IT-koncern et dansk softwareprodukt til eksklusiv forhandling

*Af Jan Horsager*

Det danske edb-program Concorde til økonomistyring i små og mellemstore virksomheder fra softwarehuset Damgaard Data skal nu som det eneste økonomisystem markedsføres globalt af IBM. Målet er en årlig omsætning af programmet på 1,5 mia. kroner i år 2000 – en tidobling i forhold til en nuværende omsætning fra programmet.

Dermed har verdens største IT-koncern for anden gang på få måneder satset eksklusivt på salget af et dansk softwareprodukt over hele verden. I november indgik IBM en aftale med danske

SDC om global markedsføring og videreudvikling af en kernesoftware til pengeinstitutter.

Efter aftalen med Damgaard Data opretter IBM en verdensomspændende salgsorganisation for Concorde med selvstændige salgsafdelinger i Europa, Nordamerika, Sydamerika og Fjernøsten. Øverst ansvarlig bliver chefen for IBM World Wide General Business Software, Larry Sheffield. Han er også formand for bestyrelsen i Damgaard International A/S, der ejer koderne til Concorde.

Damgaard International A/S blev oprettet i 1994 med Damgaard Data og IBM med hver sin halvpart. Allerede da så IBM muligheden for at gøre Concorde til en global

## Silicon Danmark

Danmark har alle muligheder for at blive Europas Silicon Valley. Softwareudviklerne er i verdensklasse. Og danskerne arbejder både ihærdigt og er helt dedikerede på opgaverne. Sådan ser Danmark ud for chefen for softwaredelen af IBM Worldwide General Business, Larry Sheffield. Han kan ikke umiddelbart få øje på nogle kvalifikationsproblemer, der skulle hindre det danske softwarebranche i at blive Europas bedste.

Selvom et par af de tilstedeværende journalister spørger chefer hos Damgaard Data godt kunne finde på nogle politiske og administrative barrierer, så er den overvejende holdning hos Damgaard Data også positiv.

– Vi har ingen problemer med at skaffe kvalificeret dansk arbejdskraft. Og det gælder både ingeniører, dataloger og salgspersonale, siger Jens Haugaard.

Han er direktør i Damgaard International A/S. Og med aftalen med IBM, skal han skaffe mindst 200 nye medarbejdere på samtlige områder.  *jaho*

software. Men efter den eksplosive udvikling i netværksteknologien har også IBM satset anderledes i softwaresammenhæng. Fra at have en lang række egen udviklede og IBM-iserede opkøbte software-produkter, satser koncernen nu på samarbejde og investering i enkelte højprofil-produkter. IBM vil alene i 1997 satse mere end 150 millioner kroner på at markedsføre og udvikle det danske økonomiprogram Concorde over hele verden.

– Det afgørende for IBM i dag er helhedsløsninger. Hver gang vi omsætter en dollar på Concorde vil vi samtidig omsætte tre dollar på andre IBM-produkter, siger Larry Sheffield og fortsætter:

– General Business-området i IBM er salg til virksomheder med mindre end tusind ansatte. Det er et 16 mia. dollars marked, der samtidig er det hurtigst voksende segment for IT-salg overhovedet, forklarer han.

## Højdepunkt

Aftalen er det hidtidige højdepunkt for brødrene Erik og Preben Damgaard, der i 1984 som henholdsvis 23- og 21-årige startede Damgaard Data for at udvikle software til økonomistyring. Sidste år var omsætningen 172 mio. kroner og medarbejderstaben på 284.

En udvikling der i år bringer Damgaard Data ind på en andenplads på Børsens Gazelle-liste for Frederiksborg Amt (se næste side).

På det danske marked har Concorde allerede succes. Ses markedet for økonomisystemer under ét, har produktet en markedsandel på 23. Men ifølge Preben Damgaard er tallet tæt på de 50 procent, når det gælder markedet for økonomisystemer til mellemstore virksomheder.

Her har Concorde dog en alvorlig konkurrent i programmet Navigator fra et andet dansk softwarehus Navision. Navigator bliver i langt højere grad udviklet sammen med forhandlerne. Derfor er Navision ikke sikre nok til at komme med på Computerworlds danske top ti liste over danske softwarehuse.

---

Larry Sheffield's appointment to chairman of the board renewed the hope that IBM would wholeheartedly roll out Concorde products globally. Thus, the smiles were huge when Larry Sheffield (left), Preben Damgaard and Erik Damgaard posed for a photograph for the press release announcing that IBM was going to spend 100 million DKK (20 million USD) a year on marketing Damgaard Data's products. This wasn't money to which the three gentlemen in the picture had direct access, but rather a summary and rounding up of the many sub-budgets that IBM expected to put into play in Damgaard International and in all those countries, which had – and were expected to have – activities. Taken together, this investment was to result in revenue of no less than 300 million USD in 2000.

It is also difficult to understand the collaboration having any problems with Damgaard Data's success, on the one hand, and the huge IBM on the other, but the situation is certainly not encouraging behind the façade. None of the countries in contact with Larry Sheffield had come any further than being positive, and in those countries where activities are already underway, the results are still disappointing. Damgaard International's board of directors has difficulty understanding why the obvious opportunities and positive responses from IBM's subsidiaries haven't been translated into concrete actions. A look over at Navision Software shows booming sales with a much higher growth rate, largely due to the success of the export markets.

The board of directors considers dividing Damgaard International up into two separate entities; one of which would be solely responsible for product development, while the other part would be responsible for international distribution. Such a construction would place more focus on sales, but it would require further investment in management – and now it's felt that the problem lies primarily with IBM.

The only positive development is in the USA, where Larry gets experienced IBM-woman Pat Falotico to prepare for the launch of the Atlanta project. After long discussions on the board, it is accepted to continue with the current construction of Damgaard International establishing the service division, while IBM will deal with marketing and recruiting resellers. It is agreed that where it hasn't gone as desired – in the countries where it has been introduced – it's because IBM hasn't allocated sufficient resources to its side of the deal.

## A lack of product marketing

However, Erik Seifert, engaged by IBM in 1996 to draft a plan for the introduction of Concorde XAL in the USA, points to another problem: a lack of product marketing. When a new product is to be introduced into a new market, it requires a solid foundation of storytelling. That storytelling has to connect customers' wishes, needs and challenges with the product's features as well as with the ability of the supplier to get the product to deliver value for customers. It must clearly demonstrate a significant difference with the established alternatives in a way that is easy to understand. The structure and maintenance of the foundation is called product marketing and it is essential for success. According to Seifert's experience, IBM can't do product marketing. And as Damgaard International can't either, there is a significant gap in the plan to ensure fast penetration into new markets.

Damgaard Data is unaware of this, because the position and history of the company and products have been built up brick-by-brick on the Danish market, since its inception in 1984. It isn't unusual for companies to forget the long journey they have endured in their home market, and to expect the journey to the export markets to pass more quickly. There is an expectation that IBM can accelerate exports for Damgaard Data, and when that doesn't happen, it is entirely due to IBM not allocating the necessary resources to reseller recruiting and care and marketing. Therefore, Seifert raises a red flag, pointing to the risk that – even with a massive effort on IBM's side in the USA – disappointing results will continue unless product marketing is addressed. Preben Damgaard understands the challenge, but is caught in the division of labour between Damgaard International and IBM. Damgaard International in Denmark can't deal with the task, and neither can the forthcoming service and support company in the USA. It's IBM's job and the expectation is that they will step up to the task. The challenge is left unattended.

## Damgaard Data gets Per Pedersen into IBM

To gain better insight into what is actually happening, and perhaps pack more punch, it is decided to appoint Per Pedersen as IBM Concorde Sales Executive in December 1996.

**Per Pedersen**
*CONCORDE Sales Executive*
*IBM General Business*
*Europe, Middle East Africa*

*IBM Corporation*
*c/o DAMGAARD International A/S*
*Bregnerødvej 133, 3460 Birkerød, Denmark*
*Phone: +45 45 99 96 53*
*Fax: +45 45 82 37 74*
*Mobile +45 40 80 95 60*
*Internet: perp@dd.dk*

IBM

In December 1996, Per Pedersen was "loaned" to IBM in an attempt to see if the experience from Denmark could kick-start sales via IBM. However, the loan was also to shed light on what was happening in IBM, and why the partnership wasn't working as it should.

Per is paid by Damgaard International, reports formally to Pat Falotico at IBM in the USA, but to Preben Damgaard in reality. He is equipped with a business card that allows him to operate on the "inside" of IBM. From here, he is to try to get IBM to do the right thing and report his observations to Preben. Per Pedersen's replacement as sales director of Damgaard Data Distribution in Denmark is Flemming Idorf Beisner, who has been sales director for the Danish part of the company since his appointment in April 1995.

## Support moves to ServicePartner

According to the ongoing satisfaction surveys, resellers in Denmark are still dissatisfied with the quality of support for Concorde XAL. Their dissatisfaction concerns both the speed at which Damgaard Data responds to questions and bug reports, and also its ability to understand the issues and come up with satisfactory solutions. The strength of being able to further develop and tailor XAL to customers' needs also makes it difficult for support staff to reproduce bugs or inconveniences so they can be resolved quickly. It is difficult for support staff to keep up with the insight gained by resellers from their everyday use of the product, and despite introducing techniques to separate those changes made by resellers from XAL's core code, the work of understanding a bug or inconvenience in a specific customer situation is in no way trivial.

To ensure better communication regarding support cases, the development of an internet-based system is implemented, where resellers themselves can log cases and communicate regularly on their status. Partners should be able to keep track of which cases are already reported and what their status is. Furthermore, it is decided to move support and system service for XAL from Damgaard Data Distribution to ServicePartner at the end of 1996. Indeed, ServicePartner, which actually operates as a reseller, running implementation projects directly with customers and even providing first level support and system service, can be assumed to possess the insight required to increase the quality for resellers.

However, this set up lasts for less than a year. ServicePartner is a project organisation designed to service individual customers and resellers, and they invoice for the amount of time spent accordingly. As no separate payment for product support is charged, Damgaard Data Distribution has to pay ServicePartner for carrying out the work. This prompts discussions on how much this payment should be and what quality should be delivered. Despite both companies being part of the same group, each has their own budget, and their respective management teams are evaluated and paid according to the extent to which they can control revenue and costs. Discussions of settling internal accounts quickly become difficult. ServicePartner isn't prepared to accept a fixed price for a task, the scope of which is difficult to define in advance, and Damgaard Data Distribution is unsure about accepting a variable payment without having a firm hold on the work and priorities. Moreover, the handling of international activities, which is managed by Damgaard International, takes on a whole new development during 1997, which, in turn, means that outsourcing support to ServicePartner becomes inopportune.

# CHAPTER 17

# A PROFIT
# OF MILLIONS
# IN SIGHT?

## Columbus IT Partner steams ahead

Whereas IBM is disappointing, Columbus IT Partner is steaming ahead on international activities. Essentially, Concorde XAL is the foundation of the company. Michael Gaardboe and Lars Andersen initially focus on production companies, which show abundant market potential especially in Jutland. In the early 1990s, many Danish companies begin to move their production to Eastern Europe. Outsourcing happens to their own newly established production facilities and to companies that perform production tasks as subcontractors. Both instances need management and communication via shared IT systems, and Michael Gaardboe sees great potential here. To support the customers, he finds business partners in those countries where production has been outsourced. When Damgaard Data enters into the agreement with IBM regarding the international distribution of XAL, Columbus decides to follow their lead and establishes an international department in 1995. In February 1996, it is certified as a ProjectPartner and is among the handful of resellers to which big leads are referred. By the beginning of 1997, Columbus has established subsidiaries in Sweden, Norway, Germany, Austria, the UK, Poland, Latvia, Estonia, Lithuania, the Czech Republic and Russia and is on its way with a subsidiary in Hungary. The company has grown to over 300 employees in total, of whom over 100 work abroad.

The model for international expansion is based on joint ventures where Columbus contributes with its brand, customers, additional products, a large package of error corrections for XAL and a project management approach. The local business partners contribute with the rest. The model doesn't require deep pockets but, in return, Columbus has to settle for about 50 per cent of the shares in the subsidiaries. With access to development and implementation resources in the newly formed subsidiaries, the company can develop local versions of XAL in those countries where Damgaard International and IBM don't operate.

In reality, they become the de facto distributor, despite not reaching an explicit agreement on this. Via their work, they experience a large and growing need for uniformity in the internal IT systems of international clients. They develop a concept of designing a core solution based on XAL, which would typically be developed with the client's parent company, and that can then be rolled out to all subsidiaries with a minimum of local customisations. The solution ensures customers a high level of uniformity in IT operations, lower IT costs, improved transparency across the entire company and, not least, faster and easier consolidation of group financial statements. The concept becomes popular first among Danish companies with international activities, but customers later come from all around the world.

Columbus fully exploits the idea of making XAL a solution for international companies and for years is the only reseller to muster an international implementation organisation. Michael Gaardboe and Lars Andersen understand how to take the maximum advantage of the possibilities and they experience great success in the 1990s.

They aren't just an important source of increasing licence revenue; they are a brilliant example of what can be achieved with Concorde products. Time and again they receive awards at international business partner meetings and always win the prize as the biggest partner. The partnership is promoted by close links between the companies' top management – not least by the personal friendship between Per Pedersen and Lars Andersen, who were former colleagues from DEC Denmark.

## The battle for the public sector

In February, Navision Software signs an agreement with Kommunedata (now KMD); from now on Financials will be offered as a standard financial management system for the country's 16,000 municipal institutions. Kommunedata decides to stop developing its own system at the same time. The announcement, coming only a few weeks after Navision Software has bought Mærsk Data out of its distribution company and is again standing on its own two feet, is an important move in the battle for the public market for financial management systems in Denmark.

In April, Damgaard Data announces it has signed an agreement with the Danish Agency for Governmental Management, under the Danish Ministry of Finance, for the delivery of XAL for the local financial management and staff administration of the state sector. The initial delivery is to 55 educational colleges, but there is also the possibility of expanding the licence agreement to other state institutions. The agreement is unusual given that the Danish Agency for Governmental Management purchases licences directly from ServicePartner and not from resellers. On the other hand, it is the partners – initially, BFC Data – who are responsible for the training and implementation.

A meeting is held in May with representatives from Columbus to discuss the development of a solution to Vejen municipality's charges for electricity, gas and water. Vejen municipality isn't satisfied with the solution provided by Kommunedata and is perhaps ready to collaborate on the development of a new system. That is a significant development and can't be financed solely by the project with Vejen municipality. However, it would also be subsequently possible to get the entire municipal market for utilities accounts, which pleases Columbus.

They would like to have Damgaard Data on board the project for several reasons. Partly as it would increase the legitimacy of their sales work with Vejen municipality. And partly so they could share the demanding investment and associated risk. Many partnership models are reviewed, including the possibility of setting up a joint company, which would own the intellectual property rights and where Columbus could have a time-limited exclusivity that would help get a reasonable return on the investment. Talks end in reduced licence prices; from there, they have to run the project themselves.

Denmark has a large public sector with many institutions, many employees and a huge need for financial management. The public sector was dominated by Datacentralen, which with Statens Centrale Regnskabssystem [The State's Central Accounting System] had lain heavily on state institutions, and by Kommunedata, which was the leading supplier to municipalities and counties. Both Datacentralen and Kommunedata had their roots in mainframes, where central bespoke solutions were developed. Dansk System Industri was, with DSI-TEKST and DSI-SYSTEM, one of the first to break Datacentralen's and Kommunedata's monopolies, introducing PC-based systems to public administration and production in the late 1980s. In the mid-1990s, this progresses to financial management systems, and in 1997, the Danish Agency for Governmental Management begins preparing a tender to determine which system will be recommended to state institutions in the future. The tender process is expected to be put into motion at the end of 1997 with the final choice of supplier being made in mid-1998. The tender is of strategic importance for Damgaard Data and its position as market leader in Denmark. Naturally, Navision Software is also interested in both the public sector and this tender, but it doesn't have to defend a leader position. Growth in export markets is more crucial to them than expanding in the small Danish market. Navision Software runs its bidding business through the Danish sales company and it doesn't receive the same attention in the company's group management, which is the case at Damgaard Data.

## Demands increase

Whereas customers in the 1980s primarily had help to move their financial systems into the Age of EDP, the market has undergone many and major changes in the meantime. At the end of the 1990s, the vast majority of new customers already have some form of IT-based solution for their administrative routines, and they only change systems to either come through the imminent turn of the millennium or get additional functions, which can improve productivity and profitability. As all information about the company's customers is already in the financial system, adding features that allow salespeople and service representatives to access that information is obvious. It will also save time if salespeople can use the company's product catalogue to write proposals. Once a potential customer accepts an offer, it is again obvious for data to be transferred directly to the customer database. For the purpose of payroll, information on all the company's employees is collected, which could also be extended to a proper staff administration system. Most companies have a number of core business processes that already link to data found in the financial system.

It is possible to add new features to products such as XAL and Financials, which customers also take great advantage of. With the regular collection of data from many of the customers' core processes, a need for generating reports, which can show the trends and status as well as evaluating the options for optimisations, emerges. All financial management systems come with a report generator, but it's seldom designed to deliver reports that can quickly shed light on all possible management issues. Customers put pressure on suppliers to offer better reporting facilities.

At the CeBIT fair in Hanover in March, Navision Software announces the Executive Insight report module, which has been developed by a reseller. Navision simultaneously introduces a new programme, Navision Add-On Center, which is to promote and use the potential of the many solutions developed by resellers. On the same occasion, Damgaard Data reveals that, as a supplement to Microsoft SQL, Oracle and its own database, Concorde XAL can now be delivered to IBM's AS/400 with the DB/2 database system and to the Informix database system. The strategy is for customers to be able to use the report generators already offered by both database providers and other suppliers.

The increased demand for more business support functions as extensions to the central administration system fits in well with Damgaard Data's and Navision Software's business models. Both companies see the potential and put a lot of effort into optimising it.

## An investment of over 20 million

Damgaard Data holds a solid position in the Danish market, reaching every nook and cranny through the hundreds of resellers. However, it is battling away on the international markets, trying to accelerate sales. Whereas Navision Software has the infrastructure in place to reap the benefits of the growth in the global IT market, Damgaard Data is stuck in a partnership with IBM that looks fine on paper but, which, in reality, isn't working. The collaboration is only beneficial in one area: IBM co-finances product development. Erik Damgaard and his team are aware which direction the new Atlanta product should take, and their ambitions are sky high. The latest object-oriented principles are to be the basis for the tools that resellers use to make extensions. The product is to be based 100 per cent on Microsoft Windows and must be able to run on the most popular databases. Resources will no longer be used on developing the native database. The product should be scalable so it can handle the workload of even large companies, and it should be useable across multiple locations, in multiple languages and in several country versions simultaneously.

The Atlanta project is an enormous investment of over 20 million USD, but IBM, which owns 50 per cent of Damgaard International, contributes both directly via injections of capital and indirectly by deducting and paying for a number of service facilities at Damgaard Data Holding. The co-financing, however, is only a little plaster on the wound. It doesn't lessen the desperation of Preben and Erik, who can see that the train is passing them by at full speed out in the big world. Each day spent with IBM as a sales partner is a day of wasted opportunities, and getting Plan B into place is more urgent than ever.

# A case of kickbacks

In mid-June, Preben gets a call from his good friend Peter Warnøe, who runs the company Complet, which resells IT products from major suppliers such as IBM, Compaq, HP and Microsoft. Peter is in the middle of a dispute with some of his former employees, who in 1994 created the competing company, Nicom Data, and both parties are now preparing legal proceedings. In preparation for the legal battle, Peter Warnøe has got an injunction on Nicom's use of Complet's customer database. During a search of Nicom, some interesting documents have come to light, which Peter believes Preben will be interested in. The documents, which are printouts of e-mails with some handwritten comments from Damgaard Data's purchasing manager to Nicom's managing director, Rene Djurslev, contain a number of gift wish-lists from the company supplying IT equipment to Damgaard Data. Peter Warnøe promises to send Preben a copy of the documents so he can take appropriate action.

Damgaard Data, which is expanding intensely and is a major consumer of computers with associated software, is a customer at Nicom, and so as to maintain customer relations, Rene Djurslev offers the purchasing manager a number of personal benefits in the form of expensive gifts and private trips. When Preben gets a copy of the above mentioned e-mails, he asks the purchasing manager to come to his office when he has a moment. When he is sitting across from Preben a few minutes later, his face grows more ashen as Preben recounts in detail what gifts he has received in kickbacks. When Preben finishes his resume by pointing at the purchasing manager's wrist, which is ornamented with a luxury Breitling watch, the latter pulls down his shirt sleeves. The purchasing manager confesses, giving his version of the case, saying it all started in the small business department. Thereafter, the generosity of Nicom Data gradually became greater and greater. The purchasing manager is fired on the spot, after which Preben contacts Rene Djurslev to get compensation for the overcharging that must have been paid for IT equipment and so on. The gifts received by the purchasing manager should have been given as discounts to Damgaard Data. Until an appropriate compensation has been agreed, Preben will withhold all outstanding payments.

At the beginning of July, *Berlingske Tidende* gets a whiff of the story, and as the episode falls in the midst of silly season, it is quickly picked up by other media. Rene Djurslev's name will now be published in all articles, while the purchasing manager remains anonymous. In August, *Computerworld* features an article that, in the wake of the Nicom case, describes how bribery and kickbacks are not uncommon within the IT industry, but it is, of course, always the competitor who is in trouble. In September, Børsen's [the Danish business daily] *Nyhedsmagasin* includes a feature story, in which Rene Djurslev is given the opportunity to comment, and it appears that Nicom and Complet are entwined in a warlike conflict. His assumption that the bribery case has landed in the media to hurt both him and his company is not without grounds.

Preben Damgaard, whose primary interest is to get the additional expenses for the purchase of IT equipment reimbursed, has no interest in a lot of media attention and, therefore, he chooses not to reveal his source. Given the evidence and confessions, he can report the case to the Fraud Squad in a split second, and there is much peer pressure on Rene Djurslev should he prove to be less willing to provide adequate compensation. When they agree on a reimbursement of 60,000 USD, all outstanding invoices are paid and the partnership wound up.

Børsen's *Nyhedsmagasin* can document that not all parties have been strictly truthful, but as, in essence, the case is about an internal relationship between Nicom and Damgaard Data, the case has played out and the article in the *Nyhedsmagasin* is the last word.

The story of Nicom is an example of what can suddenly steal time from a busy managing director. In mid-1997, business opportunities and problems are almost lining up outside of Preben's door. The demand for financial management software is in full gear worldwide; the possibilities for connecting more and more functionality to the products is endless; the internet begins to slowly show it can do more than just exchange electronic mail, and the partnership with IBM is still only limping along. Certain topics need to be dealt with to ensure that the business grows as fast as – but preferably faster – than its competitors. That Preben would choose to spend his time and energy on a plot to generally harm Nicom is highly unlikely. That he has put Rene Djurslev through the wringer and squeezed the last few dollars out of him, on the other hand, is very likely.

## C5 Light in stormy weather

Damgaard Data is now such a well-known company that newspapers are always open to writing about even small hiccups. In May 1997, the product Concorde C5 Light, launched in late 1995, finds itself in stormy weather. A journalist at *Berlingske Tidende* talks to a few unhappy customers, who are cited in an article on 27th May 1997:

*The program doesn't work like Windows 95, as all the advertisements promise, and it certainly isn't user-friendly. On the contrary, it almost requires a programming qualification to get it do even the most basic tasks of a small business. It is unbelievable that in 1997, Damgaard Data has its customers mess around with arrow keys and commands in an incomprehensible DOS interface.*

Another complains that the program makes incorrect calculations.

The problems are real enough and are due to Concorde C5 Light being marketed as a way for everyone to do their own bookkeeping. The message is illustrated with a tradesman in white overalls, enjoying a cup of coffee while he is reporting his VAT return. The company has to acknowledge that the product requires more insight into bookkeeping and accounting than suggested in the adverts and that the marketing messages need to change. Even with the many initiatives taken to make it easier to get started with Concorde C5 Light, the product is not designed for users with no prior knowledge of accounting and bookkeeping.

Despite the hard but justified criticism, the topic lasts for only a day and isn't followed by any further articles in *Berlingske Tidende* or the other media. Despite the internet moving at full speed, social media – which would have made it easy for others to know – doesn't yet exist. All views and opinions have to be channelled through the press, which, naturally, limits the debate.

## USA office opens and runs into problems

In June 1997, XAL Services opens its office in Atlanta, Georgia with a staff of seven. Five of whom, responsible for product management, pre-sales, training and support, are relocated from the office in Birkerød. IBM also allocates five people to the project. Three are partner account managers, located in San Francisco, New York and Atlanta, respectively, from where they will cover the entire USA. Damgaard International expects IBM to identify customers for beta-testing and recruit resellers parallel to the completion of the product, so there is a platform ready when the product launches at the beginning of 1998, but problems quickly arise. IBM wants a standard product where partner account managers can carry out the entire recruiting process without needing support from XAL Services in Atlanta. Only when resellers have actually signed an agreement will XAL Services be activated to provide training and support. That isn't Damgaard International's strategy. On the contrary, they develop a product with an even more flexible and advanced toolbox than XAL. It is to be sold on its customisability , and the opportunities to sell consultancy support around the product and develop features, modules and solutions for which they will receive the entire gross margin is to attract resellers.

The Atlanta product will require a team of commercially-oriented partner account managers, who discuss business opportunities with the management of potential resellers. They are to help develop business plans, which include all the elements that starting up a new business activity entails: management, organisation, go-to-market activities and training. The most notable task of the partner account managers is to convince the management of potential business partners of the business opportunity and ensure they invest as much as possible in the collaboration. Parallel to this, pre-sales consultants have to convince the resellers' technical staff of the product's excellence, so they can enthusiastically recommend it to their management. Having one person assume responsibility for all of these activities is impossible.

Discussions go back and forth, but as Damgaard International and IBM USA are equal companies, there is no "supreme judge" to cut through the red tape and make IBM understand that it's Damgaard International who defines the product strategy. The project also suffers drastically as it doesn't enjoy a high level of internal attention at IBM in the USA. In fact, by the end of 1996, IBM decided not to move into application software. There is, however, a desire to enter into partnership agreements with all software companies to facilitate the sale of as much IBM hardware as possible, regardless of which software solutions the customers choose.

Therefore, the Atlanta project is counter strategic. Those employees assigned to the venture express the desire to move to other projects with greater internal visibility. As the plans to offer the Atlanta product on AS/400 machines and the DB/2 database system aren't Damgaard International's highest priority and, therefore, will be made available after the product has been released for Microsoft Windows, it is also difficult to continue to point to the major synergies of the partnership.

## Crisis meeting with IBM

In mid-June 1997, a crisis meeting of Damgaard International's board of directors is held. The outlook for the current financial year isn't good. The countries where IBM is responsible for distribution are behind their budgets, and for the financial year, as a whole, are expected to be almost one million USD off target. On top of which IBM has stock for over 3 million USD that has to be sold before new orders can be placed. In other words, only a year after a substantial capital injection, fresh money has to be invested again.

New ideas about what can be done are now voiced. Firstly, it is proposed that IBM take over all XAL Services companies, which would significantly reduce costs for Damgaard International and, furthermore, it would clarify the placement of total responsibility for activities in the individual countries. Secondly, it is suggested that Damgaard International be reduced to a pure R&D company, which would significantly reduce both staff and costs. Such a solution could work well in Denmark given that all the features needed to handle the sales and what they entail are present. But it won't work for IBM as it has shown neither the ability nor the willingness to assume leadership in the individual countries. Finally, it is suggested that Damgaard International raise its prices for distributors, but as they can't immediately pass on that increase to customers, it isn't feasible. Moreover, an increase in the settlement prices from Damgaard International would impact hardest on Damgaard Data Distribution and, thereby, the activities owned 100 per cent by Damgaard Data.

Preben now demands that IBM commits itself to fixed minimum purchases, which can form the basis for necessary investments in product development for individual markets and cover the costs associated with building up and operating local service and support organisations.

Whereas the board of Damgaard International can discuss the issues, it can't really do anything about them. Something can be done on the Damgaard Data side here and now, but the IBM side has representatives without any mandate. Neither Larry Sheffield nor Henrik E. Nyegaard can make binding decisions on behalf of IBM. If changes are to be made, the two gentlemen face long negotiations with each country. The board doesn't make any decisions at the meeting, but it is clear that the situation hasn't at all lived up to the expectations evoked from the positive press releases just five months earlier. The possibility of generating revenue of 300 million USD in 2000 is nothing but a figment of their imaginations.

## Per Pedersen throws in the towel

Per Pedersen, who in December 1996 is appointed to IBM Concorde Sales Executive with responsibility for Europe, chooses to focus his efforts on Germany, where there are a large number of resellers on paper, and Navision Software has proven that very good results are possible with a business model corresponding to Damgaard Data's. Per travels to IBM's German headquarters in Vaihingen, near Stuttgart, every Monday morning, to assist with sales and recruit more business partners. Product-related problems are forwarded to XAL Services in Böblingen, a few miles south of IBM's offices, while commercial relations are handled directly with IBM's people. It quickly becomes quite clear to Per why IBM is unable to get the same results as Navision Software in Germany. IBM has only allocated one administrative employee to the Concorde XAL business, and when PR work or marketing campaigns are to be launched, they have to coordinate with IBM's internal departments and compete with other – and much more significant – business areas. There are no resources for visiting resellers nor for finding new partners. Per reports his observations to Preben Damgaard and Damgaard International, who take the situation to the board, but it has no influence on how IBM in Germany operates.

In July, Per asks for a meeting with Preben and Erik to discuss the situation. Over a cup of coffee in Preben's garden, looking out over Furesø Lake, he reports that he is unable to get IBM to deliver better results. It is possible that a way can be found, but he can't find it. He asks to return to the Danish organisation, or he will find another job.

After chatting about the situation, Erik's opinion is that if Per can't get the partnership to work, no one can. Therefore, it would be best if they cut their losses and take control of the international activities themselves. It's time for Plan B.

Per is asked – in confidence – to assemble a small team and prepare a report on how to proceed without IBM. The report has to contain one or more options with corresponding rough plans and budgets. Plan B has to be ready during the autumn, so its execution can begin in conjunction with the launch of the Atlanta product. Meanwhile, Per will stay in his IBM job.

## Developing Plan B

Per gathers his small team, consisting of Dorrit Overgaard, Jesper Lindhart and Hanne Haubert. They spend a couple of days together at Per's brother's summer cottage to discuss what Plan B should entail.

The situation is far from the same in every county. Norway and Sweden are under good management, have a sensible amount of staff and run, if not satisfactorily, then reasonably well. Germany, the UK, Holland, Belgium, Switzerland and Austria have been going for several years and are all severely destitute. The other Western European markets are still untouched. Columbus deals with Eastern Europe.

The activities in the USA have only been going on for a short period and it's difficult to evaluate the results yet. It's quickly concluded that the alternative to IBM is to establish their own distribution companies. This means that a basic country organisation must be established immediately in order to manage all the tasks. Plan B's development is simplified in that it follows exactly the same business model that has been used to refine things in Denmark over the last ten years. A model, which Navision Software has proven, can also be implemented with great success outside of Denmark. The plan is also simplified by the fact that, despite everything, IBM has recruited a number of resellers and Damgaard International, with its XAL Services companies, has training and support structures somewhat in place. However, experience with IBM demonstrates clearly that top management has to be in place first. That IBM in Norway and Sweden run well is due solely to the skill of management, which not only obtains the necessary resources but has put together a dedicated team.

Per's team discusses whether or not to recruit the management for the local distribution companies in the countries or to find suitable Danes instead, who are then posted abroad. The conclusion is that the loyalty to and transparency of the project is best ensured by finding Danes, who are subsequently relocated abroad for a three-year period to build up the organisation. After which, a local manager can take over and drive the business forward. The Danes are to be part of a global management team, helping to shape strategies, programmes and plans to be implemented in each country. The template used for establishing the international operation is the McDonald's burger chain, whose entire business concept is concretised beforehand and then executed locally. As very little is predetermined, the "manual" for global expansion has to be developed in collaboration with the new country managers: that way they don't need to reinvent the wheel.

Plan B requires large investments, but Navision Software has shown the way. This is not the time for half-hearted solutions, where there is no control over the implementation. No one wants a repeat of the situation with IBM. What is left of the IBM partnership is scary.

## Plan B takes form

While Plan B is being prepared, work with IBM continues. Progress is different from country to country, but is modest overall. Norway is doing well with a market share of five per cent, and as it takes approximately 15 per cent of all new projects, market share increases steadily. The team is small but dedicated and skilled. They work well with the 21 business partners, who have roughly 100 service locations across Norway between them, and they continue to recruit new resellers. Marketing is well organised, and qualified leads are continuously generated for partners.

Sweden is also doing well with two experienced people on the job. They have run extensive marketing campaigns that have generated leads, which have been used to bait new resellers. The Swedish market is difficult, but with the current staffing things are on track.

In Austria, IBM has put the tasks of support and training resellers into the hands of a small company, D&M, in Graz. There are less than ten active business partners, and – given the circumstances – they are doing reasonably well. Austria is a small market, so it doesn't make sense to throw additional resources in here.

In Switzerland, IBM has put Walter Baumann on the job, who, in spite of being only one man, has produced good results. Ten active resellers represent a good foundation, and training and support are provided by XAL Services in Böblingen, Germany, but the entire situation being dependent on a single person is fragile. If Walter Baumann leaves, everything would fall apart.

The situation in Germany is really crazy. The Concorde XAL activities are, in reality, without management. No new resellers are being recruited and there is no regular contact with the existing 50 or so partners. Per, who recently worked closely with IBM in Germany, recommends Damgaard Data themselves take on the responsibility as quickly as possible.

In the Netherlands, where there are ten resellers, IBM has allocated a single part-time employee, but there is no overall management of the market.

In the UK, almost all the world's suppliers of financial management software do battle over customer budgets. Navision Software is making nice progress, while American Great Plains Software has pumped millions of dollars into building up a local organisation and an aggressive marketing campaign without it producing any results worth mentioning. Even the Dutch Baan – successful all over the world – has trouble in the UK. IBM has allocated just one employee to managing the Concorde XAL activities and there are about ten resellers not producing many projects. There is an expectation that IBM can see the hopelessness of the situation, too and may even consider pulling the emergency brake itself if results don't improve soon.

The Belgian activities are actually run by a single reseller (EDAN), who has also been actively involved in localising the Belgian version of Concorde XAL. IBM plays no role in the Belgian activities.

Per Pedersen takes stock of the situation:

| | |
|---|---|
| Norway: | IBM can continue |
| Sweden: | IBM can continue |
| Germany: | Damgaard Data should take over |
| The UK: | IBM can continue for now |
| Holland: | Damgaard Data should take over |
| Austria: | IBM needs to go, D&M will be sounded out about taking over distribution |
| Switzerland: | IBM can continue for now |
| Belgium: | No change – EDAN can continue |
| Eastern Europe: | Columbus continues |

## Towards the euro and the new millennium

For the first time, in November 1997, the printed annual accounts and the accompanying report are published in Danish and in English. Immense satisfaction with the current situation, the achieved results and, not least, with Damgaard International is expressed – the latter isn't actually included in the consolidated financial statements – which can now show an export share of 50 per cent. What isn't mentioned is that 34 per cent of those exports are stockpiled at IBM's subsidiaries. Once that is taken into account, exports are only around 6 million USD, which corresponds to 14 per cent of total revenue for the entire group or 23 per cent if you set aside ServicePartner's service turnover. Earnings from Columbus in Eastern Europe are also included. When compared to Navision Software, which has an export of about 18 million USD (70 per cent of total revenue), which is more than double that of the previous year, it clearly illustrates the on-going challenges. Damgaard Data is still far greater than Navision Software in Denmark, but what help is that when 99.5 per cent of the world market is outside of Denmark? Whereas expectations were sky high in 1994, when the first partnership agreement with IBM was signed, and whereas IBM's Larry Sheffield, chairman of Damgaard International's board, announced a turnover target of 300 million by 2000 as late as January 1997, there is now a vast discrepancy between the official announcements and the harsh realities. The board uses the following wording in its description of the international activities:

*"In the future, the group will also invest substantial resources in continued internationalisation – an investment that can be taken on several fronts and in different ways, but all of which aim to strengthen the company's position in the international arena".*

IBM isn't mentioned here at all. Work on Plan B is happening at full speed. Parallel to this is an attempt to get the best out of the partnership with IBM. This is particularly critical in the USA, where preparations are underway for the introduction of the new Atlanta product.

The ambition is still to be one of the three leading suppliers of administrative business solutions in Europe by the year 2000. If that is to be achieved, then things are going to be busy. A market analysis from IDG estimates that the European market for this type of software is around 2.4 billion USD, and Damgaard Data is deemed to occupy 27th place, while Navision Software is at number 33.

## Positive problems

The coming millennium puts a lot of additional pressure on the demand for new IT systems. The unusual change of date carries a risk of computer-crashes, the consequences of which are difficult for customers to get their heads around. The market is further stimulated by the forthcoming introduction of the euro in a number of European countries. And finally, the rapid spread of the internet, which enables software-based optimisation of many business processes, gives everything an extra boost. The IT industry is enjoying good times.

At Damgaard Data, there are no restrictions on the issuing of new licences, but it's different for the resellers. They have to bind consultants to the increasing number of projects – they can't just be cloned. The strong demand creates a phenomenon, which the industry calls "positive problems": it can be difficult to find enough people to help implement and operate the systems for the customers.

XAL projects, in particular, need highly skilled labour. As a rule, for every dollar paid for software licences, 15 to 20 USD has to be invested in consultancy support. The strongly increasing demand for skilled labour up to the turn of the millennium becomes a bottleneck for the completion of new projects by resellers, but it could also affect Damgaard Data. If partners have to politely decline projects, customers may have to choose a competitor instead and, thereby, Damgaard Data loses out on licence income as well as the subsequent long-term extension and subscription business. The lack of skilled labour is the main theme when Preben Damgaard is interviewed for *Computerworld* in November 1997.

*Software company Damgaard Data increased its profit by 20 per cent in 96/97 financial year, but could have sold more if there had been more skilled resellers. "We could have sold more if there had been more employees with the right skills in our reseller channel," says Preben Damgaard, Managing Director, Damgaard Data A/S. How much more Preben Damgaard won't say, but the lack of skilled labour is allegedly a real problem for Damgaard Data.*

Damgaard Data carries out a survey of the supply and demand of labour within the IT industry in Denmark and discovers that from now until the turn of the millennium, there will be an unmet need of approximately 8-10,000 people. In an interview in *Berlingske Tidende* on 23rd September 1998, Preben says:

*"The problem is that the industry has a nerd image, which means that an unbelievable number of women don't apply for technical educational programmes," says Preben Damgaard. "That's terrible, to put it nicely. If we don't have women, we're cutting out half the potential".*

Contrary to the contemporary perception that this need for labour primarily concerns people with technical IT skills, Preben emphasises that consultants with domain expertise, and employees for marketing and sales assignments are needed just as badly. The shortage of skilled labour affects all areas.

## Damgaard Data accepts
## *Computerworld's* annual award

In September, Damgaard Data is selected to receive *Computerworld's* annual award for their contribution to the Danish IT industry. After the award ceremony, at Kontor&Data in Fredericia, the president of the Danish ITC Industry Association, IBM's Kim Østrup, is quoted in *Jyllands Posten* on 1st October 1997:

*"When they reached the point when they were to go out into the world for real, they chose to sell out some of the crown jewels and bet on an international firm. There was a lot of foresight there," said a member of the IT Prize Committee and chairman of the ITC Industry Association, Kim Østrup, about the reasons [for awarding the honour]. The Damgaard brothers sold half of their development company to the IBM Group, and Concorde products are going to be marketed by IBM in many parts of the world. "The Damgaard brothers have done well, despite the bad environment for developing and selling standard software in Denmark".*

It is unclear what is meant by "bad environment" in Denmark, but neither Kim Østrup nor anyone else present could know that the partnership with IBM, in particular, represents a "bad condition" and that IBM isn't in a position to use the international potential of Concorde products.

## Preben meets with DITEC about distribution in Germany

After Per Pedersen and his little team present their outline of Plan B to Preben and Erik and get the green light to continue working, they begin thoroughly researching the conditions in each country. It's especially urgent to get a handle on the situation in Germany.

An alternative to setting up a subsidiary could be to do something with DITEC, which is by far the largest reseller in Germany. Therefore, Preben Damgaard travels to Perlach, south of Munich, to meet Wolfgang Stübich, the head of the company, on 18th November.

Despite some initial difficulties, DITEC is quite pleased with the development of the XAL business. They have experienced constant growth and now employ 160 employees, 34 of whom are in-the-field sales consultants with a good understanding of customers' business needs. With an expected licence turnover of over 2.6 million USD for 1997, DITEC is the largest partner in Germany with potential for further growth. There are several German competitors with excellent and sometimes better solutions than Concorde XAL, but none of them have a development environment that enables resellers to quickly make extensions and customisations. The closest competitor is Navision Software, and it actually helps DITEC that they come from Denmark, too. Customers like Financials and the XAL concepts, and both provide resellers with an attractive service business.

However, Wolfgang Stübich isn't satisfied with IBM's efforts as a distributor. There is nothing wrong with the IBM name; it has helped open many doors and make new customers feel comfortable with a new product. But too many small resellers are being recruited, which devaluates the product's image on the market and involves completely unnecessary price competition. There is too little overall marketing and branding, and a complete lack of support in the everyday sales work. The technical support from XAL Services in Böblingen, south of Stuttgart, on the other hand, is working soundly.

Wolfgang Stübich offers a distribution partnership in Germany, where DITEC would take over XAL Services and be responsible for all product-related aspects, while Damgaard Data would assume responsibility for marketing, and reseller recruitment and management. In that case, DITEC would get 70 per cent of the licence price, of which 40 per cent is to go to the resellers. DITEC's own reseller activities are to get only 30 per cent of the licence price, so no one can claim that DITEC is using its distributor status for unfair advantage.

Preben listens with interest to Wolfgang Stübich's proposal, and despite it seeming advantageous that DITEC would take on the entire product customisation and support work, he isn't happy about the idea of a combined distributor/business partner. They have been down this road several times before and it doesn't work. On the other hand, he notes dissatisfaction with IBM's efforts, which fits with the overall picture that is gradually forming. Preben concludes that DITEC will – in all probability – support Damgaard Data itself taking over distribution in Germany; thereby contributing to the other partners backing an imminent changing of the guard.

## Erik surrenders management duty

During 1997, more than 90 employees and 10-15 freelancers are working on product development in Damgaard International. Concorde Økonomi, which was launched in 1986, continues to live on, XAL is the company's major cash machine, while C5 and C5 light continue to sell well to small businesses in Denmark. However, the vast majority of employees are working on the Atlanta project, which represents a brand new product generation that is to form the backbone of international expansion for the next 10-15 years.

Following the establishment of Damgaard International in 1994, the organisation of Damgaard's development activities changes. In spring 1995, Erik Damgaard is replaced by Jens Haugaard as managing director. As more employees are recruited, Erik surrenders more and more management responsibility so as to concentrate more on product development and, in particular, the Atlanta project. When the first version of the Atlanta project is nearing completion in mid-1997, Erik has no formal overall leadership role within the organisation. He is the team leader for a small group of five employees, who are responsible for the development of the core of the new product.

Every product gets a product manager, who is formally responsible for defining content in future versions. Erik still has a large say when executive decisions have to be made. He has the technical insight to make changes to the products if he deems it necessary. But he is no longer the central, unifying figure.

His enthusiasm for the Atlanta project certainly isn't misplaced, but he feels less comfortable with the many people and the bureaucracy that necessarily surround such an extensive product. He finds it difficult to maintain an overview and starts to rely on those leading the project to take charge. When technical presentations are to be held around the world for new resellers or at business partner meetings, Erik Damgaard is still the one sent for. He is difficult to control and can say things that weren't planned. However, he has a formidable ability to account for the product strategy and place it into a market perspective that leaves everyone excited and happy to be part of the process.

## Atlanta becomes Axapta

The Atlanta product is far more ambitious, employs far more people and requires far more planning and coordination than anything the company has developed so far. To help with the work, the Microsoft Solution Framework (MSF) is introduced; the set of principles that Microsoft itself uses to develop software, and which it published in 1993, so others could also benefit from them.

In autumn 1997, an English consulting firm is engaged to come up with suggestions for the name of the Atlanta project. The product is to be positioned as an alternative to the German SAP, and after a few weeks of work, the consulting firm presents their ideas, among which "SAPTA" has the most support. But Erik Damgaard thinks it is too close to "SAP", and he would like to have the "X" from XAL in the new name, so they arrive at "XAPTA". Erik Seifert, once again brought in as a consultant with special knowledge of the American market, points out that a product name starting with X will always appear at the bottom of an alphabetical list and, therefore, he proposes prefixing it with an A. And so "AXAPTA" is born. In Europe, the product is called Concorde Axapta, in the USA, just Axapta.

The core product, which is essentially a complete software development environment, complies with the latest standards within technical development, can run on the Oracle and Microsoft SQL databases, and has an architecture in which the individual user's work space is separate from the application itself, which is again separate from the database. This construction means that the system becomes technically easier to install and can serve both very small and very large companies, and even the journey from small to large enterprise.

Axapta is a beautiful product with an ultramodern user interface. The jaws of both resellers and customers almost drop at demonstrations. As development progresses and more and more people see the product, Damgaard Data receives confirmation that they have something here – something that distinguishes them significantly from competitors, no matter where they may be in the world.

## Product positioning problems

However, how the product is to be positioned and marketed poses a significant challenge. It's easy enough in those countries where Damgaard Data isn't yet represented. Axapta offers a fresh start and it doesn't need to take existing XAL resellers into account. In Denmark, the greatest interest lies in getting Axapta competing for the big customers. Concorde Økonomi, C5, C5 Light and Concorde XAL can still manage small and medium-sized businesses. But in the international markets, where Damgaard Data is already represented, the situation is completely different.

Over the last few years, resellers in Norway, Sweden, Germany, Switzerland and Austria have invested in a business based on XAL. Only a few have made back that investment so far. There are only a few XAL partners in the Netherlands and the UK, and they have hardly come up to speed. Columbus, who has been on board since 1991 and is now responsible for distribution in Eastern Europe, is excited about Axapta and is ready to switch all of its business to the new product, but this readiness to change is far from being shared by the other XAL resellers. It's a mixed bag.

## New economy; new abbreviations

The last year of the twentieth century is probably the most turbulent one the IT industry has ever experienced. The spread of the internet, in particular, forms the basis for brand new business models, particularly that which is called "the new economy". The old economy is characterised by businesses offering products and services at a price, which ensures a profit for the companies. Companies can invest those profits in product and service improvements as well as in penetrating new markets. The better a company is at making money and growing, the more valuable it is.

The new economy is characterised by the fact that you don't have to earn money and grow in a traditional economic sense to be perceived as a valuable company. For example, if a company can attract many visitors to its website, then the philosophy behind the new economy is that they can later be converted into revenue and earnings. At the end of the 1990s, lots of new businesses are actually able to attract many visitors to their websites, and investors then flock to pour money into them. There are many more investors in the market than businesses to invest in during this time. New businesses that believe they can attract many visitors or companies that have an idea for software, which can help other businesses attract visitors and serve them, suddenly present interesting investment opportunities. With a description of the good idea and some useful contacts, companies in the new economy can raise large sums to develop and put their ideas into production. To be the first to market that money has to be put to work as quickly as possible, and entrepreneurs are often assessed on how fast they can burn up the money – under the new concept of "burn rate".

At the end of the 1990s, stock listings of companies that have virtually no revenue are seen; they are assessed only on the expectation that their non-trading activities on the internet can be commercialised at some point in the future.

The massive growth in the use of the internet also boosts the development of the technology that makes it easier to use the network, which again forms the basis for telecommunications companies' massive investments in infrastructure to transport data around the network. The net result is easier and faster access to the internet at significantly declining prices. The improvements and plummeting telecommunication prices are so significant that it is now both technically possible and cost-effective to run software via the internet. Instead of running software on your own PC, it can run on computers located in large data centres, and can – over the even faster and cheaper internet – be used in an internet browser. This design, called ASP (Application Service Provider), is invented by the IT industry itself, starting as what is called a "hype" – an idea that is probably possible, but isn't currently in demand. Trade journalists throw themselves into the new phenomenon at once, and in the late 1990s, every software supplier has to decide whether they want to be part of a delivery model that customers still neither know nor need.

## Damgaard Data is "old economy"

Companies like Damgaard Data are now categorised as "old economy" and are criticised for not being visionary enough – especially in their use of the internet. Despite the investor market performing uncontrollably and venture capital almost queuing up to get out to work, it isn't attractive for a company such as Damgaard Data to undertake completely speculative projects that could end in disaster. For an entrepreneur, who has nothing, the scenario of getting external funding and quickly trying to get a business up and running isn't that risky. Worst case scenario is that they end up with nothing. Nothing gained, nothing lost. If, like Erik and Preben, you have spent 15 years building up a healthy business, you don't want to put everything at stake for a craze. Moreover, Axapta actually has the foundation to take advantage of the opportunities offered by the internet but, as and when customers are ready to use it and willing to pay for it.

## Plan B is put into operation
## – The meeting at Hotel Phønix

Immediately after returning home from the meeting with DITEC in Munich, Preben meets Erik and Per Pedersen to discuss the situation. They agree to give the partnership with IBM one last shot. From his IBM account, Per sends an e-mail directly to the top manager of IBM's activities in Europe, the Middle East and Africa, under which Damgaard International falls. He clearly recounts the challenges and points out what is needed for IBM to fulfil their obligations.

The email is sent without involving either the chairman of the board, Larry Sheffield, or Pat Falotico, whom Larry appointed to be operationally responsible for Concorde at IBM. Preben, Erik and Per know it will create waves, but as they feel they can't achieve satisfactory results by following the chain of command, they embark on this last theoretical possibility.

Not many hours pass after the e-mail has been sent to the European Department before Per has Pat Falotico on the phone. She says that was probably his last email from his IBM account. The European director is side-stepping their obligations and pushing the matter down in the organisation. They are back to where they started. It's back to the drawing board.

Preben now discusses the situation with Larry Sheffield. They agree that Damgaard Data take over distribution in Germany, Austria, Switzerland (DACH) and Benelux as soon as possible, while IBM and Columbus will continue in the other countries. They also agree that Damgaard Data itself coordinate the takeover directly with those responsible in the IBM subsidiaries. Preben then pulls Per out of IBM and appoints him director of Damgaard Data Holding instead, where he will be at the head of global marketing and sales activities.

With a green light to take over DACH and Benelux, preparations for the implementation need to be turbo-charged. Per already has a candidate for the post as head of the German-speaking markets waiting in the wings, but a similar manager for Benelux, who will be based in the Netherlands, has to be found. At the same time, a structure has to be put in place, so Damgaard Data in Birkerød can serve the newly created subsidiaries.

In early December, Per Pedersen is appointed director of Damgaard Data Holding, officially taking charge of global responsibility for international activities. In mid-December, the team that is going to move into DACH and Benelux is in place, and those who are to support the activities from the head office in Birkerød have been appointed and briefed.

On a wet and cold December morning, the entire Plan B team meet in a boring basement room at the Hotel Phønix in central Copenhagen. In contrast to the weather outside and the surroundings inside, the atmosphere is close to euphoric. The participants feel they are making a piece of Danish business history. The focus is on quick and efficient execution; the goal is to become the market leader in new markets. A huge wallet has been opened for the necessary investments. Per Pedersen gives a long speech about the company's culture and the Passat principle: the willingness to invest isn't to be confused in any way with extravagance. The money must be used with great care and will be released according to recorded progress. The take over from IBM has to happen before 1$^{st}$ March 1998.

# CHAPTER 18

# REGAINING FREEDOM

## Licences in stock

Following the takeover of distribution from IBM, Damgaard Data Distribution rebrands as Concorde Software. The name change is to create better coherence between the company name and the product names. A consistency it is believed will simplify marketing efforts in the international markets.

A distribution take over involves going through the accounts. Channel stuffing – the sale of point certificates to resellers, which haven't yet been converted into customer licences – turns out to be more extensive than before. To reach its budget targets for 1997, IBM had continued to sell point certificates on favourable terms and immediately recognised the revenue. The resellers had a similar interest in the trick in that they received a higher margin on the licences and could record the cost in 1997, while the revenue from the sale of licences to customers is recorded in the following year. This enabled them to reduce their profits and postpone corporate taxes. Overall, channel stuffing amounts to 3.2 million USD.

For Concorde Software, which now takes on all the costs associated with activities in the Netherlands, Belgium, Luxembourg, Germany, Austria and Switzerland, it means no revenue and earnings before the licences in stock are sold. In order to overcome the problem, Concorde

Software will receive compensation of 3.2 million USD. The compensation is recorded as an expense in Damgaard International's 1997 financial statements and posted as due to Concorde Software. There is no cash to be made out of the 3.2 million USD that the resellers have in stock; rather Concorde Software keeps the entire revenue for the first 3.2 million USD from new licences. Formally, IBM should have handed over its share of the profit, but as it was already posted to the accounts and used as a basis for paying bonuses, this "sleeping dog" was allowed to lie.

## Axapta for America

The work of completing Axapta Version 1.0 is moving at full speed. Everyone is highly impressed with the first prototypes of the product – with perhaps the exception of IBM in the USA, which still finds the product isn't ready to be released for sale. IBM believes there are too many Danish particularities in the product; it expects more standard functionality and finally IBM wants more comprehensive documentation accompanying the product. As IBM is responsible for both reseller recruitment and marketing in the USA, Damgaard International is dependent on their agreement to make the launch date.

The launch is scheduled for IBM's Business Partner Executive Conference 1998, to be held in San Francisco at the end of February. Since the beginning of June 1997, around 15 resellers have been recruited and trained and a dozen beta-test customers signed up. Damgaard International is convinced the big marketing machine should start, but IBM is hesitant. Moreover, the parties still can't completely agree on the positioning of Axapta. IBM already has well-established alliances with most ERP system suppliers in the American market, especially with suppliers to major companies that need quite a lot of computer capacity, which is IBM's core business. Therefore, it isn't thrilled about adding its name to a brand new product considered to be inadequate.

However, the tug-of-war ends with a compromise whereby Axapta is announced in conjunction with the San Francisco conference, while the launch and releasing the product for sale will be deferred to later in the year. On 16th February 1998, IBM sends out a press release describing the product as for companies with between 50 and 500 employees and an annual turnover of 5 to 100 million dollars:

*"IBM, in conjunction with Danish software developer Damgaard International A/S (DIAS), today introduced Axapta Business Management Solution for the North American market".*
*[....]*
*"With solutions such as Axapta, IBM and our business partners are helping growing businesses become more productive," says Steven Ladwig, general manager, network computing and software, IBM Global Small and Medium Business, "IBM is pleased to have helped another partner bring to market an application for this burgeoning customer set."*

It certainly isn't the intended product positioning in Europe, and IBM also fails to mention that it actually owns half of Damgaard International. It is a fine balance: IBM in the USA has to live up to its internal obligations, but it doesn't want this commitment to look greater than those it has with all the other ERP providers.

In conjunction with the announcement in the USA, Damgaard International contacts the Danish press, where there is a bigger toot of the horn in *Computerworld* on 20ᵗʰ February 1998:

*"We have contacted 5,000 American business partners, and the first 1,000 have responded positively," says Jens Haugaard, Managing Director, Damgaard International A/S. "At the same time, IBM has taken the new Concorde Axapta product so much to heart that it is being marketed as IBM's own financial management system for small and medium-sized companies".*

*"If IBM's expected sales figures for 1998 hold up, then the USA will be Damgaard Data's third-largest market after Denmark and Norway," says Preben Damgaard, founder and director of Damgaard Data. According to Preben Damgaard, the contribution to revenue from the USA should be measured in "large, double-digit millions".*

The optimistic declarations are based on the expectation that after the announcement in San Francisco, IBM will now take out the large marketing chequebook and hand over some of the millions of dollars it mentioned in the press releases the previous year. But it doesn't happen. The tireless discussions between IBM and Damgaard International about when and how much continue across the Atlantic even after the announcement in San Francisco is made.

## Columbus will take the lead with Axapta

Whereas IBM is hesitant, Columbus IT Partner is the exact opposite. Michael Gaardboe and Lars Andersen are convinced that Axapta is the product of the future and that a quick and massive investment would mean a leading position as the customers' preferred reseller for their many major international projects to which the product is tailored. With IBM's supposed backing and marketing muscle behind it, Michael and Lars expect a massive marketing campaign, which they can then work off. It will require a significant consultancy capacity to take on the many new customer projects; therefore, they initiate a large-scale retraining of their employees before the product is released.

The significant investments required by the bet on Axapta are primarily financed by operations, which in 1997 have a turnover of over 54 million USD, giving a profit of almost 6.2 million USD. When the company is introduced on the Copenhagen Stock Exchange on 18th May 1998, approximately 16 million USD is added in fresh venture capital. It is to be invested in further international expansion, and so as to exploit IBM's forthcoming launch in the US, offices are established in the New York area immediately after the IPO. Founder Michael Gaardboe, with a nicely cushioned, personal bank account, now moves to the USA to take charge of building up the business.

"Our goal is to be represented on all the major markets in Europe by the end of 1999 and in all relevant metropolitan areas by 2001. In this way, we expect to expand the market base and our potential for small and medium-sized enterprises in need for internationally integrated IT solutions," says managing director Lars Andersen. The planned establishment in Europe will be in France, Spain, Belgium and Switzerland. Thereby, establishing the company in 22 countries. The company expects growth in 1998 and a result significantly above that of 1997. "We also expect to be able to continue that strong growth in 1998, so that both revenue and result in 1998 will be significantly above that of 1997," says Lars Andersen to Reuter Finance on 21st April 1998.*

As a thank you for backing and supporting Axapta, the agreement on distribution rights in Eastern Europe is extended for three years, so they can invest in and expand their market position there without stress.

## Damgaard Data takes over in five European countries

Now begins the detailed planning of the takeover of distribution in DACH and Benelux. There is no problem in the partnership with IBM regarding the transfer in the areas concerned. It is happy to hand over the task. The most important resellers, whom Damgaard Data contacts informally early on, are more sceptical. They are still dissatisfied with IBM's efforts, but at the same time uncertain about how the market will react to IBM pulling out and unsure about how much Damgaard Data will be able to do on its own. The IBM logo has without a shadow of a doubt opened doors to both business partners and customers much faster than if Damgaard Data had started from scratch. Can Damgaard Data now convince the resellers and the market that they can do better?

The management of Damgaard Data is aware of the challenge and allocates massive resources to quickly and powerfully step into the role of distributor in the countries concerned. Germany is the first priority, followed by the Netherlands, Switzerland, Austria and Belgium.

The change in Germany is to coincide with the major international Ce-BIT fair in Hanover in March, so as to take maximum advantage of the event. Together with IBM, the transfer is prepared in January, including the sequence of press releases.

## Business partners are angry at IBM

In early February, every German reseller is seated at an all-day meeting in IBM's headquarters in Vaihingen, on the outskirts of Stuttgart. The change is to be announced and Concorde Software will present its plans for the future. The meeting, led by IBM, gets off to a turbulent start. A large number of resellers are obviously angry with IBM and feel they have been lured into a project on false premises, and that IBM is now sticking its tail between its legs. The business partners have been left with investments that haven't yet yielded a reasonable return, and can no longer use the IBM name as a door opener.

Among the criticisms are reports of poor product quality, poor service and a lack of marketing and sales' support. IBM is under massive pressure but can only confirm that the decision to change has been made and that after a short transition period, the company will no longer be in the picture. When Per Pedersen takes to the stand and presents the team that will lead the operation in Germany, and when they subsequently carry out their presentations in German – albeit with a touch of a thick Danish accent – the resellers' interest is piqued. The team explains how Concorde Software will tackle the challenges over the next 100 days, and calm gradually descends upon the crowd. Questions about Axapta are asked, and it is clear that there is great uncertainty regarding the positioning of XAL. Most German resellers simply aren't up to investing in a new product, because they haven't yet made back their investment in XAL.

In Switzerland, Concorde Software opens a little office in Zurich and hires Walter Baumann from IBM to continue the work of recruiting and managing business partners. In Austria, there is only a handful of resellers, who are initially managed from the office in Böblingen. They aren't particularly pleased with that, but as IBM is definitely pulling out, and Concorde Software promises to implement local marketing activities, they reluctantly accept.

In Benelux, Per Pedersen himself handles the official transfer from IBM to Concorde Software. Hans Bak, who comes from a position as product manager at DanaData, is subsequently posted abroad as country manager for the Dutch office. The official list of XAL business partners in the Netherlands is ten, but when Hans Bak visits them, it appears that only a handful is active and has the courage to continue the activities. In Belgium, the only active reseller is EDAN, but it is both competent and enthusiastic. Hans Bak decides to let EDAN carry on alone and instead focuses his efforts on rebuilding the Dutch market, where knowledge for XAL is quite limited.

## Navision is busy

Despite IBM agreeing to continue distribution in Norway, Sweden, the UK and the USA, Preben, Erik and Per are well aware that this solution is only temporary. It's going to take a medium-sized miracle if IBM is suddenly going to change gear and put all its efforts into the Concorde project. The situation clearly speaks for itself when the *Jyllands-Posten* newspaper reports from the CeBIT exhibition in Hanover in March 1998:

*... nevertheless,* Jyllands Posten *passed both Concorde Software's and Navision Software's stands six times during the two busiest Ce-Bit days. The picture was clear each time. Busy at the 500 square metre Navision stand; less busy at Concorde Software's 150 square metre stand.*

Germany, with a turnover of around 20 million USD, is Navision Software's largest export market and, yes, they have been going since 1990, but not even with the support of IBM could Damgaard Data manage to gain a somewhat significant role in the huge export market, which is highly responsive to exactly the type of solutions represented by XAL. The observation from CeBIT is actually a pretty good snapshot of the overall result of the global partnership with IBM.

Damgaard Data only taking over in DACH and Benelux for now is due, firstly, to IBM clearly having lost momentum in the two large markets and, secondly, to such a takeover requiring great attention from management as well as significant investments in building up the organisation and marketing to ensure that market share is won. Taking on too many countries at once would be too much of a strain. In addition, IBM has to agree to changes. It owns half of the shares of Damgaard International and, moreover, the distribution agreements entered into are binding. If Damgaard Data is to take over a country, both parties need to believe it's a good idea and work positively for it to happen without upsetting resellers and customers too much. Furthermore, it is important to maintain a civil tone in the relationship with IBM, with whom a solution for long-term ownership has to be found as they surrender the distribution. Therefore, the timing of taking over the other markets has to be clarified along the way.

## Navision Software wins the Agency for Governmental Management

At the end of 1997, the Danish Agency for Governmental Management sends out a public tender. The aim is to find a replacement for Statens Centrale Regnskabssystem [The State's Central Accounting System], which was put into operation in October 1976, and has since been introduced into the vast majority of Danish central administration institutions. After a prequalification round, the Agency for Governmental Management decides, in February 1998, that four companies are to be considered in the final evaluation: Damgaard Data, Navision Software, Maconomy and Oracle. CSC, who had announced that they would make a bid as a reseller of SAP, pull out of the project at the last moment.

The four prequalified companies have to submit their offers at the end of February. Thereafter, presentations are to be made and assessed. The choice of supplier is expected to happen around 1st April.

For both Navision Software and Damgaard Data, the offer, which includes delivering local financial management systems to the state's 300 to 500 institutions and is estimated to have a value of 12-14 million USD, is crucial.

In practice, Damgaard Data and Navision Software have been sharing the Danish market between them – and gaining market share from each other is almost impossible. Only a few resellers are able to handle both companies' products in parallel, and switching from one to the other would require large investments and a good explanation for existing customers. Growth in market share has to be taken from the other players in the market or by – as the opportunity now presents itself –entering the huge public market, which can't be done in small steps but has to be won in large chunks via public tender.

It ends up being ServicePartner who makes the offer. Now they have to decide whether to offer XAL, which the Danish Agency for Governmental Management acquired for 55 vocational schools in April the previous year, or offer the brand new Axapta instead, which hasn't been released yet. XAL, launched in April 1991, is a proven, solid and widespread product. Wagging tongues would probably say the product is technologically "obsolete" and hasn't been able to obtain Windows certification, which the Agency for Governmental Management would like to see. Axapta, on the other hand, is at the forefront of technology; is built on modern principles with an object-oriented design, fully encompasses the user interface used by Microsoft in its popular Outlook and is fully certified for Windows. However, as it hasn't been released yet, only a few test installations can be demonstrated – none of which are under the auspices of the public sector. Navision Software makes an offer with Financials, which was released in 1995, is 100 per cent Windows-based and certified and it has gained impressive penetration in both Denmark and abroad.

The timing is bad. ServicePartner is trapped between two product generations. In the meantime, it is estimated that the chances of winning the contract are greatest with Axapta, which will allow the Danish Agency for Governmental Management to build future financial management systems for state institutions on ultramodern technology. Axapta is the way to go.

The presentation of the offer is to take place on Monday, 2nd March, at the company headquarters in Birkerød, where Erik Damgaard outlines the vision for Axapta and gives a convincing demonstration. Preben Damgaard presents the business, the partnership with IBM and the expected financial results. However, during the subsequent discussions with the Agency for Governmental Management, it becomes evident that they can't under any circumstances choose a product that hasn't yet been released. That clear message causes management to bring forward the launch date, which is to happen later in the month at the Planetarium in Copenhagen.

On 19th March, the Agency for Governmental Management decides to cancel the entire procurement process due to legal issues. They ask the four companies to draw up new offers and quickly choose to proceed only with Navision Software and Damgaard Data. Peter Pietras, Project and Office Manager tells *Computerworld* on 3rd April 1998:

*If there is one thing the state doesn't want, it's taking part in the development of a new EDP system. Hard lessons were learned from the capsized projects at Told & Skat [Customs & Revenue] and the Ministry of Education. Therefore, the Agency for Governmental Management requires a completely finished system…*

With this announcement, Navision Software is by far the best choice. However, their Financials can't run on the Microsoft SQL-Server, which is what Axapta has been designed for as standard. Many long meetings are now held at which the products and visions are thoroughly examined. For both Financials and Axapta, special functionality has to be developed to cover the government's financial management needs, which both companies are able to demonstrate.

To the surprise of many, the Agency for Governmental Management chooses Navision Financials. The expectation had been for Damgaard Data – considered the major player in the Danish market with the support of IBM – to receive the order. But the Agency isn't sure about introducing the brand new Axapta to state institutions.

Naturally, Navision Software isn't without visions and plans, and at the meetings it explains to the Agency what it can expect over the next few years as well as development a little further down the line. Overall, the Agency for Governmental Management considers Navision Financials to be a well-established and reasonably future-proof platform from a supplier that is expected to follow up with developments. Thus, Navision Financials is perceived as the least risky alternative.

However, the final contract negotiations draw out as the Agency doesn't want to purchase the licences from a reseller, which is Navision Software's business model. Since its inception in 1985, Navision Software hasn't once deviated from its principle of not selling licences directly. The Agency stands by its demands, but it agrees to sign a reseller agreement so it has technically the same status as a business partner. After which, the Agency enters an agreement with DanaData for training, service and support.

The silver medal in the competition for supplying the state market in Denmark is a punch in Damgaard Data's gut. It's a big blow to both management and employees. It has to be acknowledged that not all customers fall head over heels with new technology, and that public sector customers, in particular, place great importance on the security of supply. The decision risks causing some of the resellers to start looking at Navision Financials. Otherwise, they will be cut off from being able to supply state institutions.

Large-scale sales effort is now applied to try to build a direct relationship with the state institutions not covered by the Danish Agency for Governmental Management's tender. At the same time, efforts are made to maintain talks with the Agency to, if possible, establish a two-supplier situation. In June, the Agency paves the way for delivering Axapta solutions to state institutions; thereby putting a little plaster on the wound. With this loophole, Damgaard Data receives recognition for its technology, and the feeling of being put through the wringer is mollified. However, in practice, the loophole doesn't mean anything as Navision Stat – the name of the Agency's solution – becomes the standard for financial management systems in Danish state institutions for many years to come.

## Money comes pouring in

Adopting IBM's distribution role in the German-speaking countries and in Benelux comes with significant costs. Expectations of entering additional countries, therefore, cause an increase in efforts to optimise all domestic revenue streams.

The subscription plans to which customers subscribe to access error corrections and new facilities aren't only profitable, the prepay service also has a positive effect on the company's liquidity. Whereas customers of Concorde Økonomi and C5 almost all subscribe, XAL customers are somewhat inactive. Due to many customer-specific adaptations, they can't upgrade to a new version easily and, therefore, don't see any great value in the scheme. The announcement of Axapta brings a new opportunity to encourage XAL customers to subscribe to update subscriptions. It will ensure customers can access the new product on favourable terms, when and if they wish to change. Update subscriptions, in general, ensure that customers can grow into a new product without having to pay the full licence fee.

The campaign to motivate more customers to subscribe to an update subscription is launched in 1998. On the one hand, a number of conditions are introduced that make it expensive to wait to subscribe. On the other, there are big discounts available if you subscribe for several years at a time.

All resellers are informed of the subscription campaign and have the opportunity to be responsible for the posting of letters and follow-up telemarketing themselves or Damgaard Data can handle the entire activity in the partner's name. Every reseller, with the exception of Columbus, chooses to let Damgaard Data take on the work.

Letters are sent out to the 20,000 customers in Denmark, who are subsequently contacted by phone by an external telemarketing company. If the customer shows interest, a written offer is drawn up and immediately sent to them.

The campaign is an unconditional success, causing both the switchboard and licence administration in Birkerød permanent overtime for several months. Money comes pouring in, and although – for accounting reasons – it can't be recognised as the total subscription sum for the year's turnover, and despite customers continuing to pay for multi-year agreements for a year at a time, it's a very attractive business. Apart from the cost of marketing and managing the subscriptions, the company has no additional costs. No software – other than what is already being developed in advance – needs to be developed, and delivering the updates happens electronically and practically without logistical costs. The marginal costs associated with an update subscription are close to zero; hence, the entire gross margin, after marketing and administration costs, is pure profit. All in all, subscription sales grow by 42 per cent from 1997 to 1998, while growth in the first half of 1999 is at 122 per cent compared with the same period the previous year.

## Internal challenges

The takeover of distribution in DACH and Benelux involves a great many changes. The intellectual property rights to the products lie in Damgaard International, which also operates the XAL Services companies in Germany and the Netherlands. As Damgaard International is 50 per cent owned by IBM, all aspects have to be dealt with using the "arm's length" principle: all agreements have to be entered into as though they were completely separate legal entities without the same ownership. To ensure against any unforeseen complications, Concorde Software wants to take over only the activities, not the companies themselves. Thus, new companies have to be set-up and all employees need new employment contracts. The cost of taking over leases, fixtures and IT equipment has to be negotiated as does brand new distribution agreements, including an agreement about who will be responsible for product management, product marketing, support and localisation.

Indeed, since embarking on internationalisation in 1994, localisation has caused considerable trouble. Attempting to understand in detail the legislation and market requirements of the individual countries for the localisation of the products from headquarters in Birkerød has proven difficult. Concorde Software, therefore, wants to hire local product managers and perhaps also local development teams to be able to respond more quickly to market demands. As the product strategy requires the same product for all markets, a structure with decentralised product managers and local developers would require significant coordination. The agreements between Concorde Software and Damgaard International now have to determine who will undertake which tasks and, as a consequence of that, who will pay for what and who will subsequently own the rights to the different product elements.

Although the formal transfer date from IBM is 1st March, negotiating the terms continues tirelessly for months. Discussions take place primarily between Damgaard Data Holding and Damgaard International in Birkerød and don't involve the country managers.

## Millions for recruiting

When a company externally recruits people in large numbers and establishes many new foreign subsidiaries in a short period of time, management culture is put through a tough trial. Both Per Pedersen and Preben Damgaard are quite aware of this challenge, and it explains why they largely post people abroad whom they already know, despite it being an expensive solution in the short term. If no qualified candidates exist within the network when recruiting salespeople and managers, then professional head-hunters are always called in. Damgaard Data bases its quite careful selection of candidates on their personal qualities, and puts less emphasis on their previous employment and academic background. In 1998 alone, after the takeover of distribution in DACH and Benelux, several million dollars are invested in recruitment. An amount that rises steadily over the following years as the organisation expands further.

## New business partner contracts

Despite partners in the new markets generally being happy with Concorde Software taking over the ropes of the distribution activities, the German resellers, in particular, use the opportunity to renegotiate their formal agreements. Whereas IBM had clout and the strength to force through its standard agreements, the newly launched Concorde Software isn't in such a position. A large group of business partners form an association to present a united front in the negotiations with their new distributor. They are absolutely against uniform reseller agreements across all countries that are formulated in English and based on Danish law. The new agreements must be in German, be based on German law and any dispute has to be settled by a German court.

The contract negotiations last for over six months, swallowing many resources, but when they are concluded, every partner signs. The new, thoroughly negotiated contracts prove to be a major advantage. New resellers, who come aboard later, understand they must enter into an agreement on the same terms as the others and, furthermore, they appreciate that the contracts have been drawn up in cooperation with their colleagues. When the agreements are in place, the Business Partner Association is dissolved and replaced by a Council of Business Partners, which Concorde Software itself appoints. Similar local agreements are now developed for all foreign markets, making partner recruitment significantly easier.

## Germany pulls its weight

When Preben visits the new subsidiaries in Germany and the Netherlands in June 1998 and participates in meetings with the resellers, he can see, hear and feel the difference in mood and tempo. There are still many challenges, but there is commitment, progress and, not least, increasing revenue.

Near the turn of the century, antiquated financial systems clearly need to be replaced worldwide, and the plan to introduce the single European currency as of 1st January 1999 has further boosted demand in Europe.

It's unclear how the market will look on the other side, so it's about taking advantage of the strong demand as much as possible now.

It's Preben's impression that the market has welcomed the change from IBM, but that Concorde Software still has limited capacity in its new subsidiaries, which limits the yield. He and Per Pedersen discuss how to get a greater share of the large market, and the conclusion is that heavier investment is needed in building up the German market.

Around 50 resellers have been recruited, of which five to ten, with DITEC as the largest, have good growth potential. The organisation is in place and via Navision Software's long-running solid efforts, the market knows that Danish financial management systems are high quality.

An aggressive growth plan is to ensure that Concorde Software has a good chance in the German-speaking markets to year-end. When the plan is approved by management, it contains the following elements:

- The introduction of Axapta to the German-speaking markets is aimed for the middle of 1999 at the earliest.
- Subsidiaries are to be established in Austria and Switzerland and local country managers are appointed, who then form part of a DACH management team, which coordinates all market-oriented activities. The country managers have to function as partner account managers, too, at first.
- A marketing department is to be established in each country.
- A joint product manager function is to be established.
- Support is to be established in Austria, while support for Switzerland will continue to be handled from Germany.
- Business account managers are to be hired (for recruitment and management) in Hamburg, Berlin, Munich and the Ruhr district.
- Funds are to be set aside for nationwide advertising campaigns and marketing and sales activities, which can be implemented in collaboration with resellers.
- Additional funds are to be set aside to ensure a continuous presence in the German trade press.

It is impossible to estimate what the plan, which requires an investment of about 3 million USD in the first year, will bring about in sales. Neither Preben nor Per thinks it makes sense to guess a number, so it's decided to implement the plan as soon as possible. The results will have to be seen. Once the plan has had time to work by the turn of the year, everyone will be wiser and it will be possible to set a real budget for targets and funds in 1999.

## Columbus and the global roll out

Columbus IT Partner puts on the pressure to boost internationalisation. It calls, for instance, for a plan for France, where it already has a number of installations through international customer projects. It would be obvious to use them as a springboard for a deeper penetration of the large market. It has also moved into Singapore and would like to achieve more in Asia, but country-specific versions of Axapta are needed as well as some technical changes to the foundation of the product so it can handle Chinese characters. Columbus has its eye on South America, too, and it would like to find a way to jointly start in the distant Asian and South American markets.

After all the problems with IBM, management in Damgaard Data is extremely careful regarding new experimental forms of partnerships and, in particular, getting too close to Columbus as it's primarily a reseller, not a distributor. Whereas there is good chemistry between Per Pedersen and Lars Andersen, things don't quite click between Preben Damgaard and Michael Gaardboe. Preben has a great deal of respect for the work they have done as resellers and, not least, for the recent stock market listing, where Michael and Lars earned 36.4 million USD for themselves and 15.6 million for the company. But he prefers an arm's length relationship. Mixing distributor with reseller isn't high on Preben's list of favourite things. The structure in Eastern Europe only came about because there were no other immediate alternatives. Columbus is awarded distribution rights in Singapore, but the rest is just talk.

## On the way to the stock market

Under the radar, Preben Damgaard starts to investigate the process of a stock market listing and he discusses the project with the chairman of the board, Henning Kruse Petersen, in early 1998.

Since the company's inception in 1984, Preben and Erik have never been accountable to anyone but themselves. They bootstrapped from the outset – an injection of capital wasn't ever a reason for the partnership with IBM; that was motivated purely by the possibility of quicker internationalisation.

Rumours circulate that Navision Software is considering an IPO, and although Jesper Balser rejects the story as a "hoax", it would make sense. But a strengthening of the competitor's capital foundation and global visibility could be a serious threat on both the domestic and international market fronts.

However, Preben's research reveals that IBM's joint ownership of Damgaard International puts a spanner in the works when it comes to a listing. It's time to get things wrapped up, so an elegant exit can be made as soon as possible.

## 18 months to a stock market listing

In early August, Per and Preben again discuss the global rollout. Experience from DACH and Benelux is good, and if they are to exploit the technological head start enjoyed by the company with Axapta, as well as rely on the wave of demand emerging from the turn of the millennium, then things need to move fast.

However, the internationalisation model of establishing their own subsidiaries is costly, but is considered the model that will ensure the fastest and most reliable results. The partnership with IBM has to be concluded, and it is only a question of when and how to achieve the most advantageous unwinding. Thereafter, there is only one way forward: a stock market listing, which can raise the capital for further internationalisation.

The assessment of the company's value, which will form the basis of pricing the shares will depend – to a large degree – on the extent to which the company can document its ability to exploit the international growth potential. The stock market listing has to happen before the turn of the millennium. The uncertainty around demand on the other side of this cut-off date is too great to wait for until post-2000. There is less than 18 months to document that the company has a business model and a base that can be scaled globally.

To set up in Asia where they aren't yet present, Per and Preben decide to move into Australia. A Dane is to be posted abroad to start up the activities. He or she must immediately find an experienced local person, who can then take charge of the subsequent expansion of the organisation and the building up of the reseller channel.

They decide to move into Spain and France according to the same model. However, here the posted Danish country managers are to establish the organisation and reseller network within a three-year period. Portugal may follow in the wake of Spain in 2000, after which the possibility of accessing the South American markets via that position will be evaluated. Italy is on schedule for 2001. In the USA, Norway and Sweden, the partnership with IBM will continue – for now.

## A young man travels to Australia

Jakob Schou lands the Australia assignment. He has been employed by the company for a year, and despite his modest experience within the IT industry, he has earned good figures as a sales consultant.

He has no idea of his new job when he knocks on the open door to Per Pedersen's office. This is the first time the two talk. Per asks him to come in, gets up from his desk, and together they go to a globe standing on the windowsill. Per turns the globe round, points to Australia and asks what Jakob would say to going Down Under and starting a subsidiary?

Thirty-year-old Jakob has a great appetite for experiences, adventure and his career, and he can hardly believe his own eyes and ears. Every employee knows that internationalisation has the highest priority and, therefore, the undivided attention of management. To be offered a front row seat to the show can't be turned down. The post is initially estimated at three months. Then a local country manager must be found to take over the activities. Jakob gets 24 hours to consider the opportunity and discuss it with his girlfriend. That same evening he says yes.

A few days before Jakob is due to leave, Per invites him to lunch. They talk about what needs to be done once he has arrived in Australia. Over coffee, when the plan seems clear, Per explains to young Jakob that he must use his own judgement in the many decisions to be taken on the other side of the globe. There will undoubtedly be a few wrong turns every so often, but Per will accept responsibility and help get things back on track. In return, Jakob will get all the praise for what goes well.

On 1st September, Jakob heads for Sydney.

## Language barriers in Spain

With the activity in Australia, a mark has been made on the other side of the globe, and with the establishment of a subsidiary, recruiting one or two handfuls of resellers as well as the first customers, the flotation prospectus could contain an expectation for scaling in this part of the world, too.

There is still no mark in the Latin countries. South America is probably the largest market, but it is both physically and mentally too far away. Spain has proven to be a good market for Navision Software and seems more approachable than both France and Italy, both of which are reputed to be quite protectionist.

There isn't a great distance from thought to action at Damgaard Data, and as there is no time to carry out long-term market research, it seems better to take the plunge and change course as challenges are encountered.

Damgaard Data jumps in with both feet, and in October, after four weeks of intensive Spanish lessons, Flemming Beisner, head of the Danish activities, transfers to Madrid, where he moves into an office hotel to start building up the organisation and activities.

He promptly invites potential business partners to an event. Fifty people turn up. As Flemming and the other Danes from the office in Birkerød, who are responsible for the presentation of Axapta, still don't speak Spanish, and as they can't be sure of the English proficiency of the participants, simultaneous interpretation is organised. It's a good idea, because the English level of the Spanish participants isn't particularly good. At the following lunch, however, the situation becomes awkward. Language barriers means it's impossible to start a proper dialogue with the aspiring resellers.

It's now clear that there are fundamental language barriers outside of the English-speaking markets that need to be addressed before embarking on activities with potential customers and resellers. Flemming recruits Spanish-speaking staff to be responsible for reseller recruitment, training and support.

Again, the activities in Spain benefit from Navision Software's solid preparatory work. There is already a great knowledge of and respect for Danish financial management software. Flemming positions Concorde Software as the "big brother" of Financials and finds it surprisingly easy to enter into talks with new resellers. Marketing activities are initiated to create awareness of Axapta and to create demand for the new partners.

However, the efforts in Spain suffer from Axapta being somewhat buggy and not available in a Spanish version. Screen displays and documentation have been translated into Spanish, but again there is a lack of features required by the local legislation, and features that support financial management practices in Spain haven't been developed and included in the standard product. The first Spanish version of Axapta comes out in summer 1999, so in the meantime, Flemming Beisner, his team and the resellers have to be content with serving those customers who can live using another central financial system and those who can wait for that part of the solution.

## Systematic PR work

The active media presence has been silent since Michael Sander stopped as head of PR in summer 1996. It hasn't resulted in a reduction in the press's coverage of the company, rather the opposite. However, it has meant that initiatives for publicity have come from the outside, and in a number of situations the angle or circumstances have been unfortunate. Preben would like to have better control of working with the media and, in particular, to pave a professional way towards the future stock market listing. Moreover, the attention continuously gained via the outbound media activity must also benefit the subsidiaries.

To accomplish the task, a new communications manager is sought, and on 1st June 1998 Regitze Reeh comes aboard. Preben proposes engaging an international PR agency that has offices in all the countries in which they are going to operate, but Regitze has another idea. Communication at home is very different compared to abroad: in Denmark, they are already a well-known brand, so it's about continuing to profile the company and laying the foundation for the future stock market listing. Essentially, the company has to expand its press coverage to the daily press and other nationwide media.

Concorde Software is an unknown entity outside of Denmark, so relationships with and coverage in the trade media have to be built up first. The business model with resellers and the company's advanced but, in principle, invisible products would be better managed by specialised boutique PR agencies. That structure would also take advantage of being a large client of a smaller business; whereas being a client of a large international agency could easily mean ending up at the end of their list of priorities. Preben gives Regitze free rein to implement her plan.

She helps the subsidiaries find the most suitable agencies, after which the local press activities are put in the hands of the country managers. Regitze handles the coordination and sends newsletters to the agencies in the countries, which include information about the news originating from the headquarters in Birkerød. From time to time, everyone in PR gathers to discuss the completed activities, the results and plans for the future. Establishing systematic PR work becomes an integral part of the activities of all subsidiaries, and the results are positive.

In Germany, Regitze engages a small public relations agency in Munich, which specialises in the IT industry. Together with the head of the German subsidiary, she systematically visits the editors from the most important German newspapers and journals and shares Damgaard's plans after the takeover of distribution from IBM.

The charm offensive works. A lot of positive articles are now featured in the media about the small Danish company that has taken over from the mighty IBM and has big plans for Germany. The initiative once again benefits from Navision Software already being a widely used and re-spected brand in the German market. In fact, Navision Software and Damgaard Data are perceived as major, internationally-oriented compa-nies that invest seriously in the German market. Despite both companies being far smaller than most local German competitors, they are held in great respect by the customers who, in many cases, would rather choose an international supplier, who can service their international subsidiar-ies, too – something the local competitors rarely can.

## Columbus "fakes" its role in Eastern Europe

At the end of August, Preben Damgaard and the management of Damgaard International take stock of the partnership with Columbus as a distributor and find that it's not looking good. The goal of the three-year exclusive agreement, entered into in spring 1998, was to safeguard Columbus's peace of mind so it could build up a distribution business and establish a reseller channel to ensure the penetration of Concorde XAL in the Eastern European markets. However, they are primarily still selling directly to their own customers. They only use their distributor status to obtain a better gross margin.

According to the agreement, they were to present business plans for the individual markets. The plans were a long time coming and when they finally did arrive, they were somewhat thin. The expected revenue was also far below the goal previously agreed. They were also to devel-op country-specific versions of Axapta and provide local versions of the product documentation. That didn't happen either.

The challenge was that Columbus's subsidiaries were established for direct project sales and had no tradition of or skills or incentives to recruit resellers, who would become competitors. The handling of the distribution would require the creation of a new business entity in each country and a complete separation from the project activities. No initiatives were taken in any of the countries, and only one person was allocated to global distribution in the Danish headquarters. It was far too little for such an endeavour.

The conditions are now discussed with the management of Columbus, which responds to the criticisms with an account of the massive product issues they experience with Axapta. The switch from XAL to Axapta has proven significantly more difficult than expected.

Firstly, the product is defective, which causes the company unforeseen costs and delays projects. Secondly, Axapta isn't on the same level as XAL in terms of functionality. That surprised Columbus and has meant it has had to add the functionality, which was contractually promised to customers, at its own expense. Thirdly, in contrast to XAL, Axapta is a completely empty product. There are neither account templates nor demo data to make it easier to get started with the implementation of the product. Both parties have underestimated what retraining and training was needed to move consultants and programmers from one product to the other. They have also underestimated the extent to which new customers would want to implement Axapta rather than XAL. The announcement of Axapta has made it impossible to sell XAL to the type of projects, which Columbus focuses on. They agree that Axapta is technologically advanced and far ahead of any competitor, but the product has bugs and lacks the basic functionality offered as standard by XAL and the competing products. For Columbus, which much more than any other reseller focuses on new markets and new projects, Axapta's quality and maturity problems hit hard. And despite the kitty being well-stocked by the stock market listing, the aggressive expansion strategy and the problems with Axapta devour both liquidity and management capacity.

Damgaard International believes the challenges of Axapta and the distribution in Eastern Europe are two entirely different things, but as they are busy getting the rest of Europe and the USA up and running, Columbus is allowed to continue with its distribution activities.

## A change of HR manager

The organisation development function, headed by HR manager Sven Tvermoes, hits a bit of an anti-climax after the completion of Learning-to-Learn in 1997. What should replace the ambitious and successful project? Inspired by his work with adolescents with behavioural issues, Sven Tvermoes initiates the Blue Vision project, where groups of employees participate in a few days' ocean sailing. But the project doesn't include all employees, and many of the participants don't fancy being on the open sea in a strong gale.

The company now has 300 employees. The intake of new employees continues to rise, including an increasing number of employees abroad. The feedback, received by Preben, on the ongoing staff development projects is mixed and with the strong growth in and the dispersion of the number of employees, he finds there is a need for new and continuous operational initiatives within HR and for ad hoc team building projects to a lesser extent.

There is a great need for recruitment to be continuously supported; for introductory programmes for new employees; for leadership development; for personal and professional development; for team building within the departments; for salary negotiations; for conflict resolution within the organisation and for dismissing staff who don't suit the culture or who aren't delivering.

Therefore, at the beginning of 1998, Preben proposes to the management team that responsibility for organisational development now be delegated to the individual functional areas, knowing full well that it isn't a permanent solution. Unsurprisingly, the hand over is received positively, giving Preben much needed respite to find a long-term solution, which ends in replacing the HR manager.

## Freddie B. Jørgensen comes aboard

Preben rings Freddie B. Jørgensen. They meet in early June to discuss the vision, work and challenges. Preben and Freddie have known each other since the early 1990s, when the latter was HR manager at DEC Denmark and helped Preben prepare for the major reorganisation in mid-1993. They have kept in touch ever since and Preben is convinced that Freddie is the right man for the strategy and organisational development job, which, from now on, will be of a completely different nature. Not least due to the impending divorce from IBM, the increased internationalisation and the approaching stock market listing.

Freddie is currently director of staff and organisational development at the Egmont Group, a job that is much greater on paper than the one Preben can offer and, therefore, he politely declines at first. But his thoughts continue to return to his conversation with Preben. He can see the obvious potential and the solidity of the company. Helping to put a small Danish company on the world map would be a meaningful undertaking. And it would include the opportunity to work with Preben Damgaard, whom he greatly respects and gets on well with.

Freddie changes his mind, and by the end of June they have agreed on the job description and terms. On 22nd June, Sven Tvermoes is laid off and the company will have to get by without a HR manager until Freddie formally starts on 1st October 1998. Freddie, who will be responsible for management and employee development, organisational development and implementation of the strategic development process, also becomes a member of the executive office along with Erik Damgaard, Preben Damgaard and Per Pedersen.

Prior to starting, Preben asks Freddie to attend a meeting in Erik Damgaard's small holiday apartment in the south of France. He, Erik, Per Pedersen and Jens Haugaard fly to Nice, where they are to meet Preben, who is finishing up his holidays. With the French Riviera as the backdrop, they discuss future strategy and organisational structure. How the company is to be organised when IBM pulls out of the partnership needs to be thoroughly deliberated.

## More criticism of IBM

With IBM out of the picture, it no longer makes sense for Damgaard International to continue as a separate legal entity with its own board, directorship and so on. It would also be natural to place the entire responsibility for distribution under Per Pedersen's Concorde Software, which is already responsible for the foreign subsidiaries. Moreover, significant savings have to be found in all corners of the group to help finance international expansion, which will no longer be co-financed by IBM. Indeed, rapid international expansion is needed if the company is to ensure an attractive evaluation prior to an IPO. It will require the company to demonstrate the ability to grow internationally. Growth opportunities in the small domestic market have been largely exhausted.

During the flight to Nice, Freddie hears Erik Damgaard be quite critical of Jens Haugaard, who, as a former IBM employee, has involuntarily been awarded the role of IBM's representative and, thus, a scapegoat for all that IBM has neglected during the, barely, five years of the partnership.

When they are gathered in Erik's apartment, the conversations quickly turn to whom is to actually leave the organisation once IBM is gone, whom will be left and what posts they should have. Preben, who employed Freddie to be responsible for personnel and organisation, expects him to take the lead in the restructuring. Erik, who is infuriated by what he perceives as IBM's failure to live up to its distribution commitment, wants everyone related to IBM out of the organisation. He believes IBM delayed international penetration with its lack of effort. Certainly, IBM's lukewarm commitment in the USA, which was to ensure solid marketing for the new Axapta, has cost momentum and market share. A thorough spring clean is now needed, according to Erik, so skilled and effective people can be assigned the posts.

Strategy isn't really discussed during the stay, but it's presumed to be contained in the overall plan. However, the future HR manager is well aware that significant organisational changes are required in connection with IBM's exit. When the group lands at Kastrup airport, a list of staff reductions has already been compiled – and Freddie brings it with him everywhere.

## Challenges in Australia

When the activities in Australia start in September 1998, Navision Software has already paved the way, proving that software from Denmark is definitely something to be taken seriously. After opening a bank account and finding office space overlooking the Sydney Harbour Bridge, work on recruiting the first resellers begins. A well-known but expensive head-hunter is engaged to find the future country manager; someone who can bring gravitas to the role. Michael Kofoed from XAL Services in the UK is called in as head of support and training. Apart from helping to recruit and train new resellers, he also has to clarify which country-specific features should be added to Axapta in order for it to work in Australia.

It isn't difficult to set up meetings with potential resellers in the aftermath of Navision's sound preparatory work. Concorde Software initially positions Axapta for medium and large businesses; thereby, avoiding direct competition with Navision Financials, which has a good grasp of the slightly smaller companies. Potential resellers and customers are amazed when Michael and Jakob demonstrate the new Axapta. Emphasis is placed on how partners can tailor the system to customers' needs, and Axapta is absolutely the best system on the market when it comes to this. How customers are to use the system in their daily work is skimmed over.

However, whereas efforts to recruit business partners go smoothly, there are major challenges in adapting Axapta for Australian market requirements. When resellers attend training, they discover that Axapta lacks basic features such as handling Australian Sales Tax and generating the reports that have to be regularly filed with the authorities. Customers are right to expect this type of functionality as standard – something Damgaard International agrees on. It just hasn't been developed yet. It's a long way from Australia to Birkerød, and the list of problems flowing into Damgaard International from all the countries is growing ever longer and longer.

An office has been opened in Australia, but when you are struggling to enter many markets simultaneously, not everything can be given the highest priority.

## Fierce competition in the UK

In late summer 1995, IBM assigned only a single employee to the task of building up an XAL reseller channel for the British market and, during the autumn, they began training the first partners. XAL was launched in spring 1996 at a hotel in the trendy Tower Bridge area of London to the theme of "The Vikings are back". The event, which was extremely well-attended, received good press coverage, and the optimism of both Damgaard Data and IBM was great.

However, both reseller recruitment and licence sales were slow, so to support the activities, Damgaard International opened a service office in Birmingham in autumn 1996. In spring 1997, the former Large Account employee, Michael Ammentorp, was appointed director of the office. Until then, IBM had only succeeded in recruiting 12 resellers. When Michael took stock of the situation in August 1998, there was, after some replacements, still only 12.

IBM's endeavours are utterly inadequate to get started in the large British market. The UK, which Damgaard Data has been trying to enter since the late 1980s, is Europe's second largest market. Apart from German SAP, which serves only the largest of all companies, the only other outsider that has managed to gain some visibility on the market is the American Great Plains Software, due to the massive investments it made in its own organisation and marketing. That IBM is undisputedly the largest IT provider in the UK isn't a decisive factor given its unwillingness to invest more than a single employee and some meagre marketing funds in the project. The Concorde XAL project drowns in IBM's gigantic organisation and receives no managerial attention.

## Michael writes a memo

Michael Ammentorp writes a long memo to Damgaard International's management about the situation in the British market. He describes how he considers IBM's efforts insufficient to achieve anything meaningful in the market, and that the activities can't justify the long-term retention of XAL Services.

When he talks to Preben Damgaard, during a visit to Birkerød, he senses that the latter hasn't seen the note. Preben would like a copy, and a few days later, Michael is told to book a meeting the next time he is in the area.

The meeting happens a few weeks later. Michael reports that after almost three years on the market, Concorde XAL still doesn't meet local requirements. Despite XAL Services being fully capable of specifying the demands, Country Specific Engineering in Birkerød hasn't succeeded in getting the British version right. IBM has allocated far too few employees to building up the reseller channel in the UK. In reality, there is only a handful of decent resellers actively selling projects with XAL. With the enormous competitive pressure on the UK market, XAL – and soon Axapta – will never play any part with IBM at the helm. Not because IBM is doing the wrong things. It's just doing too little. And it's doing it half-heartedly. Michael also believes that Damgaard International in Birkerød lacks international experience, experience dealing with subsidiaries and management with charisma and clout. They are friendly, nice people, but there is too little drive. Either they don't share the same concern over IBM's lack of effort or they are lacking the ability to do something about it.

Preben thanks Michael for his thorough and candid briefing. Michael can't know that his input will have a decisive influence on the outcome of a number of strategic considerations regarding a few people in top management. Neither does Michael know that despite the miserable results, management hasn't dared to cut ties with IBM in the UK. They were nervous about starting a domino effect that would pull IBM out of the activities in the USA before a solid Plan B was in place. Plan B has now been implemented in DACH and Benelux, and the results have evoked confidence in Damgaard's ability to achieve its goals in the UK and the USA.

The partnership with IBM in the UK continues and, in October, IBM issues a press statement on the release of Axapta, announcing that the large, nationwide commercial system company Fraser Williams, with almost 700 employees, is one of the first resellers.

## Late nights at the office

At a rough estimate, the Damgaard Group uses around 20 million USD on the development of Axapta until its release in March 1998. The product is probably the world's most technologically advanced financial management system, but a number of problems quickly come to light, some of which surprise management.

Damgaard Data has launched four products since 1984: Danmax (1984), Concorde Økonomi (1986), Concorde XAL (1991) and Concorde C5 (based on XAL) (1995). Concorde Økonomi replaced Danmax, and almost every reseller accepted the new product immediately. Concorde XAL was designed for large projects and aimed at a different customer segment than Concorde Økonomi. Most resellers continue to sell Concorde Økonomi while only a dozen take on XAL, after which several new, large and professional resellers come aboard in the following years. Thus, no significant competition arises between Concorde Økonomi and XAL. When Concorde C5 is released, almost all Concorde Økonomi resellers add the new product to their catalogues, while the XAL resellers maintain their focus. Yet again, there is only minimal competition between the products.

Axapta starts out as Concorde XAL 3.0, which it is intended to replace from the start. At this point, Damgaard Data is dealing with customers who are very much aware that their future investment in a new financial management system will see them through a number of years. Therefore, they aren't thrilled about acquiring a system that is about to be phased out. Moreover, in spite of its maturity, robustness and extensive functionality, XAL is perceived as technologically obsolete, particularly with regard to the development tools that don't run on the market-dominating Windows operating system.

When they hear news of a new product on the way, customers are reluctant to invest in XAL. Furthermore, XAL becomes known as "the old system" and Axapta "the new system" – and who would want to invest in or work with the old system?

After working on the development of Axapta for some time, Erik Damgaard decides to drop its compatibility with XAL. This definitely puts an end to the idea that those customers, who are considering starting with XAL, can move, relatively painlessly, over to the new product. Therefore, to avoid a fall in revenue from XAL, without having a replacement stream, getting Axapta to market is urgent.

Whereas the Danish resellers are ready to accept the XAL replacement, it is completely different in those countries where IBM is or has been responsible for distribution. There is major opposition to having to invest in a new product again in Norway, Sweden, Germany, Austria and Switzerland, in particular, as resellers there have only had a couple of years to see any return on their XAL investments. The competitive situation in the German-speaking markets is completely different from Denmark, and XAL's slightly dated technology doesn't really factor. There isn't the same opposition to Axapta in the UK and in Benelux, probably helped by the fact that there aren't yet any resellers committed wholeheartedly to XAL. In the USA, and the other countries where the activities have to be started first, Axapta will be the only product marketed.

But when Axapta is released, massive problems emerge. The XAL resellers, with Columbus at the head, underestimate the amount of training needed to reach the same level of skill as they have with XAL. The development tools work completely different than in XAL; it's a new data model and the standard functionality of the application modules is far from that of XAL. This means resellers end up with off-scope customer projects, which take longer and require more consulting resources than those allocated in customer contracts. Moreover, the first versions of Axapta are delivered without demo data and standard templates, which makes it difficult to set up a test system and get users trained in the most basic elements. There are also a disproportionate amount of bugs in the product that require documentation and reporting to Damgaard International to be corrected. Simultaneously launching in several countries puts huge pressure on getting the country-specific versions in place.

Actually, the situation isn't unusual for a software company going through international growth. This is just the first time the company is trying a product change on such a large scale, while taking over from IBM, moving into a number of new countries and preparing a stock market listing all at the same time. The pressure on the organisation is immense and there are many late nights at the offices in Birkerød and its subsidiaries around the world.

However, there are also a number of conditions that play in favour of the company. Firstly, it's financially very well-cushioned. It's possible to assign extra resources where they are most needed without running into liquidity problems. Secondly, the many challenges aren't immediately visible to new resellers and customers. Externally, Damgaard Data is a successful company in strong growth, and Axapta is a product at the forefront of technology. Once new resellers and customers have decided to invest in a partnership and in the new product, it isn't easy to get out of. In the vast majority of cases, it may be better to roll up the sleeves and make it work rather than ending the collaboration, stopping the project or finding any other alternative.

After the summer holidays in 1998, when the first feedback of Axapta comes in, a number of new initiatives are taken. The continued development and support of Concorde XAL is officially announced as is the product's ability to handle the euro when it becomes legal tender on 1st January 1999. It is emphasised that Axapta *isn't* a replacement for XAL but is a new product with a different purpose, different technology and many other new features. That's not quite historically accurate, but as more resources are assigned to XAL, the new positioning and announcement can be vouched for. Management decides to wait until 1999 to introduce Axapta outside of Denmark and in the USA. To that end, an extraordinary effort must be made to have the product completely ready when it's released for sale. It is decided to focus on recruiting new resellers for Axapta and not to put pressure on XAL resellers to make the change before they themselves believe they are ready. And lastly, it's decided to establish a team of consultants based in Birkerød, who can travel to new resellers at short notice and help them get their first Axapta customers into production. The group is nicknamed "the SWAT team" – *Special Weapons And Tactics* – forces sent in when the shit hits the fan and the situation gets critical.

The initiatives actually create calm among the resellers, and customers continue to buy XAL. The level of internal pressure is unchanged, but with these announcements, the marketing and technical challenges have once again been separated. The recruitment of new Axapta partners is intensified. The general marketing focuses on the company; not on the products. Thus, the marketing benefits all business partners.

Discussions among the resellers continue regarding the positioning of the products, but there is no desire for blunt announcements; rather they rely on it being the customer's own choice. Customers continue to ask resellers about the markets and type of work at which the products are aimed, but the answers no longer come from Damgaard Data.

## New logo; new name

Navision Software has had the clear advantage of the company and product names being identical. Damgaard Data has enjoyed a great level of brand awareness in Denmark for both Concorde and Damgaard Data. Therefore, there is no pressing need to change the name. When IBM and Columbus were responsible for distribution outside of Denmark, there was no need to market the name Damgaard Data either.

The establishment of foreign subsidiaries at the beginning of 1998 was done under the name Concorde Software in order to create recognition between the products and the company behind them. However, there is a risk that the name Concorde could cause problems when it comes to a stock market listing. With a thick bankbook, the company could find itself the target of expensive lawsuits with high claims for damages.

Thus, after consulting an advertising agency, management decides to standardise all the companies under the name of Damgaard in October; a new logo is introduced at the same time.

*"We are so well-known today in Denmark that we can delete the word "data".*
*It is a slightly old-fashioned word now, too. But we were unsure, which*
*company name we should use outside of Denmark," says managing director,*
*Preben Damgaard. "The choice fell on Damgaard, a family name with a*
*story attached. And that's far better than some new-found fancy name that*
*no-one knows or can relate to," says Preben Damgaard* (Computerworld,
*27th November 1998*).

A few weeks later, Damgaard Data ServicePartner A/S changes its name to Damgaard Consulting A/S, and to further emphasise that the company isn't competing with the resellers, Per Pedersen steps in as chairman of the board.

## Exit IBM

In April 1998, Larry Sheffield, who is to take another job at IBM in the USA, steps down from the board of Damgaard International. He is replaced by Michel Boussard, head of all IBM's activities aimed at small and medium-sized businesses in Europe, the Middle East and Africa. At the operational level, it is Pat Falotico, based in Atlanta, in the USA, who continues to try to make the partnership work.

As Damgaard takes over distribution in DACH and Benelux and opens offices in Australia and Spain, the contrast to the effort made by IBM becomes even more pronounced. The disagreement regarding the necessary investment in the marketing of Axapta in the UK, and especially in the USA, intensifies over the first half of 1998, and as Damgaard International is simultaneously running out of money, IBM is forced to decide whether or not it will continue as an active investor.

At a meeting on 8ᵗʰ October 1998, where IBM is represented by Pat Falotico and Carsten Jørring, they announce that IBM wants to withdraw from all markets and that it no longer wants to be an active partner in the project. It wants to keep its equity share, but it will be a passive investor. This also means that it won't participate in the forthcoming round of funding in which Damgaard International is to be provided with fresh capital.

The ownership of Damgaard International is no longer strategic for IBM, and the collaboration has obviously become a shackle for both parties. It's agreed at the meeting that Pat Falotico will submit a draft contract for the termination of the partnership, while Carsten Jørring will ask IBM's finance department in Paris to draw up a proposal for the terms under which IBM can retain or divest its equity share. The meeting proceeds without any drama. Both parties see a divorce as the best solution. How the divorce of the shareholder plan is to be implemented in practice lies in the hands of IBM's M&A department in Paris.

## Have to put their hands in their pockets

A few weeks later, Preben is contacted by Henrik E. Nyegaard, who tells him that IBM in Paris has forwarded the basis for the handling of its equity share of Damgaard International. They should meet as soon as possible to get an agreement in place. When Preben is sitting in Henrik's office a few days later, the latter has to regretfully acknowledge that there isn't much to discuss. The M&A department in Paris have given three options and they are non-negotiable:

1. IBM retains its equity share of Damgaard International, but doesn't participate in further funding rounds.
2. The equity share of Damgaard International be swapped for 15 per cent of Damgaard Data Holding, which includes all of the group's activities.
3. 15 million USD be put down in cash for the 50 per cent of Damgaard International. After which, IBM is out.

Preben returns to the office in Birkerød and puts Erik in the picture. They agree that Damgaard should aim for a stock market listing. That plan won't be possible if IBM continues as co-owner in any shape or form. According to the shareholders' agreement, IBM can be bought out in 2000 at the earliest and Damgaard can't wait that long. So, the first option isn't feasible.

If Damgaard is to be listed on the stock exchange, it would be at an evaluation significantly above the estimated 200 million USD, at which Columbus is presently quoted. This would mean that IBM could make at least 30 million USD on a 15 per cent stake. Given IBM's announcement that it will no longer be active in the partnership, Erik and Preben can't see why it should be rewarded for initiatives taken by Damgaard on the way to the IPO. Option two isn't viable either.

That leaves option three.

Despite owning shares in Damgaard, the brothers aren't particularly liquid. They might both drive Mercedes-Benz sports cars, but they were bought used in Germany and subsequently imported with a reduced vehicle registration tax. There is enough on the bankbook to pay outstanding invoices, but they certainly don't have 15 million USD in cash. A stock market listing is six to nine months away, and there is no guarantee that the market and other conditions will allow it to happen then. Draining the group of their liquidity to buy out IBM would limit the internationalisation initiatives that are to contribute to the success of the stock market listing, and taking out loans on the companies would still require a personal guarantee from the owners.

After considering the possibilities, a few minutes of silence pass, before Erik says:

*"We have to put our hands in our pockets".*

Preben feels it's the right choice, too. He contacts and briefs the chairman of the board, Henning Kruse Pedersen. Henning promises to help get the credit in place, after which Preben calls Henrik Nyegaard at IBM, telling him he will drop by within the next few days with a cheque for 15 million USD.

Damgaard's legal department draws up the purchase agreement, which simultaneously annuls all other agreements between the two parties and on 4th November 1998, IBM is officially out of the picture.

Over the weekend of 7th and 8th November, the country managers of the foreign subsidiaries are informed of the decision, and on Monday, 9th November, all employees – at home and abroad – are called to an all-hands meeting, where they are informed of the divorce, its grounds and what is going to happen now. Later that day, press releases are issued and, over the course of the following days, the separation is read about in the daily and trade press around the world. *Computerworld* writes on 13th November 1998:

*On Monday, Damgaard's 400 employees were immediately informed at a joint meeting in Birkerød. The buying back of IBM's 50 per cent share of the [software] development company behind the 15-year-old financial management system, Concorde, Damgaard International A/S must have been a*

*popular decision. Staff received the news with a round of applause. [Being*
*in bed with IBM] was never really the employee's "cup of tea".*

A few weeks later, Pat Falotico visits the office in Birkerød to say goodbye and thank you for the partnership. She tells Erik and Preben that IBM was quite amazed they chose to write a cheque of 15 million USD. IBM had expected Damgaard to opt for the second choice, which didn't require any cash. People at IBM were, yet again, convinced that the brothers knew something that IBM didn't.

But Erik and Preben don't know anything that IBM shouldn't know. The dissimilarity in the perception of the situation is found in the difference in the mentality of managers, who are also entrepreneurs, and managers, who are also white collar workers. Only a few senior executives in a company such as IBM could ever imagine taking out a personal loan of 7.5 million USD to achieve business goals. Most salaried managers aren't educated in that scenario; incentives don't work like that at all in a large company like IBM. But Erik and Preben are the owners and executives of a company they started fourteen years earlier. They know the company inside and out, and they believe that they, together with the employees – now released from IBM – can deliver unusual results. Therefore, they choose to take the personal risk associated with borrowing 15 million USD, which is the prerequisite for the next step of the stock market listing becoming a reality.

The excitement at escaping IBM is immense among most of the employees, while management can see the positive in IBM and fully understand the challenge at now having to handle the major task of internationalisation alone. Navision Software has proven that a life without IBM need not be so bad. The experiences of establishing their own subsidiaries also bodes well. All in all, the future seems bright, and the optimism is great.

## Quick international adjustments

With IBM's exit, Damgaard International no longer needs to be a completely separate organisation with independent management and its own sales organisation. All sales and marketing activities are, therefore, assigned to Per Pedersen, who is already working on the divorce negotiations to ensure continuity once IBM lets go of the reins. Peter Wagner, sales director of Damgaard International, is sent to the USA as the new country manager. Otto Strandvig is named as country manager for the UK (he moved from his position as country manager for competitor Great Plains in Germany to a job as a partner account manager for Damgaard GmbH in northern Germany in April 1998). Tommy Ødegaard and Michael Uhman of IBM are appointed country managers of the newly established subsidiaries in Norway and Sweden respectively, where most of the existing employees are taken on, too. Jens Haugaard, who has been managing director of Damgaard International since spring 1995, returns to a position at IBM.

The company changes its name to Damgaard Development, but is run as an internal development department with Erik Damgaard as Chief Technology Officer, assisted by Jakob Hahn Michelsen and Carl-Erik Nielsen, who are responsible for personnel, coordination and planning. Damgaard is once again a whole company.

## What went wrong for IBM
## and right for Damgaard?

Retrospectively, it's a wonder the world's greatest IT company couldn't get the job done and fulfil its own aims of rolling out Concorde XAL globally. The explanation contains several factors. The most basic was that the gamble on OS/2 was an absolute disaster. The spread of OS/2 was supposed to have been supported by XAL, but IBM never succeeded in making any headway in the market that was to use the product. Thus, XAL lost its connection to a strategic IBM product and, therefore, it had difficulty gaining interest internally in IBM. There were several attempts to getting XAL to run on AS/400 and DB/2, but both technical challenges and the lack of sufficient demand among small and medium-sized businesses led to the initiatives not finding fertile soil.

Another factor was that the agreement was signed with IBM in Denmark and with people, who had only management responsibility in Scandinavia. Outside of the Nordic region, it was up to the individual IBM subsidiaries if they wanted to join. If they chose to, there were no accompanying resources. Any business areas from which resources were appropriated still had to deliver on their existing budgets. In other words, the activities were to finance themselves as early as the first year. It takes between three to five years to establish a position on a new market with a product such as XAL, and the subsidiaries weren't geared towards that type of long-term project.

IBM was primarily a hardware and service company in the 1990s. It had a wide range of software products, but they were all so-called middleware and tools. When it came to application software, such as XAL and Axapta, IBM worked closely with every supplier to ensure its hardware were included in as many projects as possible.

After the OS/2 project capsized, IBM has no general strategic interest in owning Damgaard International. The strategic mismatch becomes most apparent in the USA, where IBM very cleverly avoids mentioning that it actually owns half of the company behind Axapta at the product's announcement.

There was also a strong lack of synchronicity on the Damgaard International board. Damgaard Data's representatives had short chains of command and great authority to execute the decisions made, while IBM's representatives had no execution authority at all. For example, they couldn't influence the activities in the individual countries in any way, and despite being in contact with both top area and regional managers within IBM's organisation, it turned out that even their execution authority was limited.

When the partnership began in 1994, Damgaard International was in no way ready to deliver national versions of its products to a standard of quality, a schedule and with the level of documentation expected by IBM. It took several years for the processes to be put somewhat into place so IBM could be told what was coming when. Did that level of immaturity impact on the partnership's lack of results? The situation certainly didn't make it any easier for the few IBM people, who were to build up the market in each country. Had IBM got more customers and resellers started sooner, both the pressure and the basis for improving processes and products would probably have secured more resources and greater urgency internally.

Damgaard International didn't lack the technical skills to get the job done, but rather the commercial incentive to spend time on those variants for which there was little demand. A combination of a company like Damgaard International, which is at the forefront of technology with its products and, therefore, willing to put them to the test on the market early, and a company like IBM, which, wearing both belts and braces, will create major challenges. And it did.

Should management have predicted these factors when they entered into negotiations with IBM in 1993? Had Preben Damgaard consulted Jesper Balser from Navision Software, he might have learned something about the inner workings of IBM. Preben couldn't do that for good reason, and Jesper Balser certainly wasn't thrilled about the situation during the first months after his break with IBM. Keep in mind that Damgaard had been trying – unsuccessfully – for years to find the way onto the international markets and that in 1993-1994, despite enormous deficits in the previous years, IBM continued to enjoy quite special status and respect within the IT industry. That status is greatly eroded during the years of partnership with Damgaard International.

Moreover, IBM in Denmark was significantly different from IBM in the rest of the world. IBM Denmark was the most successful of all IBM's subsidiaries. In the market for PC-based solutions for small and medium-sized businesses alone, IBM in Denmark, through its Business Centers and Navigator from PC&C, had acquired unusually high market shares. Thus, in 1993-94, management in Damgaard had every reason to see a partnership with IBM as not only an opportunity to give competitor PC&C a punch in the gut, but as simultaneously giving an extra boost to international growth.

Should the management of Damgaard have called off the partnership earlier on? Actually, only six months pass before Preben Damgaard suspects something is wrong. However, the delays were well explained, and IBM's representatives on the board were optimistic, too. There was always the expectation that it would probably get better soon. When Larry Sheffield came over from the USA and laid big plans and figures on the table, hope and belief that a breakthrough was coming were once again renewed, and when IBM agreed to help start up in the USA, there was yet again good reasons to wait and see. When compared to reports of Navision Software's strong growth abroad, the partnership with IBM in Germany and the UK deteriorated rather than improved, which prompted Per Pedersen being sent in as a mole with an IBM business card to find out what was going wrong. When he reported six months later that it was an impossible task, Plan B was set in motion. Things moved fast from that point.

## The press guesses and speculates

As the break-up becomes common knowledge, more articles are naturally published in the daily press, but as both IBM's and Damgaard's representatives talk about the end of the partnership in positive terms and openly explain why the divorce makes sense, it's difficult for the press to write anything sensational. It, of course, speculates about how the divorce has happened in practice; how Damgaard bought IBM out and how much it cost, but both IBM and the Damgaard brothers keep quiet here. The press guesses and it guesses wrong. When Damgaard announces in December that they are planning a stock market listing, focus naturally moves to when it will happen, how much the company is worth and how much money Erik and Preben will earn on that occasion. The unfortunate partnership with IBM is quickly forgotten.

## Finally free

Internally, the mood after the break from IBM is close to euphoric. That Preben and Erik went to the bank personally and borrowed millions (no one knew then exactly how much) to present IBM with a cheque to buy it out evokes respect among the employees. The financial results are extremely reasonable, and even with the massive investment in product development and internationalisation, Damgaard is able to maintain a profit ratio of over ten per cent. Damgaard is in the technological lead with Axapta and, with IBM out of the picture, it can decide both the direction and speed.

For Preben and Erik, who once again own 98 per cent of the shares in the group, the coast is clear to an IPO. It is to raise the funds to repay the private loan of 15 million USD. But more importantly, it is to procure the capital that aggressive internationalisation requires.

Both Erik and Preben are convinced that Damgaard has the product and managerial potential to become a global supplier of ERP systems. They are also convinced that things will be significantly easier for the company, which is capable of becoming a market leader, than for the companies in third and fourth place or even further down in the ranking list.

They hold meetings with advisors and banks in mid-November to help with the valuation of the company and the marketing of the shares. It is estimated that the market value of the Damgaard Group is approximately 400 million USD; that roughly one third of the stock needs to be traded on the stock market and that the listing itself can happen in the second half of 1999, provided that the capital market is somewhat favourable at that time. Most important for the valuation and the demand for shares is that the company can show constant and significant growth, including, in particular, that Axapta shows progress in all markets.

A new board of directors is appointed in November with Hans Kristian Werdelin, former managing director of Sophus Berendsen, as chairman; Englishman Dennis Keeling, who is director of a kind of international trade association for financial management system suppliers; Peder Max, former head of Microsoft's sales company in Denmark and corporate and commercial lawyer Vagn Thorup, who has been on the board since 1993. Henning Kruse Pedersen, who has played a major role as chairman and mentor of Preben Damgaard since 1991, can't, as managing director of Nykredit, continue on the new board for technical reasons. Following the appointment of the new board of directors, a press release is issued, which also announces Damgaard's intention to seek admission on the Copenhagen Stock Exchange (now Nasdaq Copenhagen).

## The strategy

In December, intensive work is carried out on the strategy that is to form the basis for the IPO, which is to be described in the forthcoming flotation prospectus and which is to deliver visible growth results in the period up to the stock market listing. The strategy must also ensure that future expectations, as described in the prospectus, can subsequently be met. The work has to be completed by mid-January 1999, when a two-day strategy and kick-off event is to be held for the senior management of the company.

The strategic elements are:

- During the partnership with IBM, Damgaard International and the rest of the Damgaard organisation grew apart, which resulted in different company cultures. Damgaard needs to be a single company again with the same goals, strategy, values and culture.
- Problems regarding product quality need to be resolved, otherwise the aggressive growth measures may cause backlash when resellers and customers hit the brakes or publicly express their dissatisfaction.
- The challenge will be to read market developments correctly and not be too early too often.
- Internationalisation is the basis for future growth, so it needs to be further intensified.
- The foundation of the company's ambitions is employees, who can think for themselves and who dare and can take initiatives to solve the many challenges that are an everyday part of life in the turbulent software industry.

- It is management's job to recruit, lead and create the framework for the type of employees, which the company wishes to employ, which is why new and individual management development initiatives will be implemented.
- Finally, the company must push through the stock market listing and learn to work as a listed company with the opportunities for accessing capital that opens up, but also with the increase in visibility and demand for predictability and stability that doesn't quite suit a company in growth within the software industry.

When reviewing the company and auditing the strategic basis, it becomes clear that Damgaard Consulting with its direct customer sales doesn't really fit into the future business model. With the ability to recruit large well-established resellers that are able to invest significant sums and allocate many employees to working with Damgaard's products, time has run out on the need for a function like Damgaard Consulting. The department must be divested, but it can wait until the time is right.

# CHAPTER 19

# THE ROLLER COASTER STOCK MARKET LISTING

## Growth ahead of a stock market listing

The global growth forecasts for the markets served by Damgaard are estimated to be between 20 and 40 per cent in 1999. With a growth in sales of 35 per cent from 1997 to 1998, Damgaard isn't in a high enough position to be a clear winner of market share. In other industries, a growth of 35 per cent and a bottom line of 12 per cent would be cause for much celebration. But the rules are different in the IT industry. To ensure a high valuation and a reasonable yield on the impending stock market listing, Damgaard's growth rate needs to increase even further.

At the end of December 1998, the executive team, now composed of Preben and Erik Damgaard, Freddie Jørgensen and Per Pedersen, meets. All conceivable sources of rapid growth that could affect the results as early as in the first half of 1999 have to be identified.

The ensuing list contains 26 points, some of which are somewhat creative, such as directly invoicing for large projects and subsequently paying the commission to resellers. That set-up would immediately increase Damgaard's revenue and, although the change in account settlement principles would need to be explained in a flotation prospectus, the figures would look instantly and significantly better. However, most of the proposals fall within the existing business model and include price increases on all products and consultancy services from Damgaard Consulting, lower reseller profit margins, campaigns to help resellers win new orders, launching C5 overseas, large-scale support to get new Axapta partners started quicker and a dedicated effort to close the big orders already in the pipeline in the first half of 1999.

The many ideas are now discussed with the sales managers, all of whom are scared stiff at the thought of tampering with the business model. However, the unorthodox move causes everyone to be even more creative and motivated to actively work on new initiatives within the business model.

One of the results is the launch of a pilot project in Germany in which all small and medium-sized enterprises are contacted and their investment plans registered, so they can be contacted when the time is right. This is to ensure that XAL and Axapta are considered when a new financial management system is to be acquired. Resellers are invited to participate in the project, which is funded on a fifty-fifty basis. Participation is on the "first come, first served" principle: once a reseller has reserved a postcode district, it can't be assigned to another reseller. Damgaard GmbH, which now has business account managers throughout Germany, discusses the project with the resellers, who then promptly sign up so as to avoid another partner running off with customers in their district. In those areas not well represented, recruitment activities are initiated. The investment-mapping project is used as an extra incentive to get new resellers on-board. To deal with the many thousands of calls and forwarding of information material, which is expected to result from the vast majority of the conversations, Damgaard engages an external tele-marketing company.

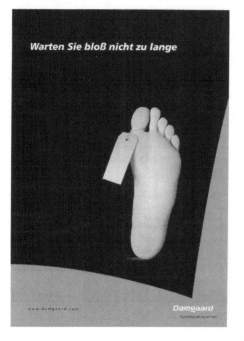

Warten Sie bloß nicht zu lange

Damgaard

Taking the company's size into account, Damgaard invested significant sums in marketing, including in full-page advertisements in foreign trade journals. The adverts, which supported the many sales-oriented activities happening in partnership with the resellers, focused on Damgaard as a brand and didn't promote the individual product. The creative presentation and production of the ads took place in the marketing department in Birkerød, but with the participation of the subsidiaries throughout the entire process. The advertisement with the foot gave rise to a number of angry letters, whose authors believed Damgaard had crossed the line. But that was also the ad, which received awards for its layout and message.

## Axapta is launched in Germany

Based on previous experience with Axapta, the German subsidiary isn't thrilled about introducing the product to the German market before 2000. XAL sells well; there are no problems or lost cases from customers assessing the technology as out-dated. Damgaard's people in Germany consider that country, in particular, to be unsuitable as a test market, and those resellers, who came on-board in the period 1996-98, aren't at all happy about having to invest in a new product.

However, Damgaard in Birkerød can't accept skipping such a large market and it would be difficult to explain that decision given the forthcoming stock market listing. It's agreed to release Axapta in Germany in 1999, but no final date is set before a version has been matured for the market. To support the work, Damgaard GmbH employs a dedicated Axapta business developer, a product manager and three technical staff. They are to assist in preparing and testing the forthcoming German version including obtaining certificates, in conjunction with an external auditing firm, to show the product complies with German accounting standards. Sales and marketing activities can now be maintained with XAL, while new Axapta resellers are recruited.

The plans for release of Axapta on the German-speaking markets are announced by Preben Damgaard and the German country manager, Hans Peter Bech, at a press conference at the CeBIT fair on 19th March 1999. Preben is careful to emphasise that XAL is continuing and that demand for the product remains quite satisfactory. Axapta has its sight set higher, especially at companies that need to correlate international subsidiaries and production sites in the same IT system. The press conference is held in collaboration with Microsoft in Germany; it is further announced that from now on both XAL and Axapta will be delivered with Microsoft SQL Server Version 7.0 as standard. Damgaard is still a small company in Germany, but can, via the partnership with Microsoft, seem both bigger and more important than it actually is. The press conference receives good press coverage at home and abroad.

Both XAL and Axapta are showcased at CeBIT; XAL by the resellers and Axapta by Damgaard. Interest in the new product is picking up but visitors from smaller companies are primarily forwarded to the XAL-resellers, who have small demo modules on Damgaard's stand, while larger companies are also offered an introduction to Axapta. It's clear that smaller companies are far more concerned about features, which match their business processes precisely, while larger companies, where the IT department is often a completely independent company, are much more interested in the development tools and support for their international activities.

With that positioning, Damgaard doesn't offend any of the current resellers, all of whom – with the exception of Columbus's subsidiaries in Germany, Austria and Switzerland – have only local representations. It's common knowledge that once Axapta is released, it will compete directly with XAL, but the former won't present a problem by that time. Customers will be able to choose the product they prefer. On the other hand, resellers who opt not to join Axapta will find themselves under pressure as the new product gains ground. Thus, the official positioning is purely for appearances. It's to calm the market and give resellers the opportunity to sell XAL until Axapta is ready.

## Axapta for every kind of business

Axapta is packaged in three versions: Standard Edition, Professional Edition and Enterprise Edition. The purpose is to allow resellers to offer the technologically-leading product to as many kinds of customer as possible.

| **AXAPTA** | Technology | Adaptability | Storage | Functionality |
|---|---|---|---|---|
| **Enterprise edition** | 3-tier Client / server | Complete | MS SQL serve Oracle | Financials, trade, logistics production, project market solutions, partner solutions |
| **Professional edition** | | | | |
| **Standard edition** | 2-tier Client / server | Limited | MS DE | Financials, trade, logistics production, project market solutions |

Despite Axapta being designed for large companies, the product's packaging was to help resellers sell it to small and medium-sized companies, too.

Distinguishing between large and small businesses is far too simplistic. As early as 1998, when Axapta was released in Denmark and the USA, there were enquiries from software companies interested in using the platform as the basis for their own solutions. One software developer, that supplies IT solutions to pharmacies, finds Axapta to be a suitable platform for a new generation of their products. Another enquiry comes in from a major international group that would like to develop a financial solution for its hundreds of smaller subsidiaries. Damgaard learns quite quickly to be careful about making statements regarding positioning. It could go wrong no matter what you say. Despite being constantly asked by the press, the resellers and the customers, it gradually decides to say as little as possible.

## Navision Software goes public

On 15th February, Navision Software announces its plans for an IPO. As early as 4th March, a thoroughly prepared prospectus is ready for interested investors. Purchase orders have to be submitted in the period from 11th to 25th March with the first day of the listing expected to be 29th March. The goal is a stock market listing of 28 per cent of the company's shares with estimated proceeds of approximately 160 million USD, of which about 100 million will go to the company's founders, senior executives and board members, while the remaining 60 million USD will go to the company's kitty via the newly issued shares.

On 26th March, the company announces that the offer of shares has been over-subscribed by six times the amount and the price will, therefore, be set at 25 USD. On 14th April, an option is exercised for the sale of an additional 700,000 shares from the "old" shareholders to bring in extra proceeds of around 17.6 million USD.

The valuation of the realised price of 25 USD per share is 640 million USD, equivalent to an average value increase of more than 40 million USD a year since the company was founded.

Impressive results are the reason for the stock marking listing. Revenue rose by 33 per cent in 1995/96, by 55 per cent in 1996/97 and by a grand 136 per cent in 1997/98. Part of the realised increase in revenue in 1997/98 and the expected growth in 1998/99 is due to acquiring distributors, but they are particularly impressive growth rates nevertheless.

Navision's Revenue for the first half of 1998/99 is expected to exceed the total revenue of the previous year, and here the acquisition of the distribution in Germany plays an essential role. Turnover outside of Denmark is at 78 per cent and that Germany, with a turnover of almost 18 million USD is the largest single market, testifies to the company's global scaling ability and potential.

Hardly anyone reads Navision Software's flotation prospectus or follows the process more closely than the Damgaard IPO-team. For the first time, they have full insight into the company they have always measured themselves against, and they can see they have been overtaken without warning. In Denmark, Damgaard – with a turnover of approximately 40 million USD – is significantly greater than Navision Software's nearly 12 million dollars, but in the financial year preceding the IPO, the company in Vedbæk overtook Damgaard's nearly 45 million USD with a total revenue of almost 52 million USD, and when it comes to the stock market, international scaling capacity is absolutely crucial.

## Charm offensive on the international press

In preparation for the stock market listing, the work of building up relationships with the trade and daily press is escalated, and in May 35 journalists from the nine countries where Damgaard has its own companies fly to Copenhagen for a briefing. They participate in a full-day's event with the theme *"Axapta – the world's most advanced ERP system"*. In addition to the journalists, Damgaard's top management, country managers, local PR agents and a few developers, who give demonstrations of the product, participate.

The event starts early morning at a hotel in Copenhagen, where a journalist from the leading German financial newspaper *Handelsblatt* has an exclusive interview with Preben Damgaard. Preben tells the story of how he and Erik started the company in 1984, and outlines how it has developed since. The journalist is clearly fascinated by the young and informal Danish entrepreneur, who also managed to enter into a partnership with the multinational IBM only to buy them out again; open subsidiaries around the world, including Germany; and, along with Navision Software, give German competitors a run for their money and who is now preparing for a "Börsengang" [stock market launch].

The official press event takes place at the Eksperimentarium science centre in Hellerup, where the journalists are seated for a couple of hours listening to company and product presentations, followed by questions. Lunch and the afternoon are spent on a schooner in the Øresund [The Sound], where the participants can chat and get to know each other better, and the day ends at the Tivoli Gardens, where dinner is held at the Fregatten restaurant, which has hoisted a flag with the Damgaard logo to its mast in honour of the occasion. For the Danish press representatives, it is a repetition of already known material, but for the foreign press there is plenty to write about.

Major American IT companies regularly hold similar types of events, but it isn't commonplace for a small European company to take such an initiative. The informal, relaxed tone and opportunity for socialising closely with Erik and Preben at the event obviously make a big impression on the foreign journalists, who return home and write long, positive articles for their respective magazines.

## The international partner conferences

After Damgaard initiated the establishment of its own subsidiaries in 1998, it was decided to hold an annual event for the best-selling business partners. Participants, from each country, were invited to a combination of professional and social activities over three to four days in an attractive location.

In 1998, the Damgaard Topperformer Conference was held at the end of May in Nice in the south of France, where the participants attended Formula 1 racing in Monaco's narrow streets from the best stands. Some years previously, Damgaard had informally invited more select Danish resellers to Formula 1 in Monaco, and in 1998, the event was extended to include business partners in Germany, Austria, Switzerland, the Netherlands and Belgium.

It's a huge success. The vast majority of resellers are smaller companies whose employees aren't used to being invited on luxury stays in exotic locations all expenses paid. During the conference, business partners are waited on hand and foot. They can get close to Preben and Erik, meet their foreign colleagues and get to feel what it's like to be surrounded by a respect they probably don't get to experience in their everyday work.

The conference ends with a black tie dinner, where "awards" are presented according to a number of different criteria. Afterwards, the winners are photographed with Per Pedersen, Preben Damgaard and the country managers, so they can take advantage of the distinction in their own marketing.

Upon their return from Nice, a competition is announced for invitations to attend the 1999 conference, which is set for Catania, Sicily, in May. The resellers really put their backs into the contest. Once they have attended an event, they would go through fire and water to attend again the following year. During the year, the conference is expanded to include participants from the new subsidiaries in Norway, Sweden, the UK, the USA, Spain and Australia, and when it takes place about 125 people attend of which 100 are guests and 25 are from Damgaard.

## A party goes off the rails

After the black tie dinner in Sicily, some of the participants move the celebrations out onto the town. A group of employees, from one of the major resellers, has a few too many and continue the party into the early hours back at the hotel. For whatever reason, the party goes completely off the rails and it ends in the hotel room being trashed and some of the furniture being thrown out of the window. The hotel's management is deeply offended and threatens to stop the conference and send all the participants home. Per Pedersen has to use all his diplomatic abilities and he ensures that a large sum is deposited to remedy the damage from the derailed party. Running a business based on self-employed and independent resellers requires many talents! The episode is contained and the vast majority of the participants never discover it.

## Next year: Mexico

On the last day of the conference, the time and location of next year's seminar is announced, and the excitement is great as it is revealed that the destination for the 2000 conference is Puerto Vallarta in Mexico. For the European participants, Mexico is definitely exotic, but it is primarily chosen out of consideration to the increasing number of American participants that it has been decided to alternate between the two continents for now.

It's crucial to maintain just one conference. The size itself is quite motivating for the participants, but the need to minimise the time demanded from Erik and Preben, whose participation is absolutely crucial, plays a part, too.

In light of taking steps for the good of the stock market listing, additional preparations are made for the conference in Mexico. The number of places increases and the promotion material for the resellers is made more colourful and sent out more frequently.

## Gold fever rages again

In 1999, a real gold fever rages once again in the global IT industry. The euphoria is primarily expressed in the increase in share prices on the New York Stock Exchange. Shares rise by almost 24 per cent in just four months – from the beginning of the year until the end of April – due, not least, to the introduction of companies from "the new economy". Every company that prefixes their name with an "e" automatically sees a dramatic increase in value.

The party atmosphere also affects the forecasts for the ERP market. Analysts estimate growth rates to be about 40 per cent a year, which is quite unheard of when compared to traditional industries. But it's an everyday occurrence within the IT industry.

However, the euphoria doesn't stretch to the individual ERP suppliers, which are mainly locally-owned companies.

Among the international companies, Dutch Baan runs into massive problems in 1998 after being exposed in a form of channel stuffing, whereby it posted the sale of products not yet delivered. The scandal rubs off on customers' confidence in the company, leading to a subsequent drop in turnover and a deficit of billions. In 1999, Swedish Intentia has to report failing profits several times as a result of an unsuccessful venture trying to enter the American market and German SAP also reports a downward adjustment later in the year.

The Danish stock market isn't affected by the same euphoria as in the USA. It is simply too small a market for start-up companies to reach a size that justifies a stock market listing within just a few years.

## Navision shines

For this reason Navision Software, with its phenomenal results and proven ability to expand internationally, shines like a star and is warmly welcomed onto the Copenhagen Stock Exchange, which, thereby, gains an IT comet. Not even reports of major foreign ERP suppliers entering and competing in the Danish market have any bearing on the potential seen in companies such as Navision Software and Damgaard.

## Damgaard Technical briefing in London

With the sharp growth in the number of new resellers abroad, the transfer of knowledge of the products becomes a critical bottleneck. The challenge is also due to Damgaard releasing more functionality more frequently than ever before with its over 100 developers working on XAL and Axapta. The traditional process of offering courses in the various modules can't deal with the training needs satisfactorily on its own, which is why the doors open for the first "Damgaard Technical Briefing" at the Holiday Inn Hotel, London-Nelson Dock, by the Thames, on 21st May 1999. Over four days, the over 300 participants from 18 countries are offered a cornucopia of presentations and workshops on Axapta and XAL, which are delivered directly by Damgaard's developers and technical support staff. The main topic is Axapta Version 2.0, which now includes an Internet Connector that makes the system suitable as an e-commerce engine and is to be released the following month. In addition, Version 2.0 includes project management modules, CRM modules, HR features and facilities to integrate with other IT systems also based on Microsoft's technologies. With Version 2.0, Axapta can also offer – as standard – country-specific features for Denmark, the UK, the USA, Norway, Sweden, the Netherlands and Australia.

Partners Microsoft, IBM, Compaq and Oracle are sponsors and, therefore, also make presentations at the conference. Moreover, Compaq sets up islands of PCs connected to the internet, where participants can check their email and keep in touch with the outside world. Unlike at Topperformer conferences, participants of the technical conferences pay an attendance fee of roughly 2,000 USD and must cover their own travel and accommodation costs.

## Project Dambuster

Since the end of November the previous year, Preben and his closest employees have been negotiating with potential advisors. On 10th May, the team, codenamed "Dambuster", which is to take Damgaard to the stock exchange is ready to start work on the actual preparations. The Damgaard participants are Preben and Erik Damgaard, Per Pedersen, Freddie Jørgensen, CFO Peder Grau, Regitze Reeh, newly appointed director of relationships with shareholders, Hans Henrik Pontoppidan, as well as jurists Marianne Nyegaard and Marianne Wier. Goldman Sachs has been chosen as the leading bank, while Enskilda Securities and Nykredit Bank are included as complementary issuing banks. Law firms Kromann & Münter, Bech-Bruun & Trolle and Brokeck Hale & Dorr (London) are affiliated to the project, while PricewaterhouseCoopers (PwC) and Andersen Hüberz Kirkhof have been chosen as the auditors.

In preparation for the stock market listing, all of the company's rights are gathered in Damgaard A/S, which is the company to be listed on the stock exchange, while Damgaard Data Holding, which owns all the shares, changes its name to ERP International A/S.

A little phonebook with the names, phone numbers, fax numbers and e-mails of the participants and their respective secretaries and assistants is published. The book contains the contact information of 44 people, of which only nine are from Damgaard, not including secretaries and assistants. The cost of the IPO is estimated at around 6 per cent of the amount to be raised. As the figure is expected to be in the order of 200 million USD, the cost of the many people and activities will be in the region of 12 million USD.

The preparations have to be published in the form of a flotation prospectus, which describes the "Damgaard" investment opportunity to interested shareholders to such an extent that they are, in principle, equally as well-informed about the company's past, present and future as the company's current owners and management. The flotation prospectus is to be presented to potential investors around the world by the company's top management in the week leading up to the end of the subscription period.

The work of the flotation prospect is made somewhat easier by Navision Software's stylish and thoroughly-prepared prospectus, which receives the following review in the *Nyhedsmagasin* of the Børsens daily newspaper on 22nd March 1999:

*Grade: 4 stars.*
*Strengths: clear and thorough description of the market, competitors and products, firm strategy, good language in general, nice section on employees, comprehensive prospectus. Weaknesses: vague section on the future, poor description of where growth should come from, no pro forma calculation, internal people on the board, nothing about pricing policy".*

Of course, the two companies are quite different; some of which isn't so advantageous for Damgaard in relation to a stock market listing.

On the plus side, Damgaard in Denmark is significantly larger than Navision Software. Due, in particular, to Damgaard having a broader product range and, thereby, appealing to a larger share of the market. But it's also due to Damgaard being better able to recruit resellers and better able to create demand more efficiently with its partners. Navision Software's early partnership with IBM limited its market access to IBM's resellers and that restriction was only lifted when IBM ended the partnership in 1994. In addition, Damgaard has a stronger value proposition for production companies with XAL and Axapta and, thus, has a larger market. Furthermore, Damgaard has a brand new product with Axapta, which, with the latest technology, is deemed to be the foundation for significant growth for many years to come.

On the minus side, growth potential in Denmark is limited, and Damgaard has only shown a small degree of growth abroad. Moreover, Damgaard is in the middle of a product shift, and Axapta hasn't yet demonstrated itself to be the comet of growth it was expected to be.

While Navision Software was able to lay some particularly impressive growth figures on the table before its stock market listing, Damgaard has to, parallel to preparing the flotation prospectus, ensure the business moves up a few gears. Prior to the IPO, it has to demonstrate solid half-year results.

During the discussions with the advisors, the possibility of listing the company in the first half of 1999 on the basis of the 1998 annual accounts is considered. However, it's advised that the valuation be 50 per cent lower than if the company were to be listed in the second half of 1999, based on better growth figures from the first half of the year. As management expects very good results for the period of January to June 1999, it's decided to bet on this timing.

## Damgaard's "data room"

Preparing for an IPO is a major burden of work on the top management of the company, which has to simultaneously see to the everyday running of the business. Whereas Navision Software kept the period, during which the company was under review prior to the listing, to less than six weeks, Damgaard announced, the previous November, a significantly longer – though informal – observation period. Parallel to preparing the flotation prospectus, good results have to be produced, which can support the valuation and interest in the shares. Banks, lawyers and auditors have to probe each and every business relationship, so every right, obligation and risk can be examined and assessed. To this end, the company creates a so-called "data room" where all of the company's contracts and agreements are collected. They are reviewed minutely by the advisors to assess the extent to which they are to be mentioned in the flotation prospectus.

The advisors also need access to the company's financial information in order to provide an adequate description of its historical development; that task is complicated by the fact that Damgaard changed its financial year to the calendar year in 1998. It is, therefore, necessary to re-periodise previous financial years, so it's possible to compare the historical figures on a calendar-year basis in the prospectus.

When reviewing the company's obligations and rights, the advisors also check whether or not Damgaard has all the rights to its products. There are problems here. Both XAL and Axapta contain elements to which Damgaard doesn't own the rights. It's quite common in the software industry to use tools and software fragments that others have made available for free – something Damgaard's developers have also made use of. When a business is listed and eventually becomes extremely valuable, it automatically also becomes a target for compensation cases. Such cases are, regardless of their character and whether they are won or lost, time-consuming and costly. If Damgaard's products contain elements they don't own, the financial compensation requirements of the copyright holder must be 100 per cent clear and it must be ensured that they can't demand Damgaard immediately ceases using them. An external specialist is now engaged, who is to carefully examine all the products and identify any and all elements owned by others. Damgaard can either develop something similar itself or enter into an agreement with the copyright holder, which would disallow the latter from making a later claim against Damgaard. The extensive work means the prospectus doesn't need to include a section on that risk.

## Many uncertainties

However, the greatest challenge in compiling the flotation prospectus is making a fair assessment of how the company will develop in the near future. While growth potential – and the ability to exploit it – is crucial to the value of the stock market listing itself, the ability to predict the company's year-to-year development is vital for price development and management's reputation in business on the whole. The prospectus has to include an assessment of the results for the current financial year and as the listing is to happen a few months before the end of the financial year, the estimate has to be on the button. That challenge is particularly great for Damgaard due to a combination of several factors. The product switch from XAL to Axapta creates uncertainty about how quickly demand for XAL will decrease and how quickly the reseller channel can change to Axapta. After divorcing IBM, Damgaard establishes its own subsidiaries that are just about falling into place. How fast can an organisation be built up? How fast can the markets be penetrated? How quickly can new resellers be recruited? How quickly can selling start? What effect will the millennium have on demand? Will a slowdown be seen before or after the turn of the century, or will the high growth rates continue? What will the new business opportunities via the internet mean for demand, and how quickly will the possibilities break through?

The many uncertainties make it meaningless to make a simple projection of the previous years' results. Growth potential with new subsidiaries, better control and new products are far greater than before, and the global market share is still so small that the market itself doesn't constitute a limitation. The two factors that matter most for the immediate future are the company's own ability to execute its strategy and whether the market is playing for or against the high ambitions for growth. The many considerations are formulated in the prospectus as follows:

*Based on Damgaard's results in the first half of 1999 and the volume of orders, Damgaard currently expects a growth in net turnover in 1999 that corresponds to net turnover growth in the first half of 1999, compared with the first half of 1998. Despite possible fluctuations in some operational costs, no significant changes in total operational costs are expected in relation to turnover for the 1999 financial year when compared to the first half of 1999.*

On review the figures in the prospectus can be translated into the following expectations:

Turnover 1999: 114 million USD (growth of 60%)
Operating profit 1999: 8.74 million USD (growth of 72%)

To find the same growth rate in revenue, it's necessary to return to the period 1986-89, despite there being several years when the net profit grew significantly more. In the immediate expanding paragraph, the prospectus notes:

*Damgaard's expectations with regard to the development in turnover are subject to a range of risks and uncertainties, which Damgaard itself has no control over, cf. the section "Risk factors".*

The uncertainties faced by the company are described in detail. At the very front of the prospectus – from pages 14 to 20 – the 25 risk factors, which the board considers most significant, are described. The list includes competitive pressure, market development (not least what the turn of the millennium will bring), the dependence on Microsoft's technologies, the acceptance of Axapta, the performance of the resellers, the ability to grow and lead the organisation, the consequences of serious bugs in the product, challenges enforcing trademarks, fluctuations in exchange rates and the risk of litigation and liability for damages. 'The gloomy outlook doesn't scare away all potential investors because the company has demonstrated that it has been able to navigate between these uncertainties and deliver growth and profits every single year since its inception in 1984. In other words, there is confidence that management can handle the conditions and will deliver good results to the shareholders in the future.

## Positioning is a delicate balancing act

Damgaard's ambition of becoming one of the world's leading suppliers of integrated business solutions for medium-sized enterprises, defined as companies with a turnover of between 5 and 500 million USD, or which requires solutions for between 5 and 250 simultaneous users is emphasised in the flotation prospectus. The company has no plans to strive for globalising the solid position enjoyed by the company in the Danish market for financial management software for the very small companies with less than five users. Neither is there any longer an ambition to become a leading supplier to large companies, where German SAP,

Dutch Baan and a number of primarily US software companies, such as Oracle and PeopleSoft, already enjoy solid positions. The market delineation doesn't mean the resellers are barred from selling to whomever wants to buy, regardless of their size, but it does mean that Damgaard in its development of products, in its marketing and in its recruitment of resellers, will prioritise highest the chosen market segments in relation to its position. There are several reasons why both Navision Software and Damgaard choose small and medium-sized businesses as their core segment.

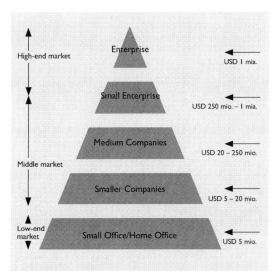

Market segmentation of the high-end, middle and low-end markets is based on the companies' turnover.

This illustration is from the flotation prospectus and shows a simple division of the market for ERP systems. Damgaard's focus is the middle market, defined as all companies with a turnover of between 5 and 500 million USD. The middle market is estimated to account for about half of the total market and annual growth rates are expected to be between 18 to 32 per cent.

Just as Damgaard owns the Danish market for solutions to very small businesses, there are competitors in every other county, which dominate the market in a similar manner. They are dependent on chartered accountants recommending the solution, and for good reasons, accountants often recommend the solution that already has the greatest distribution. Resellers play a different role in selling to very small companies, which don't have much need for consultancy, customisation or implementation. Customers demand standard solutions and would prefer a solution from the market leader. Therefore, business partners standardise solutions so they can be sold at both a lower price and to many customers. Entering that market requires a very special situation where customers, chartered accountants and resellers have good reason to consider completely new and unproven alternatives.

Selling to large companies has to happen in competition with already well-established competitors and will require direct involvement in the individual customer cases – something neither Navision Software nor Damgaard desires.

Both companies have shown very good results in serving small and medium-sized companies. The interaction between customers' needs and wishes, the resellers' roles and Navision Software's and Damgaard's products have proven extremely competitive precisely in these markets. They have both demonstrated they have the products, business model and management power to beat competitors on their home turf. When compared to the analysts' expectation of the greatest growth being exactly in that market, Damgaard has quite unusual potentials for growth and earnings. At the time of publishing the flotation prospectus, Damgaard is a company with over 71,000 customers, who use the company's four products and are served by 1,000 resellers in 28 countries. The staff amounts to 448 people, of whom almost 100 are employed abroad. 120 work with research and development; 198 with marketing and sales (via resellers); 50 carry out consultancy work for customers and resellers and 80 deal with management, administration and internal IT.

## Dissatisfaction with Goldman Sachs

The preparation of the flotation prospectus, which ends up being 110 pages, is headed by Goldman Sachs as chief editor, while the research and copywriting are done by members of Damgaard's own Dambuster team. Coordinating the many people and work turns out to be an unforeseen challenge, which isn't made any easier by Goldman Sachs changing project manager in the middle of everything. Damgaard isn't particularly pleased overall with Goldman Sachs' way of running the project. Therefore, Preben calls the top management of Goldman Sachs in for a crisis meeting, after which things are more under control.

The prospectus is published on 20th September in both Danish and English. The offer price will, depending on demand, be between 280-320 DKK (56-64 USD) per share of 10 DKK (2 USD). 1,350,000 new shares are offered, while Damgaard Data Holding will sell 1,650,000 shares, with an additional option to sell 450,000 shares. In other words, 34 per cent of Damgaard shares will be floated, and if the price succeeds in increasing to 320 DKK (64 USD), it would correspond to a market valuation of 660 million USD and a total capital increase of 220 million USD, of which 134.4 million USD would go to ERP International A/S, owned primarily[10] by Erik and Preben and the remaining 86.4 million USD would go to Damgaard A/S. Interested investors can submit offers from 27th September to 4 pm on 6th October 1999. They are further invited to the initial investor presentation on Monday, 27th September, at 9 am, at the Eksperimentarium science centre in Hellerup.

## The beauty contest

That same week and the week after, a traditional roadshow goes on tour, where the executive team travels by private jet to Stockholm, Amsterdam, Frankfurt, Zurich, Milan, Paris and London and then, by regular scheduled airliner, to Boston and New York to present the company and the investment opportunity. Many questions are asked at the meetings, especially regarding revenue expectations. Investors are aware that a software company has to be assessed on its ability to increase revenue and become a leading player in the global market. If it could manage that, the shares could be extremely attractive. The business model used with resellers to serve customers is extremely scalable, but it also depends on the company's ability to recruit and develop them. It's primarily Per Pedersen who answers these questions and explains what Damgaard can do that IBM can't. Investors also question Damgaard's predictions for the market's demands, including whether they are in direct contact with

---

10   Erik and Preben each own 49 per cent of the shares, while ASER Ltd, owned by lawyer Anders Schrøder, owns just under 2 per cent and Michael Sander owns 0.4 per cent.

customers to hear their wishes. It's a tricky question given that it's the resellers who primarily hear customers' wishes, while Damgaard looks into the future and develops tools to make resellers more productive and adds functionality, which all customers are expected to need. Erik explains Damgaard is a company that creates the market, while resellers follow the market. He words it so it sounds like Damgaard deliberately doesn't listen to the customers. It takes some explaining to get the investors to understand Erik's philosophy, which Steve Jobs showed the true potential of many years later.[11]

In principle, nothing more can be said at investor meetings than what is already available in the flotation prospectus or accessible via other public sources. Nonetheless, the meetings are of great importance for potential investors, who want to see the faces behind the company and assess whether or not they are a team in which they can have confidence. In the IT industry, in particular, where development happens much faster than in almost every other industry, the quality of a management team is crucial to whether or not investors will put their hands in their pockets.

## Price 320 DKK

The offer window closes on 7th October and as it seems that demand is 16 times greater than what is available, the price can be set at 320 DKK (64 USD). All bids to purchase up to 20 shares are fully met, after which other interested parties are granted shares according to a number of specific criteria in that purchasing orders of more than 6,700 shares are assessed individually. On 12th October, Goldman Sachs utilises the option of the purchasing and selling of the 450,000 shares, after which the stock market listing is concluded. On 12th November, the Damgaard share price has risen to 540 DKK (108 USD), and the company's value is equivalent to 1.1 billion USD. Had IBM managed to retain its 15 per cent share of Damgaard Data Holding in November last year, it could have sold its shares now for 165 million USD. In other words, the 15 million USD borrowed by Erik and Preben from the bank to buy out IBM the year before

---

11   "It's really hard to design products by focus groups. A lot of times, people don't know what they want until you show it to them." – Steve Jobs

has turned out to be a gold mine of a business. At the same time, Navision Software's share price has risen to over 250 DKK (50 USD), with which its market value has passed the 1.4 million USD mark. Woohoo! Things are looking good in the Danish IT industry.

## Damgaard and Navision are worth the same

The difference between Navision's price 125 DKK (25 USD) and Damgaard's price 320 DKK (64 USD) is primarily due to the number of shares in the companies. Damgaard has fewer shares, but each share is ten Danish kroner. If Damgaard's shares are converted to one Danish kroner per share, the total rises to 17.6 million USD against Navision's 4.6 million USD. The companies achieve the same value and issue roughly the same number of new shares to the market; thereby achieving the same price on the whole.

## The stock exchange party 20th November

The IPO, with a value of more than 600 million USD and an oversubscription 16-times greater than what is available, has to be characterised as being almost a Danish record. The process prior to the IPO imposed greatly on many of the employees who, already stressed in everyday life due to the intense internationalisation, had long working days and short weekends. To mark and celebrate the event and thank the employees for their contribution, Preben and Erik Damgaard invite every single employee to a grand gala at Øksnehallen, in Copenhagen, on Wednesday, 20th November. And it is every single employee. The cost of the event is paid out of Erik and Preben's own pockets.

Erik and Preben Damgaard acknowledge the hard work that employees have put into the company over the years; not least, in the period up to the listing, by inviting them all to a black tie event in Øksnehallen on 20th November 1999. With bands, such as Michael Learns to Rock and Henning Stærk Band, the party goes on until the early hours.

It's an incredible party that opens with a group photo being taken of all the participants, after which the guests are guided to their preassigned seats at the dinner tables. Master Fatman is hired as DJ, and the job of MC goes to Michael Carøe, who after the main course, enters the room on a small truck with a band on the back that plays songs requested by the audience.

After dinner, there are cigars and an open bar, while the music is first provided by Michael Learns to Rock and then by Henning Stærk Band. After midnight, with the number of guests still impressively high, the party moves to a more intimate venue where a third rock band continues the entertainment. And when it's time to collect coats and wraps from the wardrobe in the early hours, a copy of the latest CD with Michael Learns to Rock is given as a party favour. Everyone is a little sore the next morning, but they have memories of a once-in-a-lifetime party, which is much talked about among the employees.

## A storm is brewing

As in all other companies, the sales managers send a monthly status report to the company's top management. The fourth quarter is by comparison the busiest three months of the year in terms of sales of financial management software. But this time, the volume of incoming orders aren't increasing as expected. Growth in revenue, which was already declining in late October, decreases further in November.

As early as October, meetings with and telephone calls to resellers are implemented. Partly to better understand the situation; partly to identify opportunities for getting customers, in the process of buying, to decide quicker. No great price reductions will be offered to make customers – who are going to buy anyway – expedite their purchases. That practice is widely used by American software companies listed on the stock market. It results only in customers getting used to buying when they know they can push for big discounts. Damgaard has no desire for that culture to spread. If you can win a customer, who has yet to pick a supplier, to choose a solution based on a Damgaard product, then you are willing to work hard to make it happen quickly.

Whereas software licences are the primary source of income for Damgaard, it's not the same for resellers. The strength of Damgaard's business model is that licences for 1,000 dollars generates between 7,000 and 10,000 dollars of service revenue for the resellers. Whereas Damgaard runs a product business, resellers run a consulting business. Therefore, a slowdown in licence sales isn't necessarily as big a problem for the individual reseller. They do, by far, the most business by selling services to their existing customers. Companies, such as Columbus and DITEC, bank absolutely on the sale of new licences and have established professional sales departments that are held to their targets. But the vast majority of business partners don't focus on new sales. They take whatever comes, when it comes.

Damgaard's crystal ball for seeing what is in the resellers' pipelines is extremely cloudy. It actually only has a few knobs it can turn to make customers and resellers buy more right now.

The channel stuffing trick, whereby licence points are sold to business partners, which they then stockpile for the following year, and which IBM and Damgaard International previously used to embellish the results, can't be used by a listed company. Only licences delivered to the end customer and where the right of use is finally transferred may be included in the turnover.

With the effect of the turn of the millennium, the growing need for internet-based solutions and international expansion, there was no reason to expect, just a few months earlier, that revenue growth in the first half of the year wouldn't continue in the second half. The results in October, and especially November, say something else entirely. As the reports from the sales managers are consolidated, a bleak picture of a notable slowdown in revenue growth forms. With just four weeks of the financial year left, it's impossible to affect the costs, most of which are personnel. Therefore, safeguarding profits via cost reductions isn't possible.

## The storm hits Damgaard on 3ʳᵈ December

By the end of November, Damgaard's executive team has to acknowledge that they are most likely looking at a fourth quarter that can't meet the expectations described in the flotation prospectus published just two months earlier. It's not that revenue doesn't grow, it just doesn't grow as much as expected. Nor is it the case that the company is facing a deficit, the profit will be just less than expected. And the long-term growth perspectives certainly haven't changed; it's just a probable temporary drop in demand.

Had Damgaard not been listed, the situation wouldn't have given rise to specific measures, but the company now has an obligation to share its knowledge of the state of the company with the entire stock market and, therefore, there is no alternative but to disclose a so-called profit warning. Damgaard isn't the first company in history to make a profit warning, but doing so only seven weeks after the listing is highly unusual and gives rise to much speculation.

On Wednesday, 1ˢᵗ December, the board sends a notice to the Copenhagen Stock Exchange, and on Thursday, 2ⁿᵈ December at 8:10 am a fax ticks in.

The flotation prospectus had estimated that sales for 1999 would reach a level of around 114 million USD with an operating profit of 8.6-8.8 million USD. After the adjustment, an interval revenue of between 91-94 million is expected as well as a lower operating profit. On 3ʳᵈ December, Damgaard issues a specific stock exchange announcement, which indicates that the operating profit is expected to be between 4.55 and

4.7 million USD. Thus, growth in revenue will amount to 28-33 per cent, which most companies would be proud of. But Damgaard is in a market that is estimated to grow 40 per cent a year. Just a few months earlier, competitor Navision Software was able to present its best-ever accounts with a turnover of 122.2 million USD, corresponding to an overall growth of 136 per cent (88 per cent, if the effect of acquiring the German distributor is deducted), and an operating profit of no less than 28.2 million USD, corresponding to an impressive profit margin of just over 23 per cent. Parallel to releasing the specific stock exchange announcement, Damgaard calls an open investor meeting on Friday, 3$^{rd}$ December, at 2 pm, at the Hotel SAS Royal in Copenhagen.

Friday morning at 8 am, the board and the executive management team meet to agree what will be presented at the investor meeting later in the day. Hans Werdelin, who stepped in as chairman of the board in November 1998, is the first to arrive. When Per Pedersen, who has just flown back from a business trip in Norway that very morning, enters the room, he gets the greatest scolding of his life. When you are the sales director of a listed company that has just ascertained that the sales expectations have to be drastically scaled back, there isn't much to say. Per Pedersen is tight-lipped. When the other participants arrive, Hans Werdelin is finished getting his frustration off his chest, after which he constructively engages in preparing those who are to attend the investor meeting for what they will face and he makes sure they are agreed on whom will comment on what.

Preben Damgaard looking exhausted in the picture featured in Berlingske
Tidende the day after the press conference wasn't without reason. A downward adjustment just seven weeks after an IPO was unheard of and risked
damaging Preben Damgaard's reputation. Not even the decorated Christmas
tree in the background could help elevate the mood. The media was turning
all its spotlights to Preben and his company, when help suddenly came from an
unexpected source (Photo: Mogens Ladegaard).

Preben Damgaard and Hans Werdelin, who lead the meeting, explain the
dismal circumstances, the broad slowdown across all markets as a result
of the turn of the millennium and that demand is expected to normalise
the following year. The press coverage is significant and the verdict is
harsh. The shares crash to price 240 DKK (48 USD). It's a decline of 88
per cent and a loss of value of 600 million USD since the top listing of
520 DKK (104 USD) the month before. Calculated on the introductory
price, it's a decline of 25 per cent and a loss of value of about 160 million
USD. Damgaard is criticised for waiting an entire month, from when the
first signs of crisis were noted, to making the downward adjustment and
it's also rumoured that some shareholders will demand an investigation
to clarify whether they have been misled in connection with the stock
market listing itself.

A cunning reporter from *Reuters Finance* contacts Navision Software
and reports as early as 2nd December that the latter isn't experiencing
a slowdown, but still expects revenue of around 200 million USD and

an ordinary result, after tax, of 20.2 to 25.66 million USD. However, an industrial analyst comes to Damgaard's rescue, reporting to *Berlingske Tidende* on 3rd December that *"everyone who makes financial software is having problems. Sales have been stalled for the past six months"*. Though, the really helpful hand comes from a completely unexpected source:

A devastating hurricane hits Denmark that afternoon, leaving behind massive destruction, seven dead and 800 injured. The windmill on the island of Rømø measures a Danish wind record of 51 metres per second before it completely subsides. The storm steals the entire media spotlight, and despite Damgaard not escaping critical articles during the days that follow, the storm shifts the focus of the journalists, after which the peace and calm of Christmas befalls Denmark.

The price has already risen to 360 DKK (72 USD) by the end of January 2000; on 9th February it passes 450 DKK (90 USD) and the misery of the downward adjustment fades gently into oblivion. Some comments are passed in the press when the financial statements are made available at the end of March, and on 10th May, Preben Damgaard takes stock of the situation in a long article in the broadsheet *Jyllands Posten*. The darkest chapter in Damgaard's history seems to be coming to an end.

## Navision Software wants a finger in the resellers' pies

Despite Navision Software being able to bask in its outstanding results, it doesn't completely escape the media's interest. A leak, in September 1999, reveals that Navision is planning to change the way in which its resellers buy and sell the company's products. The new concept includes business partners receiving free training and a larger share of licence sales, in return for Navision receiving 15 per cent of the service revenue stemming from customers actually using the software. The idea for the model comes from sales and marketing director René Stockner, who in 1992 assumed responsibility for the activities in the USA after Erik Seifert.

In 1994, when René launched Navision Financials in the USA and had to establish a reseller channel, he faced a number of challenges. Navision Software was a small, unknown company with few resources, but with an excellent product. René travelled around the USA to find new resellers. He needed them to make quick decisions, and what is more stimulating than a cheaper admission ticket? Therefore, he offered them free training and a 50 per cent reduction in licence fees, which are quite unheard of and attractive terms within the IT industry. In return, he was to get a 15 per cent share of their service revenue, which stemmed from the Navision business. With that concept, resellers were able to get started without having to put their hands in their own pockets, and as they earned only a little service revenue at the beginning, it seemed like a good deal. As the resellers grew and their service revenue increased, it also became good business for Navision Software. Indeed, it was such good business that even if business partners didn't sell new licences, Navision Software continued to earn from the resellers' service revenue. The genius of the model was that it made it easy for partners to get started, and despite the vast majority of resellers actually stopping once they reached a certain number of customers, they continued to contribute positively to Navision Software's business.

When René Stockner was recalled from the USA in December 1998 and became responsible for all of the company's global marketing activities, he discussed how to implement the above model in every country with Jesper Balser. There were three main challenges to be overcome. Firstly, the model was quite unusual in the industry and, like everything else new, was met with considerable scepticism. Secondly, the established resellers were uncertain whether or not the model would also be to their advantage. And thirdly, the arrangement meant that Navision would have access to their accounts, which most partners certainly didn't care for. Thus, there was – if not massive resistance – at least considerable scepticism in the European reseller channel. So the scheme was initially voluntary.

Despite the scheme being unusual, it is essentially quite fair and can help protect the overall ecosystem. The products are at the heart of both Damgaard's and Navision Software's business models, where resellers can build up very solid businesses without having to deliver a lot to the two producers. Indeed, an overwhelming majority of resellers stop once they have reached a certain size and continue to live mainly on the service business generated by Damgaard's and Navision Software's products. Thus, they contribute little to the development of the ecosystem keeping them alive. Competition within the software industry is tough and both Damgaard and Navision Software are extremely sensitive to price competition on their licences. A share of the resellers' service business eases this sensitivity, which, in turn, benefits the entire ecosystem. Despite René Stockner's model being quite fair, the initiative to change the existing format creates widespread uncertainty and the media coverage isn't exactly positive.

## *Ekstra Bladet* sets out to cause trouble

On 14th November, *Ekstra Bladet* (a Danish tabloid) sets out to cause trouble for Jesper Balser, who, with a stake worth almost 400 million USD, has, according to the Danish tabloid, sought out a tax haven in Hamburg. Michael Gaardboe, who has moved to the USA to build up Columbus IT Partner there, gets a turn in the media on the same occasion.

In December, the story of Navision losing a lawsuit brought by former director Erik Seifert breaks. Seifert, who started Navision in the USA, claims to be entitled to a share of the profits the company gained from the deal with the American software company, Peachtree, which he found and introduced to Navision. Both the Danish Maritime and Commercial Court and the Supreme Court rule on the side of Erik Seifert, and Navision has to pay 2.6 million USD in damages and costs. Navision can easily pay the sum, but it leaves a little scratch on the otherwise perfect finish. Whether or not Jesper Balser acted in good faith, it never sounds good when former employees have to go to court to collect that to which they are entitled.

# CHAPTER 20

# THE MERGER WITH NAVISION SOFTWARE

## Great expectations

The internet received a major boost in 1994 when Netscape launched a user-friendly browser, and Digital Equipment Corporation launched the Alta Vista search engine. Both were free to use. With Alta Vista and Netscape, ordinary people without specific IT prerequisites could search, find and use information on the internet. When Microsoft included their free browser, Internet Explorer, in Windows 95 in 1995, anyone who bought a PC had immediate access to the internet. And when Google launched their search engine in 1996, it became even easier to search for and find information.

Parallel to the development of the internet itself and the software components necessary to make it available to everyone, the telecommunications industry invested in technologies that facilitated faster, easier and, above all, cheaper connections.

In the early 1990s, connecting to the internet was via a modem coupled to ordinary telephone lines. With ISDN technology, the speed increased, making it possible to talk on the phone and be on the internet at the same time, and with ADSL, the speed increased by a factor of eight, and, moreover, it did away with annoying connection rituals.

## Record growth

The simultaneous development of the many technologies ensures the rapid penetration of the internet and forms the basis for new businesses that achieve unprecedented growth in record time. While the total share index on the New York Stock Exchange rises 85 per cent in 1999, the value of technology companies rises by no less than 800 per cent, and despite a slight decline in early January 2000, expectations for growth in IT companies are still high.

In Denmark, Navision becomes the model for the unusual growth potential. By mid-January, when the price of its shares passes 1,000 DKK (200 USD) and a stock market value of 3.2 billion USD, it stands shoulder-to-shoulder with longstanding, renowned companies such as Carlsberg, ISS and Danisco. Actually, Navision now warns that it will be difficult to find sufficient resources for new sales activities in the second half of 2000 because resellers are busy installing and implementing all the solutions that have already been sold. The optimism could hardly be greater!

## Excitement at Damgaard

The excitement is great when Damgaard again holds an investor meeting on 28th January 2000; this time in a more modest location – the company's address at Bregnerødvej 133 in Birkerød. Management confirms that the company's turnover for the 1999 calendar year, as announced before Christmas, is expected to be in the region of 94 million USD, while earnings before financial items are expected to be just above the previously stated level of 4.6 million USD. Software licences and update subscriptions account for about 80 per cent of sales in 1999, of which roughly 55 per cent that pertains to XAL and Axapta comes from abroad. The total sales of software licences and update subscriptions rises by almost 20 per cent in Denmark and by about 80 per cent outside of Denmark compared to 1998.

Management continues to be cautious in its assessment of the market, which is expected to only gradually normalise during the coming year. Estimated revenue for the first half of 2000 is 50-52 million USD, while revenue for the entire year is expected to increase by 30 per cent when compared to 1999, equivalent to around 122 million USD. Software licence sales are expected to increase by about 45 per cent. The somewhat lower increase in the company's total turnover is due to a lower rate of growth in the sale of Damgaard's other services, including update subscriptions, services and activities in Damgaard Consulting.

About 60 per cent of the revenue from Axapta and XAL licences and update subscriptions is expected to come from abroad in 2000. As a result of the strong investments in sales, marketing and product development, earnings before financial items are expected to be around zero in the first half of 2000, while for the entire 2000 financial year they are expected to be around 12 million USD.

In 1999, Damgaard recruited 105 new Axapta Business Partners, which is 20 more than estimated. Therefore, in 2000, Damgaard will focus on the breaking-in of the many new resellers. Investments in sales and marketing will account for 35-40 per cent of turnover in 2000, which represents an increase of more than 35 per cent compared to 1999. The focus will initially be on the emerging markets and key markets such as the USA, Germany and the UK.

## New product name and a new entity

To ensure brand consistency, Damgaard changes its product names to Damgaard Axapta, Damgaard XAL, Damgaard C5 and Damgaard C4. Furthermore, the company will work on spreading knowledge of its technologies among the more than 7,000 sales consultants, which the company has at its disposal in its global reseller channel, comprising over 1,100 independent and authorised Business Partners.

To that end, the company establishes a business development unit, Damgaard Business Development, composed of about 50 employees, with both technical and marketing backgrounds. Moreover, knowledge of the company's technologies is enhanced by the fact that employees from Damgaard Consulting are posted to a number of foreign subsidiaries. Investment in product development amounts to around 15 per cent of total revenue in 2000.

Despite Damgaard being quite tarnished by the downward adjustment in December and having to watch itself fall well behind Navision Software, confidence in the company is slowly improving. The bottom line is still positive; there is plenty in the kitty and, not least, there is the ambition of taking internationalisation further.

## Full speed on Axapta

Before Christmas, Damgaard announces that Axapta has been awarded Windows 2000 certification. When Microsoft holds a major launch event in San Francisco in February, Damgaard is among the select 19 companies from around the world participating as exhibitors and the only provider of ERP software supporting both the client and server side of the new operating system. Navision Software, which gained great success as the first ERP system certified for Windows 95 with its launch of Financials in 1995, has finally been overtaken. With Windows as the dominant operating system for both large and small businesses such an announcement calms the nerves of every IT manager.

On 11th January, Damgaard Axapta Version 2.1 is launched, which, besides a number of e-commerce facilities, also includes country functionality for Spain, Germany, Austria and Switzerland.

## Roadshows in all major cities

In autumn 1999, the subsidiaries, together with the newly established Business Development department in Birkerød, implement an Axapta roadshow in all major cities in the countries where it's represented. The purpose is to recruit more resellers. As early as at the beginning of the year, a large IT reseller was recruited in Switzerland, and a senior employee from the company now participates in the roadshow, explaining how and why they chose to bet on that exact product. Interest is great, but the decision-making process is often long given that the investment was significant and strategic. All Navision Software business partners are also contacted. The majority are curious and would like to hear about the new Axapta, but nobody apparently feels an immediate need to supplement their business with a new product.

## Damgaard Consulting is sold to Aston

At the end of March, the final accounts for the 1999 calendar year are made available. As revenue hits the middle of the predicted range, the result is slightly better. Expectations for 2000 are sustained. In other news, plans to start up activities in Finland are mentioned as is that the partnership with WM-Data now encompasses the entire Nordic region and that the German company Würth is going to introduce Axapta into its subsidiaries in more than 70 countries.

A few days after the presentation of the accounts, the Damgaard Consulting business unit, with its 50 employees, is sold to the Aston IT Group for 7.4 million USD. Aston was founded by entrepreneur Peter Warnøe in August 1999 and is now Navision Software's largest business partner in Denmark. With the sale of Consulting to Aston, Damgaard hits two birds with one stone. It had already assessed, prior to the stock market listing, that the business unit was no longer of any strategic significance. As there is a vast difference between running a product business, such as Damgaard with its ERP systems, and running a consultancy business that implements those systems, it makes sense to dispose of the activity. Consulting was still a thorn in the side of the large Danish resellers, who felt it imposed direct and unfair competition on them. The business demanded the ongoing attention of management to ensure it wasn't unduly bothering business partners, but also to ensure it was contributing positively to the company's overall results. It was a delicate balance. Damgaard gets a new powerful reseller in Aston, and avoids overlooking any of its existing partners at the same time. That would have been the case had it been sold to, for example, Merkantil Data, the EDB Group, Thy Data Center or Columbus IT Partner.

Sales are expected to reduce the annual turnover by 5.6 million USD, while the operating profit isn't expected to be affected. The sale of Damgaard Consulting is assessed positively by market analysts, and there is also great satisfaction at the spinning off within the company as it leaves Damgaard with a completely clean channel strategy.

## ASP: Software-as-a-service

With the standards introduced as a result of the spread of the internet, and with the greatly improved telecommunications connections, technical possibilities emerge for running software via the internet. Axapta was actually designed for precisely this mode of operation: providing computing facilities to customers, who use their own PCs for data entry, but gain access to major central computers for computing and database access via a network. This transmission mode is called Application Service Provider, ASP, and it quickly becomes the foremost topic of discussion within the IT industry. Every trade journalist asks suppliers if and when they will offer their software like this. A press release from Damgaard in January 2000 reads:

*The benefits of hosting [ASP] are that the costs of the company's ERP (Enterprise Resource Planning) system are easier to understand because payment is made per user per month. It's easy to set up new users and problems of response times, overloading, backing up data and the need to make quick changes and upgrades are also avoided by outsourcing the ERP system. Damgaard's technology makes it easy to customise e-commerce solutions and connect new offices, subsidiaries and mobile employees.*

Damgaard enters into an agreement with Compaq, which as a "hosting provider" can offer hosting facilities to Damgaard's business partners and specialised ASPs. The press release states:

*Damgaard's hosting concept opens the possibility of specialised ASPs, for example, chartered accountants and industry associations could adapt Axapta to the needs of specific customer segments and then distribute that solution with significant economies of scale. Damgaard views hosting as an essential market trend, derived from a new business structure in which the internet is the catalyst. It is, therefore, strategically important for Damgaard to be among the first providers of ERP solutions, which can offer a complete hosting concept, to the middle market. However, Damgaard's hosting activ-*

*ities aren't expected to account for a sizeable part of Damgaard's revenue*
*and earnings in 2000.*

ASP is also the topic on the lips of exhibitors and the trade press at the
CeBIT fair in March. Customers don't seem half as taken with the phenomenon, which analysts forecast to grow from 2.6 million USD in 1999
to 3.36 million USD in 2003.

In reality, Damgaard and the resellers aren't particularly excited about
the subscription model that is expected to accompany a hosting solution. The long-term effect may will be increased revenue and earnings
on the software, but restructuring from prepaid licences to a monthly
subscription payment will have a negative effect on liquidity in the short
term and companies undergoing rapid expansion are always in need of
liquidity.

Moreover, Damgaard doesn't want to run a hosting company that
follows a completely different business model, and significant changes
would also need to be made to the software so it could be delivered in a
true ASP format, which would steal resources from the development of
more functionality for users. Every established software supplier pro-
claims it's following the hype, but they are hesitant and secretly hope
development doesn't happen too fast.

## Business partner meeting in Mexico

The business partner meeting is to be launched in Puerto Vallarta, Mexico, in April, and once again Damgaard endeavours to provide the participating resellers with an unforgettable experience. Due to the distance
and time difference, the programme is extended to four days, and the
vast majority of participants arrive the day before the official opening.
The first day commences after lunch with various business presentations and a welcome dinner in the evening. The second day has a shorter
morning programme, after which participants can choose between horse
riding in the surrounding mountains, swimming with dolphins or a jeep
safari along the coast; all followed by a themed dinner that evening at the
hotel. The third day's itinerary is an excursion for everyone to a nearby
island, which Damgaard has organised for the occasion. Canoeing, snor-

kelling, scuba diving, massages in secluded clay huts and just relaxing on the beautiful beaches around the island are all available. That evening dinner is held for the individual country delegations in restaurants throughout the city. The business programme continues on the morning on the fourth day, after which the afternoon is free. A black tie award dinner is held on the last evening at a restaurant located on a cliff top with a magnificent view of the sun setting over the Pacific Ocean. When the prize-giving is about to start, Per Pedersen and Preben Damgaard, sporting ponchos and sombreros, enter the stage on vintage motorbikes and the evening ends with the announcement of Top Performer 2001, which will take place in Puerto Banús, near Marbella, in Spain.

## Damgaard Technical Briefing in Berlin

The annual Damgaard Technical Briefing takes place in Berlin. From 15th to 18th May more than 500 participants gather from the 23 European countries where Damgaard is represented as well as from the USA, Canada, Singapore, Hong Kong, Australia and South Africa. Over the course of four days, developers and support staff from Damgaard carry out a wide range of technical presentations of Axapta 2.1 and XAL.

## Damgaard World Compass 2000

A similar arrangement entitled "Damgaard World Compass 2000" takes place for the top management and sales staff of business partners in Miami Beach, Florida, from 6th to 9th September.

A cornucopia of presentations and demonstrations is provided by both Damgaard employees and business partners over four days. The conference attracts over 500 participants from around the world and is such a huge hit that it's decided to repeat the success every year at the same time.

## Columbus runs into problems

That Columbus IT Partner is, without comparison, the reseller, who goes home with the most awards in its suitcase from the Mexico reseller seminar, doesn't really surprise anyone. The company publishes impressive annual accounts in February 2000. Revenue has increased by 23 per cent to 116.44 million USD – 76 per cent on consulting services, 19 per cent on software including its own software solutions and five per cent on hardware. Operating profit increased by six per cent, amounting to 5.28 million USD.

During 1998 and 1999 half of the company's employees are retrained for Axapta and, consequently, they could take on about half of the market in Denmark. Furthermore, as a distributor, it releases Axapta in the Baltic countries, Poland, Russia, the Czech Republic, Hungary, Turkey, Slovakia and Singapore just as it now has more than 50 resellers, according to its own statements. During 1999, the company expands its international activities with new offices in Spain (Barcelona), the USA (Baltimore and Los Angeles), Switzerland (Zurich), Linz (Austria), Sweden (Motala and Gothenburg) and Germany (Nuremberg), while the activities in Norway are expanded via additional acquisitions.

There is increasing demand for e-commerce solutions and customer relationship management, so from now on Columbus will invest further in becoming a global player in the market for such systems.

The massive investments in Axapta have certainly given a competitive advantage, but they have also had a negative impact on efficiency. Columbus is primarily a consulting business, where both turnover and earnings are dependent on invoicing for as many hours as possible. Thus, benching the consultants would have an immediate negative effect on both revenue and earnings. Many projects have a fixed price, where estimates are based on experience from the XAL business, but as Axapta is different and brand new for consultants, it takes some time before the company returns to the normal level of efficiency. Due to competition, it isn't always possible to pass the lower efficiency onto the customer, which is why Columbus has to take on the additional costs.

## Columbus is at a disadvantage

Prior to the presentation of the final annual accounts in April, Columbus has to issue a stock exchange announcement warning of disappointing results in the first half of the year. But there is reason to expect that the loss can be made up in the second half of the year. However, the reality is that the company is at a serious disadvantage. The market for new projects isn't just declining, it has come to a complete standstill. This hits a company dedicated to selling to new customers extremely hard. A large part of the Axapta projects won in 1998 and 1999 are loss-making, and some customers are so dissatisfied that they choose alternative resellers. The customer decrease is doubly painful as Columbus has to write off its sales costs, taking the loss on the implementation, after which the competitor gets a profitable customer from day one. The management has serious talks with their colleagues in Damgaard, whom they believe carries some of the responsibility for the capsized projects. Damgaard can't deny that the first versions of Axapta were buggy, but according to the licence and the reseller agreements, they bear no legal responsibility for the consequences. Moreover, it's impossible to estimate what impact it would have had on Columbus's business; besides, other resellers haven't experienced the same challenges.

There is an attempt to compensate for the severe slowdown in sales to new customers by increasing the sales efforts aimed at existing customers. This does show results but not enough to provide for the large body of staff employed during the frenzy in 1998 and 1999. The effect of the acquisition of all subsidiaries is finally fully realised in 2000, when the senior executives change from being co-owners running a financial risk to being full-time permanent employees with well-padded wallets.

In May, Lars Andersen, managing director of the group, discusses the situation with Michael Gaardboe, who, based in New York, is building up the American market, informing him of the challenges now beginning to cause liquidity problems. Lars doesn't see himself as the one to take charge of the company's clean up, and he suggests that Michael find someone else for the task. As there is no one waiting in the wings, they agree that someone must be found before the end of the year. Until then it's a job for Lars.

## Things get worse

The situation is further exacerbated at the end of June and the company finds itself in a real liquidity crisis. Talks with Damgaard resume, and Columbus makes it clear that if no solution is found, it may have to file for bankruptcy. After many long and difficult discussions, it is agreed that Damgaard will acquire the rights to a number of modules that Columbus developed for Axapta for a sum of 2.4 million USD. The intention is that by including the modules in the standard product and pricing them separately in the price list, Damgaard can make back its money.

This never happens for many reasons. The code and documentation are placed in a drawer and never again used. But Columbus gets a much-needed cash injection, which helps it ride out the crisis, and that in itself is of great value to Damgaard.

When the chairman of Columbus learns that Lars Andersen would like to step down, he makes it clear that it can't wait until the end of the year. It's not good to have a senior executive, who wants to leave the company, holding the reins. It is, therefore, agreed that Lars Andersen resign at the end of July and that Michael Gaardboe act as group managing director until a replacement has been found.

This is made known on 11th July in a stock exchange announcement, which also explains that the market has come to a complete standstill and sales for the first half of 2000 are now expected to be 24 per cent lower than for the same period the year before. The consequence is a loss of between 7 and 8 million USD. Revenue for the entire year is expected to be at the same level as the previous year and, with an expected result of close to zero for the second half of the year, there will be no catching up on the deficit for the first half year.

## New strategy

As early as the presentation of the 1999 financial statements in April, management presents a new strategy to supplement the products from Damgaard with other products, which are specifically aimed at e-commerce and CRM. The company also announces it has agreed to offer products from Damgaard's nemesis, Navision Software. The agreement covers all countries where Columbus isn't currently a distributor of XAL and Axapta.

The pact certainly hasn't been entered into out of desire, but since the listing, they have been continually criticised by analysts for being a "one-product-company" and, thus, linked to an unfortunate shared destiny with Damgaard. Management had always seen the sharp focus as a clear strength, ensuring that all of the company's resources were allocated to one and the same product. Therefore, the financial problems were primarily blamed on market conditions and not associated with Damgaard's ability to produce technologically advanced products (despite the troubles with Axapta). Thus, the agreement with Navision is primarily entered into to improve the relationship with analysts and put an end to the criticism.

## Welcome to the club

After the downward adjustment in December 1999, the management of Damgaard suffered an extra blow when Navision Software was able to report record revenue and earnings. Since its stock market listing in March 1999, Navision Software has conquered new markets in Poland, Finland and Portugal as well as establishing regional offices in Malaysia and Singapore. At the mid-February announcement of the expectations for results for the period January to June, the situation still looks positive. Navision expects a turnover of around 94 million USD and a net profit of almost 18 million USD, both corresponding to impressive growth rates of over 70 per cent. However, on 15th May 2000, the company's management has to make a downward adjustment due to a strong decline in revenue, which is now estimated to be 28 million USD lower than previously expected, giving a distinct deficit in the first half of the year.

Damgaard's management can now breathe a sigh of relief and welcome the competitor to the club. Given that Damgaard, Columbus and now even Navision Software are concurrently reporting slower growth, the difficulties in predicting development can't be attributed solely to poor management in the individual companies.

The lower turnover combined with major investments in expanding the sales and marketing capacity as well as a new and ambitious development project code named "Jamaica" hit hard, causing Navision Software to expect a loss in the second half of the financial year of up to 14 million USD. With a revenue of 68 million USD in the second half of the year, the company can still achieve a total turnover of well over 160 million USD, which represents growth of more than 30 per cent and with a net profit of 17.3 million USD in the first half of the year, the bottom line won't be red. Nevertheless, the company is treated roughly by the media

Listed companies are very visible, and if a company doesn't reach its own estimates, the punishment on the share price and in the media is relentless. As early as 22nd May, Børsen's *Nyhedsmagasin* features a large-scale article speculating on Damgaard and Navision Software's anticipated fate. Apart from the figures obtained from companies' accounts and stock exchange announcements, the many pages of text are pure speculation. Developments in the market as well as for the two companies will prove a completely different direction.

## Erik lacks the desire to manage

After the divorce from IBM, the stock market listing and, not least, the downward adjustment, there have been personnel-related problems with Erik Damgaard. He doesn't focus enough on managerial tasks and can even be challenging to work with. These issues have led to a number of resignations and, finally, Jakob Hahn Michelsen, responsible for overall coordination in the development department, chooses to say yes to an outside offer. The core problem is that Erik Damgaard isn't interested in the many diverse management tasks of a development organisation. Having more than 100 employees means there is a need for inter-departmental communication, for planning future products, for coordinating the various development teams, for quality assurance, for drawing up documentation, for preparing product releases and for many other administrative jobs.

Erik's interest lies in the development of the core technology of Damgaard's products and his great strength is his ability to understand – and even anticipate – what customers and resellers need, and then to quickly incorporate the new technology into the products using a select team of skilled developers. Everything outside of that in terms of planning, coordination and administration doesn't get his attention. He is too impatient to wait to have his ideas discussed by committees, and especially not by people whom, he considers, to be lacking the professional knowledge to judge what is right and wrong. Therefore, Erik simply does what he finds is most appropriate without discussing it, and often without informing the rest of the organisation.

As his decisions mostly affect areas for which other managers in the development department are responsible, frustration builds up. Moreover, Erik doesn't exactly have the best diplomatic skills; he shoots from the hip, often with annoyance in his voice when he feels that someone hasn't acquainted themselves properly with the issues at hand. Employees, who know him well, can handle his manner, while employees who aren't so close to him often become confused and demotivated.

The situation is aggravated by the launch of Axapta and the continuation of XAL, where there is an evident need to respond quickly to the requirements of and problems experienced by customers. Erik feels the culture of the development department has become too much "9 to 5". When the company was small and the product was manageable, his way of working was one of the company's major strengths. But now that the product is more extensive and requires a development organisation of over 100 employees, it causes constant conflicts and frustrations among several managers and employees, who depend on his work and that he follows the agreed plans to a tee.

Damgaard can't do without Erik's overview, insight and technical skills and, therefore, a structure must be found that can compensate for his lack of desire and skills for HR management and administration.

It is Hanne Haubert, head of Damgaard's support activities, in collaboration with Freddie Jørgensen, who is to smooth the situation and ensure that the development machine keeps running and that any "episodes" are dealt with. The operation is somewhat successful and a considerable amount of calm descends on the working conditions of the development department, but it isn't a long-term solution.

## Heading for a deficit

Damgaard's financial results for the first half of 2000 are available at the end of August, and for the first time in the company's history, it's heading for a deficit. Whereas management predicted a profit of 12 million USD for the entire year in March, an operating loss of between 0 and 4 million USD is now expected. The net profit is only positive due to a one-off imbursement of 6.6 million USD from the sale of Damgaard Consulting to Aston. In spite of renewed investment in XAL and the release of Version 3.0, more customers switch to Axapta and presumably to competing products, too. Sales of XAL decline by 35 per cent in the first half of 2000, while turnover from Axapta increases by 162 per cent. However, the net effect is that licence sales as a whole fall by four per cent.

Whereas market analysts in 1999 expected customer demand to grow by 40 per cent per year until 2003, the reality is already completely different in 2000.[12] Fewer companies invest in new ERP systems in 2000 compared to the previous year and they take longer when deciding to make a purchase. With the turn of the millennium behind them, companies no longer have a hard deadline for their decisions, while the possibilities of the internet and new technology make decisions even more comprehensive and, thus, even more time consuming.

12  The market analysis company IDC reduces its expectations for growth in the ERP market to 12 per cent in July 2000, while other analysts go down as low as 4 per cent.

## The dot-com bubble bursts

The dot-com bubble bursts in March and April. The price of technology shares on the New York stock exchange plummets. The new economy has been massively overestimated, and many of the companies that had attracted significant investments only a few years earlier must either make massive cuts or shut up shop.

The unrest among IT companies spreads throughout the entire market, and many customers choose to wait and see. Every ERP supplier is affected by the slowdown. That Damgaard is hit harder than Navision Software is due to Damgaard starting internationalising late, so it, therefore, hasn't achieved the same level of acceleration. Damgaard is also caught in the major product shift from XAL to Axapta. Despite persevering to keep the flag flying high on XAL, the company can't avoid competitors consciously describing it as an old product. An investment in a new ERP system is an investment in a new central nervous system for any company, so it has to last for the next five to ten years. Who would want to choose an old system? It's certainly not every XAL reseller, who can offer Axapta instead, which is why Damgaard loses even more projects to its competitors. Most companies prefer an already well-proven solution to a brand new product. In other words, Damgaard often finds itself in situations reminiscent of the experience with the Danish Agency for Governmental Management, which, in 1998, chose the proven Navision Financials over the technologically advanced, but brand new, Axapta.

However, the turnover being reached is mainly due to the massive investments in international markets and, for the first time in the company's history, Damgaard notes in its interim report that close to 60 per cent of total revenue now comes from outside of Denmark. The situation has been helped along by a distinct decline in revenue in Denmark and the rest of Scandinavia, while foreign subsidiaries can all report progress. The progress isn't due to demand abroad growing more than it has in Denmark, but to the competitive situation making it easier for the subsidiaries to win market shares from competitors. For that reason, the management of Damgaard decides to maintain the high level of investment in product development, marketing and sales, despite the risk of facing an operating deficit.

Damgaard could probably cut costs to make a profit, but cutting costs won't generate continued growth. A dollar saved now is deemed to come at too great a price in the long run. Damgaard's crisis fund in the form of liquid assets of 74 million USD is expected to work hard and, therefore, tightening the belt won't be of any help. A deficit certainly doesn't look good on the newly listed company, and it troubles the management, but they are convinced that the challenges are temporary. Damgaard will be best served by standing stronger when the state of the market turns again.

## A meeting of country managers

The many new subsidiaries established after the divorce from IBM in 1998 enables Damgaard to build up an organisation with a growing number of new employees with different cultural backgrounds, a native language that isn't Danish and, not least, in offices quite far away from its headquarters on Bregnerødvej in Birkerød. This challenge has been clear from the outset and the stationing of Danes abroad to establish the subsidiaries as well as build up and manage the local organisations is one of the initiatives that is to ensure that the culture of Damgaard spreads to the countries and that feedback on progress is more accurate.

Per Pedersen visits the subsidiaries once a month to follow up on plans and discuss how to handle the challenges and problems that have arisen. To that end the European country managers, in particular, travel regularly to Birkerød to discuss all kinds of matters directly with those responsible.

## The meeting in Böblingen

To ensure a united front across the organisation, a biannual two-day "country manager" meeting is introduced in early 1999, in which all country leaders, the company's senior management and a number of functional managers participate. The first meeting is held in March 1999 in Böblingen, in Germany. Despite there being a high degree of centralisation in Damgaard's structure for determining the strategy of the sales activities, each country manager has significant freedom to run their subsidiary. Damgaard's management is aware that good ideas can be born elsewhere than on Bregnerødvej in Birkerød. Thus, the biannual meetings with all the country managers become a forum facilitating two-way communication for the global management team.

## The meeting in Amsterdam

From 30th August until 1st September 1999, a country manager meeting is held in Amsterdam. There are two major topics on the agenda: the rolling out of Axapta and the stock market listing.

Turnover for the first half of the year shows a growth of over 60 per cent, and the estimates from the countries for the rest of the year are well over budget. So management can breathe a sigh of relief for now. The major challenges are: firstly, recruiting a few new resellers for Axapta and, secondly, getting those, who are on board, to start selling quicker. Efforts are needed on several fronts in order to accelerate incoming orders. There are still too many bugs in the product. Indeed, at the end of August, the number of bugs is 80 per cent higher than the previous year. This isn't due to the developers getting worse at programming, but to more resellers and more customers coming on board, leading to a deeper exploration of the product's nooks and crannies as well as the product being constantly expanded with new facilities. For competitive reasons, it isn't possible to put development on hold, so a bigger and better effort is implemented instead to validate and classify the bug reports, many of which aren't bugs, but a lack of insight and experience on the part of the resellers. Investments are also made in IT systems in which resellers can report their problems and search a database of bug reports already submitted. If a solution already exists, it's quicker for all parties if the resellers themselves can find and implement it. With the many initiatives, the number of so-called "bombs" (bug reports not handled within the time frame promised by Damgaard) has been reduced from 300 earlier in the year to 15 for Axapta and 3 for XAL at the end of August. The country managers don't view the situation with Axapta's bugs as especially positive. They are of the opinion that head office is too quick to close the bug reports without the real problems actually being resolved for the sake of statistics.

However, it is agreed that the situation surrounding and the handling of bugs shouldn't burden the business account managers. Product and service managers in the subsidiaries and headquarters in Denmark have to work closely to solve 99 per cent of the problems, so the business account managers and country managers need only be involved occasionally. Preben promises that head office will keep a close eye on the problems and ensure that the sales and marketing staff of the subsidiaries won't spend too much time on this type of productivity-hampering repair work.

## Recruiting everything and everyone

Axapta's strength is also its challenge. The product is new and extensive in every way, making the learning curve both long and steep for Damgaard's own employees, for business partners and for customers. Apart from traditional class-based teaching, plans are made to offer online learning (e-learning). But teaching material for every part of the product has to be developed first, and then made available in English, German and Spanish. The other main languages will have to wait until the company plans further international expansion. Per Pedersen gives each country manager a few pep talks to get them to put aside their reservations and recruit more Axapta resellers. The motto is: "recruit everything and everyone; we'll find out who's working along the way".

## The meeting in Miami

Once the company's general situation after the downward adjustments has stabilised, a two-day country manager meeting is implemented again – this time prior to the business partner conference in Miami in September 2000, which Preben Damgaard opens with the following statement:

*"1999 was far more difficult than we expected – 2000 is just as difficult as we feared"*

There is now significant growth in all the international markets. External Axapta training centres are established in Denmark and Germany and a global certification programme for Axapta is introduced. In May, the first distance learning modules for Axapta are offered, and knowledge transfer via workshops and the central SWAT team works. The number of new Axapta resellers exceeds targets, and intense efforts are now made to get the individual partners started. In the first half of the year, more than half of the sales on Axapta come from new resellers, recruited in 1999 and later. The global marketing campaign, which is to create awareness of the Damgaard name and connect it with ERP and e-business, produces good results. Awards have even been won from a German media organisation. How demand will progress remains uncertain, and the latest projections from analysts are down 4-12 per cent in 2000 and 2001.

Unlike most of its colleagues within the industry, Damgaard has more products at play, and whereas C4 is on its way out, both C5 and XAL are still cash cows, while Axapta is a baby that is well on its way to becoming a star. It's a reassuring situation.

## Full speed ahead

Preben Damgaard shares his gut feeling at the meeting of the Miami managers. He is convinced Damgaard has the right products, the right strategy, the right business partners and the right organisation. It just needs to be executed:

*"Therefore, we're accepting a deficit in the current year. We're not wasting time on cost-cutting measures and we're not laying off staff. We're not cutting back on our investments in development, marketing or sales. We are going full speed ahead and harvesting the fruits of 2001 and the subsequent years. If anyone offered me double the price for my shares, I'd say no thanks".*

Preben is convinced the Damgaard shares will soon be worth significantly more. He urges everyone to act in the situation and use their intuition.

*"We are in unknown waters without a chart, but we can absolutely increase our speed, because there's enough water under the keel."*

The mood is high when the meeting closes. Everyone feels they are the one who will get the project to succeed.

## Heading for a merger

During the 1990s, Erik and Preben Damgaard met several times with Jesper Balser and Torben Wind for an informal chat over dinner. In August 1998, Preben calls Jesper, asking to meet over coffee. During the initial small talk at Jesper's office, Preben talks about the imminent divorce from IBM and the challenges they have faced since the start of the partnership. Jesper, in contrast, recounts the significant success of the international activities, and mentions that it looks like Navision Software's revenue in the current financial year will pass the 100 million dollar mark. Preben notes dryly that it was very lucky for Navision Software that IBM bought into Damgaard Data, after which he comes to the purpose of his visit.

What if they merged? The two companies work with the same type of products, aimed at the same markets. A merger could consolidate a whole range of operations; thereby, saving quite a lot of costs. Despite the products being competitors to some extent, they also complement each other. Navision Software doesn't target the very small companies that Damgaard Data does with its C5 and Light products. Financials and XAL overlap to some degree, while Axapta targets a market where

Navision Software rarely shows up. There is plenty of room for the two companies to easily continue with their products in the export markets in which they both operate, and Financials and Axapta can be positioned in the new countries so they cover a large part of the ERP software market.

Jesper likes the idea, and promises to think about it and discuss it with his co-founders. When a few weeks pass without Preben hearing anything, he calls Navision Software's office again and is told that Jesper has gone on leave for a few months. Preben is busy preparing for the divorce from IBM and the subsequent listing and doesn't follow up on the opportunity. Navision Software is in the midst of forthcoming listing preparations, which is why the timing for discussing a merger isn't great.

## NavisionDamgaard is born

In connection with the stock market listing, Eric Rylberg, financial director of the ISS Group, joins the board of Navision Software in March 1999, but when he is appointed managing director of ISS in August 2000, he can no longer give the board work the same level of attention. Eric asks his predecessor, Waldemar Schmidt, who would like to pursue a new career at board level, if it might be something for him and as it is, Eric puts Waldemar in contact with Jesper Balser.

On Wednesday, 16th August, Waldemar Schmidt is on his way to meet Jesper Balser at Navision Software's headquarters in Vedbæk. He wonders what value he can bring to the company. He doesn't have any detailed insight into the IT industry or any experience in running a software business, but from his many years as head of the ISS Group, he has a solid insight into the strategic importance of IT as well as the hopeless problems that often emerge. Moreover, he has observed that Navision once had a market value that exceeded ISS's, so despite the recent plummet in prices, there has to be interesting potential in the company. From his research prior to the meeting, he knows that, regardless of the still very impressive results, Navision Software faces a number of challenges. The market is breaking up and it's impossible to predict how it's going to develop. The extreme growth rates experienced up to the turn of the century will hardly return. Future growth has to come from massive internationalisation implemented by capable management.

Outside of Denmark's borders, the company is up against the major players, such as SAP and Oracle. They aren't direct competitors, but they have deep pockets and can buy up competitors and make life difficult for little players like Navision Software. Acquisitions can also happen in the domestic market, thus increasing competition for resellers, customers and employees. International expansion is the primary priority, and when he tries to place the competitor Damgaard in the picture, he envisions a biscuit war. Small Danish biscuit producers around the world competed hard with each other at great harm to themselves, but to the great advantage of their international competitors, who watched from the side-lines as the Danes slaughtered each other, especially in the large markets in China and Japan. If Navision Software and Damgaard were to be combined, they would be much stronger on both the domestic and global markets. They would immediately be able to cut a good chunk off their capacity costs. They would need only one finance department, one HR department, one sales organisation and so on. Staff and management functions could be merged in the same way in the subsidiaries and more invested in marketing and more salespeople instead.

The meeting with Jesper Balser proceeds positively. The chemistry is good and they quickly agree that Waldemar Schmidt is the future chairman of Navision Software's board of directors. With the formalities in place, Waldemar asks Jesper how he would view a merger with Damgaard. Jesper tells him about the PCPLUS partnership in the 1980s and about the talk he had with Preben Damgaard in 1998. He confirms that the owners of Navision Software are positive about discussing such a structure. Waldemar is to meet Hans Werdelin, chairman of Damgaard's board of directors, a few weeks later regarding another matter and decides to use the occasion to toss around the idea with him.

When the two meet on Monday, 25th September at 10 am for a cup of coffee at Waldemar Schmidt's office, Hans Werdelin is immediately in favour of the idea. Damgaard released its interim results just a month earlier, which clearly showed the great potential of the company, but also that it's in a critical phase. A merger with Navision Software would solve a number of Damgaard's problems.

On his way home from the meeting, Hans calls Preben and asks a little curiously if there was something he forgot to tell his chairman? When Preben hears about Waldemar Schmidt's proposal, he confirms the talk he had with Jesper Balser at the end of 1998 and the good relations that were built up in the 1980s. As Preben is still positive about the idea of a merger, they agree that he talk to Erik about the situation. If he gives the green light, they can meet and go deeper into the details.

Erik, however, isn't overly enthusiastic. He can absolutely see that a merger would solve a number of short-term problems and probably provide further acceleration for the spread of Axapta, but at what price? He would prefer they continue as an independent company, but given the uncertainty of the market and the need for increased internationalisation, he won't oppose a merger.

On Wednesday, 14th October, Preben Damgaard and Hans Werdelin meet to discuss the situation. Werdelin has extensive experience in business acquisitions and mergers and, therefore, he can also explain what decisions need to be made quickly and how the formal process should be organised now that both companies are listed on the stock market.

The financial situation and distribution of ownership shares should be straightforward, precisely because the two companies are listed on the stock market. And a cut-off date for the merger means that part of the deliberations can be left to the auditors. The vital question – that has to be decided first – is who should be the managing director. There are three possibilities: Jesper Balser, Preben Damgaard or an external candidate. The meeting ends with Preben being asked to consider the management question.

That evening, Hans Werdelin calls Waldemar Schmidt, announcing the go-ahead. They briefly discuss the board issue and agree that Waldemar Schmidt, who took the initiative and represents the largest company in the merger, be chairman with Hans Werdelin in the role of vice-chairman. They also agree that if the merger is a good idea, it should be implemented as quickly as possible and preferably before Damgaard completes its financial year.

Parallel to Jesper Balser and Preben Damgaard thinking about who should be the forthcoming managing director, the search for suitable external candidates begins. It doesn't help that the question of managing director ends in an impasse and it takes two to three months to find a suitable outside candidate.

## Joint managing directors

It becomes clear from Waldemar Schmidt's individual conversations with Preben and Jesper that they would both accept resigning and leaving the helm to an outside director. But Jesper won't accept Preben being assigned the post and Preben won't accept Jesper being assigned the post. However, in mid-October, Jesper and Preben themselves come to Waldemar Schmidt with a solution. Put simply, they will be joint managing directors and lead the company together. This structure is normally unacceptable, but as the two have known each other for years, the chemistry between them is good and as they come with significant owners' shares, Waldemar Schmidt and Hans Werdelin have to admit that it just might work.

Late in the afternoon of Wednesday, 25th October, Waldemar Schmidt and the five main owners – Torben Wind, Peter Bang, Jesper Balser and Erik and Preben Damgaard – meet in Hans Werdelin's kitchen at Hveensvej 2, in Vedbæk. They quickly agree that out of consideration for the employees, for whom the merger will come as a great surprise and even as an outright shock for many, the new company will have to be called either NavisionDamgaard or DamgaardNavision during the transition period. Neither name is optimal, but it wouldn't do to rush the selection of a brand new name, and only choosing one of the existing names would send the wrong signal to employees, business partners and customers. As NavisionDamgaard sounds best, they choose to go with that.

There is general reluctance at the idea of a two-managing-directors set up, but Hans Werdelin comes to Preben and Jesper's rescue. If the merged company is to be named NavisionDamgaard and if Navision Software, the larger of the two companies, is to be the continuing company and fill the position of chairman (as has been agreed) and now also the position of managing director, it won't look like a merger. Two managing directors, which, according to business school practice is unacceptable, could be a good solution here, as it's a founder of each company. Moreover, Jesper Balser lives abroad while Preben Damgaard lives in Copenhagen. With Jesper Balser as one of the directors, Damgaard's employees could rightly feel they have been passed over. That wouldn't be good for the subsequent working environment. Everyone is aware that a merger can easily focus the employees' attention inwards, causing long and fatal conflicts over almost everything, especially regarding who is to have what position. A new managing director, from the outside, would need a long time and a lot of energy to gain the necessary insight before they could make crucial decisions. The advantage of having both Preben and Jesper as directors is obvious. They have both proven capable of leading their businesses from their fragile beginnings to what they are today. They have many years of experience in the market, enjoy great respect among employees as well as the resellers and have detailed insight into their respective companies. Furthermore, they are both the bearers of distinctive cultures and identify to a large extent with their companies, both internally and externally. As it's vital that the new company quickly translate the potential synergies into external impact forces, the risk will be substantially reduced if continuity on the top floor can be ensured. Actually, it may be conducive to the necessary merger of the cultures of the two companies and even motivate the employees with Jesper and Preben being role models for how the partnership can work.

Hans Werdelin's arguments find fertile soil, and it is accepted that Jesper and Preben share the post of managing director. The search for external candidates is called off.

Jesper will be responsible for the capital markets, IT and communication (PR), while Preben will deal with sales and marketing, including the subsidiaries and products. They will both be responsible for strategy.

The other managerial positions are assigned as follows: Niels Bo Theilgaard from Navision Software becomes head of development. René Stockner will be sales and marketing director as well as director of all the subsidiaries, while Damgaard's Freddie Jørgensen and Lars Larsen are HR director and financial manager, respectively.

Project Hveen, eponymously named after the site of the epoch-making meeting, has begun.

## René forgets to breathe

Jesper Balser walks into René Stockner's office the next morning and asks if Damgaard is still the most annoying competitor. René confirms that it most certainly is. Jesper says that things should become easier on that front now, because the two companies are going to merge. Moreover, responsibility for the total sales of all products will be René's.

René is momentarily speechless, and Jesper has to remind him to breathe before something bad happens. More time passes before René utters a word. However, it doesn't take him long to understand the huge potential of such a merger. There may well be a thousand practical things to clarify, but the result will be a quantum leap towards fulfilling the ambitions that René has, too. That he will be responsible for the entire sales side of the project makes it even more exciting.

## 14 days to get things in place

On Thursday, 26th October, the boards of the two companies are formally notified of the merger plans, and on Friday, Waldemar Schmidt and Hans Werdelin stick their heads together to draw up the timetable. The merger team consists of the two chairmen and Eric Rylberg. Preben Damgaard, Erik Damgaard, Lars Larsen and Freddie Jørgensen participate from Damgaard, while Jesper Balser, Torben Wind, René Stockner, Niels Bo Theilgaard and Investor Relations Manager Lars Plesner Hamann participate from Navision Software. To avoid anything leaking out prematurely, it's agreed that Damgaard be referred to as Denmark and Navision as Norway. Enskildas Securities and ArosMaizels (now Nordea) are chosen as financial advisers; Kromann Reumert are the selected lawyers; KPMG, Mortensen & Beierholm and PriceWaterhouseCooper are brought aboard as the chartered accountants; McKinsey & Company are the advisory consultants and the PR advisors are Jøp, Ove & Myrthu ApS.

A merger prospectus now needs to be drafted so all shareholders and the public can gain insight into the purpose of the merger; the vision and the strategy of the new company as well as clarify what shares the shareholders will own from now on. Moreover, as many management positions in the organisation as possible should be determined in advance, so the company loses as little momentum as necessary and can immediately start harvesting the synergy.

On Saturday, 4th November at 10 am, Jesper Balser, Preben Damgaard, René Stockner, Waldemar Schmidt, Freddie Jørgensen and Niels de Coninck-Smith from the McKinsey & Company consulting firm meet for a full-day's meeting at the home of Hans Werdelin on Hveensvej. There is much to be discussed and clarified prior to the announcement of the merger to the management teams of the two companies, which is scheduled to take place on Saturday, 18th November. The public will be informed the following Monday via a stock exchange announcement and an investor and press conference. That means the team has 14 days to get as many details as possible in place.

## Per and René come to think of a difficult task

When Per Pedersen is on his way from his home in Herfølge to the office in Birkerød on Monday, 6th November, he receives a call from Preben Damgaard, who informs him of the situation and tells him he has to yield the post of director of marketing and sales and, therefore, won't be a part of the executive office of the merged company. Furthermore, he is to agree his future role with René Stockner and assist him in putting together the future marketing and sales organisation, including how the merger should be implemented in all the subsidiaries.

Per now heads for a location in Copenhagen, where he is to meet René Stockner and start work. The chemistry between Per and René is good. They immediately agree that Per will be responsible for the overall activities aimed at the Danish market and that his new organisation will be housed in Damgaard's premises in Birkerød. After which, they start on the other positions – that turns out to be somewhat more complicated.

There are subsidiaries in 16 countries in all, distributors in another 15-20 countries and then the central sales and marketing organisation. The most pressing thing is distributing the management positions in the subsidiaries and in the central sales and marketing function. They can discuss how to deal with the distributors later.

Despite the fact that Navision Software has the greatest revenue and is currently growing fast, their central marketing organisation is less developed than Damgaard's. The reason is that Navision Software chose to hand over marketing and reseller management to external distributors from the start, which, in turn, means that the latter largely decided how to organise and implement Navision's market management. Only immediately prior to the stock market listing in 1999 did Navision Software acquire distributors and employ the former owners as country managers. The principle of independence was carefully adopted here, and as that principle is still producing very good results, there is no great incentive to change the concept.

Damgaard's internationalisation progressed completely differently. Following the divorce from IBM and in preparation for listing, Damgaard quickly established subsidiaries in a long list of countries. With that as the starting point, the concepts of marketing and sales work were organised centrally, after which they were implemented in the various countries. Damgaard's country managers are used to working closely with the central marketing organisation on preparation and execution. Given the fundamental differences in the way the companies operate, it is difficult to choose the managers before the future modus operandi (either Navision Software or Damgaard's principles) on which the company is to be built has been decided. René and Per agree that in time the company will have to head more in the Damgaard direction, but they are aware that this will be met with resistance in Navision Software's subsidiaries and perhaps also by Jesper Balser, who believes independence is a major strength. However, they do agree that Damgaard's marketing manager, Jette Børsting, will be head of the new central marketing function in the merged company. She is to be responsible for the development of NavisionDamgaard's new brand and associated global campaigns.

When René and Per are about to address the distribution of management posts in the subsidiaries, Per tells René that Damgaard is in the process of introducing a regional structure. The number of countries has simply grown too great for Per to have all the country managers report directly to him. René is sceptical about the structure. He would like to avoid an expensive middle management layer for as long as possible. When that initiative is finally implemented, its tasks and powers will have to be thoroughly discussed.

As Hans Peter Bech's contract in Germany is about to expire and he is to return to Denmark, Damgaard's activities there can immediately be placed under Navision Software's German subsidiary. The same can be done with Flemming Beisner when his contract in Spain expires, and he is to be moved to another position. But what are they do in the meantime? After some discussion, René accepts the establishment of two regional manager positions: one for Central Europe for Hans Peter and one for southern Europe for Flemming. Responsibilities and powers will have to be addressed along the way.

The purpose of the entire exercise is harvesting the synergy. This means that some country managers will no longer be on the payroll. If anyone can be transferred to and fit into other position, which needs to be filled anyway, then that is a natural option, but country managers usually earn highsalaries, so their current salary and employment terms can't automatically follow a job change. Despite both René and Per approaching the task with an open mind, it is hampered by them not knowing each other's employees.

Per and René, therefore, agree to delegate responsibility for the combining and coordinating of the activities of the European subsidiaries to the two newly appointed regional managers, while they deal with laying off Damgaard's country managers in the USA, Australia and the UK as well as Navision Software's country manager in Sweden. Damgaard's country manager in Norway can continue, after which Navision Software's distributor will have to be phased out over time. Navision Software's country managers in the USA, Australia, Germany, the UK, Italy, Spain and France will remain.

Lars Larsen and Freddie Jørgensen review the rest of the company organisation, and it's estimated that 100 positions can immediately be scrapped, while the 50 current vacancies need not be filled. Along with other merging opportunities, the overall synergy will amount to around 28 million USD a year. The costs of the merger and the subsequent integration process is estimated to cost a one-off 45.8 million USD of which 13 million USD pertains to fees for advisors, chartered accountants and lawyers in connection with preparation and implementation. Charges include costs for the outplacement packages offered to all employees being made redundant.

## Every product continues

One of the major questions is how to position the merged company's products. Despite the management of both companies agreeing that all product lines should continue, a merger always creates speculation in the press, among resellers and customers as well as among the employees. Product consolidation or phasing out might be possible in other industries, but in an ERP business, experience has shown that it equates to signing your own death sentence. It's the customers who decide when they will change systems. If a supplier tries to push through a shift, they are typically penalised by their customers going over to the competitors. To eliminate any suspicion of trying to force a product change onto their customers, it must be made clear in the merger prospectus and all other communications that all product lines are being continued. One of the strengths of the merger is that the two companies serve practically the same type of customer and have completely identical business models. Similarly, there is also a great overlap between XAL, Axapta and Financials. And, surprisingly, it's rare that they are in direct competition with each other for the same projects. Even in Denmark, where both companies have large market shares, they are only occasionally in direct competition. Abroad, both companies have small market shares. Here they are often up against the local competitors. In Denmark, customers often choose a product first, after which they contact the resellers, who can help them understand the implementation.

Therefore, there is no great risk that a merger would lead only to an increased product substitution.

However, employees, resellers, customers, analysts and journalists all ask which customers the three products will be aimed at in the future, and it will certainly seem a little tame if the company doesn't have a good answer for that question.

In the long term, it makes no sense to outside parties that Navision-Damgaard continues to develop products with similar content, aimed at exactly the same customers. This understanding is correct for products that are immediately replaceable – something ERP products aren't. Naturally, customers, who are to choose a new system, have considerable freedom of choice, but once a system is implemented and put into operation, it has significant associated costs, inconveniences and risks at being switched to another system. The resellers have also invested significant sums in training and building up their organisations and, with a few exceptions, they don't handle products from both companies.

Therefore, the merged company has many more good reasons to continue its product lines than to try to save costs by pushing to get customers and resellers to switch from one product to another.

On Sunday, 12<sup>th</sup> November, Jesper Balser, Preben Damgaard, Erik Damgaard, Torben Wind, René Stockner, Per Pedersen and Niels Bo Theilgaard meet at McKinsey & Company in Copenhagen city centre to clarify the issue of product positioning. Apart from Damgaard's C4 and C5, which are for the very small companies, and exclusively marketed in Denmark, there is – in theory – a great overlap between XAL, Financials and Axapta. Axapta's technology means the product can handle complex business processes for customers with many users, but both XAL and Financials are also being used in large installations and Axapta is even in operation at small customers. XAL and Axapta contain facilities for manufacturing companies – something Financials doesn't immediately do. Though a number of Navision Software's resellers have developed modules so the product can actually be used for production and project management. The positioning task is complicated by the fact that it's ultimately the resellers, who decide which customers they will target and they are free to add whatever facilities necessary to be attractive and competitive.

Damgaard has experienced a significant decline in turnover on XAL since the announcement of Axapta. The merged company would probably experience something similar on revenue on Financials, which is why it's especially important to place the two products differently on the market. The conclusion of the talks reads as follows in the final prospectus:

*Damgaard Axapta*
*Damgaard Axapta is technologically the most advanced, comprehensive and scalable product in the shared portfolio of products and is delivered to medium and large companies with up to 1,000 concurrent users. Damgaard Axapta features most of the applications demanded by medium-sized production companies and also offers a good web-enabling architecture.*

*The many possibilities mean that the product has the longest sales cycle and implementation time of NavisionDamgaard's products. Damgaard Axapta requires a partner network that understands production and/or distribution companies. NavisionDamgaard will position Damgaard Axapta selectively in relation to the most advanced partners in the joint network of authorised partners.*

*Navision Financials*
*Navision Financials is positioned as NavisionDamgaard's product for the broad market, focusing on light industry, trade and service with up to 300 users. The majority of end users are typically companies with 5-50 users. NavisionDamgaard will continue to expand and add functionality to this solution, which, among other things, is characterised by a high level of user friendliness and relatively short implementation time.*

*Damgaard XAL*

*Damgaard XAL is targeted at the smaller companies in the middle market with typically 5-50 users. Damgaard XAL is tailor-made to meet the requirements of a number of sectors within production, distribution and service. NavisionDamgaard will continue the product and continue to support and maintain the installed base and partner network.*

*Damgaard C5 and C4*

*Damgaard C5 and C4 are the company's smallest solutions for small businesses with up to 5 users. The products are marketed in Denmark alone. Damgaard C5 has so far sold more than 30,000 licences and will continue to be marketed and maintained. Whether there is a basis for marketing the product internationally will be investigated. Support of Damgaard C4 will continue.*

An illustration supplements the explanation, showing the positions of the products in the overall market.

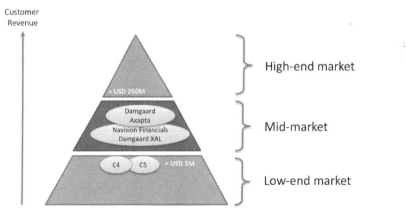

The pyramid, which illustrated the market for ERP software and placed NavisionDamgaard's products solely according to the customers' turnover, proved too simple and led to many misunderstandings among employees, resellers, customers and journalists.

Most people, who read the extensive text, notice the following:

- Navision Financials: 5-50 users
- Damgaard XAL: 5-50 users
- Damgaard Axapta: 1-1,000 users
- Damgaard C5: 1-5 users

This simplification will result in many challenges.

## The merger is announced

Preparations for the merger are successfully kept secret; thus, the invitations to information meetings on Saturday, 18th November can be sent out as planned to the top middle management. A plan has been worked out for who should contact whom and when; on Thursday, managers, who work outside of Europe, will receive a call. European leaders will be contacted on Friday. Everyone is asked to book a plane ticket so they can be in Copenhagen on Saturday afternoon before 3 pm.

Damgaard's group will meet at the SAS Globetrotter Hotel in Kastrup, while Navision's group will meet at the SAS Hotel Scandinavia on Amager Boulevard. The two venues are just a few miles apart. The travel plans have been carefully arranged so the managers from the two companies won't be on the same flights to Copenhagen and, therefore, won't have an opportunity to speculate on the mysterious meeting.

At precisely 3 pm all leading Damgaard employees – with a few exceptions – are sitting in the meeting room of the SAS Globetrotter Hotel in Kastrup. Preben Damgaard welcomes them briefly and thanks everyone for coming at such short notice. Then he gets straight to the point: Damgaard is going to merge with Navision Software. Outside a bus is waiting to transport everyone to the SAS Hotel Scandinavia, where they will meet their new colleagues. There, a presentation of the merger plans will be made, after which there will be an opportunity for questions.

The meeting at the SAS Globetrotter Hotel takes less than ten minutes, whereupon the somewhat perplexed staff get on the bus. They meet an equally as puzzled group from Navision Software at the SAS Hotel Scandinavia about fifteen minutes later.

Jesper Balser and Preben Damgaard stand together on the podium and alternate in explaining the plan. It's clear they get on along well with each other. The interaction between them is natural and relaxed. The rationale behind the merger is easy to understand, so everyone sits impatiently as they wait to see the organisational chart. Who will be let go? Who will be taken on? What jobs will they be assigned?

Fortunately, Preben and Jesper get to the overview without delay, and everyone in the room breathes a sigh of relief. Those colleagues, not present at the meeting or not appearing in the overview either have already been notified.

The participants will all receive the presentations by e-mail after the meeting so they can inform their respective employees on Monday morning. Despite everyone being sworn to secrecy, the rumours start to trickle out as early as during Sunday, but when all employees are informed Monday morning at 9 am at the same time as a comprehensive stock market announcement and press release, the communication remains under control. An open investor and press conference is held at Arkitekternes Hus [The Danish Association of Architects] in Copenhagen city centre on Monday, at 1 pm. Due to a number of formalities, including approval by the competition authorities, the merger officially first falls into place on 21st December. This means that those employees, who still don't know their future role must wait until after this date to discover their destiny. In the period from 21st to 31st December 2000, 100 employees will be made redundant. It's not a nice time to be given a redundancy notice, but letting employees take their Christmas holidays without knowing if they have a job to return to in the company in the New Year is considered to be even more unacceptable.

All formalities are in place on 21st December, and at the AGMs of the two companies, the merger is finally confirmed. The new Navision-Damgaard is born.

When the new board is subsequently assembled for the constituent meeting of the board, an employee interrupts the happy atmosphere, reporting that Microsoft has announced they intend to purchase the

American competitor Great Plains Software. The meeting room falls completely silent until the new chairman, Waldemar Schmidt, remarks the merger now seems to have been perfectly timed.

*"Had we merged after this announcement had taken place, our initiative would have been viewed as a response to it. Now we can just recognise a change in the competitive landscape."*

## Merger technicalities

Technically, Navision is the continuing company, which means the company's capital is increased by 10,030,772 shares of 1 Danish krone, and as the price on the cut-off date[13] is the same for both companies, Damgaard's shareholders can exchange their shares (at ten Danish kroner per share) at the ratio 1:1. Thus, following the merger, the former Navision Software shareholders own 72 per cent of the total company, while the Damgaard shareholders hold 28 per cent.

## The merger's rationale

Why is a merger between Damgaard and Navision Software only a reality in December 2000 when Preben Damgaard and Jesper Balser both liked the idea as far back as 1998?

It was a good idea back in 1998, but the timing was poor. The situation had changed fundamentally by autumn 2000. Both companies had had a few scares. Whereas prior to their respective stock market listings the previous year they found themselves in a market with enormous growth rates, the future was suddenly more uncertain. For Damgaard, the merger was a major boost to internationalisation in that it utilised Navision Software's broader and better established network of subsidiaries. At the same time, Damgaard was able to avoid having to finish the year with its first ever deficit. The new company could instead report that turnover for the financial year 1 July 2000 to 30 June

---

13   The cut-off date is 10 days before the official stock market announcement (20th November 2000), when Navision's price is 227 DKK and Damgaard's is 226 DKK.

2001 was expected to show growth of approximately ten per cent. The primary operating profit, before goodwill depreciation allowance, was estimated to be around ten per cent of revenue after factoring in that part of the estimated synergies expected to be realised in the second half of the 2000/2001 financial year.

Both companies were obvious candidates for acquisitions. Indeed, Damgaard shares were probably the more attractive here. If you wanted to enter the Danish market, Damgaard had the largest market share. If you wanted to buy new technology, Damgaard – with its new Axapta – was the best buy. And, even better, Damgaard could be purchased at a much lower price. If you wanted to buy market share in Europe, Navision was probably the best, but obviously more expensive, option. Jesper Balser actually considered the imminent risk of Damgaard running into further downward adjustments with subsequent new falls in prices. The cheaper the price became, the greater the possibility of a foreign company ac-quiring Damgaard and, thus, the risk of a new and not very attractive competitive situation in the Danish market. The only safeguard against this situation was Navision Software itself taking the initiative to acquire or merge with Damgaard.

Last but not least, they had both experienced the difficulty and risk of expanding internationally. Thus, Navision's great success in Germany wasn't only a consequence of the size of the market, but a result of three highly skilled and persistent entrepreneurs. Not only did the trio of Lars Damgaard Andersen, Jesper Bowman and Per Grønfeldt have the idea of taking Navigator to Germany, they did the hard work of adapting the product themselves, and they themselves drove the German Autobahns to get resellers and customers to use the products. It took three years from when they started until they could make a living from it. The huge success only came when Navision Software launched its Windows-com-patible Financials in 1995. The future expansion strategy can't be based on there being corresponding unsolicited endeavours from enthusiastic individuals or teams; rather it has to be implemented by establishing and investing in new subsidiaries. It's an expensive strategy, both in terms of setting up and operating the subsidiaries, but also with regard to the infrastructure that has to be in place in the headquarters to carry out and lead the expansion.

With the merger, each company could almost halve its sales costs and a large part of its administrative costs. Despite both companies having had ambitions to become global market leaders, it's made more clear than ever for Preben Damgaard and Jesper Balser in 2000 that actually fulfilling such goals would require even greater investments if the companies are to grow faster than the many hundred local competitors, who might not have the same ambitions but who weigh heavily on the national markets. Moreover, the industry expects a consolidation, whereby the smaller, local suppliers are bought by major international players, such as SAP and Oracle, by which they suddenly have grander aspirations and more muscle.

When the merger becomes a reality, it's also due to both companies being Danish and their headquarters being less than ten miles apart. But the crucial factor is undoubtedly the executives of both companies. There is a 100 per cent correlation between Preben Damgaard and Jesper Balser's personal and business interests. Neither of the two see a division of power as a threat to their career. Financially, they are both extremely well cushioned. Their motivation isn't to be found in remuneration packages, job titles or areas of responsibility, but solely in making the company the world's leading supplier in the market. They are open-minded as to how that position is to be reached. That they both can continue in the top management of the company makes the merger extra appetising and when the board agrees (reluctantly) it's due to their special background as founders and co-owners. Jesper Balser and Preben Damgaard are both slightly reserved, introverted people, who are quite ambitious and competitive, but neither of them has a huge ego to be continuously tended to and which would stand in the way of practical solutions being found. They have learned they can count on each other, and, from the start, they trust they are each solely governed by the company's interests.

## Christmas peace descends

In mid-December, both companies must again report their expectations for the half-year and full-year earnings to the Stock Exchange. While Navision Software pretty much meets its expectations, it's a little more difficult for Damgaard, which is hit hard by the recessive Danish market and the product shift from XAL to Axapta. However, the media's attention is focused on the merger, its main characters and the new company's overall performance and expectations. After which Christmas peace descends upon Denmark. Everyone goes on holiday to catch their breath and gather their strength for a new year in which their sleeves will have to be rolled up to meet the expected revenue and earnings projected by the merger. Efforts also have to be made to resolve the hundreds of awaiting internal tasks associated with the merger as soon as possible.

# CHAPTER 21

# FULL STEAM AHEAD ON ALL FRONTS

## A thousand questions demand immediate answers

NavisionDamgaard starts the New Year as a highly effective company. Revenue for the previous financial year (the merger means the financial year is July to June) is nearly 260 million USD, the operating profit is almost 26 million USD, the staff is over 1,000, the customer base comprises roughly 130,000 installations, the international network has more than 2,300 resellers and the company has its own representation in 25 countries. An increase in revenue of 10 per cent is expected for the current financial year against a target of almost 280 million USD and an operating profit of 28 million USD. NavisionDamgaard has become a shining beacon in the Danish business landscape.

Whereas top management has had several months to get used to the idea and work intensively with the overall strategy, employees, business partners and customers first have to understand what the merger will mean for and to each of them. Navision Software is the largest company and also the most successful. Their name comes first in *Navison-Damgaard*. Formally, Navision Software is the continuing company, and with the decision that the new headquarters will be in its premises in Vedbæk, many Damgaard employees view the merger as more of a takeover. As decisions regarding who is to remain in positions of management in the subsidiaries are made, that belief is strengthened.

Management, therefore, consciously tries to counteract that perception of the takeover by involving the employees in the hundreds of considerations and decisions, which a merger gives rise to. It's also aware that camaraderie isn't exercised when positions are to be filled with internal candidates. Yet it's also inappropriate to prevent a manager from choosing the candidate they prefer. Although Navision Software and Damgaard have completely different cultures, neither of them has the tradition of micromanaging. That a manager may have difficulty assessing the appropriate candidates from the other company is unavoidable and, therefore, they prefer to go with staff they already know. As Navision Software has more employees and, thus, more managers than Damgaard, there is a natural imbalance.

## Mergers seldom come at opportune moments

The merger will affect some employees more than others: those employees, whose positions are abolished, are hit worst of all, but others also feel the squeeze from the merger. For example, Damgaard had decided to set up a subsidiary in Italy the year before. Michael Graves, sales manager of the American subsidiary, was offered the position as country manager. Therefore, he and his family head to Milan in autumn 2000, so he can begin preparations and find a place to live. The entire family take an intensive language course, so they can get by in the local language as quickly as possible. He winds up his work and obligations in the USA and packs the contents of his home into containers to be shipped to Milan to coincide precisely with when the merger is announced. Navision Software already has a well-functioning subsidiary in Milan, and there is no need for additional senior executives. However, there is a need for Michael to remain in the USA where Damgaard has dismissed its country manager and, therefore, needs someone to help merge the American activities. The moving containers are returned to the USA and Michael, together with his family, has to start looking for a home, choosing a school for the children, buying a car, opening bank accounts and so on all over again.

## Mergers are generally subject to risk

Mergers are generally subject to risk. They create uncertainty about the future among employees, partners and customers. That uncertainty is then actively used by competitors and is, thereby, felt all the more by resellers and customers. Head-hunters are also aware that employees in newly merged companies can be unsure of where they stand and systematically go after the best people. Despite both Damgaard and Navision Software enjoying a high level of visibility within the Danish media, in particular, the new NavisionDamgaard by the very nature of its size is even more interesting, and an increasing number of critical articles emerge, which management has to respond to. While there is plenty to attend to externally, the practical details on the inside are also beginning to mount up.

The two companies not only have different cultures, but also very different remuneration and employment conditions. Policies for employee benefits and other employee conditions are also different. When the new HR function reviews the situation, the list of significant differences to be reconciled is no less than 50. In principle, every employee is employed on an individually negotiated basis, but paying people, who carry out the same work with the same qualifications and enthusiasm differently isn't sustainable. The challenge is, naturally, that everyone is ready for improvement, while nobody wants be downgraded. Formally, any and all changes in salary and employment conditions must be noted with an employee's termination period. If the employee doesn't accept the new terms, then, in practice, they are fired. Management naturally wants to avoid that situation as far as possible. But having to negotiate with over 1,000 individual employees is an impossible task. Choosing the most advantageous common denominator for each of the 50 points would be extremely expensive, but after having struggled with the problems for a couple of months, it's the only remaining option that can be swiftly implemented.

Apart from the salary and employment conditions specified in the employment contracts, the company's other HR policy conditions need to be coordinated. At Navision, a large buffet is served every morning, where employees can start the day with a cup of coffee, freshly squeezed orange juice, muesli, fresh fruit, eggs and bacon, freshly baked bread rolls and so on over a cosy catch-up with colleagues. Should this now be introduced at the offices in Birkerød, too? Navision also has free sweets in the kitchenettes in every department – should that now be introduced in Birkerød, too? And what about Navision's free bottled water, lemonade and ice tea in the fridges? What size car can be rented when travelling for business? Are hotel rooms going to be shared at business events? When can you fly Business Class? The list of issues to be coordinated is long and as not all of them can be resolved in advance, quick decisions are often made when a concrete example arises.

Of course, with new teams and new managers, the all-round chemistry isn't great. Instead of discussing the disagreements directly with the parties involved, they are often discussed with previous managers and colleagues. In many cases, managers further up in the organisation or the HR department have to get involved, so as to solve the problems and get things settled down, so progress can be made on those tasks, which actually create value for customers and resellers alike.

The further away from the headquarters in Birkerød, the greater the uncertainty, and the more often speculative stories of the merger's aim and consequences surface.

## A million for miscellaneous consulting

The merger activities and the work on the many open questions require external assistance. Firstly, there is a need for people, who are completely neutral in relation to the outcome of a given question. Secondly, there is a need for people, who can help facilitate the analysis process that is to lead to well-founded decisions. Both management and employees are busy with their everyday work. Moreover, they are also parties affected by the questions discussed, and are, therefore, too biased to be running the clarification and justification process with sufficient neutrality. When the merger preparations started the previous year, Waldemar Schmidt had put the consulting firm McKinsey & Company into the position of assisting with this type of task, but Jesper Balser, in particular, wasn't overly excited about the work they carried out in relation to product positioning. Therefore, he asked Freddie Jørgensen to inform McKinsey that they were being taken off the project. Naturally, this didn't sit well with the world's most reputable consulting firm, but the decision was irreversible. A few days later, Freddie Jørgensen received an invoice for one million Danish kroner with the laconic text "miscellaneous consultancy work". It now turned out that no agreement had been signed with the consulting firm about how it would be reimbursed for its work but Freddie thought paying 200,000 USD for a couple of meetings and a few proposals was expensive. Jesper Balser doesn't want to get involved, so he asks Freddie himself to find a solution, which is that they get their one million Danish kroner. In doing so, they were also most definitely removed from the project. Instead, PWC Consulting is engaged for the strategy work and Kjær & Kjærulf for the organisational development.

## A change of name

NavisonDamgaard was chosen as a temporary name only. A new name and a new graphic identity, which can form the basis for future communication, needs to be found quickly. Neither part can give the impression that Navision Software took over Damgaard or vice versa. Jette Børsting, global marketing manager, asks the two companies' advertising agencies to come up with proposals for a process, which can lead to the wording of the "brand promise", including the new graphic identity, as soon as possible.

Young & Rubicam gets the job. They assign their global branding expert, Sue Mizera, from the Geneva office to the task. Sue and her team interview a number of customers, resellers and NavisonDamgaard employees to find the core values that the company is understood to represent. After which, they recommend that the merged company shortens its name to simply Navision. Navision Software merged with Damgaard and became NavisonDamgaard. Now, it's just Navision that is to continue, which sounds good and builds on the level of brand awareness that Navision Software managed to create. Damgaard also sounds good. However, it doesn't enjoy the same level of recognition in the global markets, and it's also too closely linked to Erik and Preben given the sensitive merger context.

Top management agrees that Navision is the best name. But it will undoubtedly reinforce Damgaard employees' perception that the merger isn't a merger but an acquisition. Preben sends out a feeler via email regarding the name choice to a number of select Damgaard employees and has it confirmed that the choice of name and, in particular, the retention of Damgaard in the company's name is of great significance.

When all the Danish employees are gathered in the canteen at the head office in Vedbæk on 15th March, Preben summarises why the name NavisonDamgaard isn't working and why it's urgent that a new name be found. The new name has to be at the core of a common identity, which is to enable a quick launch of new and effective marketing campaigns. He explains that the work of the advertising agency has ended in an impasse, because he and Jesper Balser can't agree. They decide to toss a coin to choose the company's future name. Preben wins.

An artistic pause follows, allowing the curiosity of the audience to intensify. Preben continues: *"Therefore, our new name is..."* a second pause for effect, before he moves on to the next PowerPoint slide.

# *NAVISION*®

## *The Way to Grow*

The name change from NavisionDamgaard to Navision was the right choice
in terms of the market, but it hurt many of the former Damgaard employees.
Only Preben Damgaard emphasising that it was his wish, and he, who pushed it
through, mollified the upset staff.

He examines the rationale behind the decision and gives the word to
marketing manager Jette Lundquist, who reviews the elements in the
new corporate identity as well as the new payoff *"The Way to Grow"*.

It has to be asked: why is the Damgaard name apparently more important to the employees than it is to Preben and Erik? The explanation
lies, first and foremost, in the fact that it was possible to create an entirely exceptional identification between the company and its employees,
who simultaneously developed a special loyalty to the two brothers as
individuals. Navision Software had been Damgaard's nemesis for years,
and its great success prior to the merger was especially tough on the
self-belief of Damgaard's employees. There was a clear feeling of being
beaten in the merger, and many perceived the choice of the name Navision as an attempt to beat Preben and Erik, too. Intellectually-speaking,
everyone understood that Navision was the right name, but it's only
due to Preben communicating the decision as one he himself pushed
through that feelings are calmed and everyone moves on. Navision Software's employees had a similar affinity for their company, but when it
came to the balance of feelings, there was more at stake for Damgaard's
employees. They were the underdogs, who had suffered the most before
and during the merger.

The name choice is right one and the new payoff *"The Way to Grow"*
is nothing short of genius. Firstly, it speaks to every stakeholder with a
promise of being on the way to something better. Secondly, it captures the
essence of the company's ambition. Growth – faster growth than that of

both competitors and markets – was Navision Software's and Damgaard's ambition. That remains the main priority of the new Navision.

With the new name and the brand identity in place, Jette Lundquist now begins the laborious, but necessary, task of establishing and creating support for a common communication strategy. The new Navision has to wipe the slate clean and start afresh, and it has to leverage the clear economies of scale by running the same types of campaigns across all markets. The need for coordination is further strengthened by the fact that the English-language communication taking place via the internet has a major global spillover effect. Inconsistent messages would only cause confusion. Jette and her team frequently visit the subsidiaries to get to know their colleagues and gain insight into and understanding of the local market conditions and marketing initiatives. After which, new concepts are gradually introduced, which bring together and replace the local ones. It doesn't always go smoothly when the subsidiaries in differ-ent countries have to adapt. The major subsidiaries, in particular, resist. However, Jette and her team manage to glean much inspiration from the respective countries and ensure, via the constant and close communica-tion, that everyone feels a part of the team and can influence both the form and content of the marketing strategy. Therefore, the new Navision is quickly released from the vacuum that often follows a merger in which none of the old marketing concepts can be continued. With the founda-tion in place as early as mid-March 2001, marketing efforts again start to move up a gear – unusually fast.

## Product positioning causes confusion

Both competitors and Navision's own resellers consciously spread ru-mours that the company is going to reorganise, merge and cut product lincs. Competitors actively use Navision's own product positioning, in particular. They make potential customers aware that Axapta is only for very large installations; that Financials isn't for projects of more than 50 users and that XAL can handle 25 users at most. It greatly annoys the resellers. Never before have they had to respond to these type of claims that have no base in reality. Axapta could be quite relevant for a custom-er with only a few users, while XAL and Navision Financials could be relevant for 25 and 50 users, respectively. That assessment has been in the hands of the resellers and customers until the merger. Only if there were reasonable doubts in a specific case, were Damgaard and Navision Software consulted in turn.

Even the company's own employees wonder a little too much from time to time. They talk about or hint at decisions with colleagues, journalists, resellers and customers, who then repeat those stories, launching a kind of game of Telephone, where the stories eventually make their way back to the employees, who don't recognise them. And energy has to be spent on addressing those misunderstandings.

On 8th December, the German weekly, *Computerwoche*, publishes an article speculating on the significance of the merger for Navision's products. Market analysts claim the company's ambitions for savings can only be met if the number of products is reduced. The article fails to mention which analysts exactly reached that conclusion and on what basis, but goes straight to reporting that Navision Financials is intended for customers who have between 5 and 300 IT users; that Axapta is targeted at major customers with up to 1,000 IT users, while XAL is a low cost alternative to businesses with between 5 and 25 IT users. The article asks why the company would continue to provide products that are allegedly the same, and then quotes a Navision reseller, who was promised that the user limitation on Financials would be lifted and, thus, would cover the same segment as Axapta.

Both the German XAL resellers, with DITEC at the forefront, and the German Axapta resellers are furious and the Navision headquarters has to quickly make a corrective statement.

The positioning polemic creates complications for the business partners. There are still no plans to reduce the investments in product development, and neither are there plans to stop any product lines. The synergy only concerns a reduction in the number of middle managers and employees where there is an overlap. And, actually, there isn't any on the development of products.

However, the outside world can't grasp that Navision doesn't have such consolidation plans when they themselves have announced that the products – with the exception of the number of IT users – are exactly the same. Management quickly becomes aware that the product positioning, which they conceived in haste with McKinsey & Company in November the previous year, is creating far more problems than it's solving. Another type of positioning – one that isn't related to customer turnover or to the number of IT users, but more to the type of task the ERP system is to solve – is needed.

The job is placed in the hands of marketing manager Jette Lundquist. With the help of an external consultant, an analysis is made of which customers use which products, and via interviews the incentives for their choices are elaborated upon. A clear picture now develops of how customers of Financials and Axapta differ from each other, and with that knowledge, a new and far more nuanced storytelling is prepared.

Financials is compared to a VW Passat and Axapta to a Range Rover. The Passat is the solid workhorse that delivers predictable and reliable work to handle the known everyday routines. The Range Rover can do the same, but it's also suitable for comfortable driving in impassable terrain, where the roads aren't marked on a map. A number of senior executives receive a thorough briefing in the new positioning principles, after which they travel around to the subsidiaries in the second half of 2001, explaining how the story is to be disseminated to resellers and customers. At this time, however, more calm has befallen the subject. Customers have learned that no products have been discontinued. Actually, new versions of all of them have been released.

## Too many products

The new Navision does, however, have too many products, which, generally speaking, can all do the same thing. Moreover, C4/C5 and XAL are considered technologically outdated. That there is still life in C4 (Concorde Økonomi), which was launched in 1986, is due to 26,000 Danish companies using the product and paying about 1.4 million USD annually for maintenance subscriptions and 600,000 USD for licence extensions. C5, which has a customer base of more than 40,000 Danish companies, brings in 12.2 million USD annually, and XAL, used by almost 10,000 businesses in ten countries, brings in about 21.6 million USD.

Many software companies would be quite pleased with such earnings, but as Axapta is expected to bring in around 100 million USD and Financials, 300 million, the desire is to get all C4/C5 and XAL customers over to product lines that have a future potential of millions. The challenge of retaining the 66,000 customers using C4/C5 is that neither Axapta nor Financials lend themselves to them. With Navision's strategy of serving customers with a revenue of between 5 and 250 million USD, the C4/C5 segment could be dropped. But Navision is nervous that competitors would take over that market and, thus, threaten the company from below, while SAP and the other major competitors put on the pressure from above. Both Damgaard and Navision Software started out with the very small companies. Actually, over 5,000 companies still using Navision Financials have just a single user. Therefore, having a product for the very small companies makes sense, despite it at first appearing to be a weakening of the strategic focus. But if Navision is to serve the very small businesses, it needs to be global and not, as is the case with C4/C5, only be sold in the small Danish market.

## New Line

Even before the merger, Navision Software had implemented an initiative that, under the project name New Line, was to lead to a new offer for the very small companies. The product, which is delivered as a hosted service, needs to be able to verticalise, so that industry solutions can be offered and it must be possible to access those solutions from mobile devices. New Line is to make Navision one of the first companies to have a dedicated platform for the ASP format. In spring 2001, 25 developers are employed for New Line, and the first test version – aimed at electricians – is expected to be ready in January 2002. The official launch is expected in April and is initially limited to Denmark. New Line will be released for sale in the rest of the world in 2003, and it's expected to earn 100 million in revenue as early as in 2004.

The challenge with ASP is that despite it being a topic on the lips of journalists and analysts, demand is limited. Both Damgaard and Navision Software had initiated pilot projects with a number of partners prior to the merger, and although the enthusiasm is great, the financial outcome is hard to see. Furthermore, Navision wants someone else to be in charge of hosting and in loyalty to its business model would like for its customers to continue to be served via resellers.

When Navision Software and Damgaard embarked on creating solutions for very small businesses, the prices they demanded were far higher than what can now be expected from an ASP offer, where customers pay a monthly subscription and, by the way, can cancel it at short notice. Entering the market with an ASP solution means finding a new formula for how to quickly scale it. There is no existing established infrastructure of resellers and hosting partners taking on the task, and compared to the modest demand, it's a project with high risk.

## A new role for Axapta

To support product positioning after the merger, the Standard Edition of Axapta is removed. The division of Axapta into Standard, Professional and Enterprise Editions meant Axapta was able to meet the needs of both small and large companies, and pricing was tailored to ensure the versions were competitive in each of the three segments. However, it's obvious that with that structure Axapta competes directly against Financials (which, with the merger, and after being released with expanded functionality, changes its name to Navision Solutions and later, when every product is renamed, to Navision Attain). In principle, such a substitution has no great effect on the company as a whole, but it's a serious threat for the Attain resellers, which is only reinforced by their supplier now also directly recommending and profiting from Axapta.

Above all, Navision has to avoid Attain being perceived as "an old product" as it may cause customers to consider alternatives – the result of which won't necessarily be Axapta. The Attain channel is both larger and far better established than the Axapta channel, which is why there is absolutely no capacity to cope with a drastic substitution. There is good reason to protect Attain and the product's well-established reseller channel. When Navision raises its prices on its strategic products in mid-2001, product differentiation is supported by giving Attain a 10 per cent price increase, while the price of Axapta Professional increases by 20 per cent and Enterprise by 12 per cent.

Axapta becomes more exclusive with the initiatives, but now there is a serious lack of a product for companies with five to ten users. An analysis reveals that 65 per cent of all companies using Navision Financials have less than 10 users. Therefore, the idea of introducing a Small Business Edition is tossed around, which is what the Axapta Standard Edition really was initially intended as. To avoid having to introduce additional product platforms, it's decided that a Small Business Edition business case will be prepared based on the Attain platform, and if that is received positively, the product will be launched in January 2002.

## Navi-Hub

Navi-Hub is a project that provides information services directly to customers via the internet, regardless of which Navision product they use. The project employs six developers and is in need of more resources. There is no deadline for when the service is to come to market, but the expectation is that initiatives will be announced at the forthcoming business partner meeting at the Bella Center in Copenhagen in May.

## Siebel Connector for Navision Attain

A partnership with Siebel CRM Systems, which entails developing a connector for Attain, employs 15 developers. So far, it hasn't produced any great results. There are quite a few divided opinions on whether it makes strategic sense for the project. The rumour is that Siebel is considering incorporating ERP functionality into its solutions, and if that happens, then Navision would be giving a competitor access to its own customer base via the partnership. There might well be an agreement with Siebel in place until mid-2003, but it doesn't contain any obligations. It's decided to wind down the project and move the resources over to the more strategically important areas.

## Navision is to be Number 1 world wide

In February 2001, René Stockner calls a meeting of his regional executives and a number of staff members. Budgets need to be discussed for the coming financial year beginning 1st July. Navision now has to show the world that it's heading towards the leadership position. Many of the competitors feel challenged and some customers delay their purchase decisions, but millions are still being invested in new ERP and e-business solutions. If, in the coming financial year, Navision can move faster than all its competitors, the company will have demonstrated that the merger has been successful and that the new company is well on its way to taking the position as the global market leader. René shows an illustration of Navision's target revenue for the coming financial year:

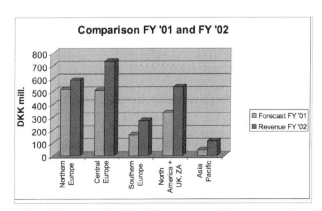

You could have heard a pin drop when René Stockner presented the regional managers with management's growth ambitions for the 2001/2002 financial year in February 2001. With a combined target of 46 per cent, it was four times greater than the most positive assessments of growth in the market.

If Navision can deliver growth of 46 per cent, the company will be number two in Europe, only surpassed by SAP, but in the middle market – its home turf – it would be a clear number one. The growth target is spread: 44 per cent in Central Europe, 14 per cent in the Nordic region, 70 per cent in Southern Europe, 60 per cent between the USA, the UK and South Africa and a whopping 153 per cent is expected to be delivered in Asia/Pacific. In light of the expectations for overall growth within the market for ERP systems, these are extraordinarily aggressive growth targets.

But the ambitions haven't been pulled out of thin air. Since the end of December the previous year, management has been working on a detailed analysis of the company with the help of PwC Consulting. 43 interviews have been carried out with the company's key figures, including all regional managers and select country managers. Every business partner and all ongoing initiatives are thoroughly reviewed. Compared with the situation on the market, the conclusion is that there is significant growth potential, and it must be exploited now.

The aggressive goal is to ensure that the last remnants of old animosity between the company's managers responsible for revenue generation are removed. Given that the bar has been set so high, it can't be reached by sub-optimising only those products that each manager worked with before the merger. Every single product must come into play and all hostility be set aside.

## A new course of action

In the days leading up to Easter, Navision's top executives meet with all regional and country managers in Cairo, Egypt, to assess the situation, discuss plans for the coming financial year and review the product positioning once more. At the meeting, each country manager receives an envelope with the expectations for their results for the coming financial year. The targets are now broken down into quarters and products and include a number of intermediate goals, too, such as the number of new resellers to be recruited, the number of training days to be completed and the total cost budget available. This budgeting approach is new to country managers and goes against the principles that have so far been in place in Navision Software, in particular. Previously, country managers had sent in their expectations, upon which the total budget was built on the sum of the contributions.

Top management, however, believes that the potential is far greater than what the country managers have individually assessed. With a growing organisation comes the increased risk of too much "sandbagging" in the budget.

The meeting reveals significant opposition to both the targets and processes, and some of the country managers openly challenge the 46 per cent growth in revenue. A heated discussion ends with the country managers being asked to come back with what they think is achievable. It becomes clear at the meeting that the new organisation with regional managers isn't working. Navision's country managers in Southern and Central Europe won't report to the new regional managers. It leads to continuous conflicts, because there is no agreement as to whom should handle what tasks. Here, the ways in which the two companies drive their subsidiaries are made clear. Navision Software's subsidiaries were started many years earlier as independent distributors, who built their businesses from the bottom up at their own expense and risk. It took several years before they made reasonable profits, and they were only acquired prior to the stock market listing, where the entrepreneurs were employed on normal country manager contracts. They had been used to considerable autonomy and independence and given the results they had achieved, no one could say that this modus operandi wasn't working brilliantly. Damgaard's country managers had a much different story in that they were employed on normal country manager contracts from the get go and were used to and supported a much more top-down way of working. Moreover, Navision Software's German subsidiary had a unique history and had made an extraordinary contribution to the company's success. Therefore, Lars Damsgaard Andersen, managing director of the German subsidiary, had received a seat on the board of the parent company and only stepped down in connection with the merger. It's difficult for Navision Software's country managers to understand why they now have to run their plans and initiatives past a regional manager, and similarly the regional managers can't understand why it should be done if nobody – including Navision's top management – actually wants it done.

The Southern and Central European regional managers are now removed from the budgeting process, and management completely changes the structure in June, so that all regional manager posts – with the exception of Per Pedersen in Scandinavia – are assigned to country managers from Navision Software. This means the subsidiaries can better follow the tradition of Navision Software, soothing the management of the subsidiaries.

## A provocation

The goal of communicating the 46 per cent growth was to open everyone's eyes to the potential of the new joint company. Management was aware that no country would report such a high percentage itself. The tendency was to focus on the problems of the merger instead of on the opportunities. Navision's country managers were particularly sceptical of Axapta and couldn't see any possibilities at all with the product. It required a powerful and well-documented "provocation" to change that position.

The challenge of jumping from 19 per cent growth in the 2000/01 financial year to 46 per cent in the following financial year is primarily that the reseller channel has to be scaled to handle such growth. It's the resellers – not Navision – who sell and implement the licences. More customers can probably be obtained for the resellers via investing in the general marketing, but 46 per cent growth requires both an increase in the number of resellers and further professionalisation of the entire reseller channel. There is actually a decline in the recruitment of new business partners in the first half of 2001 – probably due to the organisational unrest related to the merger – which means that recruiting resellers needs to move faster in the second half of 2001 and that the new resellers need to be trained and win their first projects before 30th June 2002, when the financial year ends. A growth target of 46 per cent in a market that only grows about ten per cent per year means many potential customers have to be wrestled from competitors.

## Navision and the resellers

After reviewing all products and product initiatives, management concludes that revenue growth in the 2001/2002 financial year is to come primarily from Attain and Axapta, and in order to grow by 46 per cent, equivalent to close on 140 million USD more than the year before, effort needs to be made in a number of areas. Marketing and especially branding need to be heavily invested in so as to lead a large part of the potential demand to the reseller channel. The reseller channel needs to be extensively expanded. The Axapta channel, in particular, needs to be expanded and professionalised. Damgaard's reseller recruitment strategy, whereby almost anyone with a pulse was signed up, had resulted in 110 out of the 336 resellers not having sold a single licence in the first year. The channel needs to be pruned and more productive business partners recruited. With the distinctive dominance of former Navision Software people in managerial posts within the sales organisation, including, and in particular, the management posts of the subsidiaries, there is a risk that it will be easier for them to opt for earning the short-term growth on Attain rather than embarking on the longer and harder task of strengthening the Axapta channel.

But management isn't interested in the subsidiaries using weights and pulleys to bring in the extra revenue. Instead, it wants to build a foundation so that growth can continue at the same pace in the subsequent years until Navision reaches its position as the global market leader. After the merger, some employees skilled in Axapta resigned from their jobs, and if that were to continue, it would pose a threat to the potential represented by the product, which top management wishes to exploit. If Axapta is to achieve the same strength as Attain, it requires that additional staff be employed for recruiting resellers, transferring knowledge from Vedbæk to the subsidiaries and from there to the new resellers as well as moving business partner support to the subsidiaries.

One of the major questions after the merger is precisely the management of business partners as the two companies each have their own reseller contracts and programmes. The differences mean that the competitive conditions aren't the same for each of the company's products.

It's somewhat inconvenient and also places great demands on those employees, who deal with the resellers as they constantly have to be aware of the many differences.

Navision Software had been working on completely reforming its partner programme, so as to give a higher discount on the products and reduce the prices on a number of services, such as training, against 15 per cent of the reseller's total service turnover. Before the merger, Damgaard had used this unusual model as an argument for new resellers to choose Damgaard instead of Navision Software, and it would be difficult to change course now and suddenly believe that it's a fantastic arrangement. The 15 per cent model wasn't popular among Navision Software's subsidiaries and, thus, was only introduced in the USA, Denmark, Sweden, the Netherlands and Belgium, while resellers in Germany, Spain and the UK stubbornly resisted. With the many inevitable other changes and the increased unrest that come with a merger, it's decided to freeze all business partner agreements for a few years. If a reseller wishes to engage with more Navision product lines, they must accept that the terms are different, but as only a small number actually want to do this, the problem is manageable.

Globally, Navision has more than 2,300 resellers in 60 countries, serving more than 130,000 customers in 90 countries. In Denmark alone, Navision has almost 800 resellers, of which 750 offer earlier Damgaard products, while 50 sell Navision products. The number of resellers in Denmark needs to be thinned, while it's estimated that another 500 new partners need to be recruited globally in the coming financial year.

The global reseller channel for ERP products is divided into three layers. At the top are multinational companies, such as IBM Global Solutions, Cap Gemini, Accenture, KPMG, CSC, Siemens Business Solutions and EDS. These companies are suitable for managing large projects, especially large projects with international dimensions, whereas they aren't interested in developing industry solutions and running smaller projects. Moreover, they are characterised by orienting themselves primarily according to customers' preferences. Getting this type of business on board requires the potential large project customer showing a clear preference for a Navision product.

The second layer includes companies such as Columbus IT Partner, Mærsk Data, Steria, Aston, Vanenburg and Grant Thornton, who also have global ambitions and are able to handle international projects, but are more sales-oriented. And in a third layer we find the many, small local IT companies that actually account for 80 per cent of Navision's current business.

Work now commences on recruiting a good handful of the 500 new partners from layer two, while the rest are to come from layer three. Naturally, Navision is also interested in top-level resellers, but without concrete projects, management estimates the interest to be limited and the risk of wasting the scarce sales resources considerable. You have to be ready to move when a concrete project comes along. To motivate country managers into giving the recruiting of new resellers the highest priority, 25 per cent of their bonus is linked to that goal.

## The final budget falls far short of the 46 per cent

The 46 per cent target is unrealistic and the entire negotiating process doesn't inspire confidence in the relationship between Navision's top management and its subsidiaries. Following this experience, the country managers are wary during the subsequent year, when management announces how the growth ambitions are to be built into the budgets. But there is no doubt about management's growth ambitions and that they will go far to exploit the company's potential.

When the accounts are settled the following year, revenue for 2001/02 shows a growth of 18.7 per cent, while the operating profit increases to 70 per cent to 77.8 million USD. Growth of almost 19 per cent on a market that grows by 10 per cent is very impressive. Had the budget target of 46 per cent been insisted upon, then growth of 19 per cent would have been a complete fiasco.

## The Method

Management has demonstrated a strong ambition to build up a global scalable business platform. Therefore, it's decided to align and streamline the principles used to recruit and work with the resellers. Damgaard had to some extent uniform principles for its subsidiaries, whereas Navision's companies ran more independently. On the initiative of Navision's Spanish subsidiary, a comprehensive methodology was developed for dealing with resellers, and it's decided to introduce it in all subsidiaries.

The methodology, called simply the "The Method", covers all activities within management, business development, marketing, sales, implementation and support. The initiative is to ensure that better resellers are recruited; that resellers get started faster, grow faster, make their customers more satisfied and achieve better growth and better earnings overall. A more productive reseller channel would obviously be strongly conducive to Navision reaching its own growth goals. The Method has already been introduced in subsidiaries in Denmark, Spain and Austria, and the results are promising. To keep track of the spread and application of the Method, a certification programme has been developed for the various types of tasks that need to be solved by both the subsidiaries and the resellers. Therefore, specific targets are set for individual subsidiaries to ensure that the Method is introduced broadly. To manage the comprehensive training activities required by the programme, the methodology department is expanded from 5 to 20 people.

## Joint business partner conference at the Bella Center

Unlike Damgaard, Navision Software didn't have an annual Top Performer conference where the business partners competed to participate. As Damgaard announced Top Performer 2000 the previous year, which is to be held in Marbella in Spain in April, the event will go ahead as planned, but will only be open to the XAL and Axapta resellers. However, it's agreed that such an event is important for fostering reseller-loyalty, and that once things have settled down, the best resellers will be brought together at such an event annually.

Damgaard already faced major challenges arranging professional events that included C4, C5, XAL and Axapta resellers prior to the merger. Hardly any business partners are interested in all four products, and only a few are interested in both XAL and Axapta. Adding yet another product line will only make it even more challenging to offer a programme that is equally exciting for all participants. Neither does the new Navision have any interest in too many resellers adding more products to the programme as it would put too much pressure on their scarce resources and weaken their focus. A few large resellers may have sufficient resources to follow a multi-stranded product strategy, but the vast majority won't. Nevertheless, the conclusion is that, from now on, the business partner meetings will be run collectively for all resellers.

To get the ball rolling with a good example, headquarters organises the first collective global business partner conference on the 18$^{th}$-19$^{th}$ May at the Bella Center in Copenhagen. As both resellers and employees are still extremely sensitive to even the slightest uncertainty in communication, it's vital that all messages are clear and that there is a good balance between the different product lines. Moreover, the conference is to confirm the power of the merged company and the benefit of being involved in the ecosystem for both resellers and employees.

To set a high standard from the start, none other than British comedian John Cleese is engaged to open the conference with an hour's sketch on the challenges of providing good customer service. John Cleese outlines how he arrives late at a hotel in the USA and asks the receptionist to make sure he gets breakfast in his room early the following morning. When he tells the receptionist that he doesn't want white bread toasted for his breakfast, the receptionist over-reacts, as white toast is a standard ingredient in the hotel's breakfast and isn't to just be removed. The skit is certainly funny, but more impressive is affording to fly in such a celebrity as John Cleese for an hour's show. The price is the net sum of 200,000 USD, but the investment emphasises that Navision is a world elite.

Over 1,000 people, from all over the world, attend the conference, and for the first time it's realised just how big the company has become. Both resellers and employees are excited about the event, which presents a united Navision with a common voice, a common strategy and where there are no traces left of either Navision Software or Damgaard. Business partners enjoy the experience of being part of something so grand and successful.

## Erik expresses his regret

Erik Damgaard now expects top management to start looking at the direction for the company's future technology platform. As Damgaard has invested over 20 million USD in the development of Axapta, he finds it natural to use that as his starting point. However, prior to the merger, Navision Software had already initiated another technology project, under the code name Jamaica, for a new family of products to supersede Attain when it retires. One of the project's aims is to include tools that will enable customers to describe their business processes, after which the system itself will generate code to perform those work processes, generate the related screen displays and set up database fields at the touch of a button.

Erik believes, firstly, that it's too ambitious technically and, secondly, that the resellers won't be able to handle such facilities properly. Furthermore, he deems Jamaica to have been running too long as a technology project without demonstrating anything that can be used in practice. In his opinion, it's dangerous to let technology projects run too long given that new things are constantly emerging within the IT industry, which then have to be integrated, so the projects never become production ready. Last but not least, he is also disturbed by the large investments being made in something that won't see the light of the day for many years.

His views don't resonate with his colleagues in the development department. He also raises the issue via his seat on the board; some members find it difficult to understand what his protests are really about, but there is also a broad consensus that such matters don't belong there.

Erik doesn't find large organisations easy, and neither his nature nor his experience help him with the politics necessary to change something in an organisation that has become as big as Navision. Facing resistance on all fronts, he gradually retreats from his role as self-appointed chief architect and concentrates instead on further developing Axapta. He doesn't share his dissatisfaction with his employees, but just complains about his plight to Preben. At one stage, his frustration is so great that he directly expresses his regret at having ever agreed to merge the two companies. He can see the great advantage of the merger in the short term, but he is convinced that Navision Software would have broken its neck on the Jamaica project – it will soon realise that the market ran away from Attain and that it wouldn't be ready with a replacement in time. At that point, the ambitious Jamaica project would have drained the company's kitty, so it wouldn't have the degree of freedom to compensate for the mistake. Parallel to this, Damgaard would have come through its product change from XAL to Axapta and could now be accelerating ahead with an ultra-modern product. Of course, the merger can't be undone, so he begins to quietly consider whether his future may lie somewhere other than in Navision.

## Preben goes into cardiac arrest

Despite sharing the top job of managing director with Jesper Balser, there is an enormous burden on Preben Damgaard. On top of dealing with the hundreds of loose ends that have to be tied up, he is constantly on the go talking with customers, analysts, resellers, subsidiaries and journalists. In spite of being a good speaker, Preben is a little reserved and quite an empathetic person, who makes an impact on all levels. When conflicts arise, he takes the time to listen to the parties involved in the dispute before making a decision, which is always based on what he perceives as being in the company's overall interests. After which, plasters are put on the wounds of those who have been refused or put into a tight corner. Preben strives to do the right thing and to ensure that everyone is treated fairly. There is an inexhaustible amount of conflicts in a newly merged business; moreover, a company with over 1,000 employees is a tad more complicated than a company with only half as many. After the stock market listing, and especially after the merger, the company is under the media's constant surveillance. Results have to be delivered to shareholders and despite him and the other founders owning more than 55 per cent of the company and being more than financially independent for some time, it's crucial for him to prove to himself and to the outside world that he is able to lead the new and bigger business successfully. For the first time in his life, Preben Damgaard feels stressed. He struggles to sleep properly and often has a knot in his stomach. The success is taking its toll. Charlotte – his wife – tells him he looks worn out and tired, and that often, despite him being physically present, he seems to be somewhere else mentally.

In May, Preben is diagnosed with a minor hernia and a few weeks later is hospitalised for routine surgery, which goes ahead without complications. When he slowly comes to in the recovery ward a few hours later, he suddenly goes into cardiac arrest. The alarm is immediately raised, and the staff get his heart started again quickly. He barely registers what has happened before he is conscious again, and the doctor informs him of what he has gone through. Less than an hour later, Preben goes into cardiac arrest again, and again the alarm is raised, but this time the defibrillator can't resuscitate him. Only when a doctor injects adrenaline directly into his bloodstream does his heart start pumping. When he wakes up again, he has a massive pain in his chest due to the cardiac massage and a migraine-like headache that hurts so much he cries.

The headache gradually wanes as the hours pass, after which the rest of his hospital stay proceeds as normal and he is discharged a few days later. He takes a few more days off, during which he only checks his emails now and again, while he contemplates the longevity of this life. When a patient is transferred to a recovery ward after an operation, it's precisely in order to deal with any complications arising from the anaesthesia, but cardiac arrest isn't a frequent event post-surgery. He is, therefore, more than lucky that the episode occurs while he is in recovery, wearing electrodes to constantly monitor his condition. Had he been sitting on a plane or in a car, it would have been a completely different story. The incident is a reminder that dramatic things can happen; things you have no control over – even death. Maybe he should be a little more selective about how he spends his time? Is a conversation with a customer, journalist, analyst, reseller, employee and so on more important than a conversation with his wife and children? Is it absolutely necessary to attend all those meetings? What is important now and what can wait?

When Preben returns to work, the only noticeable difference is a slight limp during the first few days when he walks up and down the stairs, but, inside, his priorities have changed.

## With the wind at your back

As early as the beginning of January 2001, management realises that as the total sales for December 2000 are far better than expected, the expectations for the half-year result can be adjusted upwards, both in terms of revenue and earnings. Actually, it's the biggest turnover in a single month ever. Despite the result not being affected by the merger, it's still a very comfortable situation to be in. If things had headed in the opposite direction, management would have had to spend its time explaining and meeting with analysts and the press. Now it can focus all its energy on moving on.

There is good news again at the end of February. Revenue for January is also quite satisfactory and it has even been possible to get most of the layoffs out of the way quicker than expected. Salaries for those made redundant or who resign during the notice period can be taken from the accrued merger costs, after which the operating profit is immediately improved. In the first half of the 2000/01 financial year, revenue has risen by just over seven per cent compared with the same period the previous year, while the operating profit has fallen from 28.8 million USD to 17.2 million USD, but when the company's continued heavy investments in product development, sales and marketing are taken into consideration, the situation is extremely satisfactory. The many costs of the merger, such as consulting services, new company identity, new signs, new business cards, relocation of offices and the termination of contracts are paid from the amount set aside from the first half of the year and, thus, don't affect the operating profit.

As the end of the financial year is approaching in June, the figures show that it's continuing to go far better than expected. It's been possible to implement the cost-related synergy effect much faster than initially assumed, while revenue has simultaneously increased much faster. Indeed, it's going so well that Navision risks drastically surpassing its own announcements. Listed companies have to deliver on their predictions. Delivering a little over is fine, but if they dramatically exceed expectations, they will be criticised for not having reported it earlier and will, thereby, be accused of not having their business under control. Management, therefore, chooses to stop issuing licences at the end of June, so that those orders coming in during the final weeks of the month will be fulfilled in July; thus, counting towards the turnover of the subsequent financial year. This is to guarantee that the previously announced expectations and actual results don't end up being too far apart, while also ensuring that turnover is already being recorded in the books when the new financial year begins. The manoeuvre creates a little more administrative work as those employees, who have part of their salary linked to the revenue and operating profit, can't be affected by the artificial postponement. Therefore, the first couple of weeks in the new financial year are included in the performance-related pay statement for 2000/01.

The first annual accounts for the merged company are nothing short of impressive. Revenue has risen almost 19 per cent to just under 300 million USD, and with a growth in the primary result of about 80 per cent to around 60 million USD, which, thereby, accounts for 15 per cent of the turnover, the conclusion has to be that the merger was the correct choice; that it has succeeded and that the new company is being well-managed. The growth in revenue comes from the international activities alone as the contribution from the Danish market has fallen by six per cent compared to the previous year. Market growth in the rest of Scandinavia is a modest five per cent, while Germany turns out a 24 per cent growth and the USA, 27 per cent. The rest of Europe grows 38 per cent and the rest of the world 63 per cent.

With these great results, Navision has moved a giant step closer to meeting its ambition of becoming the leading provider of integrated ERP systems for medium-sized businesses with a turnover of between 5 and 250 million USD. It's clearly the market leader in the small Danish market, where the main challenge is maintaining the high market share. Via its strong position in Germany, Navision is leading in Central Europe, but is also becoming well established in the rest of Europe and experiencing strong growth in North America and South Africa as well as in Asia and the Pacific. Market coverage is so good in Scandinavia, Germany and Spain that Navision is now working intensively on getting resellers to develop and focus on industry solutions. With industry solutions, Navision products become more attractive to customers and can be implemented faster, whereby resellers can sell more licences. At the same time, the specialisation reduces competition between the individual resellers and, therefore, enables Navision to recruit more partners; thereby, further increasing its market share.

## Double distribution

After the merger, Navision ends up with double distribution in several countries. In numerous other countries, Navision is represented by Columbus IT Partner, which distributes XAL and Axapta, and by Mærsk Data, which distributes Attain. There are also distributors in Finland, India, Norway (Attain), Latin America (focusing on Brazil, Argentina, Mexico and Chile) and in Iceland. In some cases, Navision owns a minor interest in the distributors' businesses.

The primary strategy is for Navision to take over distribution itself, but getting established in the distant markets, in particular, has proven to go faster if local entrepreneurs take on the task at their own expense and risk, though with a view to a significant capital gain. Therefore, all new distribution agreements, which are by nature exclusive, contain precise terms for maintaining exclusivity as well as for when and how Navision can buy back the distribution rights. All parties know from the outset that Navision intends to buy the distributor eventually, who can calculate their own price based on the results they are able to create.

In August, Navision buys back the rights of XAL and Axapta from Columbus IT Partner in Singapore, Turkey, Hungary, Russia, Poland, Belarus, the Czech Republic, Slovakia, Ukraine, Estonia, Latvia and Lithuania. Likewise, in October, it buys back the distribution rights for Attain from Mærsk Data in Russia, Poland, Bulgaria, Hungary, Romania, Turkey, India, Kenya, Uganda, Nigeria, Saudi Arabia, the United Arab Emirates and Tunisia. As a result of the takeovers, 100%-owned subsidiaries are now established in Russia, Poland, Lithuania, Hungary and Turkey. Representation offices are set up in Estonia and Latvia, but the scheme is to gather all the products under the same distributor in each country. Navision doesn't want distributors to compete against each other, but rather, like the philosophy before the new Navision, that they join forces to create a strong brand and leave the resellers to deal with the competition for customers.

## A nice quarterly result

Despite the bloody battle for the 46 per cent growth target in the spring, management can report in November that the first quarter of 2001/02 shows a growth of 23 per cent. Whereas there was an operating loss of 3.4 million USD for the same period the year before, there is now a profit of 10 million USD. The total licence revenue for the quarter is 60.8 million USD of which 65 per cent comes from Attain, while 35 per cent comes from C4/C5, XAL and Axapta of which the latter shows a growth of no less than 82 per cent and now amounts to 12.4 million USD. Germany, which was quite uncooperative before the budget was set, shows a growth of no less than 38 per cent and – given the continued lull in Denmark – with a turnover of 14.4 million USD is once again the largest single market for the company. The rest of Europe is also going well with a growth of 67 per cent, some of which comes from the acquisition of distributors. It isn't that the market has returned to the rate of growth experienced up to the turn of the millennium; rather this is the result of the meticulous work carried out over the last few years combined, not least, with the solid market position achieved by the new Navision. Whether or not potential customers are considering investing in a solution based on XAL, Attain or Axapta, it's about choosing a well-consolidated supplier, who is growing faster than the market and represented by an experienced reseller channel.

Investing in a new ERP system comes with significant risk and, therefore, customers tend to choose a supplier, who can show the longest list of references and which appears to be the most successful. The new Navision is apparently well on its way to a so-called "tipping point", where growth in brand awareness and revenue in itself creates increased demand, because more and more customers choose, of their own accord, to put the company on the list of suppliers to be considered for future investments.

## A lack of acquisitions

In relation to the stock market listings of both companies, an intention to achieve part of the growth ambitions via acquisitions is expressed, but even after the merger is completed at the end of 2001, nothing other than repurchasing the distribution rights for its own products has been done. With the reseller-based business model, which both Navision Software and Damgaard use, it doesn't make any sense to acquire a competitor, who exercises a different business model. In that case, significant surgical intervention in the acquired organisation would be needed, which is done at high risk.

In theory, a competitor with the same business model could be purchased, for example, in Italy, after which the company's revenue can be immediately consolidated into the acquirer's own accounts; thereby, enabling them to show growth. But as the company is in another country, it's difficult to harvest the synergy. The Italian company could, of course, be split up so as to consolidate the distribution activities, leaving a development department and a product that can only be sold in Italy. What should happen next? If it's shut down, customers will immediately penalise the parent company by seeking out other suppliers in anger. If it's allowed to continue, the Italian market itself is too small to bear the costs of maintaining the competitiveness of an ERP product. If it's allowed to quietly waste away, the employees will also start to depart and there is still no guarantee that the customers will stay.

Moreover, those being acquired typically have quite different expectations for a purchase and the price to be paid than the buyer has. The Italian owners expect the acquisition will secure the future of the product, including internationalising the sales and marketing. In light of this, expectations are high, but buyers are rarely prepared to pay for a value, which they believe they themselves have to add. The theory that companies with outdated systems in need of replacement exist isn't wrong. The challenge is that the management of such companies rarely has a realistic perception of its own situation, including the lack of competitiveness of its products. It sees a takeover as a project to save – not phase out – their product.

Buying ERP companies simply to continue running them as independent entities isn't Navision's strategy and doesn't suit the company's DNA at all. Making acquisitions requires capital and the attention of management, and the question is whether or not investing resources in organic growth until the right opportunity comes along would yield a better and more secure return.

The Siebel project, which is scrapped shortly after the merger, isn't successful. The assumption that companies in Navision's market segment will invest heavily in CRM and e-business solutions doesn't come to pass. Rather it appears that most customers are quite pleased with the extensions that Navision continues to add to its products. Such extensions, which are already closely connected to the central modules, such as purchasing, stock control, order management, invoicing, bookkeeping, accounts payable and receivable, project management and so on, can be introduced regularly, requiring fewer investments and fewer disturbances to the customers' organisations.

The many new opportunities that technology and, not least, the internet allow, take far longer for customers to embrace than journalists, analysts and even the IT industry imagine.

## Microsoft makes a direct enquiry

While Damgaard and Navision Software are discussing the merger in autumn 2000, Microsoft is implementing its decision to move into the market for ERP systems. Microsoft, which is the undisputed global leader in a wide range of IT markets, needs more growth than its current business areas can deliver. Therefore, it's seeking out new markets that are large enough to deliver measurable growth rates to the already gigantic company. Given that all companies need to use IT to support their business processes, the ERP market, estimated to be worth close to 30 billion USD in 2001 and to grow by just over 10 per cent a year from now until 2005, is one of the largest markets for the IT industry and, therefore, a natural candidate for a growth area for the company. The expansion is to happen via acquisitions, and in June 2000, Microsoft opens discussions with Great Plains Software, which is already developing solutions for Microsoft's technology, and with whom the latter already enjoys a good relationship. Microsoft is aware that the entry into that market will raise the eyebrows of a number of its business partners, who also rely on the company technologies. However, Great Plains Software doesn't compete directly with the very large partners, such as Siebel, SAP, PeopleSoft and J.D. Edwards, so the assumption is to come to an agreement with the latter and not send them into the arms of competitors.

Despite Microsoft announcing its purchase of Great Plains Software on the very day the NavisonDamgaard merger is formally approved, they are two completely different transactions with two completely different sets of motives. Funnily enough, the new NavisonDamgaard, via the merger, becomes a company that corresponds to Great Plains Software in many ways. On 20th November 2000, Great Plains Software has a market value of 956 million USD, while NavisonDamgaard is listed at 925 million USD. Great Plains Software employs approximately 2,000 employees, has an annual turnover of roughly 240 million USD, develops products for businesses with a turnover of between 1 and 500 million USD, operates a reseller-based business model, has ambitions of becoming a global market leader and is still managed by the company's original founders. NavisonDamgaard certainly views Great Plains Software as a serious competitor in the USA, but outside of North America the latter finds it much harder to gain a foothold – market penetration is particularly slow in the non-English speaking countries. The situation is expressed succinctly by a journalist writing of his visit to the major international CeBIT fair in Hanover for the Danish website Finans.dk on 29ᵗʰ March 2001:

*"Microsoft's acquisition of Navision's rival Great Plains has attracted a lot of attention in the press. But many a thumb was twiddled at Great Plains at the world's biggest IT fair, while Navision's stand was like Piccadilly Circus at times".*

Actually, while discussing their own merger, Jesper Balser and Preben Damgaard had already spoken of contacting Doug Burgum from Great Plains Software to get an idea of the interest in a strategic partnership. The merger of Damgaard and Navision Software was only the first step on the way to being the global leader, and getting Great Plains Software on board would be an advantage for both parties. Thus, it's perhaps not surprising that only a short time passes before Jesper Balser's phone rings. Jeff Raikes, president of the Microsoft division responsible for the acquisition of Great Plains Software, is coming to Copenhagen and would like to invite both Jesper Balser and Preben Damgaard to dinner.

A few weeks later, after the main course has been served in a secluded area of Hotel Sheraton's (now Hotel Scandic Copenhagen) restaurant, by the lakes in Copenhagen city centre, Jeff says that Microsoft is interested in buying Navision, which, with its strong international position outside of the USA, could help secure the Seattle-based company a good global foundation for its entry into the market for ERP systems. Jesper and Preben thank him for the initiative and promise to get back to him in a couple of weeks with their position once the company's board has discussed it.

To be courted by the world's largest software company is obviously very flattering, but both Jesper and Preben have been through this before and have to keep their hair on for now. That Microsoft is serious about its intentions of joining the ERP market is without doubt. Paying just over 1.4 billion USD for Great Plains Software and creating a new division for the purpose testifies to its seriousness. The initiative isn't driven primarily by a desire to simply support the sale of its other products, but by wanting a share of the enormous ERP systems' market, which could help keep the company's – recently slightly sluggish – growth rate up. The president of Great Plains Software, Doug Burgum, is at the forefront of a new division, known as Microsoft Great Plains Business Solutions, and that's a good signal, too.

Navision already enjoys a very close partnership with Microsoft in a wide range of technical areas and bases its products largely on the latter's technologies. Just as the merger of Navision Software and Damgaard made customers feel more secure in choosing Axapta and Attain, having Microsoft behind them would further strengthen their market position. On the other hand, Navision has got off to a good start with the merger and all the lights in the control room are green. Great Plains Software is really only a serious competitor in the USA, and Navision might be able to achieve equally good results without Microsoft. However, if Microsoft were to decide to buy another competitor instead, then the entire picture would suddenly look quite different.

Another crucial point is whether Navision's founders actually want to sell. With the merger, the company remained in their hands, and they are still solidly seated at the table when it comes to strategic decisions and the daily operations. With Microsoft as the owner, their owners' shares would be exchanged for employee contracts. Despite it bringing more money into the bank, none of the partners is financially constrained and neither do they dream of fancy job titles. Preben thinks it might be exciting to be part of a set up where Microsoft is the owner, while Jesper Balser, who is also well aware of the market potential, is more uncertain about what his own role would and could be.

After sleeping on the opportunity and discussing it with the board, everyone agrees that from a purely shareholder perspective, the offer has to be pursued and the board listen to what Microsoft would do with the company in the future and, not least, what they are willing to pay for it. Therefore, the feedback to Microsoft about beginning a due diligence process is positive. The Americans acknowledge receipt, but can't officially enter into negotiations until they have finalised the acquisition of Great Plains Software, which happens on 5th April. After that, the purchasing process can start.

But nothing happens. Weeks go by, and management in Navision grows uneasy. Should they push for a response, thereby showing their enthusiasm, or should they just wait? Contact is made, but nothing that is supposed to happen when you want to buy a company happens, namely initiating due diligence and a drafting a term sheet. If agreement can be reached on this, both parties can choose advisors, and the buyer can begin thoroughly investigating the company for the purpose of preparing the final offer. None of this happens. There are sporadic meetings when Microsoft's top executives are in Europe anyway, but there is no momentum in the process. People at Navision grow irritated as the situation prevents the company from making a number of capital decisions, such as issuing additional employee shares given that the board now possesses knowledge that the capital market doesn't.

Nothing happens for good reason during the summer holidays, and when Navision is to resume contact in September, the Islamist terrorist organisation al-Qaeda flies two passenger aeroplanes into the World Trade Center, in New York, on Tuesday, September 11th. A third aeroplane hits the Defense Department's Pentagon Building, in Arlington, near Washington, D.C., while a fourth plane, which was also intended to hit populated buildings, crashes into a field in Stonycreek Township near Shanksville, in the state of Pennsylvania. The event sends shock waves throughout the West, and a few days later, Navision receives notification from Microsoft that it has cancelled all acquisition projects and can't say what projects will be restarted or when it will happen.

Navision can now proceed with its own plans. Autumn 2001 is devoted to internationalisation: acquiring distribution rights and entering into several new markets. The uncertainty and worldwide economic slump in the aftermath of the tragedy of September 11th doesn't affect Navision as badly as feared; solid growth and increased earnings can still be noted.

# CHAPTER 22

# NAVISION LANDS IN AMERICAN HANDS

## Microsoft calls again

The lack of progress in the purchase process is due to an internal disagreement among Microsoft's top echelon. Doug Burgum, Jeff Raikes and Steve Balmer are ready to take out the big chequebook, but Bill Gates believes the same result could be achieved by investing in organic growth. In May 2001, the price of Navision rises to almost 1.6 billion USD plus the premium that has to be paid to obtain all the shares at once; Bill Gates is of the opinion that by investing that money in products, organisation and marketing, it would be possible to break through on the international markets in the way Microsoft has always done. Having only one product would benefit that strategy, whereas if Microsoft acquires Navision, it would end up with at least three product lines plus XAL and C4/C5, both of which are in their dotage.

As all acquisition projects are reset after September 11th, there is time to rediscuss the two scenarios thoroughly. The ERP market doesn't resemble anything Microsoft has ever grappled with before, which is why the analogy of previous strategies is a tad tenuous. The market for financial management systems for major companies is dominated by only a few players, such as SAP, J.D. Edwards, PeopleSoft and Oracle, whereas the market Microsoft is going after with the acquisition of Great Plains Software is extremely fragmented and the competitive situation varies widely from country to country. Localising ERP software is much more extensive work than Microsoft is used to from its other products, and requires significant resources in both the respective countries and centrally. Expanding the necessary organisation quickly enough represents a significant risk in itself. Doug Burgum has been working on these challenges for years and could recount in detail issues that even unlimited funds couldn't solve. Moreover, Navision has gained impressive momentum, and it is highly likely that they will grow even faster in that period in which Microsoft is struggling to enter the international markets. The discussions lead to the conclusion that acquiring Navision is a safer way to a global platform for entry into the ERP market than if it were to build up everything from scratch. The result may well be more product lines, but they are based primarily on Microsoft's technology and could subsequently be linked even closer and help strengthen the company's overall position with small and medium-sized businesses.

In January 2002, the phone at Navision in Vedbæk rings once again with Doug Burgum on the line. Based on experience from the previous year, Navision's executives ask for confirmation of the intent to purchase from Microsoft's top management and a schedule for the process. This time there is a prompt reply – signed by Steve Balmer. The initial strategy clarification confirms that Microsoft intends to continue all product lines and utilise Navision's international organisation as a platform for expansion into the ERP market. Navision's international organisation will gradually be integrated into its own organisation; hereby continuously reaping significant synergy benefits, while Navision's development activities, which were gathered in Vedbæk after the merger in December 2000, will continue and will be Microsoft's largest development department outside of the USA. How Navision's long-term technology projects can be coordinated with Microsoft's will have to be examined after the acquisition.

With the assurance that the company's products will continue, the deciding group of owners, comprising of Jesper Balser, Torben Wind, Peter Bang and Erik and Preben Damgaard, who each have a de facto veto, arranges to investigate the possibilities of selling Navision to Microsoft, which would also require them agreeing on a reasonable price. The market's assessment of the price of Navision is set daily on the stock market, so if Microsoft wants to buy all the shares at once, a premium must be paid, too. Via its financial advisors, Navision's board sends out feelers to a number of other major IT companies, including SAP, with the message that Navision might be interested in discussing a closer strategic partnership. The purpose is to create a bidding war to force Microsoft into paying a higher price, so as to prevent a competitor from getting the spoils. Unfortunately, no serious responses are forthcoming, but on 15th February, Navision announces a strategic partnership with none other than good old IBM, with whom it shares a somewhat chequered past. This time the deal is more in line with the agreements IBM prefers when it comes to software applications, and it assumes that Navision's products will be packaged with IBM's hardware and sold via IBM's resellers. However, the agreement also contains a clause stating that a version of Navision Attain, which can run on IBM's iSeries machines (the successor to AS/400), must be developed. That solution will compete directly with Microsoft.

As a listed company, Navision is very well-documented and, in relation to the only one year-old merger, additional official analyses of the company were carried out to which Microsoft can also gain access. Based on this, Microsoft can give a price indication for the main shareholders to consider. The final quote will depend on the due diligence process that Microsoft has to implement. Every single stone in the company has to be overturned to determine whether there are conditions that would completely prevent a purchase or that would represent such a high risk that it would have to be reflected in a reduction in the price. Microsoft sends a small army of lawyers and accountants to Copenhagen, and as the process has to be kept secret until it's likely the transaction will take place, they rent an entire floor of the Marriott Hotel near Copenhagen's harbour and Navision sets up a "data room", containing any and all documentation, which Microsoft would like to gain insight into. To assist in preparing and implementing the purchase, Microsoft engages Goldman Sachs as its financial adviser and Gorissen Federspiel Kierkegaard, Preston Gates & Ellis and Linklaters as its legal advisors. Navision contracts

Nordea Securities and Schroder Saloman Smith Barney as its financial advisors and Kromann Reumert as its legal advisors.

Naturally, Microsoft doesn't want to base the acquisition only on what it can see in hindsight; rather it needs to be informed about the company's forward-looking ambitions, strategies and concrete plans, too. But as Navision is a listed company, there are limits as to what can be said and, furthermore, Navision is unwilling to provide Microsoft with too much information, because if the deal should go down the drain, Microsoft will be its main competitor.

Navision's management visits Microsoft in Seattle repeatedly to present and discuss their plans for the future and hear the buyer's more precise intentions for the company after an acquisition.

Preben and Erik Damgaard had faced a similar situation in the years when IBM had tried to buy Damgaard. Now, they must once again consider whether they really want to swap their company for a bag of money, because no matter how big that bag of money would be, they wouldn't be able to undo the swap. Following the stock market listing and the merger with Navision Software, there are more owners and more considerations to be taken. Jesper Balser, Torben Wind and Peter Bang each have enough of an owner's share to prevent Microsoft from acquiring the 90 per cent of shares required for the purchase to happen, but if a majority of the founders would prefer to sell, it makes no sense for them to sit on their hands.

As top management in a listed company, the founders also have to look beyond their own noses and assess what is the best opportunity for all the shareholders and employees in the long term. Despite not all the founders being jubilant about relinquishing control, they believe the company's products will be stronger with Microsoft as the owner, which, in turn, would be beneficial for many employees, who would be able to continue their work in the world's largest software company. The price that Microsoft is willing to pay would probably be a fair compensation to the shareholders for relinquishing ownership, but it would be nice if it happened in a bidding round with some of Microsoft's competitors.

## Strategy for a future without Microsoft

Despite a lot of time being spent on meetings with Microsoft, there are still everyday things to be taken care of and a future to be prepared for, especially if the deal doesn't go through. Spring is already a busy period: the current financial year has to be closed off and plans and budgets for the next year, starting 1$^{st}$ July, prepared.

During the merger preparations, a three-step strategy is formulated, whereby the first year is to be used to harvest the synergies and bring the organisation into place. The platform for increased growth is to be established in phase two, estimated to take about two years, so the company can grow significantly faster than its competitors. Navision wants to gain market share during phase three, estimated to take three years, to assume the position as the global market leader of ERP systems for medium-sized enterprises.

The illustration of the merger process, which earned the internal nickname "the butt cheek diagram", was used in numerous internal and external presentations to depict the company and explain its status and plans. The chart was introduced by the consultancy firm McKinsey & Company, which was briefly associated with the merger project in autumn 2000, but was later replaced by the consultancy firms PwC Consulting and Kjær & Kjærulf.

Phase one of the merger goes much faster and better than expected, and by mid-2001 – after only six months – not only is the foundation in place but market share has been gained, too. After the 2001 summer holidays, Jesper Balser and Preben Damgaard initiate the development of the next strategic framework for how the ambitions of becoming a global market leader can truly be realised. In mid-February 2002, they send a 20-page strategy paper to the board for discussion. By mid-2005, the company – measured according to the statements of the American advisory company, Gartner – is to be number two in Europe, number five in the USA and number three worldwide. The proposal, the goal of which is to double revenue over the next three years and then reach a level of one billion euro by the end of the current decade (2010s), contains descriptions of all the initiatives that need to be taken on the path to achieving the goal of global market leadership. Attain and Axapta are both "immortalised" and will continue to constitute the company's core products targeted at the lower and the upper tiers of the intermediary market, respectively. In time, the products will be moved onto the new Jamaica platform, with Attain expected to move in 2006 and Axapta in 2008. The proposal recommends replacing C5 with a new C6. With New Line, now entitled ACE, they would become a so-called "first mover" with ASP, which has changed its name to Software-as-a-Service, for the small businesses with a turnover of half a million euro and upwards. Navision will continue to introduce a Small Business Edition of Attain, now named CE for Channel Entry, which can serve companies with 5-10 users. Some of those companies can grow into Attain and Axapta in time. XAL and C4/C5 will carry on until customers can voluntarily change to Attain, Axapta, C6, ACE or Attain CE. Via Navi-Hub, Navision will deliver web-based information services directly to customers and develop mobile solutions for all products parallel to this platform being developed. Apart from continuing to recruit more resellers and dismiss those partners not retaining their certifications or selling anything, Navision will spread its partner development approach, now called OnTarget, which helps resellers to professionalise all aspects of their businesses. As part of the efforts, a database of anonymous data, where resellers can measure where they themselves lie on a number of key parameters in relation to the other resellers, is to be established. With these tools, Navision's partner account managers can motivate and help resellers to constantly develop their business, which, in turn, means increased licence revenue and market share. The global leadership position can only be achieved if Navision continues to expand its presence across the globe, and that depends specifically on the North American market, estimated to account for almost half of the world market by the analysts. North America is the market in which both Navision Software and Damgaard have had the most difficulty gaining traction – even after the merger, advancing fast enough is a struggle. If the ambitions are to be achieved, North America has to go from accounting for about 13 per cent of the company's revenue to accounting for 28 per cent, corresponding to revenue of roughly 200 million USD in the 2004/2005 financial year. The plan is based on the condition of organic growth and voices Navision's wish not to purchase direct competitors, but rather to find independent distributors, who can then be acquired after the establishment phase and merged into the organisation.

During the review of the critical success factors of the plan, internal organisational matters are pointed out as the most important. The good results mean arrogance and smugness could easily spread throughout the organisation; similarly, the rapid increase in the number of employees means there is a risk of mounting politicisation in internal relationships. Management is convinced the company has a unique opportunity – the market is more attractive than ever before, and technology and products are under control. Realising the great ambitions now rests primarily on the ability to lead the company at every level and ensure that the high ambitions sink into every corner of the company.

# The interim financial statements

At the end of February, Navision publishes its interim financial statements, which also contain adjusted expectations for the entire financial year. In addition to some very nice results – an increase in revenue of 19 per cent to 169.8 million USD, which isn't far from 400 million USD on a yearly basis – Navision also notes an increase in earnings of no less than 127 per cent, corresponding to 23 per cent of revenue. A total growth in revenue of 18 per cent is expected for the financial year as a whole of which a minimum of 17 per cent will be profit. Axapta again shows the greatest percentage growth: 67 per cent, while Attain, which contributes over 100 million USD, shows 21 per cent growth. Revenue on XAL declines eight per cent, while C4/C5 grows by 15 per cent.

| Revenue per product | First half of FY 2001/02 | | |
| Mill. DKK | 2001/02 | 2000/01 | Change |
|---|---|---|---|
| Navision Axapta | 149  18% | 89  12% | 67% |
| Navision Finacials/Attain | 520  61% | 428  60% | 21% |
| Navison XAL | 67  8% | 73  10% | -8% |
| Navision C4/C5 | 44  5% | 39  5% | 15% |
| Total licenses and updates | 780  92% | 629  87% | 24% |
| Services | 69  8% | 85  13% | -19% |
| Total Revenue | 849  100% | 714  100% | 19% |

The engine in Navision is still Financials/Attain, which accounts for 66 per cent of software revenue. The sales of services, which are associated with much higher cost-of-goods-sold than software sales, have fallen from 13 per cent to 8 per cent of total revenue, actually contributing to increasing the company's market value.

Geographically, revenue growth in Scandinavia and the USA is limited, while Germany delivers growth of 19 per cent. Turnover in the rest of Europe and the world is affected by acquiring distribution rights and shows growth rates of 32 per cent and 109 per cent, respectively. The partnership with IBM gets another shot in the ring: Attain will be delivered preinstalled on all of IBM's iSeries machines from the second quarter of 2002 *"according to the agreement, IBM will urge its worldwide network of Business Partners to become certified Navision Solution Centres".* (Interestingly, the partnership with IBM is mentioned only peripherally and not assigned any significant importance in the 20-page internal strategy plan that the board and senior management are putting the final touches to.)

Somewhat unusually, the report also contains a number of sections on the company's long-term plans and strategy, which stem from the strategy paper and, obviously, form part of the negotiations with Microsoft.

| Revenue per region | First half of FY 2001/02 | | | |
|---|---|---|---|---|
| Mill. DKK | 2001/02 | | 2000/01 | Change |
| Denmark | 192 | 23% | 187 | 26% | 3% |
| Rest of the Nordics | 62 | 7% | 59 | 8% | 6% |
| Germany | 173 | 20% | 146 | 20% | 19% |
| Rest of Europe | 264 | 31% | 200 | 28% | 32% |
| USA | 92 | 11% | 90 | 13% | 2% |
| Rest of the world | 66 | 8% | 32 | 5% | 109% |
| Total Revenue | 849 | 100% | 714 | 100% | 19% |

Once again, in the first half of the 2001/02 financial year, there has been growth in the Danish market, making it yet again the largest single country in the group. The growth in Germany remains impressive.

## The final offer is made

With the good results, the well-developed strategy for an independent future and with feelers out to other potential buyers, Navision's board is well-equipped for its negotiations with Microsoft. Until the final offer is made, there is no guarantee that the transaction will be go ahead, so management doesn't want to announce anything publically. But given the number of people involved in the project, the risk of a leak is significant, and on Wednesday, 30th April at about 2 am, Jesper Balser's phone rings. A journalist from *The Financial Times*[14] would like to have his comments, if any, on an article that the British newspaper is printing later that day, reporting on Microsoft's negotiations to acquire Navision. Jesper has no comment, but rings Navision's PR manager instead, asking him to send out the already prepared stock exchange announcement, which in its simplicity reads as follows:

*As a consequence of rumours in the market, Navision's board can confirm that it is considering a potentially strategic transaction.*

*The board of Navision has decided to investigate the potential of such a transaction. These investigations may – or may not – result in an agreement regarding a potential transaction. Navision has no further comments unless/until the circumstances demand further announcements.*

On the basis of that, the board asks the Copenhagen Stock Exchange to transfer the company's shares to the observation list that very same morning.

The announcement triggers an avalanche of articles in the media, speculating in all directions, even trying to answer the question of whether the purchase would be good or bad for Navision. This is a complex question whose answer requires defining who Navision really is.

Navision can only be sold with the founders' permission as they are also major shareholders and together hold more than half of the shares. If they choose to sell, it has to be because they consider it a better option than continuing themselves. Despite the founders being able to lodge a nice sum in the bank, their acceptance depends on Microsoft intending to continue the business, but naturally control passes to the new owner with a sale. From now on, all strategic and operational decisions will be in the hands of Microsoft, and the former owners won't have any influence on what it chooses to do. It will mean a new culture for all staff, and only the future will show whether that is good or bad for the individual employees. Indisputably, Microsoft offers great career opportunities for

---

14   Navision's management is convinced the leak comes from Microsoft, who would like get the market's reaction to the initiative.

many employees, while others don't particularly want to be a tiny cog in such a big machine. It's undoubtedly a great advantage for resellers as they now have an even more solid supplier behind them. Microsoft has 100 per cent brand awareness and no one can question the company's solid survival capability or that it has the deepest pockets within the IT industry. Only time will tell how a takeover will affect the capacity for innovation and long-term competitiveness. Large companies are rarely as innovative as small businesses; however, they do have more muscle to get their products accepted on the market.

The negotiations take place at the law firm of Gorissen Federspiel Kierkegaard on City Hall Square, Copenhagen, which has meeting rooms large enough to accommodate the entire negotiating delegation and rooms to which each party can withdraw to discuss the counterparty's play. When a point is to be negotiated, the parties meet in the large meeting room, where one party presents its views while the other party listens, asks clarifying questions and takes notes. Subsequently, both parties retire to their respective rooms and, next time, it's the turn of the other party to present their views. The meetings run this way from morning to evening every single day for several weeks. Between 6 and 7 pm, food is brought in to the participants, served as a buffet in an adjoining room. Jesper Balser has scheduled the meetings so that Navision finishes its presentation just as the food is being brought in. While Microsoft is dealing with the latest play, the Navision delegation sits down to dinner and Jesper suggests that they eat all of the food. After a few days, Microsoft catches on to the feint and ensures that there will also be food for its delegates.

One evening, the negotiations come to an impasse and the Microsoft delegation announces that they can't continue on a number of points without concessions. As Navision won't meet the demands, the counterparty packs up its papers and leaves. Navision now stations a number of observers at their hotel and at the airport to see if they really are checking out and going home, and as that isn't the case, the Navision delegates wait patiently for a couple of days after which negotiations resume.

On Sunday morning, 5th May, the parties are once again gathered for ne-gotiations in the large meeting room at City Hall Square, Copenhagen, and work all day on finding solutions for the last details. After lunch, when the participants are quite tired, loud laughter suddenly erupts from down on the square. The delegates flock to the windows and see thousands of people laughing their heads off.[15] The Americans wonder aloud if this is something that happens every Sunday, but the Danish participants say no. The occurrence evokes smiles from the serious lawyers and auditors, and the atmosphere in the meeting room relaxes. That evening, senior executives receive their new employment agree-ments from Microsoft, and Freddie Jørgensen is tasked with ensuring they are signed no later than the next day so as to stick to the schedule. When he reviews the agreements on Monday night, they are all signed except for Jesper Balser's. When Freddie reminds him, he is told that Jesper won't sign. He is offended at getting the contract at the last min-ute and doesn't care to enter into agreements he has no influence over, in general. The employment contracts are part of the package, and if they aren't signed, the entire deal will go down the drain. After several reminders and attempts at talking him into it, Freddie finally manages to wrench a signature from Jesper Balser just thirty minutes before the deadline. On Tuesday, 7th May, Microsoft makes known its final offer of 300 DKK (60 USD) per share via a stock exchange announcement from Navision, which, thereby, gives shareholders a premium of more than 40 per cent in relation to the average price over the past six months before the share was placed on the Copenhagen Stock Exchange's observation list on 30th April.

---

15  On Sunday, 5th May 2002, between 2 pm and 5 pm, the Danish contribution to World Laughter Day is held at Rådhuspladsen [City Hall Square], Copenhagen.

The three entrepreneurs (from left) Preben Damgaard, Doug Burgum (Great Plains Software) and Jesper Balser dressed for the occasion of the press conference presenting Microsoft's acquisition of Navision to the world media on 7th May 2002. At the beginning of the meeting, Preben and Jesper are notably tired after the long negotiations, but as the questions are answered, the adrenaline gets pumping, bringing a smile to their lips and colour to their cheeks.

When Navision Software was listed in March 1999, it was at price 125 DKK (25 USD), while Damgaard received a price of 320 DKK (64 USD) the same year. With the merger, Damgaard's shareholders had their shares exchanged for NavisionDamgaard shares at a price of 227 DKK (45.4 USD). Since the stock market listing, Navision Software's shares have been listed at a price of 1,000 DKK (200 USD) and Damgaard's at 640 DKK (128 USD). The assessment of whether the Navision founders have made a good deal depends, therefore, on which price you choose for comparison – and there are plenty to choose from. When it comes down to it, it's those, who own the shares, who determine whether they think the offer is good or not and time shows that they almost all believe the former.

## The sale falls into place

The deciding factor for the purchase falling into place is Navision's shareholders giving their joint approval before 5<sup>th</sup> July 2002 to sell at least 90 per cent of the shares to Microsoft at the offered price. At the time of the offer, the principal shareholders, who represent 56.4 per cent of the shares as well as a number of other shareholders accounting for an additional 3.6 per cent, had already given their consent.

The shareholders are entitled to withdraw their approval if a better offer from another potential buyer is submitted during the period up to the cut-off date, just as Microsoft can retain its purchase option if such an offer is matched at a minimum. Approvals must now be obtained from the competition authorities in the relative countries where Navision has subsidiaries, and despite speculations of competitors trying to prevent the sale in Børsen's *Nyhedsmagasin* on 31<sup>st</sup> May, the transaction is lower than the amount that the competition authorities normally concern themselves with.

The approvals are issued on 4<sup>th</sup> July, and on 5<sup>th</sup> July, Microsoft receives consent from what amounts to 98.8 per cent of the shares, and as no better offer has been made in the meantime, the most important steps in the purchase process have fallen into place. Navision's shareholders are welcome to exchange their shares for cash or shares in Microsoft. On 25<sup>th</sup> July, the company's AGM decides to redeem the last shares by force and initiates the process of delisting the company from the Copenhagen Stock Exchange. The remaining 1.2 per cent of the shares are acquired on 13<sup>th</sup> August, and on 22<sup>nd</sup> August, the company's shares are removed from the stock exchange. The board and almost all of management – except Preben Damgaard – resign on 28<sup>th</sup> August, and on 30<sup>th</sup> September, Navision changes its name to Microsoft Business Solution and is simultaneously changed to an ApS (a small private limited company).

All employees continue in their jobs. Those, who were employed on executive contracts, have received new salaried employee contracts. Jesper Balser resigns as managing director and accepts a position within global strategy development for Microsoft Business Solution, which is housed in Vedbæk after the merger. Preben Damgaard continues formally as managing director; his main task being to help with the dividing up of the company into sections, which can then be incorporated into Microsoft's existing worldwide organisation. In continuation of the acquisition, the Microsoft Great Plains Business Solutions division is also renamed Microsoft Business Solutions, while the products are initially renamed Microsoft Navision Axapta®, Microsoft Navision Attain®, Microsoft Navision C5® and Microsoft Navision XAL®.

This is the story of Brødrene Damgaard, which became Navision and eventually Microsoft. At first, almost everyone remains – with Microsoft printed on their business cards – but eventually several executives and employees voluntarily or otherwise take their leave. The culture changes rapidly, and despite Microsoft being among the most valued workplaces in many countries, working for an American company with 50,000 employees is quite different to working for a Danish organisation with 1,200. Some prefer the former; others, the latter.

# EPILOGUE

## After the sale to Microsoft

As the sale to Microsoft happens just before the summer holidays, no major changes ensue in the first few months. But when the practical merger is to be implemented in autumn 2002, many in Navision realise they haven't been acquired by Microsoft, but by Great Plains Software, and their business models aren't quite as similar as they seem to be on the surface. Attain, XAL and Axapta are more flexible products than Great Plains' Dynamics, which, in turn, contains more standard functionality. This means that Navision's resellers provide far more functionality and have greater consultancy businesses than Great Plains Software's partners.

Navision's ambitious Jamaica project is dropped shortly after the acquisition as Great Plains Software is planning an even more ambitious project under the codename Green, which is to be a common platform for all Microsoft's ERP products in the future. Despite the development department in Vedbæk being maintained, the strategic decisions and longer-term technology projects are moved to the USA. When all the jobs have been allocated, no one from Navision is part of Microsoft's top management team, which comprises approximately 100 people – the strategic decisions have been moved out of Denmark.

PREBEN
DAMGAARD

179855

*Microsoft*

For the first time in his life, Preben Damgaard is on a full-time permanent employee contract, complete with the title "Employee" on his staff card. Despite his position at Microsoft having many more employees and the responsibility for a significantly higher turnover on paper, it also comes with a 50 per cent reduction in salary and exclusion from the company's strategic management team.

As Navision's subsidiaries are to be placed under Microsoft's control, there is a significant dilution of management. Many of the directors of Navision's subsidiaries are used to running their businesses entirely independently. Only a few have the desire or patience to take on an intermediary role, answering to managers who have no experience of the kind of business operated by Navision. Preben Damgaard remains for a year, while Erik Damgaard leaves Microsoft in spring 2004. In June 2003, René Stockner takes over Preben Damgaard's role as responsible for the business in Europe, the Middle East and Africa, but the job isn't the same as before and the managerial room to manoeuvre is growing ever narrower. In 2004, René leaves Microsoft, too.

Jesper Balser receives the newly created position of director of strategy development, and when he arrives at the Seattle office after the summer holidays, he is told that ten management consultants from McKinsey & Company have been engaged. They are to help him develop the strategy that will increase revenue across the entire MBS division from the current 700 million USD a year to ten billion USD by 2010. When, after a few months, he learns that the costs of his little strategy department amounts to over six million USD a month, he sends the McKinsey consultants home and recruits a few employees himself to help prepare the presentation that Microsoft's top management will need to make its decisions. It results in a few meetings with Bill Gates, Steve Ballmer and Doug Burgum, but when Microsoft begins splitting Navision up by placing its employees under its own general organisation, he can see how his skilled employees are being squeezed out and he loses faith in the ability of the new organisation to live up to the ambitions of top management. Even the most well-though out plans will flounder if the implementing organisation doesn't have energetic, experienced and skilled managers.

It's different further down the ranks, where the work, for the most part, continues as before and where the new business cards feel both effective and prestigious. Management and administration positions are abolished as Microsoft already has that organisational infrastructure in place. Nevertheless, many of Navision's employees continue with Microsoft for several years.

Microsoft's entry into the ERP market doesn't go smoothly by any means. Apart from the usual difficulties in incorporating smaller acquisitions into a large organisation, both Great Plains Software and Navision operate businesses that, in their very nature, differ significantly from Microsoft's traditional activities. Microsoft delivers standard products such as the Office suite as well as basic software and middleware on which other software companies build their solutions. These products require only minimal localisation, minimal customisation and can be sold in large quantities. Microsoft Business Solution becomes the second-smallest division (the smallest being mobile activities), experiences declining sales after the takeover and has to report a loss of over 200 million USD in the second half of 2003. Rumours of Microsoft's plans to resell the division even surface in 2005. The rumours fade, and to this day Damgaard and Navision Software's products are the basis for Microsoft Dynamics AX, NAV, XAL and C5.

## Erik Damgaard

Erik Damgaard tries to buy the Concorde C5 business from Microsoft upon his return to Denmark in 2004, but doesn't succeed. Instead, he becomes an investor with a portfolio that includes real estate and renewable energy. The 2008 financial crisis pulls the rug out from under his investments, and in 2009 he begins to develop software again.

His first software project is a trading platform for currency and securities, which is marketed by a number of brokers. The market for this type of trading platform is niche-driven, but the system doesn't achieve wide penetration. Nevertheless, the work provides Erik with insight into new development tools and gives him practical experience in developing and operating cloud-based solutions. He also learns how to put together and lead virtual development teams that exist in different time zones around the globe.

In 2015, he founds the company UniConta, to develop a cloud-based financial management system for small businesses. His many years of experience in developing ERP systems combined with his newly acquired skills in hosting systems together with the help of his virtual development team, means he spots a growing gap in the market. Time is running out on the systems he himself helped to develop in the 1980s and 90s, but he believes a proper supply of systems, based on new technology, that can substitute the earlier systems, has yet to be established.

UniConta is launched in Denmark in spring 2016 as the replacement for Concorde C5, and there is interest among both resellers and customers. As Erik is a well-known face, enquiries are quick to come in from abroad.

In spring 2017, Erik and his new team succeed in raising 12 million USD from external investors, and the work of internationalising UniConta begins. With UniConta and a team of people he knows well and who know him well, too, Erik has gone back to his roots: a product aimed at the millions of small businesses worldwide that require a financial system that suits their needs and wallet. And a business model that can be scaled via resellers.

Today, Erik Damgaard lives with his wife in Madrid, Spain.

## Preben Damgaard

With the sale to Microsoft, Preben goes from being primarily known within the IT and entrepreneurship industry to being known in the wider public domain. He becomes synonymous with a generation of successful entrepreneurs who, with a combination of hard work, business acumen, leadership skills and a good idea, suddenly become multimillionaires.

There is immediate and great demand to get him on boards. Listed companies, such as the technical plumbing, heating and sanitary wholesale company, Brødrene A&O Johansen; renowned and much respected companies, such as Rockwool International as well as Bang & Olufsen, and later the TDC Group, are after his insight into IT, business and organisational development as well as buying and selling businesses.

However, the desire to work with entrepreneurs and entrepreneurship is more appealing to Preben Damgaard. An obvious career as a professional board member of listed companies is replaced with a role as an investor and active board member in smaller technology companies with global growth potential.

It's a combination that works well; he gets involved in business model development, which, within a few years, earns other young entrepreneurs – and himself – million dollar profits.

To date, no single business deal has exceeded the value of Navision's sale, but after the divorce from Microsoft, Preben Damgaard invests money, time, effort and experience in projects that lead to business transactions in the millions: the network company Axcess is sold to Atea for 64 million USD; the IT security company Secunia is sold to the American Flexera Software for almost 100 million USD; as chairman and shareholder of the training app, Endomondo, he, and the rest of the management and founders, are responsible for selling one of the biggest Danish app successes to the American Sportswear apparel company Under Armor, for nearly 120 million USD; as chairman of Cirque A/S, he helps to build up Denmark's leading provider of Skype for Business, which is sold to the TDC Group for over 20 million USD. Most recently, Preben has become part of the Too Good To Go company. This company is fighting food waste via an app by linking restaurants, supermarkets, bakeries and sushi chains, which would like to sell off the day's produce of fresh bread and ready meals, with customers, who would like to "eat well with a clean conscience", helping to minimise food waste and reduce $CO_2$ consumption by millions of tonnes – annually – and all at a good price.

Today, Preben Damgaard lives with his family in Holte, Denmark.

# THE AUTHOR'S ROAD TO DAMGAARD AND A SAD ENDING

## From civil servant to sales consultant

Despite me starting in the IT industry on 2nd January 1980, Damgaard Data's first years completely passed me by. From a comfortable, but quite stressful position as a civil servant in the then Danish Ministry of Employment, I allowed myself to be talked into a significantly better paid job as a sales consultant for large computer systems in the Danish subsidiary of the American Control Data Corporation (CDC) by a close acquaintance. CDC was (unfortunately it later proves) in a completely different place on the market than where Erik and Preben Damgaard started their business four years later.

## Skandinavisk Dataco

Michael Mathiesen called me in spring 1986 to hear if I would like to join his company, Skandinavisk Dataco, which was in the process of completing a new series of products to connect PCs and other computer systems. He rang me specifically due to the fact that since 1982, some good colleagues and I had built up a number of local businesses, which compensated for our parent company's lack of ability to supply us with competitive products. The latest business area we had established when Michael Mathiesen called was with local area networks for connecting

PCs, where we had won the first big order from Jernets Arbejdsgiver-forening (now the Confederation of Danish Industry].

To put it lightly, things weren't going at all well for CDC in 1986, and I had difficulty seeing how they were going to get back on track, but smaller companies, such as Skandinavisk Dataco, whose foundation was the PC, were soaring and growing quickly. Despite Dataco having no history and most definitely posing a great risk, I had enough insight to know that the products on their drawing board were going to hit a huge niche in the market. Furthermore, I would be part of the top management in Dataco and the whole world would be my market. I started as sales and marketing director in Skandinavisk Dataco on 1st April 1986, and from then until 1989 was busily concerned with selling Danish IT products abroad, so my attention wasn't focused on what was happening within the Danish IT industry at home.

## A well-paid job that was going nowhere

Despite CDC's Danish subsidiary being a very good workplace, I promised myself upon my resignation in 1986 to never again work as a "sergeant" for a large international group. Three years later I reneged on my oath and accepted an offer to become the head of the Danish subsidiary of the American company, Data General. My vanity simply couldn't resist the temptation of becoming a managing director before the age of forty. Without comparison, the job was the best paid job I had ever had, and – not only did it lead to stock options and money in the bank – it also introduced me to Preben Damgaard. Damgaard Data's distribution agreement with Novell meant that we had to enter into a local agreement with them in order to obtain sales rights to Novell on Data General's machines in Denmark. And the signing of the agreement entailed meeting with Carsten Kaae and Preben Damgaard at the latter's office in Birkerød in March 1991. I was astonished at how big the company really was but didn't quite understand how it all hung together.

## My unsolicited application

The agreement between Data General and Damgaard Data never generated any business, and other than one additional meeting with Carsten Kaae and Preben Damgaard, I had nothing more to do with the company until mid-1997. I was then sales and marketing director of the Danish firm, RE Technology, which was acquired by the Belgian company Barco in spring 1997. I was dismissed as an extension of this, and was to leave by the end of March the following year. I now had to contemplate my future and came to the conclusion that I either had to start or buy a company myself or get a job in a Danish company where I would be responsible for global sales. Regarding the latter, I compiled a list of names of the companies to consider, and as I wanted to stay within IT, there weren't many names on the list. Navision Software and Damgaard Data were at the top.

In September, I rang Preben Damgaard, who remembered me, and we agreed to meet at his office. I didn't know anything about Damgaard's challenges with IBM nor did I realise that one of my old colleagues from CDC, Per Pedersen, now held a key position in the company. The meeting with Preben got off to a good start, and he asked me what my plans were for the future and what kind of job I was looking for. I had thought carefully about this and was able to answer that I wasn't looking for a job as such, but more of a project where something that wasn't working needed to be fixed. It should be international and closely linked to marketing and sales. Preben asked if I could speak German and when I said yes (without blushing), he asked if I would be willing to move to Germany. Again, I said yes, but that I had to discuss it with my family as they would be moving with me in that case. Preben said there might be an opportunity, and that I should talk to Per Pedersen, head of the group for future international plans. A week later, I was sitting in Per Pedersen's office being briefed on the state of things. That Damgaard Data itself should enter the German-speaking markets was already on the drawing board, but nothing had yet been decided. Should it go ahead, I was now a good candidate for heading up the operation, but I would have to go through Damgaard's formal recruitment process before it could offer me a job. It was going to take four to eight weeks for the decision to be made, so I was going to have to exercise some patience. In the meantime, I received a few offers to become the Danish sales and marketing director in a few foreign companies as well as being offered the purchase of a small but well-established PR company. I also sent a feeler out to Navision Software, but didn't hear anything.

## An opening in Germany?

After discussing a move to Germany with my family and getting the green light from my wife, Sue, and our daughter, Maria, who would both move with me (our son Daniel, an apprentice electrician, would remain in Denmark), I chose to give the job my all if something were to come out of it. I could tell how hard Per Pedersen was working on taking over distribution in Germany, Austria and Switzerland from IBM from our conversations, and I had faith he would succeed. Therefore, I held out on all other options by explaining that there were other offers in the pipeline and I needed time to think. The decision, backed by IBM, was eventually made in November, and I was now able to start the recruitment process, which included various interviews and personality tests.

I was offered the job at the beginning of December. The negotiation of the employment and posting conditions was so efficient that I was able to participate in the historic planning meeting at Hotel Phønix on that rainy day in December 1997.

## Europe's Asshole

As early as January 1998, I flew to Stuttgart to meet with my future German employees and start finding a place to live. Despite having travelled and worked extensively in Germany over the years, I had never been to Stuttgart, so my excitement was great as the SAS plane touched down at the airport near Echterdingen, a little south of the city. I rented a VW Golf and drove directly to ADAC to buy some maps, so I would orientate myself in the area. I had the day to myself as I wasn't meeting Per Pedersen until the next evening at the Marriott hotel in Sindelfingen, where I was going to be introduced to Susi Pfaff, acting manager of the German support office, too.

On the way to ADAC, I was surprised to see that Stuttgart is beautifully surrounded by high hills with vineyards and large, attractive houses. The road from the airport over Degerloch and down to the city is aptly named Weinsteige and as I drove along the winding road overlooking the city on my left, I was already sold and looking forward to calling Sue at home and telling her what was awaiting us. The department in southern Germany had earned the nickname "Europe's asshole" back at Damgaard Data in Birkerød, so my expectations weren't high, but when I drove to Böblingen the next day to see where the office was located, my surprise was again great.

There was nothing "asshole" about either the location or the facilities. The office was located at Hans-Klemm-Strasse 5 in the Hulb business area, a little south of Böblingen. The building was a futuristic office complex with a large, spacious atrium garden at its centre. XAL Services had rented a few hundred square metres on the 3rd floor of the southern wing. Daimler-Benz had major development and production facilities in the area, while Hulb houses many high-tech companies, including the German branch of Hewlett-Packard.

A little north of Böblingen, on the other side of motorway 8, which runs from Karlsruhe in the west to Salzburg in the east, is Vaihingen and IBM's German head office. I visited there later in January to begin planning the handover and had to admit that here, both the buildings and atmosphere, could have inspired the name "Europe's Asshole".

After being introduced to Susi Pfaff, a young, gifted and beautiful woman, my mood was great. Susi was energetic, positive and clearly looking forward to taking over the activities in Germany. Next day, in the office, I had the opportunity of meeting the other employees, and again the outcome was positive. My predecessor, Lars Balle, had hired a super talented team, who were clearly motivated by the fact that they were to be responsible for the entire business.

## The dance school

I moved to Böblingen in February 1998 and rented a furnished apartment from Frau Hohensee, a retired secretary from IBM Germany. After a disagreement with her daughter, she moved out of her own house and was renting out her apartment on the first floor, while her daughter lived on the ground floor and ran a dance school in the basement. I landed completely unawares right in the middle of a family drama in which I was perceived as a pawn in something I neither understood nor had interest in. Thankfully, I was hardly ever home, and succeeded in building polite and friendly relationships with all parties.

My family remained in Denmark at this time, so Maria could finish her Danish 7th grade. I flew home every weekend to be with them. Monday to Friday, when in Germany, I mainly worked and slept and went for the occasional jog in the woods. This set-up wasn't that bad. The takeover from IBM involved an inexhaustible list of tasks to be dealt with that didn't get any shorter once Germany was designated a growth market.

## Diestlerstraße

The entire family came to visit for Easter 1998, and we went house-hunting in the area. We engaged a real estate agent who, after being given a description of our preferences, was determined to find us a suitable home. It wasn't that we were picky but when moving a family abroad for a short period of time with the expectation of working many hours and having to often stay away from home, it's crucial that the base is in order. The day before the family was due to return to Denmark, we went to a small residential area in the Frauenkopf district to look at an apartment in a newly built block. The building had a forest on one side and overlooked the vineyards down towards the Neckar River on the other. The apartment was on the first floor, had a nice terrace and thankfully no garden. We jumped at it, and as the owner wanted to let it for a limit of three years, we went straight to the front of the queue and signed the lease a few days later. Diestlerstraße 28, 70128 Stuttgart/Frauenkopf was our address from then until September 2001.

After the summer holidays of 1998, Maria was starting in a private German school, ten minutes by bike, from where we lived, while Sue was starting a three-year Master's Degree in Health Informatics at Aalborg University. So we all had things to look forward to in our everyday lives. At the weekends, we used our base in the middle of Europe to go to Strasburg, Schaffhausen, the Alps or the Black Forest.

## The division of labour

There were many loose ends after the takeover from IBM. Preben Damgaard and Per Pedersen took the general and principle ones. My energy was to be invested in market-oriented activities, such as building up a marketing, sales and service organisation, recruiting several more resellers and developing those resellers acquired from IBM. My most important tasks were, firstly, to ensure the short-term revenue via business partner management and secondly, to build the foundation for long-term growth via PR, marketing and reseller recruitment. I was confident that Per Pedersen and Preben Damgaard were working to negotiate the best possible terms with Damgaard International. From time to time, I was consulted for my views. Therefore, I was convinced that the outcome would also serve our interests in the markets for which I was responsible for the results. I didn't have to spend my time and energy on keeping track of the negotiations.

It might not be easy for an outsider to understand the importance of the way in which Damgaard Data was managed, but the clarification of the many details of the transfer of distribution from IBM clearly showed the strength of the culture. I was certain that management in Birkerød was taking care of our interests in DACH in the negotiations with Damgaard International. At my end, I had free rein to act on a market twenty times greater than that of Denmark, and I had to decide when to ask first, when to inform later and when to do my own thing. Not everything succeeded, but management helped out when things went wrong. First and foremost, it was crucial to quickly stop what wasn't working and then move on in another direction. No time was wasted placing blame. "You live and you learn" was an expression often used in the top management teams. There was deep trust that everyone was working in the company's interest.

## The plan for growth

While developing the plan for growth for Germany in June 1998, it was impossible to estimate the return on the project, which cost approximately 3 million USD in the first year. As neither Preben nor Per believed it useful to guess an amount, I was asked to implement the plan as fast as possible so as to see its effects. Everyone would then be wiser once the plan had had time to work by the turn of the year, and it would then be possible to set a real budget for goals and fiscal resources in 1999.

When I was sitting in the plane on my way home to Stuttgart, I had a cheque for 3 million USD in my briefcase. The Passat principle had been refreshed and I had been instructed to put the money to work as quickly as possible and that I would be measured on my ability to execute the plan with care. Despite the fact that how that could be accurately measured wasn't clear, I hadn't an inkling of doubt that we could produce visible results and that we would be fairly judged at the end of the day.

## Maria wants to go home to Denmark

After 18 months, Maria has had enough of the private German school and wants to return to Denmark. After a quick consultation with my boss, Per Pedersen, an extra subsidy will be awarded so she can attend the International School Stuttgart, after which calm befalls the family once again. We all learn German, and Maria sharpens both her English and her French at her new school.

## On my own two feet

The parting from IBM and the stock market listing are the basis for the wildest international expansion I had ever been involved in at that time. The combination of a market in exceptional growth, a company with grand global ambitions and a well-cushioned bottom line creates a quite unusual working environment. The stock market party in November 1999 is the culmination of two years of whirlwind business development on my part, but the mood is unusually high that evening among all the party guests.

I have been asked to give the employee's speech to Preben and Erik, which is quite the honour. I have had nothing but positive experiences with Preben and Erik, who have both personally helped with the challenges we have had during the course of my work for the company. For instance, just a few weeks earlier, those of us in Germany had forgotten to sign up for next year's major CeBIT exhibition. It was a colossal blunder. CeBIT is the largest international IT fair, so it could have major consequences for the entire company. The embarrassing situation was realised at a press conference held by the Danish representative of CeBIT in Copenhagen, where those journalists present are informed that Damgaard hasn't signed up for next year's exhibition.

Immediately afterwards, I receive a call from a *Computerworld* journalist wanting to hear what it's due to. My surprise is just as great as theirs, so I promise to ring back once I have figured out what is going on. It turns out the registration form has been placed in a stack of papers in our marketing department in the office in Germany. It is, indeed, correct that we haven't signed up in time. It's my responsibility and I have to quickly find a solution. While my German marketing director and I bombard CeBIT's management in Hanover with calls, Preben calls to see if there is anything he can do. Not once does he criticise me or my people. On the contrary, he praises our work and makes himself available to help in any way he can. Fortunately, we are able to quickly get in touch with the fair's top management, who promises to do everything they can to get us in, and a few days later we are notified that a large stand in the grand Hal 1 is available.

It's not as good as being in Hal 6 with Navision Software and our other colleagues, but it's certainly good enough. Now it's up to us to make the most of the location. We receive great praise for our handling of the matter, and despite being red-cheeked over the slip-up, we come out the other side of the episode with even greater loyalty to the Damgaard company.

I also have only good things to say about Erik. He comes to Germany whenever we need him to solve a critical product issue, when we would like to have a contribution from "himself" at business partner meetings or when we are trying to land a special deal with a customer or new reseller.

## The profit warning hurts

We have barely managed to sleep off the party before the profit warning comes. It hurts. Every year my wife and I write Christmas letters to our friends and family. I write the following at Christmas 1999:

*It's hardly surprising that 1999 was a busy year for Damgaard GmbH and for me. We started the year by opening subsidiaries in Vienna and Zurich. The Austrian company is now running on schedule after appointing a director. We expanded the German company with additional sales consultants and are now operating from Munich, Saarbrücken, Hamburg, Berlin and Dortmund.*

*At the end of April we held our annual "Top Performer Conference", this time in Sicily. Due to the great success we enjoyed in 1998, a large contingent of resellers, from my countries, participated.*

*We delivered results in the first half of the year that far exceeded our budgets and the spirit was close to euphoric. Success can make you blind and we didn't see that the good sales in the first half of the year would commandeer all the resources of our resellers in the second half.*

*Since the summer holidays, we have spent many hours every day on pulling in turnover. Despite the Germans not caring for military metaphors, I have chosen the following image anyway: "We have forsaken the comfortable seats of our high-flying bombers for fighting door-to-door on the streets". It requires readjustment to go from a situation where revenue comes in of its own accord to one where it has to be tugged and pulled. It is my job to ensure such a readjustment happens quickly.*

*In October, we carried out a very successful IPO. With a share price of 320 DKK (for DKK 10) [64 USD], Damgaard got an injection of over 200 million USD. It was an A+++ IPO. However, the market's expectations for our short-term growth potential were completely out of sync with reality; we, therefore, had to scale down the expectations in a stock exchange announcement. This almost led to a panic on the Copenhagen Stock Exchange. It was nice to be 1,200 km away in such a situation! Our long-term growth potential remains enormous, and I am convinced that we will deliver.*

*I have dropped my weekly German lessons as I feel quite comfortable with the language now. When you speak German for ten hours every day, more and more starts to stick. Two days every fortnight, I work from our office in Zurich, so I am even getting to grips with Swiss German.*

*I am incredibly happy for my job, which offers new challenges and tasks every day. It is exciting to work in new cultural environments and find a style and methods that work in view of local conditions.*

## The difficult merger

In autumn 2000, we start preparations for finding my replacement and my return to Denmark. I am not happy about it, but my family would like to return to Denmark when school finishes in June 2001. Maria is starting upper secondary school after the summer holidays, and Sue would like to use her newly acquired knowledge after graduating with her master's degree. Neither of them wants to stay in Germany. I have to respect that.

After the merger with Navision Software in December 2000, I immediately landed on both feet with the title of Vice President with responsibility for marketing activities in Central Europe. As regional manager, I participate in the February 2001 meeting, where the very ambitious growth target of 46 per cent is presented. My region is to provide a growth of 44 per cent.

After René Stockner has shown the figures, you could have heard a pin drop in the meeting room. I look around at my colleagues and can see that they are thinking what I am thinking: should we attack now to reduce the figure or should we take on the challenge and show what we can do? We are all entrepreneurial types who love challenges, but we also know that if we accept those numbers, our own and not least our employees' bonuses will be built around those targets. If we achieve a growth of 20 per cent, which would be outstanding, we would have failed to reach the target and nobody would be paid their bonus. If we accept the goal, we will have to support the ambition for all the country managers. If they resist and refuse to accept the goals, then we are, in fact, powerless. It's in the countries that the results are achieved and, actually, our contribution and influence as regional managers is quite limited. If truth be told, we don't know our power as the work on defining them is still ongoing. If a country manager doesn't want to participate in the project, do we then have the authority to fire him? As it currently stands, we can't and it enables the country managers to simply ignore our proposals and suggestions.

I don't know René Stockner and Navision's culture particularly well and wonder if the gambit is a kind of invitation to haggle. Is the expectation that we stand up and drive down the percentage? Are we chickens if we don't say anything? In Damgaard, Preben would have said, "Let's drop the disguises", and then I would have known the numbers couldn't be changed, and that we would all have come up with a strategy and plan for how they could be reached. When we had then laid out our plans and asked for 10 million USD to complete them, Preben would have asked what we could be done for 5 million USD.

The thoughts whirl around my head, and I can see my colleagues' cogs turning, too, but before anyone can respond, René says there is no point in questioning the numbers – they haven't been pulled out of thin air.

Since the end of December the previous year, management has been working on a detailed analysis of the company with the help of PwC Consulting. 43 interviews have been carried out with the company's key personnel, including all regional managers and selected country leaders. All resellers and all ongoing initiatives are thoroughly analysed. Compared to the market situation, the conclusion is that there is a significant growth potential and it must be exploited now. Within a few weeks, we receive a copy of the report, after which we discuss the growth targets with the country managers.

Some of the others in the room make a few noises, but they are brushed off with the message that now we are to show what we are worth. That is exactly my attitude, but maybe René's play is just a part of the ritual? As none of my colleagues from Navision challenges René any further, I, too, accept that management wants us to formulate strategies and develop plans to reach the 46 per cent together.

Later, when I'm on the plane on my way back to Switzerland, where I am going skiing with my family and some friends, I wonder if René should be negotiated with individually. I had been through enough budget meetings in my life and experienced all kinds of play for ensuring that the lowest possible revenue target and the highest possible cost budget are agreed without regard for the company's interest. At Damgaard, it was possible to remove the worst political pretences from the budget planning. I had even experienced the budgets being adjusted for the benefit of employees when it was realised that market development was making it impossible to reach the original targets.

I have no idea what the new Navision culture entails or expects. I can discuss that, as appropriate, with my country managers when I present them with the 44 per cent growth, which we are to deliver together.

When I am finished merging the companies in my region, I realise that my job as regional manager isn't a long-term solution. The chemistry between me and my boss, René Stockner, isn't good and I don't get properly acquainted with Navision Software's history – in particular, the vital role of the German company in the organisation's success. In the battle for the budgets in spring 2001, I play my cards completely wrong and end up with the management in Germany against me.

## The return to Denmark and a dismissal

As time goes by, I can see that despite the impressive job title of Vice President, I am not delivering the worthy contribution reflected in my salary. There is no desire for the independent management team of Flemming Beisner and me between René Stockner and the country managers. From neither the country managers nor Navision's top management. And even if there were, it wouldn't be a job suited to my profile.

When I meet with René on 23rd June to discuss my future upon my return to Denmark on 1st August, I am not at all surprised to be dismissed. It's a shame it's ending that way, but I know the terms, and as Navision treats me more than fairly, I can't complain about the outcome.

Being sacked that way pushes my dream of starting my own business. Given the dismissal package I receive that dream can now be realised. The job of Vice President Central Europe at Navision will be my last job as a full-time permanent employee.

My years with Damgaard Data and Navision, from 1997 to 2001, were a very special experience; one I feel privileged to have had. The company was accommodating and the ambitions were high. And it had the products, the management and the financial strength to pursue those ambitions. I experienced and learned much in the barely four years that I was part of the team.

Even my somewhat unsuccessful achievement after the merger with Navision Software taught me something about myself that I was later able to use constructively.

You live – and you learn.

# BACKGROUND MATERIAL

## Product overview

Damgaard Data product chronology overview:

## 1984:

Maxisoft, which changed its name to Danmax after its launch in October 1984. An invoicing and financial management program for very small businesses with only one or very few users. The product was developed for CP/M, but could also be delivered to PC/MS-DOS.

## 1986

Concorde. An invoicing and financial management program for small and medium sized businesses with 2-5 users. The product was developed for PC/MS-DOS and used Novell Netware for multi-user solutions.

## 1987:

Production of own network cards via the joint ownership of Connect A/S. The activity is abandoned in September 1989. Damgaard Data takes over the distribution of PCPLUS from Sophus Berendsen Computer Products.

## 1989:

Concorde Version 4 with the possibility of customised solutions. Partnership with DSI commences and a connector for DSI-SYSTEM is launched.

## 1990:

The toolbox for Concorde Version 4 is released. Distribution of third-party products activities are intensified.

## 1991:

Concorde XAL released. A program for managing financial and other business processes in medium-sized businesses. The product comes with a separate development environment that enables customers and resellers to develop customisations and extensions. The program can be delivered to PC/MS-DOS and OS/2 as well as a wide range of variants of UNIX.

## 1993:

Concorde XAL Version 2 is released with a whole range of improvements, including enhanced functionality for production and material management as well as support for the Oracle database system.

## 1994:

Concorde C5. Considered a replacement for Concorde for small businesses. The product is built on Concorde XAL technology and can be delivered on PC/MS-DOS and OS/2. Distribution activities of third-party products are spun off.

## 1995:

Concorde C5 Light for Windows. Replacement for Concorde Light, which is sold through DIY centres and computer retailers.

## 1998:

Concorde Axapta. First thought of as a Concorde XAL substitute, but launched as an independent product for managing financial and business processes in medium and large companies with international activities. The product is developed solely for Microsoft Windows and requires a database system from either Microsoft or Oracle.

## Damgaard Data turnover 1984-1999

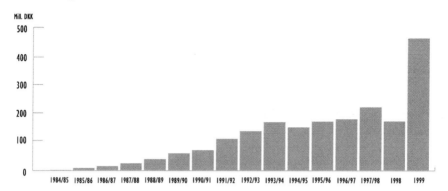

## Damgaard Data operating profit 1984-1999

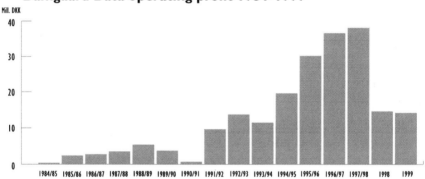

## Damgaard Data number of employees 1984-1999

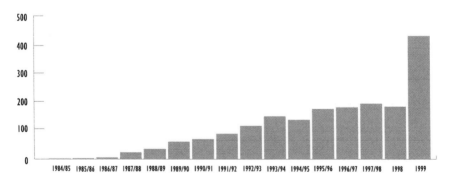

Comments:

1984/85 are estimated figures

1996/97 covers the 14 months May 1996 to June 1997

1998 covers only the 6 months July 1998 to December 1998

For 2000-2002 the figures are included in the merged company
NavisonDamgaard, which changed its name to Navision in 2001.

## Navision Software turnover 1985-2002

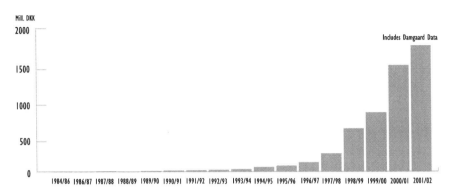

## Navision Software operating profit 1985-2002

## Navision Software number of employees 1985-2002

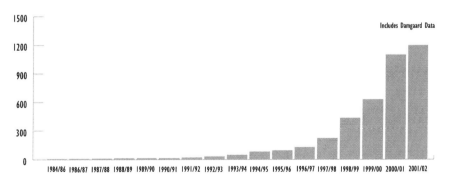

Comments:

1984/86 covers the 18 months November 1984 to April 1986

1994/95 covers the 14 months May 1994 to June 1995

2000-2002 contains figures for the merged company NavisonDamgaard, which changed its name to Navision in 2001.

# ACKNOWLEDGE-MENTS

## A huge thank you to the many contributors

The book is based largely on the memories of people involved in some way or other with Damgaard Data and Navision Software from 1983 to 2002. I am grateful for the immense kindness shown by all those I was in contact with; not least, for their willingness to be interviewed and answer any follow-up questions I had. Without access to Erik and Preben Damgaard's archives as well as their active and patient involvement, it wouldn't have been possible to delve into the many nooks and crannies I deemed necessary for describing Damgaard Data's opportunities, challenges, decisions and development. Having access to Preben Damgaard's notebooks, in particular, was invaluable for determining chronology, who was involved in what events, which subjects were discussed and what decisions were made.

I am privileged to live in a country with a unique library system. The Royal Danish Library and Allerød Library gave me access to all public sources regarding Damgaard Data since 1984. The Infomedia database helped my research of the period 1990 and later significantly. I owe special thanks to Bob Vagn Hansen, Hans Christian Markvardt Pedersen, Morten Gregersen, Michael Sander, Casper Guldbrandsen, Vagn Sanggaard Jakobsen, Per Pedersen, Anna Eskelund, Søren Fink-Jensen and René Stockner. Not only did they contribute with their memories, they also supplied valuable photographic and text material: press releases, company newsletters, brochures, annual reports, flotation prospectus, business presentations and other documents.

I would also like to thank the following people for sharing their insights and memories: Allan Mathiassen, Anders Lehmann, Anne Grethe Pind, Birgit Hildebrandt, Birgitte Munch, Bo Nielsson, Carsten Glem, Carsten Kaae, Casper Guldbrandsen, Claus Grevsen, Claus Winblad, David Tykskov, Dorrit Overgaard, Egon Østergaard, Eric Burkel, Erik Seifert, Erik Ørum Hansen, Finn Kusk, Flemming Idorf Beisner, Flemming Louw-Reimer, Flemming Østergaard, Freddie B. Jørgensen, Garth D. Laird, Günther Sabeck, Hanne Haubert, Hans Bak, Hans Henrik Pontoppidan, Hans Kierulff, Hans Månsson, Helle Lunde, Helle Lynge, Helle Baarts Vang, Henning Nielsen, Henrik Albertsen, Henrik Klinkvort, Henrik E. Nyegaard, Henrik Rose, Henrik Steen Pedersen, Horst Fischer, Irene Steffens, Jacob Michelsen, Jacques van Branteghem, Jakob Schou, Jan Hjelm, Jan Månsson, Jan Olesen, Jan Radoor, Jan Vinjebo, Jan-Elling Skaugerum, Jeanette Storm, Jens Haugaard, Jens Svanholdt (nee Riis), Jens-Peder Vium, Jesper Carl Hansen, Jesper Falkebo, Jesper Lindhardt, Jesper Pedersen, Jette Ankerstjerne, Jette Lundquist, John Holdt, Jørgen Holck-Christensen, Kaj Jensen, Kim Kasperek, Kim Kruse Petersen, Kirsten Larsen, Larry Sheffield, Lars Andersen, Lars Balle Andersen, Lars Damsgaard, Lars Kafton, Lars Larsen, Lasse Zäll, Leif Arildsen, Lennart Jönsson, Louis Burdulis, Mads Westermann, Majbritt Rossau, Marianne Nyegaard, Marianne Scheufens, Marianne Wier, Martin Glob, Michael Ammentorp, Michael Dyrberg, Michael Graves, Michael Kofoed, Michael Laursen, Michael Lerche, Michael Uhman, Morten Løgager, Morten Vedel Nielsen, Pat Falotico, Peter Åkerwall, Peter Bastholm, Peter Colsted, Peter Perregaard, Peter Wagner, Peter Warnøc, Pia Glavind, Poul Schilling, Poul-Jørgen Brinck, Preben Westergaard, Regitze Reeh, René Vernon, Sigurd Flydal, Steen Bindslev, Stine Laforce, Sven Jochimsen, Sven Tvermoes, Søren Dolberg, Søren Printz Christensen, Thomas Bang, Thomas Hejlsberg, Thomas Neergaard, Tina Beisner, Tine Haagensen, Ulla Kjærsgaard, Vagn Thorup and Waldemar Schmidt.

The manuscript was read and commented on by my good friend Esben Stubager, who provided encouraging feedback and remedied many errors. There are some anonymous sources in the book though I know their identity. Some people wished to participate, but didn't want to be named in either the book or as a source. I have respected that.

Annie Hagel's thorough and merciless editing saved the readers an extra 100 pages, lowered the readability index to a reasonable level and ensured a much better flow than I hoped.

Mette de Fine Licht from Skriveværkstedet was a great support and help, offering practical advice regarding the book itself and the preparation of the book's launch.

A thank you to Niels Borgen, who, in the course of my writing, willingly provided his extensive experience from the publishing world. Thank you, too, to my kind neighbours, Birgitte Borgen and Claus Secher, who are far better versed in literature than most of us – me included – and who followed the book's development, giving me good advice along the way.

I am indebted to my wife, Sue, and my friend and brother-in-law, Wilfred Burton, both native English speakers, whose help fine-tuning and polishing the manuscript has been invaluable.

My biggest thank you goes to Sue and our two children, Maria and Daniel, who, together with their spouses, Jetmir and Maria, and our grandchildren Selina, Oliver, Mathias, Bella, Laura, Anik and Adrian, have shown great patience and ensured my thoughts were away from the project when I got bogged down. There's nothing like a game of Uno or a walk in the woods for seeing things afresh.

Hillerød, May 2018

# BIBLIOGRAPHY

(In chronological order)

Hølge, Palle, and Vibeke Bagge. 1985. 'PC'erne vil fortsætte deres eksplosive vækst', *PC world Danmark*, 1985/01/15, pp. 22-24.

Knudsen, Lars H. 1985. '1984 var et spændende data-år: – men i 1985 kan alt komme til at ske!', *Datatid*, 1985/02/15, pp. 24, 26-27.

Ottenheim, Freddie. 1985. 'Analyseinstitut: 16.500 PC'er solgt i Danmark i 1984', *PC world Danmark*, 1985/02/15, pp. 6.

Knudsen, Lars H. 1985. 'Store problemer i databranchen', *Datatid*, 1985/07/15, pp. 8-9.

Knudsen, Lars H. 1985. 'Brugervenlighed i højsædet', *Datatid*, 1985/10/15, pp. 34-35.

Annonce. 1986. 'Damgaard Data', *Datatid*, 1986/01/15, pp. 2.

Knudsen, Lars H. 1986. 'Klar trussel mod minibaserede systemer', *Datatid*, 1986/02/01, pp. 2.

Damm, Henrik. 1986. 'Halvdelen af erhvervslivet har ikke edb', *Computerworld*, 1986/04/11, pp. 20-21.

Knudsen, Lars H. 1986. 'Afskyelig stor og flot: CeBit 1986 i Hannover', *Datatid*, 1986/04/15, pp. 28-30, 32.

Rybner, Torben. 1986. 'Datamaten i nettet', *PC world Danmark*, 1986/04/15, pp. 18, 20, 24.

Hølge, Palle. 1986. 'HERA-SOFT – et administrativt system til den mindste eller mellemstore virksomhed', *PC world Danmark*, 1986/05/15, pp. 50, 52.

Hølge, Palle, and Helmuth Rasmussen. 1986. 'Den fantastiske historie om HERA-DATA', *PC world Danmark*, 1986/05/15, pp. 80, 82, 84-85.

Knudsen, Lars H. 1986. 'Hele bordet op på skærmen: PC Plus administrativ programpakke', *Datatid*, 1986/05/15, pp. 30, 32.

Jensen, Bent Reno, Henrik Stanley Madsen, and Herbert Nathan. 1989. 'Focus på kreditorregnskab: vi ser på håndtering af kreditorer og tester Admiral, Concorde og System Svendsen', *PC world*, 1986/06/15, pp. 76-78, 80-86, 88, 90, 92.

Editorial. 1986. 'PCPLUS', *Kontorbladet*, 1986/06/15, pp. 24, 50.

Olsen, Lars. 1986. 'Lille vestjysk softwarehus tager ordrer fra de store', *Computerworld*, 1986/08/08, pp. 14.

Ebbesen, Jens Erik. 1986. 'PC-administration der går nye veje', *PC world Danmark*, 1986/08/15, pp. 53-54, 57-58.

Hølge, Palle. 1986. 'PCPLUS ØKONOMI: et administrativt program i særklasse', *PC world Danmark*, 1986/09/15, pp. 110-18, 23-24.

Advertisement. 1986. 'Polydata A/S', *Datatid*, 1986/11/15, pp. 2.

Knudsen, Lars H. 1986. 'Ikke de store nyheder', *Datatid*, 1986/11/15, pp. 16-17.

Madsen, Knud Erik. 1986. 'Her rullede de store penge', *Datatid*, 1986/11/15, pp. 18, 20, 22.

Østergaard, Mikael. 1986. 'Startet af syv fallerede studerende', *Datatid*, 1986/11/15, pp. 64-66.

A/S, Brendsen Computer Products. 1987. 'Brendsen Computer Products A/S', *Datatid*, 1987/01/15, pp. 1.

Data, Damgaard. 1987. 'Concorde (Damgaard Data)', *Datatid*, 1987/01/15, pp. 1.

Editorial. 1987. 'Årets dataprodukter 1986', *Datatid*, 1987/01/15, pp. 2.

Koch, Jens. 1987. 'Et billigt lokalnet kan sagtens være godt: test af PC-netværk', *Datatid*, 1987/03/15, pp. 20-21, 24.

Munk, Ivan. 1987. 'PC'en er ikke skabt til et liv i isolation', *Datatid*, 1987/03/15, pp. 16-20.

Moan, Øystein. 1987. 'Token Ring bliver ny markedsstandard: local area network', *Datatid*, 1987/07/15, pp. 22-24.

Data, Damgaard. 1987. 'Ja Tak til rapporter om Concorde (annonce)', *Datatid*, 1987/09/15.

Østergaard, Mikael. 1987. 'Danske programmører laver verdens bedste software', *Datatid*, 1987/09/15, pp. 52, 54.

Jensen, Palle Bruus. 1987. 'EDB-folk skal holde fingrene væk', *Ehverv/København*, 1987/10/15, pp. 2.

Madsen, Knud Erik. 1987. 'Nyt dansk adm. program sælges gennem IBM', *Datatid*, 1987/10/15, pp. 1.

Schwanenflügel, Ditlev. 1987. 'Et program i sværvægtsklassen: Concorde PC-administrationssystem', *Datatid*, 1987/10/15, pp. 110-12, 14.

Hosny, Curt. 1987. 'Lettere administration med mange muligheder: vi tester det første bogholderi-program det danske Danmax', *Aalborg stiftstidende*, 1987/10/17.

Bomberg, Leif. 1987. 'Nu falder dommen fra 330 PC forhandlere', *Datatid*, 1987/11/15, pp. 2.

Bomberg, Leif. 1987. 'Image i top, service i bund: 330 forhandlere om PC-leverandørerne', *Datatid*, 1987/12/15, pp. 10-11.

Christ, Bjørn. 1988. 'Fattigmandsfinans', *Alt om data*, 1988/01/15, pp. 34-35, 37-38.

Data, Damgaard. 1988. 'Concorde skaber basis for effektiv økonomistyring', *Datatid*, 1988/01/15, pp. 1.

Kusk, Finn. 1988. 'FK-Data annonce', *Datatid*, 1988/01/15, pp. 1.

Pind, Anne Grethe. 1988. 'Dansk System Industri ApS Annonce', *Datatid*, 1988/01/15, pp. 1.

Editorial. 1988. 'Kort og soft – en succes', *Direct Office*, 1988/02/15.

Editorial. 1988. 'Nytænkning er vejen til succes i softwarebranchen', *Aktiv Erhvervskommunikation*, 1988/02/15.

Schwanenflügel, Ditlev. 1988. 'Underskud på betalingsbalancen', *Datatid*, 1988/03/15, pp. 10, 12, 14.

Olsen, Lars, and Jens Michael Damm. 1988. 'PC-verdenen vil fortsat være blå: Danmarks fem største PC-forhandlere', *Computerworld*, 1988/03/18, pp. 16-18, 44-45.

Nathan, Herbert. 1988. '10 gode råd der er guld værd, før du skal vælge administrative PC-software', *PC world Danmark*, 1988/05/15, pp. 27-29, 31.

Bomberg, Leif. 1988. 'Åben strid mellem FK Data og Damgaard Data', *PC world Danmark*, 1988/09/15, pp. 2.

Damm, Jens Michael. 1988. 'Regnecentralen og den multinationale partner', *Computerworld*, 1988/10/07, pp. 30.

Lindknud, Peter. 1988. 'Over-smart og frustrerende: en bruger anmelder Kontor & Data 88', *Computerworld*, 1988/10/14, pp. 34-35.

Data, Damgaard. 1989. 'Concorde økonomistyring er nummer et i Danmark', *Datatid*, 1989/01/15, pp. 1.

Jensen, Bent Reno, Herbert Nathan, and Niels Strange Nielsen. 1989. 'Stor sammenlignende test af 15 økonomisystemer til PC'er', *PC world*, 1989/01/15, pp. 10-15, 18-19.

Pind, Anne Grethe. 1989. 'Dansk System Industri ApS', *Datatid*, 1989/01/15, pp. 1.

Kargård Nielsen, Søren. 1989. 'Vi kan jo godt i Danmark!', *PC world*, 1989/03/15, pp. 44-46.

Hilbert, Poul, and Povl Erik Gedde. 1989. 'Nu flyver Albatros igen: efter økonomisk ruin er PolyData på markedet med ny ledelse og ny udgave af det danske program Albatros', *Børsen*, 1989/05/09.

Barnholdt, Christian. 1989. 'Branchen, alle savner data på: dansk software i krise', *Datatid*, 1989/06/15, pp. 18, 20, 22.

Persson, Lars. 1989. 'Danskere med vokseværk', *Datatid*, 1989/06/15, pp. 51-52, 56, 58.

Jensen, Bent Reno, Henrik Stanley Madsen, Herbert Nathan, and Ole Arboe. 1989. 'Stortest af økonomisystemer – konklusion', *PC world*, 1989/07/15, pp. 80-83, 85-86, 88-89, 92-94.

Forchhammer, Peter. 1989. 'Som brødre vi dele', *Penge og privatøkonomi*, 1989/10/15, pp. 14-15.

IBM. 1989. 'IBM Personal System/2 med OS/2: Dagen er for kort til langsomme computere', *Datatid*, 1989/12/15, pp. 2.

Pind, Anne Grethe. 1990. 'Dansk System Industri', *Datatid*, 1990/01/15, pp. 1.

Christensen, Mads. 1990. 'Tolv års højtflyvende eventyr: PolyData satsede for voldsomt', *Computerworld*, 1990/03/09, pp. 18-19.

Data, Damgaard. 1990. 'Netværk', *Datatid*, 1990/04/15.

Redaktionen. 1990. 'Værsgo: her er en PC', *Politiken*, 1990/05/09, pp. 1.

Bomberg, Leif. 1990. 'Vi kunne nok ikke gøre det een gang til', *Datatid*, 1990/08/15, pp. 30-32, 34.

Noter. 1990. 'Damgaard Data, ICL Data og Sun indgår samarbejde', *Berlingske Tidende*, 1990/09/07, pp. 1.

Mulvad, Nils. 1990. 'Når mødet med edb ender i dyb afsky. Uddrag af en oliesælgers edb-dagbog', *Computerworld*, 1990/10/05, pp. 20.

Bruhn, Erik. 1990. 'Kan man stadig tjene penge på at sælge edb?', *Datatid*, 1990/10/15, pp. 46-48, 50, 52.

Grünbaum, Ole. 1990. 'EDB-succes begyndte hjemme i kælderen: to brødre udviklede økonomiprogram til PCer', *Politiken*, 1990/11/21.

Datanyt. 1990. 'Digital Equipment og Damgaard Data har indgået et strategisk samarbejde', *Dagbladenes Bureau*, 1990/11/23.

Noter. 1990. 'Damgaard Data har fået en millionordre på software fra Singapores største edb-virksomhed PET Computer', *Berlingske Tidende*, 1990/12/31.

Larsen, Ove. 1991. 'Damgaard Data bliver autoriseret Novell distributør', *Dagbladenes Bureau*, 1991/01/31.

Larsen, Ove. 1991. 'Damgaard Data bliver CA-Cricket distributør', *Dagbladenes Bureau*, 1991/03/27.

Bech-Andersen, Peik. 1991. 'Navigator 3 kræver en god styrmand', *Datatid*, 1991/04/15, pp. 5.

Bauer, Allan. 1991. 'Hos Oticon pusler man med fremtidens edb-kontor', *Datatid*, 1991/05/15, pp. 3.

Bomberg, Leif. 1991. 'Hvem sælger flest PC'er hertillands', *Datatid*, 1991/05/15, pp. 1.

Larsen, Ove. 1991. 'Damgaard Data bliver Lotus-distributør', *Dagbladenes Bureau*, 1991/06/06.

Larsen, Ove. 1991. 'Damgaard Data A/S blandt de store udstillere på Mikrodata 91 i Bella Center', *Dagbladenes Bureau*, 1991/09/13.

Jørgensen, Asbjørn. 1991. 'Danske firmaer kan ikke følge edb-kamp', *Berlingske Tidende*, 1991/10/24.

Malmgreen, Henrik. 1991. 'Runder 100 millioner i omsætning: Historien om en softwarevirksomhed i 3D – Damgaard – Data – Dansk', *PC world*, 1991/11/15, pp. 93-95.

Pedersen, Helle Skou, and Henrik Nellager. 1991. 'Bogholderi for alle pengene', *Alt om data*, 1991/11/15, pp. 10-11, 13-14, 16-17, 20, 22-23, 25-26.

Larsen, Ove. 1991. 'Concorde XAL godkendt af revisorer', *Dagbladenes Bureau*, 1991/12/05.

Jørgensen, Asbjørn. 1992. 'Danske edb-firmaer jager nye forhandlere i Europa', *Berlingske Tidende*, 1992/03/11.

Jørgensen, Asbjørn. 1992. 'Dansk forsøg på fælles edb-eksport', *Berlingske Tidende*, 1992/03/14.

Bech-Andersen, Peik. 1992. 'Her kan administrationen programmeres', *Datatid*, 1992/03/15, pp. 78-82.

Editorial. 1992. 'Concorde på Oracle', *Berlingske Tidende*, 1992/04/13.

Redaktionen. 1992. 'Damgaard Data, ICL Data og Sun', *Berlingske Tidende*, 1992/09/07.

Jensen, Bent Reno, and Herbert Nathan. 1992. 'Stor analyse af administrative systemer', *PC world*, 1992/10/15, pp. 16-20.

Larsen, Ove. 1992. 'Ny WordPerfect distributør', *Dagbladenes Bureau*, 1992/12/09.

Larsen, Ove. 1992. 'Dansk edb klarer sig fint', *Dagbladenes Bureau*, 1992/12/23.

Editorial. 1993. 'Jan Løwe og Kurt Bertelsen er ansat i Damgaard Data', *Computerworld*, 1993/02/12.

Bomberg, Leif. 1992. 'Danmark legestue for de store?', *Datatid*, 1993/03/15, pp. 20-22.

Schade, Dag Holmstad and Christian. 1993. '300.000 mulige kunder er for lidt', *Politiken*, 1993/06/16.

Editorial. 1993. 'Software på vej op', *Berlingske Tidende*, 1993/09/10.

Sørensen, Niels Møller and Torben B. 1993. 'Elektronisk post breder sig eksplosivt', *Computerworld*, 1993/09/17.

Sørensen, Torben B. and Niels Møller. 1993. 'Forskellige nettjenester til forskellige priser', *Computerworld*, 1993/09/17.

Jørgensen, Asbjørn. 1993. 'Kamp om kanalerne', *Berlingske Tidende*, 1993/10/25.

Thomsen, Jens. 1993. 'Sophus Berendsen taber sag om økonomi-system', *Computerworld*, 1993/10/29.

Larsen, Ove. 1993, Damgaard Data og Microsoft har indgået samarbejde, *Dagbladenes Bureau*, Press Release, 1993/11/16.

Morsing, Finn. 1993. 'For 110 mio. kr. økonomi-systemer i Danmark', *Computerworld*, 1993/12/10.

Morsing, Finn. 1994. 'PC&C sagde nej', *Computerworld*, 1994/01/24.

Larsen, Ove. 1994. 'Fremtidens Windows er på vej', *Dagbladenes Bureau*, 1994/01/26.

Morsing, Finn. 1994. 'Concorde skal til udlandet', *Computerworld*, 1994/01/28.

Marfelt, Birgitte. 1994. 'Græsrods-post boomer', *Ingeniøren*, 1994/02/18.

Bomberg, Leif. 1994. 'Hvem har fat i rorpinden: Damgaard Datas og PC&C's chefer i duel', *Datatid*, 1994/03/15, pp. 28-30.

Jørgensen, Asbjørn. 1994. 'Eksport og ung sex', *Berlingske Tidende*, 1994/03/21.

Morsing, Finn. 1994. 'IBM Danmark har købt sig til en guldgrube i Concorde-aftalen med Damgaard International.', *Computerworld*, 1994/03/25.

Editorial. 1994. 'Datalog Data bliver Damgaard ProjektPartner', *Computerworld*, 1994/03/25.

Nathan, Herbert and Claus Wøbbe. 1994. 'Endnu en Concorde er lettet', *PC world*, 1994/04/15, pp. 48-49.

Vad, Kasper. 1994. 'Regnskabets time', *Alt om data*, 1994/04/15, pp. 27, 29-30.

Sørensen, Torben B. 1994. 'Damgaard satser millioner på markedsføring af Concorde', *Computerworld*, 1994/05/13.

Hansson, Leif. 1994. 'Edb-systemer tilpasses internationalt (POSIX)', *Ingeniøren*, 1994/05/20.

Editorial. 1994. 'Hop på nettet', *Ingeniøren*, 1994/06/17.

Editorial. 1994. 'Erik og Preben Damgaard har fået prisen "Årets Bernhard" af Erhvervs-Bladet', *Computerworld*, 1994/06/24.

Sørensen, Torben B. 1994. 'Kunder giver karakterer', *Computerworld*, 1994/06/24.

Holmstad, Dag. 1994. 'Damgaard sælger en afdeling fra', *Politiken*, 1994/06/30.

Christensen, Claus Bulow. 1994. 'Velkommen i Cyberspace', *Berlingske Tidende*, 1994/08/02.

Editorial. 1994. 'Produkter på vej (C5)', *Computerworld*, 1994/08/05.

Olesen, Dorte. 1994. 'Kronik: Et universitet for os alle', *Politiken*, 1994/08/12.

Nellager, Henrik. 1994. 'Det kan også blive for let', *Alt om data*, 1994/08/14, pp. 4-6.

Tovgaard, Jens. 1994. 'Light-versioner eller bare dyre demo'er', *Datatid*, 1994/08/15, pp. 62-64.

Andersen, Klavs. 1994. 'Nyt mps-modul kan styre både ordre og serieproduktion', *Computerworld*, 1994/08/31.

Morsing, Finn. 1994. 'Damgaard Data voksede nær 25 procent i 1993', *Computerworld*, 1994/10/07.

Morsing, Finn. 1994. 'Navigator får ny distributør', *Computerworld*, 1994/10/07.

Thestrup, Allan. 1994. 'Danskerne skal ud af nichen', *Datatid*, 1994/10/15, pp. 5-10.

Holmstad, Dag. 1994. 'IBM opsluger dansk EDB', Politiken, 1994/11/09.

Grünbaum, Ole. 1994. 'Gates: Vi kan æde de andre', *Politiken*, 1994/11/17.

Holmstad, Dag. 1994. 'Navigator skifter IBM ud', *Politiken*, 1994/11/17.

Sørensen, Torben B. 1994. 'Uændret omsætning trods frasalg (halvårsregnskab fra Damgaard Data)', *Computerworld*, 1994/11/25.

Larsen, Ove. 1994. 'Der vælter god dansk software frem på markedet', *Dagbladenes Bureau*, 1994/11/30.

Toft, Dorte. 1995. 'Overskudsdeling hos Damgaard', *Computerworld*, 1995/01/06.

Toft, Dorte. 1995. 'Store eksportforhåbninger til Navigator Financial', *Computerworld*, 1995/01/13.

Editorial. 1995. 'Damgaard til Medialog', *Markedsføring*, 1995/01/18.

Sørensen, Torben B. 1995. 'Firmaer møder kunderne gennem Internet', *Computerworld*, 1995/01/20.

Toft, Dorte. 1995. 'Damgaard Data vil rette software på samlebånd', *Computerworld*, 1995/01/27.

Bauer, Allan. 1995. 'På Internet med DanaData', *Berlingske Tidende*, 1995/01/31.

Clausen, Rolf Ask. 1995. 'Konvergens (Netscape)', *Ingeniøren*, 1995/02/03.

Sørensen, Torben B. 1995. 'Danske softwarehuse holder sig fra OS/2', *Computerworld*, 1995/02/10.

Editorial. 1995. 'Damgaard Data indfører overskudsdeling', *Berlingske Tidende*, 1995/02/14.

Tovgaard, Jens. 1995. 'Med og uden mus i økonomien', *Datatid*, 1995/02/15, pp. 68-69, 71.

Editorial. 1995. 'Ejendomsmæglere anskaffer Concorde Home (C5)', *Computerworld*, 1995/02/24.

Toft, Dorte. 1995. 'Nye Concorder med valgfrihed', *Computerworld*, 1995/02/24.

Andersen, Pia Lykke. 1995. 'Pæn dansk deltagelse på Cebit', *Computerworld*, 1995/03/03.

Editorial. 1995. 'Erik Seifert har forladt PC&C efter uenighed om arbejdsbetingelserne', *Computerworld*, 1995/08/18.

Lahrmann, Finn B. 1995. 'Pædagogik for private penge', *Politiken*, 1995/08/20.

Larsen, Ove. 1995. 'Kun popstjerner og borgerkrige har fået en tilsvarende ...', *Dagbladenes Bureau*, 1995/09/05.

Morsing, Finn. 1995. 'Damgaard Data rykker op', *Computerworld*, 1995/09/08.

Bech-Andersen, Peik. 1995. 'XAL – et administrativt system, du kan nå', *Kontorbladet*, 32: 2. 6-7.

Toft, Dorte. 1995. 'Den risikovillige kapitals blinde øje', *Computerworld*, 1995/10/06.

Toft, Dorte. 1995. 'Økonomisystemer til eksamen i brugervenlighed', *Computerworld*, 1995/10/06.

Toft, Dorte. 1995. 'Damgaard retter blikket mod Holland', *Computerworld*, 1995/10/20.

Toft, Dorte. 1995. 'Byrden skal automatisk på de bredeste skuldre', *Computerworld*, 1995/11/03.

Toft, Dorte. 1995. 'Farvel til PC&C – goddag til Navision Software', *Computerworld*, 1995/11/17.

Toft, Dorte. 1995. 'Økonomistyring til under 2.000 kr. fra Damgaard (C5 Light)', *Computerworld*, 1995/11/24.

Wirgowitsch, Lisbeth. 1995. 'Stor TV-kampagne til lille målgruppe', *Markedsføring*, 1995/11/29.

Wihre, Dorte Skovgaard. 1995. 'Ærlighed som et ledelsesværktøj', *Berlingske Tidende*, 1995/12/28.

Editorial. 1996. 'Ny dynamo i dansk teknologi-forskning', *Berlingske Tidende*, 1996/01/07.

Toft, Dorte. 1996. 'Et spørgsmål om ærlighed', *Computerworld*, 1996/01/19.

Toft, Dorte. 1996. 'IBM var en vendekåbe, siger svensk distributør', *Computerworld*, 1996/01/19.

Toft, Dorte. 1996. 'Mudderkastning mellem Damgaard og Visual Business', *Computerworld*, 1996/01/19.

Toft, Dorte. 1996. 'Ægteskabet med IBM gav vækst i Concorde-salget', *Computerworld*, 1996/01/19.

Editorial. 1996. 'Columbus IT Partner bliver Damgaard Data Projekt Partner.', *Computerworld*, 1996/02/16.

Wang, Anne-Lise. 1996. 'Økonomistyring præget af lokale leverandører', *Computerworld*, 1996/03/08.

Sihm, Malene. 1996. 'Fokus på tilfredse kunder', *Markedsføring*, 1996/03/20.

Toft, Dorte. 1996. 'Navigator-ejerne sagsøgt for millionbeløb', *Computerworld*, 1996/03/22.

Toft, Dorte. 1996. 'Fælles-europæisk udgave af Concorde på vej', *Computerworld*, 1996/03/29.

Høyer, Peter. 1996. 'Firma trækker i maraton-løbetøj', *Politiken*, 1996/04/01.

Morsing, Finn. 1996. 'Ameridata tror på en fremtid for Intranet i Danmark', *Computerworld*, 1996/04/19.

Wessel, Lene. 1996. 'Spidse albuer klarer sig stadig bedst', *Ingeniøren*, 1996/05/31.

Svendsen, Susanne. 1996. 'Sjov og ballade for virksomhedens skyld', *Berlingske tidende*, 1996/07/03.

Svendsen, Susanne. 1996. 'Det handler om personlig udvikling', *Berlingske Tidende*, 1996/07/03.

Frank, Søren. 1996. 'Håb forude', *Berlingske Tidende*, 1996/08/11.

Frank, Søren. 1996. 'Damgaard Data – Privat sponsor for institution', *Berlingske Tidende*, 1996/08/11.

Editorial. 1996, *Damgaard Data deler ud af overskud*, RB- Bureau, Press Release, 1996/08/29.

Editorial. 1996. 'Rekord i Damgaard Data', *Berlingske Tidende*, 1996/09/03.

Kyrø, Øjvind. 1996. 'Fallerede studenter skaber millionindustri', *Politiken*, 1996/10/02.

Editorial. 1996. 'Rambøll vandt (sammen med Columbus IT Partner)', *Berlingske Tidende*, 1996/10/31.

Editorial. 1996. 'Per Pedersen udnævnt til ansvarlig for IBM's Concorde XAL aktiviteter i EMEA', *Berlingske Tidende*, 1996/12/01.

Editorial. 1996. 'Per Pedersen skal stå i spidsen for IBM's europæiske Concorde-salg', *Jyllands-Posten*, 1996/12/11.

Egholm, Kurt. 1997. 'Concorde skal ud i hele verden', *Erhvervsbladet*, 1997/01/10.

Horsager, Jan. 1997. 'Dansk software skal skaffe IBM succes', *Børsen*, 1997/01/10, pp. 10.

Møller, Niels. 1997. 'Dansk EDB erobrer verden', *Berlingske Tidende*, 1997/01/10.

Mulvad, Nils. 1997. 'IBM satser på dansk EDB-firma', *Jyllands-Posten*, 1997/01/10.

Toft, Dorte. 1997. 'IBM satser 100 millioner årligt på danske Concorde', *Computerworld*, 1997/01/10.

Lund, Oskar. 1997. 'Edb-gazelle skaber 300 nye arbejdspladser', *Børsen*, 1997/01/16, pp. 10.

Horsager, Jan. 1997. 'Fra kælder til kvist', *Børsen*, 1997/01/17, pp. Bagsiden.

Evert, Eigil. 1997. 'Brødrene Concorde', *Børsens nyhedsmagasin*, 1997/02/07, pp. 40-43.

Toft, Dorte. 1997. 'Kommunedata vælger Navision til institutioner', *Computerworld*, 1997/02/28.

Sørensen, Torben B. 1997. 'Økonomisystemer udvides med ledelsesinformation og databaser', *Computerworld*, 1997/03/14.

Sandøe, Niels. 1997. 'Damgaard indtager USA', *Jyllands-Posten*, 1997/03/17.

Sandøe, Niels. 1997. 'Concorde-økonomisystem mere fleksibelt', *Jyllands-Posten*, 1997/03/19.

Editorial. 1997. 'Sven Tvermoes personaledirektør for Damgaard Data Holding A/S', *Computerworld*, 1997/03/21.

Editorial. 1997. 'Finansministeriet køber Concorde XAL', *Berlingske Tidende*, 1997/04/11.

Toft, Dorte. 1997. 'Staten vælger Concorde XAL som lokalt økonomisystem', *Computerworld*, 1997/04/11.

Bach, Kim. 1997. 'Strid med politi, foged og retssager', *Berlingske Tidende*, 1997/05/01.

Hjorth, Lise Leonhard. 1997. 'Regnefejl til 67.000 kr.', *Berlingske Tidende*, 1997/05/27.

Hjorth, Lise Leonhard. 1997. 'Concorde Light C5 var lige lovlig "light«', *Berlingske Tidende*, 1997/05/27.

Hjorth, Lise Leonhard. 1997. 'Damgaard vildledte kunderne', *Berlingske Tidende*, 1997/05/27.

Bach, Kim. 1997. 'Dyre gaver koster EDB-chef jobbet', *Berlingske Tidende*, 1997/07/03.

Editorial. 1997. 'Indkøbschef bortvist for at have modtaget returkommission', *Ritzau*, 1997/07/03.

Sandøe, Niels. 1997. 'Bestikkelse i EDB-branchen', Finans.dk, 1997/07/08.

Simonsen, Torben. 1997. 'Eks-direktør opfordres til at sælge aktiepost', *Computerworld*, 1997/07/11.

Larsen, Ove. 1997. 'Concorde XAL til Microsoft SQL', *Dagbladenes Bureau*, 1997/07/30.

Toft, Dorte. 1997. 'Selvransagelse efter rygter om bestikkelse', *Computerworld*, 1997/08/08.

Olsen, Michael. 1997. 'Edb-firmaer i kold krig', *Børsens nyhedsmagasin*, 1997/09/05, pp. 30-33.

Editorial. 1997. 'Kontor & Data Messen: IT-pris for succes-software til Damgaard Data', *Jyllands-Posten*, 1997/10/1.

Hilbert, Poul. 1997. 'Concorden startede i forældrenes kælder', *Computerworld*, 1997/10/03, pp. 14-15.

RB-Børsen. 1997. 'Damgaard Data øger overskud', *Børsen*, 1997/11/18.

Krabbe, Klaus. 1997. 'Salget hæmmes af for få kompetente forhandlere', *Computerworld*, 1997/11/21.

Editorial. 1997. 'Ny mand i ledelsen', *Børsen*, 1997/12/02, pp. 6.

Arentoft, Hanne. 1998. 'Gave til Columbus', *Berlingske Tidende*, 1998/02/05.

Davidsen, Lotte. 1998. 'Ønskes: 10.000 IT-folk', *Computerworld*, 1998/02/06.

Rechnagel, Ursula. 1998. 'Damgaard Data foran stort gennembrud i USA', *Børsen*, 1998/02/09, pp. 9.

America, IBM. 1998, *IBM Announces New Force in Small and Medium Business*, IBM, Press Release, 1998/02/18

Krabbe, Klaus. 1998. 'IBM satser på dansk software i USA', *Computerworld*, 1998/02/20.

Simonsen, Torben. 1998. 'CSC ude af ordre om lokalt økonomisystem', *Computerworld*, 1998/02/20.

Mejlvang, Mette. 1998. 'Damgaard Data introducerer nyt system', *Jyllands-Posten*, 1998/03/11.

Mejlvang, Mette. 1998. 'Systemproducenter skærper konkurrence', *Jyllands-Posten*, 1998/03/11.

Lund, Oskar. 1998. 'IT-komet på vej mod 700 medarbejdere', *Børsen*, 1998/03/12, pp. 8.

Abild, Lars. 1998. 'Dansk IT-komet til USA', *Berlingske Tidende*, 1998/03/16.

Sandøe, Niels. 1998. 'IBM stopper salg af det dansk økonomisystem fra Damgaard Data', *Jyllands-Posten*, 1998/03/25.

Sandøe, Niels. 1998. 'Navision satser på mindre virksomheder (Tyskland)', *Jyllands-Posten*, 1998/03/25.

Simonsen, Torben. 1998. 'Damgaard overtager Concorde-salg', *Computerworld*, 1998/03/27.

Simonsen, Torben. 1998. 'Kultureksport', *Computerworld*, 1998/03/27.

Hilbert, Poul. 1998. 'Navision og Damgaard i kapløb om at levere statens økonomisystem', *Computerworld*, 1998/04/03.

Hansen, Uffe. 1998. 'To firmaer i opløb om statens økonomisystem', *Børsen*, 1998/04/15, pp. 8.

Haun, Jesper Bille. 1998. 'Axapta med Java look-alike', *Computerworld*, 1998/04/17.

Abild, Lars. 1998. 'Lovende ordre til Columbus IT Partner', *Berlingske Tidende*, 1998/04/20.

Editorial. 1998. 'Columbus IT Partner børsnoteres', *Reuter Finans*, 1998/04/21.

Hilbert, Poul. 1998. 'Dansk software vandt slaget om statskassen (Navision)', *Computerworld*, 1998/04/24.

Abild, Lars. 1998. 'En iværksætter på farten (Michael Gaardboe)', *Berlingske Tidende*, 1998/04/27.

Christensen, Peter Møller. 1998. 'Børsintroduktion skal sikre fortsat ekspansion', *Børsen*, 1998/04/28, pp. 8.

Bredsdorff, Magnus. 1998. 'Lønboom sætter danske virksomheder tilbage', *Computerworld*, 1998/05/22.

Editorial. 1998. 'Certified Solutions til Concorde produkterne', *Computerworld*, 1998/05/26.

Hilbert, Poul. 1998. 'Genistreg forhindrer monopol på stats-edb', *Computerworld*, 1998/06/26.

Dyrekilde, Birgitte. 1998. 'Columbus får første ordre til kommunale sektor', *Reuter Finans*, 1998/07/01.

Editorial. 1998. 'Columbus har flere mio-ordrer på beddingen', *Reuters*, 1998/07/01.

Editorial. 1998. 'Axapta til Dansk Industri', *Computerworld*, 1998/07/03.

Toft, Dorte. 1998. 'Navision tilbageviser rygter om børsintroduktion', *Computerworld*, 1998/07/24.

Editorial. 1998. 'Farum dropper Kommunedata', *Ritzau*, 1998/07/29.

Toft, Dorte. 1998. 'IBM skuffer på Concorde-fronten', *Computerworld*, 1998/08/07.

Toft, Dorte. 1998. 'Farum vil have Kommunedata ud', *Computerworld*, 1998/08/07.

Høst-Madsen, Kristoffer. 1998. 'Dansk software på spansk', *Børsen*, 1998/08/24, pp. 9.

Editorial. 1998. 'Columbus IT får stadig større marked i udlandet', *Reuters*, 1998/08/24.

Andersen, Klavs. 1998. 'Nyt MPS-modul kan styre både ordre og serieproduktion (Navision)', *Computerworld*, 1998/08/31.

Høst-Madsen, Kristoffer. 1998. 'Går efter international erfaring [Flemming Idorf Beisner]', *Børsen*, 1998/09/08, pp. 16.

Wahlers, Allan. 1998. 'IT-branchen skriger på flere ansatte', *Berlingske Tidende*, 1998/09/23.

Stokdyk, John. 1998. 'IBM launches Axapta (in the UK)', *AccountancyAge*, 1998/09/30.

Stokdyk, John. 1998. 'IBM launches Axapta', *AccountancyAge*. http://www.accountancyage.
com/aa/news /1780930 /ib m-launches-axapta.

*Newswire*, PR. 1998. 'IBM announces new mid-market global business management solution (in the UK)', Press Release, 1998/10/01.

*Newswire*, PR. 1998. 'IBM partners with leading reseller to bring axapta to channel', Press Release, 1998/10/01.

Rechnagel, Ursula. 1998. 'IT-bøvl bremser små selskaber', *Børsen*, 1998/10/01.

Høst-Madsen, Kristoffer. 1998. 'Det globale slagsmål', *Børsen*, 1998/10/02, pp. 12.

Krabbe, Klaus. 1998. 'År 2000 truer 10.000 danske virksomheder', *Computerworld*, 1998/10/02.

Toft, Dorte. 1998. 'Brixtofte på gyngende grund', *Computerworld*, 1998/10/02.

Hilbert, Poul. 1998. 'Egmont-direktør går til Damgaard Data', *Computerworld*, 1998/10/09.

Morsing, Finn. 1998. 'Messen var to dage for lang', *Computerworld*, 1998/10/09.

RB-Børsen. 1998. 'Damgaard Data ind i Australien', *Børsen*, 1998/10/09.

Heiberg, Anni. 1998. 'Mennesket i Centrum', *Børsen*, 1998/10/13, pp. 16.

Nystrøm, Kristian. 1998. 'Columbus er landet i Singapore (i oktober 1997)', *Jyllands-Posten*, 1998/10/13.

Editorial. 1998. 'Damgaard Data til Australien', *Berlingske Tidende*, 1998/10/17.

Editorial. 1998. 'Damgaard Data skifter navn', *Computerworld*, 1998/10/27.

Editorial. 1998. 'Columbus ser kun lille effekt fra Damgaard-ændring', *Reuters*, 1998/11/09.

Svith, Flemming. 1998. 'Damgaard køber IBM ud af udviklingsselskab', *Jyllands-Posten*, 1998/11/10.

Hilbert, Poul. 1998. 'IBM fik et godt tilbud', *Computerworld*, 1998/11/13.

Morsing, Finn. 1998. 'Damgaard blev træt af IBM's bureaukrati', *Computerworld*, 1998/11/13.

Morsing, Finn. 1998. 'Damgaard slipper gratis fra skilsmisse', *Computerworld*, 1998/11/13.

Lund, Anders. 1998. 'Farvel til IBM endte lykkeligt', *Berlingske Tidende*, 1998/11/18.

Bertelsen, Anja. 1998. 'Piger kan også programmere', *Aktuelt*, 1998/11/19.

Høst-Madsen, Kristoffer. 1998. 'Børsens næste IT-komet', *Børsen*, 1998/12/08, pp. 4.

Krabbe, Klaus. 1998. 'Afleverer IBM-direktør tilbage', *Computerworld*, 1998/12/08.

Toft, Dorte and Poul Hilbert. 1998. 'Damgaard på børsen', *Computerworld*, 1998/12/11.

Andersen, Mads Cordt. 1999. 'Danmark takker nej til amerikanske rammesystemer', *Computerworld*, 1999/01/19.

Toft, Dorte. 1999. 'Verdens mægtigste mand', *Computerworld*, 1999/02/09.

Simonsen, Torben. 1999. 'Kommuneløsning klarer år 2000-problemet', *Computerworld*, 1999/02/12.

Software, Navision. 1999, *Navision Software offentliggør planer om Børsnotering*, Press Release, 1999/02/15

Bredsdorff, Magnus. 1999. 'Navision vil være synlige', *Computerworld*, 1999/02/19.

Bredsdorff, Magnus. 1999. 'Børskapløb mellem Damgaard og Navision', *Computerworld*, 1999/02/19.

Editorial. 1999. 'Navision øger antallet af døtre til 13', *Reuters*, 1999/02/26.

Simonsen, Torben. 1999. 'I seng med fjenden', *Computerworld*, 1999/02/26.

Toft, Dorte. 1999. 'Gør det selv, siger Damgaard', *Computerworld*, 1999/02/26.

Hilbert, Poul. 1999. 'Navision Software A/S køber sig selv i England og Spanien', *Computerworld*, 1999/03/05.

Editorial. 1999. 'Rollerne fordelt blandt børsaspiranter', *Reuters-Børsen*, 1999/03/08.

Lai, Jens Kristian. 1999. 'Kundens behov bestemmer produktet [Columbus]', *Berlingske Tidende*, 1999/03/11.

Lai, Jens Kristian. 1999. 'Columbus vender pilen mod Spanien', *Berlingske Tidende*, 1999/03/11.

Lund, Anders. 1999. 'Navision rydder op', *Berlingske Tidende*, 1999/03/11.

Editorial. 1999. 'Navision vil være på global top tre', *Reuters*, 1999/03/11.

Editorial. 1999. 'Navision vil ekspandere på nye markeder', *Reuters*, 1999/03/11.

Iversen, Jens. 1999. 'Damgaard parat til at introducere Axapta på det tyske marked', *Børsen*, 1999/03/19.

Borring, Ghita. 1999. 'Godt gået navigatører', *Børsens nyhedsmagasin*, 1999/03/22.

Krabbe, Klaus. 1999. 'Kedsomhed gjorde dem til millionærer', *Computerworld*, 1999/03/23.

Lund, Anders and Jens Kristian Lai. 1999. 'År 2000-frygt giver øget salg af software', *Berlingske Tidende*, 1999/03/23.

Editorial. 1999. 'Navision udsolgt', *Erhvervsbladet*, 1999/03/29.

Ascarelli, Silvia. 1999. 'Navision Software Beats the Odds with IPO amid Sagging Sector', *The Wall Street Journal*, 1999/03/30.

Troelse, Ole. 1999. 'USA afgørende for Damgaard', *Børsen*, 1999/03/30, pp. 1.

Lai, Jens Kristian. 1999. 'Gigant truer danske virksomheder [SAP]', *Berlingske Tidende*, 1999/04/12.

Simonsen, Torben. 1999. 'Internationalt udviklingsseminar (Damgaard Technical Briefing)', *Computerworld*, 1999/04/27.

Simonsen, Torben. 1999. 'Undervisning er sagen', *Computerworld*, 1999/05/08.

Møller, Niels. 1999. 'Damgaard-brødre går på børsen', *Berlingske Tidende*, 1999/05/10.

Data, Damgaard. 1999, (*Highlight Damgaard Technical Briefing 1999 London*), PR Newswire, Press Release, 1999/05/21.

Editorial. 1999. 'Damgaard høster på Concorde, satser på Axapta', *Reuters*, 1999/05/21.

Simonsen, Torben. 1999. 'Axapta på forkant', *Computerworld*, 1999/05/21.

Simonsen, Torben. 1999. 'Concorde-partnere samlet til teknisk seminar', *Computerworld*, 1999/05/21.

Sandøe, Niels. 1999. 'Damgaard i storoffensiv', *Jyllands-Posten*, 1999/05/25.

Simonsen, Torben. 1999. 'Det psykologiske år 2000-problem', *Computerworld*, 1999/05/28.

Simonsen, Torben. 1999. 'Koden skal vaskes', *Computerworld*, 1999/05/28.

Simonsen, Torben. 1999. 'Send e-post fra økonomisystemet', *Computerworld*, 1999/05/28.

Hilbert, Poul. 1999. 'Navision topper med 3,2 milliarder på børsen', *Computerworld*, 1999/06/25.

Hilbert, Poul. 1999. 'De danske gulddrenge', *Computerworld*, 1999/06/25.

Krabbe, Klaus. 1999. 'Bambus-produkter ligger i halen på mærkevarerne', *Computerworld*, 1999/06/25.

Sejr, Kim. 1999. 'IT-gazelle har tabt pusten', *Børsen*, 1999/08/23.

Gaarden, Hugo. 1999. 'Dansk edb-firma udnytter opbrud i tysk IT-verden', *Børsen*, 1999/09/15, pp. 30.

Høst-Madsen, Kristoffer. 1999. 'Damgaard-brødre er tre mia værd', *Børsen*, 1999/09/20.

Editorial. 1999. 'Damgaard Data forudses at få en værdi på over 3 milliarder', *Reuters*, 1999/09/20.

Editorial. 1999. 'Navision vil være global nummer 1 på mellem- marked', *Reuters*, 1999/09/23.

Editorial. 1999. 'Navision overskud steg 199 % til 85,8 mio. kr.', *Reuters – Børsen*, 1999/09/23.

Eriksen, Karin. 1999. 'Forrygende regnskab og meget store ambitioner hos Navision Software', *Berlingske Tidende*, 1999/09/24.

Hilbert, Poul and Morten Østergaard. 1999. 'Navision stikker sugerøret i partnernes pengekasser', *Computerworld*, 1999/09/28.

Editorial. 1999. 'Navision vil have del i partneres profit', *Reuters-Børsen*, 1999/09/28.

Kræmer, Steen. 1999. 'Damgaard-aktie står til kurshop', *Børsen*, 1999/10/08, pp. 30.

Sørensen, Torben B. 1999. 'Damgaard glemte CeBIT', *Computerworld*, 1999/10/20.

Editorial. 1999. 'Navision vil vokse langt hurtigere end markedet', *Reuters-Børsen*, 1999/10/22.

Sundnæs, Per. 1999. 'Navision vil overhale markedet indenom', *Berlingske Tidende*, 1999/10/23.

Aagaard, Sune. 1999. 'Damgaard ren børskomet', Børsen, 1999/11/12, pp. 33.

Davidsen, Lotte. 1999. 'Academy sikrer Navisions vækst', *Computerworld*, 1999/11/12.

Jakobsen, Søren. 1999. 'Multirige nørder på skatte-flugt', *Ekstra Bladet*, 1999/11/14.

Editorial. 1999. 'Damgaard-fremstød i Berlin til maj', *Reuters-Børsen*, 1999/11/26.

Simonsen, Torben. 1999. 'Damgaard til briefing (DTB2000 i Berling)', *Computerworld*, 1999/11/26.

Editorial. 1999. 'Navision oplever ikke år 2000-opbremsning', *Reuter Finans*, 1999/12/02.

Krabbe, Klaus. 1999. 'Seifert vinder 2-0 over Navision', *Computerworld*, 1999/12/03.

Møller, Niels. 1999. 'Damgaard i frit fald på Fondsbørsen', *Berlingske Tidende*, 1999/12/03.

Editorial. 1999. 'Navision retssag koster erstatning på 13 mio', *Reuter Finans*, 1999/12/03.

Lund, Anders. 1999. 'Damgaard afviser beskyldning', *Berlingske Tidende*, 1999/12/04.

Niels Sandøe and Keld Louie-Pedersen. 1999. 'Stærk kritik af Damgaard', *Jyllands-Posten*, 1999/12/04.

Editorial. 1999. 'Damgaard tror stadig på fremtiden', *Berlingske Tidende*, 1999/12/04.

Wichmann, Sonny. 1999. 'IT-selskab er kommet i unåde', *Berlingske Tidende*, 1999/12/04.

Krabbe, Klaus. 1999. 'Damgaard ramt overalt', *Computerworld*, 1999/12/07.

Møller, Niels. 1999. 'Den tålmodige velhaver', *Berlingske tidende*, 1999/12/13, pp. 5.

Kristensen, Søren. 1999. 'Endelig lidt medvind til Damgaard Data', *Børsen*, 1999/12/23.

Jakobsen, Søren. 1999. 'Erhvervs-fusere: Hans K. Werdelin', *Ekstra Bladet*, 1999/12/27.

Bentow, David. 2000. 'Massive aktionær-krav om IT-vækst', *Børsen*, 2000/01/10, pp. 6.

Sandøe, Niels. 2000. 'Navision på niveau med Carlsberg', *Jyllands-Posten*, 2000/01/21.

Elmose, Kim. 2000. 'Intentia fik kæmpetab i 1999', *Computerworld*, 2000/01/28.

Jakobsen, Søren Linding. 2000. 'Skyerne letter for Damgaard', *Børsen*, 2000/01/28.

Kristensen, Søren. 2000. 'Damgaard har igen kæmpet sig tilbage', *Børsen*, 2000/02/09, pp. 26.

Svith, Flemming. 2000. 'IT-selskab på stand by', *Jyllands-Posten*, 2000/03/04.

Ditlevsen, Mads. 2000. 'Columbus IT Partner prøver at justere kursen', *Berlingske Tidende*, 2000/03/12.

Lund, Anders. 2000. 'Damgaard er i vælten forud for årsregnskabet', *Berlingske Tidende*, 2000/03/23.

Sandøe, Niels. 2000. 'Damgaard sælger ud (Consulting)', *Finans*, 2000/04/01.

Krabbe, Klaus. 2000. 'Damgaard sælger konsulentforretningen', *Computerworld*, 2000/04/04.

Svith, Flemming. 2000. '70 dage i skærsilden', *Jyllands-Posten*, 2000/05/10, pp. 5.

Editorial. 2000. 'Navision på vej mod halvårsunderskud', *Reuters-Børsen*, 2000/05/15.

Elmose, Kim. 2000. 'SAP sagde nej til køb af Damgaard', *Computerworld*, 2000/05/22.

Erhardtsen, Birgitte and Martin Bundgaard. 2000. 'IT-flagskib til salg', *Børsens nyhedsmagasin*, 2000/05/22, pp. 28-29, 31, 33-34.

Simonsen, Torben. 2000. 'Damgaard leverer første ASP-løsning', *Computerworld*, 2000/05/26.

Ditlevsen, Mads. 2000. 'Damgaard går en lys fremtid i møde', *Berlingske Tidende*, 2000/06/04, pp. 6.

Erhardtsen, Birgitte. 2000. 'IT flagskibe sejlet agterud', *Børsens nyhedsmagasin*, 2000/06/06, pp. 18-22.

Editorial. 2000. 'ERP International spaltes', *Computerworld*, 2000/07/07.

Elmose, Kim. 2000. 'Lederteam forlader Damgaard', *Computerworld*, 2000/07/13.

Abild, Lars, Anders Kristian Lai and Morten Asmussen. 2000. 'IT-branchen vågnet op til ny økonomi', *Berlingske Tidende*, 2000/07/17.

Sandøe, Niels. 2000. 'Smæk til Navision', *Jyllands-Posten*, 2000/09/15.

Sandøe, Niels. 2000. 'Navision er klar til fusion', *Jyllands-Posten*, 2000/10/03.

Erhardtsen, Birgitte. 2000. 'Navision og Damgaard kørt over af e-biz', *Børsens nyhedsmagasin*, 2000/10/08, pp. 32-34.

Sandøe, Niels. 2000. 'Det trækker om hjørnerne i Navision', *Jyllands-Posten*, 2000/10/23.

Editorial. 2000. 'Damgaard tilgodeses i fusionsbestyrelse', *RB-Børsen*, 2000/11/20.

Evert, Eigil. 2000. 'Gamle drenge bag fusion', *Berlingske Tidende*, 2000/11/21.

Evert, Eigil. 2000. 'Navision opsluger Damgaard', *Berlingske Tidende*, 2000/11/21.

Evert, Eigil. 2000. 'Brødrene Concorde', *Berlingske Tidende*, 2000/11/21.

Jakobsen, Søren Linding and Kim Schaumann. 2000. 'Ny IT-gigant giver sig selv frist på et år', *Børsen*, 2000/11/21.

Krabbe, Klaus, Poul Hilbert and Torben Daarbak. 2000. '100 skal fyres i nye NavisionDamgaard', *Computerworld*, 2000/11/21.

Lai, Anders Lund. 2000. 'Software-giganterne lurer på nye fusioner', *Berlingske Tidende*, 2000/11/21.

Sandøe, Niels and Flemming Svith. 2000. 'Navision og Damgaard: Fusion aftalt på formandsmøde', *Jyllands-Posten*, 2000/11/21.

Blunck, Lars. 2000. 'Balser er ingen sprællemand', *Børsen*, 2000/11/22, pp. Bagsiden.

Evert, Eigil. 2000. 'Ros til direktør-eksperiment', *Berlingske Tidende*, 2000/11/22.

Jakobsen, Søren Linding and Kim Schaumann. 2000. 'NavisionDamgaard får opkøbsproblemer', *Virksomheder*, 2000/11/22, pp. 8.

Malmgreen, Henrik. 2000. 'Den hellige IT-flamme brænder stadig', *Børsen*, 2000/11/28, pp. 1.

Editorial. 2000. 'Muss sich SAP warm anziehen?', *Produktion*, 2000/11/30.

Myrthu, Bjarke. 2000. 'NavisionDamgaard kan stå foran et svært indtog i USA', *Børsen*, 2000/12/01, pp. 5.

Editorial. 2000. 'Navision-Damgaard führt Produktlinien vorerst weiter', *Computerwoche*, 2000/12/08.

Schaumann, Kim. 2000. 'Navision og Damgaard fyrer 95', *Børsen*, 2000/12/21, pp. 8.

Henriksen, Kurt. 2000. 'Optionsbombe underr NavisionDamgaard', *Børsen*, 2000/12/22, pp. 4.

Rasmussen, Knud Teddy. 2000. 'Microsoft-køb sender NavisionDamgaard i bund', *Børsen*, 2000/12/28, pp. 1.

Jensen, Peter Tegllund. 2001. 'Den ukendte succes-direktør', *Fyns Stiftstidende*, 2001/01/03.

Schaumann, Kim. 2001. 'Ny monopolsag kan gavne NavisionDamgaard', *Børsen*, 2001/01/03, pp. 4.

Evert, Eigil. 2001. 'NavisionDamgaard frygter ikke ulven', *Berlingske Tidende*, 2001/01/09.

Editorial. 2001. 'NavisionDamgaard has announced the release of Damgaard Axapta 2.5.', *AccountancyAge*.

Landgrave, Tim. 2001. 'Why Microsoft bought Great Plains Software', *TechRepublic*, 2001/01/11.

Schaumann, Kim. 2001. 'Microsoft rammer Navision i USA', *Børsen*, 2001/01/12, pp. 12.

Ebbensgaard, Ida. 2001. 'NavisionDamgaard vendt stærkt tilbage', *Børsen*, 2001/01/23, pp. 20.

Evert, Eigil. 2001. 'Statsministeren kom i IT-himlen', *Berlingske Tidende*, 2001/02/03.

Andersen, Mads Cordt. 2001. 'NavisionDamgaard tager opkøb roligt', *Computerworld*, 2001/02/05.

Lauridsen, Søren. 2001. 'Fusion: Navision eller Damgaard?', *Computerworld*, 2001/02/14.

Schaumann, Kim. 2001. 'Navision beskyldes for dårligt salgsarbejde', *Børsen*, 2001/02/19, pp. 5.

Schaumann, Kim. 2001. 'Navision fortsætter med at vinde markedesandele', *Børsen*, 2001/02/21, pp. 9.

Schaumann, Kim. 2001. 'Navision fortsætter med at vinde markedsandele', *Børsen*, 2001/02/21.

Evert, Eigil. 2001. 'Flovmand til Columbus for arrogance', *Berlingske Tidende*, 2001/02/24.

Jakobsen, John. 2001. 'IT-værdier for 185 mia. kr. væk', *Berlingske Tidende*, 2001/03/10.

Dietrichsen, Søren. 2001. 'NavisionDamgaard skifter navn', *Erhvervsbladet*, 2001/03/16.

Editorial. 2001. 'Biler giver Navision omsætning', *Finans*, 2001/03/29.

Buckman, Rebecca. 2001. 'Acquisition of Great Plains Software Moves Microsoft in a New Direction', *The Wall Street Journal*, 2001/04/05.

Sandøe, Niels. 2001. 'Great Plains skruer ned', *Jyllands-Posten*, 2001/04/20.

Larsen, Jens Frederik. 2001. 'SAP vil satse på SMV'er', *Erhvervsbladet*, 2001/04/26.

Bosmann, Christian. 2001. 'Navision trak KVX-indekset i minus', *Berlingske Tidende*, 2001/05/23.

Editorial. 2001. 'Navision ser opkøb i USA inden for et år', *Reuters Finans*, 2001/05/30.

Flyvholm, Flemming. 2001. 'Damgaards duel med Bill Gates', *Berlingske Tidende*, 2001/06/20.

Sandøe, Niels. 2001. 'Navision køber distributionsret i Østen', *Jyllands-Posten*, 2001/08/09.

Krabbe, Klaus. 2001. 'Navision overtager distribution fra Columbus', *Computerworld*, 2001/08/10.

Editorial. 2001. 'Navision skifter direktør i Navision Danmark', *RB-Børsen*, 2001/08/21.

Skouboe, Jakob. 2001. 'Godt år for Navision efter fusion, *Berlingske Tidende*, 2001/08/21.

Krabbe, Klaus. 2001. 'Navision-direktør tænker internationalt', *Computerworld*, 2001/08/24.

Hilbert, Poul. 2001. 'PC'en startede Danmarks største software-succes', *Computerworld*, 2001/08/31.

Editorial. 2001. 'Navision på opkøbsjagt efter god Damgaard-fusion', *Reuters Finans*, 2001/09/10.

Brok, Thomas. 2001. 'Software: ERP-udbyderne venter på Y3K', *Computerworld*, 2001/09/21.

Osmark, Leif. 2001. 'E-bogføring: Konkurrence bydes velkommen', *Computerworld*, 2001/09/21.

Editorial. 2001. 'Navision overvejer at droppe produkter i Danmark', *Reuters Finans*, 2001/09/27.

Lykke, Pia. 2001. 'Navision beholder to partnerstrategier', *Computerworld*, 2001/10/22.

Sandøe, Niels. 2001. 'Dansk IT-offensiv i USA', *Jyllands-Posten*, 2001/11/05.

Editorial. 2001. 'Konkurrenter tegner grumset billede før Navision-tal', *Reuters*, 2001/11/06.

Evert, Eigil. 2001. 'Navision overrasker med flot kvartal', *Berlingske Tidende*, 2001/11/09.

Editorial. 2001. 'Lev dine værdier', *Berlingske Tidende*, 2001/11/14.

Siegumfeldt, Helen. 2001. 'Navisions aftale med Siebel er mest til pynt', *Computerworld*, 2001/11/19.

Hilbert, Poul. 2001. 'Navision er Global Guld Partner', *Computerworld*, 2001/11/30.

Hilbert, Poul. 2002. 'Navision ude med kurven', *Computerworld*, 2002/01/25.

Editorial. 2002. 'Navision vil dominere ERP mid-market i USA', *RB-Børsen*, 2002/01/28.

Hilbert, Poul. 2002. 'SAP erklærer softwarekrig', *Computerworld*, 2002/01/29.

Skouboe, Jakob. 2002. 'Hvorfor ikke bare tale engelsk?', *Berlingske Tidende*, 2002/02/06.

Editorial. 2002. 'Microsoft skyder 4 mia. i Navision-konkurrent', *Reuters Finans*, 2002/02/11.

Editorial. 2002. 'Navision tror på partnerboom efter IBM-aftale', *Reuters Finans*, 2002/02/15.

Skouboe, Jakob. 2002. 'Skarpe sandheder på en festdag', *Berlingske Tidende*, 2002/02/27.

Editorial. 2002. 'Great Plains vil angribe Navision i Europa', *Reuters Finans*, 2002/04/16.

Bredsdorf, Magnus. 2002. 'Nøgleposition til stifterne', *Børsen*, 2002/05/01, pp. 6.

Evert, Eigil. 2002. 'Navision vil være et kup for Microsoft', *Berlingske Tidende*, 2002/05/01.

Evert, Eigil. 2002. '11 mia. kroner for Navision', *Berlingske Tidende*, 2002/05/08.

Hilbert, Poul. 2002. 'Nyt IT-kra center i Vedbæk bliver en jobmagnet', *Computerworld*, 2002/05/10.

Hilbert, Poul. 2002. 'De mutte milliardærer', *Computerworld*, 2002/05/10.

Poulsen, Per Thygesen. 2002. 'Kulturfusion i Navision', *Civiløkonomen*, 2002/05/15, pp. 30-31.

Editorial. 2002. 'EU vil ikke undersøge Microsofts køb af Navision', *Børsens nyhedsmagasin*, 2002/05/31.

Jessen, Christian. 2003. 'Damgaards vilde ridt på aktiemarkedet', *Børsen*, 2003/05/23, pp. 12, 13.

Morsing, Finn. 2003. 'Balser kunne undværes', *Berlingske Tidende*, 2003/12/04.

Erhardsen, Birgitte. 2012. *Erik Damgaard – Rigdommens pris* (Gyldendal: Copenhagen).

Rosenzweig, Phil. 2014. *The Halo Effect: ... and the Eight Other Business Delusions That Deceive Managers* (Free Press).

# GLOSSARY

10-Net

10-Net was a network product from Fox Research in Ohio, for connecting PCs. 10-Net, which was imported and distributed in Denmark by PolyData, used a cheap telephone cable instead of the more expensive Ethernet cables or coaxial cables. The product was also known for not needing a dedicated PC to act as a file or print server. The product was introduced in the mid-1980s and cost 695 USD per PC – about 1.450 USD today (2018).

8-bit processor

The emergence of microcomputers was made possible by the development of integrated circuits where the core parts of the computer were gathered into a single microprocessor that didn't take up much space, didn't overheat, didn't use much energy and finally could be produced cheaply in very large quantities. The earliest microprocessors had an 8-bit registry and data bus and address architecture, which, in practice, meant they could accommodate and handle an 8-bit byte at a time. A byte represents a single letter, number or character. However, the first 8-bit processors – the Intel 8080 and the Z80 – used a 16-bit address space and could, thereby, address, at most, a 64,000- character memory. The computer operating systems and other key software components (networking software, screen, keyboard and printer drivers, anti-virus, etc.) also had to be accommodated within the 64,000 characters after which any surplus space could be used for the users' programmes and data. If there wasn't enough room, the operating system had to send those components not being used to external media, such as floppy or hard disks, which made the computer very slow.

| | |
|---|---|
| 16-bit processor | With the introduction of the Intel 8086 16-bit processor, the address space increased to 20 bit; thereby expanding the memory area, which the central microprocessor could address, to one million characters. Despite the operating system and other key system components also growing in size, there was now more room for user programmes and data. When Intel introduced its 80286 processor, the address bar increased to 24-bit – the computer could now handle a memory of 16 million characters (see also 8-bit processor). |
| 32-bit processor | The first 32-bit processors had the same address space as the 16-bit processors and were, therefore, also limited to handling a memory of 16 million characters. Only with the expansion of the address space to 32-bit did the possible memory increase to 4 billion characters (see also 8-bit processor). |
| 4GL tools | 4GL (4th Generation Languages) was the term used to describe of a range of tools that were to make it both easier and faster to develop software. Whereas 3GL was the name given to the common programming languages, such as C, C++, C# and Java, 4GL tools offered not only a higher level of abstraction, but also report generating facilities, user interfaces, database management and, later, development for the web. |
| 5 1/4″ disk | The first microcomputers that Erik Damgaard worked with, used "floppy disks": thin and soft magnetically coated discs in a plastic sleeve. Their diameter was 5 1/4 inches. |
| Accounts payable | See creditor. |
| Accounts receivable | See debtor. |
| ACE | ACE was the name of a development project launched by Navision at the beginning of 2000, which was to be a Software-as-a-Service product with industry-wide functionality for very small businesses. The product was scheduled for launch in Denmark in spring 2002, but was delayed and then cancelled when Microsoft acquired the company. |
| ADSL | Asymmetric digital subscriber line (ADSL): communication technology enabling fast data transfer via ordinary phone lines while talking on the phone. The technology was implemented in the late 1990s and spread rapidly due to the great need for easier and faster access to the internet. |
| AL | Application Language that PC&C (Navision) used in its Navigator product, which launched in 1989. Customers and resellers could make adjustments and extensions to the standard functionality with AL. |

| | |
|---|---|
| Albatros | Albatros was the name of a multi-user finance system for MS-DOS developed by the PolySoft company, announced at Kontor&Data 1985 and released for sale in February 1986. The product received very good reviews and started off well, but the parent company, PolyData, ran into financial difficulties that demanded the management's attention. Therefore, it didn't respond quickly enough to the product's problems, which then quickly lost ground to Navigator and Concorde. |
| AltaVista | AltaVista was a web search engine developed in 1995 by researchers at Digital Equipment Corporation. It was one of the most used search engines for a number of years, but it lost ground to Google and was purchased by Yahoo! in 2003. |
| Application | "Application" is the term used to describe the program with which the user is in direct contact. Damgaard Data's programs are applications, while operating systems, database systems, network applications and so on are called system software or middleware. |
| ApS | An Anpartsselskab (ApS) is a Danish private limited company, which is required to have capital of at least 50,000 DKK (10,000 USD). |
| A/S | An Aktieselskab (A/S) is a Danish private limited company with higher capital requirements than the Anpartsselskab (ApS) and a requirement for a registered board of directors (see Anpartsselskab (Aps)). |
| AS/400 | A minicomputer from IBM. This product line started in 1983 as System/36, changed to AS/400 in 1988 and became eServer and iSeries in 2000. |
| ASP | Abbreviation for Application Service Provider, covering companies offering software solutions that customers could access via the internet. The term has now been replaced by *SaaS*: Software-as-a-Service. |
| Atlanta | See Axapta. |
| Attain | See Navision Attain |
| Attain CE | See Navision Attain CE |
| AudioScan | AudioScan was a Danish importer of hi-fi equipment that sold directly to consumers; thereby, skipping the wholesaler. AudioScan also tried to import IT equipment but couldn't make it work and closed the activity in the mid-1980s. |
| Axapta | Axapta started out as a development project under the name Concorde XAL Version 3, after which the project briefly changed its name to Royal Oaks only to get the code name Atlanta in 1996. With the help of an external advertising agency, the name Axapta was found. The product, which was Damgaard Data's largest development project, was developed during the period when Damgaard Data's development department was co-owned by IBM. Today, Axapta is called Microsoft Dynamics AX. |

| | |
|---|---|
| Azanta | Azanta was a software package with Concorde C5 and Lotus SmartSuite for OS/2, developed in 1995 by Damgaard International for IBM for marketing in Denmark, Norway and Sweden. |
| Azlan | Distributor of network and PC Products with headquarters in the UK. |
| Baan | Baan Corporation was created by Jan and Paul Baan in 1978 in Barneveld, the Netherlands, to provide financial and administrative advice. Baan launched an ERP system for UNIX in the early 1980s and gained considerable success. After winning a major contract with Boeing in 1994 and completing a stock market listing in 1995, Baan became a real threat to the market leader, SAP. It was revealed in 1998 that Baan's management was cooking the company's accounts by posting software licences, which had been transferred to a distributor, as revenue. The company had to report huge deficits and its stock price plummeted. In June 2000, Baan was sold to Invensys and, in June 2003, to SSA Global Technologies. In May 2006, SSA was acquired by Infor Global Solutions. |
| Backward compatibility | A control system is backward compatible if it can run programs that were developed for earlier versions. User programs are backward compatible if users can upgrade to a new version without having to make significant changes. Keeping a program backward compatible over extended periods of time demands significant investments. Therefore, Damgaard Data broke the backward compatibility between Danmax and Concorde, between Concorde and Concorde XAL, between Concorde Økonomi and Concorde C5 and between Concorde XAL and Axapta. |
| Ballmer, Steve | Steve Anthony Ballmer (1956) was CEO of Microsoft from 2000 to 2014. |
| Basic software | Basic software is a term for those software components, which lie under the software that the user has direct contact with. Thus, basic software includes operating systems, development tools, database systems, data communication, backup and security, etc. |
| Batch job | A batch job or batch processing is an IT job, typically initiated by an operator when there is available computer capacity. A batch job could be the monthly employee payroll or the printing of customer invoices and bank statements. The rapid expansion of computer capacity as well as the development of more user-friendly software meant that tasks no longer needed to be scheduled and processed according to when there was available capacity on the computer. The term is rarely used today. To exploit the very expensive mainframes most efficiently, the running of batch jobs was strictly prioritised in 24-hour operations, seven days a week. Data for a batch job was typically entered by a "typing pool", after which the actual calculations were performed by the computer, which then printed the results in long lists or on pre-printed forms (product lists, customer lists, invoices, payrolls, bank statements, returns, etc.). |

| | |
|---|---|
| Berendsen Computer Products | Berendsen Computer Products was a subsidiary of Berendsen A/S, which began importing and distributing hardware and software for PCs in 1984. The company obtained the distribution rights to PCPLUS from PC&C in 1985, but was passed over for IBM when PC&C launched Navigator in October 1987. |
| Beta test | It's widely known that developers can't test their own software. Therefore, an internal test (alpha test) is required before sending the product to selected customers for external testing (beta test). Normally, suppliers recommend that products being beta tested not be used for production purposes as there may be critical bugs in the product. Thus, customers, who participate in a beta test are often compensated for the inconvenience of testing the product. |
| Bit compatible | The term "bit compatible" refers to computers that are able to run the same programs without needing any changes. For example, software developed for Intel's 8080 was able to run easily on systems based on Zilog's Z80, which in the 1980s was a ground-breaking innovation. |
| Brdr. Damgaard Data I/S | Brdr. Damgaard Data I/S was the name of Erik and Preben Damgaard's first company, which formed the framework for the activities until April 1985, where the activities were transferred to Damgaard Data ApS, CVR number 77627111. |
| Brooks, Frederick | Frederick Brooks is author of the book *The Mythical Man-Month* (Addison-Wesley, 1975). The book explains why software development can't be accelerated by adding more programmers. |
| Bug | All software products contain bugs or errors. The more extensive the products become and the more customisations added, the more bugs that automatically occur. Errors are prioritised and remedied in the order in which they are considered critical. Some bugs will only be corrected in a later version of the product, and some, considered insignificant, will never be rectified. Thus, reporting and correcting bugs is a completely normal task within the software industry. |
| Bulletin Board System | A Bulletin Board System (BBS) was an electronic bulletin board that users could ring to upload or download data, read and write messages and, in some cases, even chat with each other. The emergence of Bulletin Board Systems gained serious momentum in the early 1990s, when the price of data communications fell sharply, but they were replaced rapidly as early as the mid-1990s by ordinary websites accessible via the internet. |
| Bundling | Bundling is a standard expression within the IT industry that refers to offering several products or services for sale in a combined package. |
| Burgum, Doug | Douglas J. Burgum (1956) was CEO of Great Plains Software from 1984 to 2001. After which he became Senior Vice President for Microsoft Business Solutions Group (2001-2007), under which the acquisition of Navision occurred. |

| | |
|---|---|
| Burroughs | Burroughs Adding Machine Company was officially launched in 1904 in Detroit, Ohio. The company entered the computer industry in the 1960s, achieving reasonable success with its mainframe systems. In September 1986, Burroughs Corporation merged with Sperry Corporation to form Unisys. Shortly after the merger, the amalgamated company ceased developing Burroughs' mainframes. |
| C | C is a language for software development that was used increasingly in the 1980s. C made it possible to run programs on different operating systems and computer types with only modest adjustments. Concorde XAL was written in C. |
| C4 | See Concorde Økonomi. |
| C5 | See Concorde C5. |
| Calc, the. | The Calc was a program developed by Erik Damgaard for the copy protection of Danmax. When the customer's company name was entered, the Calc generated a set of codes for each of the modules in Danmax. When customers entered the codes while installing Danmax, the modules opened and the customer's name was encoded into all the screen displays. In principle, the codes could be reused by others, but the original customer's name would still appear in all screen displays. |
| Cashcow | A company's products are divided into four stages of development: children, stars, cashcows and dogs. A company with products in all four stages is well-covered in relation to its future development. |
| CDC | See Control Data. |
| CeBIT | CeBIT (Centrum für Büroautomation, Informationstechnologie und Telekommunikation) [Centre for Office Automation, Information Technology and Telecommunications] took place for the first time in 1970 as a division of the Hannover Messe [Hanover Fair] in the newly built Hal 1. The CeBIT section grew rapidly and, in 1986, this part of the exhibition was held separately four weeks before the main exhibition. From 1986 until the turn of the millennium, CeBIT was the most important global IT exhibition with a display area of 450,000 m2 and close to one million visitors. |
| Channel | In Damgaard Data jargon, the "channel" was a term used to refer to all resellers at once. Thus, how to expand the channel, how to increase its capacity and its productivity and so on were regularly discussed. The channel was Damgaard Data's way to the customers, and there was a clear awareness that the channel was to be continuously utilised to reach the goal: the greatest possible market share (see also reseller). |
| Channel Entry | See Attain CE. |

| | |
|---|---|
| Channel Stuffing | The term refers to producers generating revenue by selling goods to their resellers, which are placed in stock and not immediately sold to customers. IBM and Damgaard International used this practice for a few years to artificially inflate revenue. |
| Christian Rovsing A/S | Christian Rovsing A/S was a Danish producer of minicomputers, who achieved some success in the 1970s and early 1980s, but went bankrupt in 1984. |
| Client/server | When PCs were seriously considered and installed in large companies in the 1990s, a new model was needed for implementing IT solutions. The model named "client-server" split tasks so that data management and special resource-demanding tasks ran on powerful central computers (server), while data entry, data presentation and less resource-demanding tasks were carried out on the individual user's PC (client). The client-server model was further motivated by being able to use cheaper PCs (thin clients), PCs from different manufacturers and not having to provide too much support for the individual user. Concorde XAL supported a partial client-server model as the database could run on an independent server, while Axapta was directly designed according to this model. |
| Cloud Computing | Cloud Computing refers to the delivery of software and other online services via the internet, where most of the computing work takes place on the supplier's computer and, thus, not on the user's computer (see also Hosting). |
| Commodore | Commodore International, with headquarters in Toronto, Canada, was a pioneer of the development and production of cheap microcomputers. Most well-known is the Commodore 64 (1982), where the entire computer (without the screen) was built into the keyboard. |
| Compaq Computers | Compaq was one of the major players in the PC market in the 1990s. The company was acquired by HP in 2002. |
| Compatibility | Compatibility meaning "co-existing". In the IT industry's youth, each supplier had its own standards, which is why hardware and software from different suppliers didn't match. Once customers had chosen a supplier, they were almost subjugated into continuing the relationship as changing to another supplier demanded completely replacing all hardware and software and retraining the IT staff. This situation impeded the innovative incentives of established suppliers, leading to very high prices. When IBM opened the PC architecture and allowed Microsoft to sell the DOS operating system to other manufacturers in the early 1980s, market forces were released that completely changed the IT market in the space of only a few years, enabling customers to reward producers who made themselves compatible with other suppliers. Customers quickly learned the advantages of compatibility and could increase the pressure on manufacturers for both better products and lower prices. |

| | |
|---|---|
| Compilation | See compiler. |
| Compiler | A compiler is a software program that can collect and translate source codes written in one programming language into another programming language and typically into binary form or machine code. Typically, software is written in a language with a high level of abstraction, while computers can only run programs in machine code. Compilers collect and translate the code modules written by the programmer into a language that the computer can understand. |
| Concorde | See Concorde Økonomi. |
| Concorde Business | In the early 1990s, Damgaard Data bundled Concorde Økonomi with software for word processing, spreadsheets, presentations, e-mail and calendar, etc. The package was marketed as Concorde Business with attractive price tags. |
| Concorde C4 | See Concorde Økonomi. |
| Concorde C5 | Concorde C5 was launched by Damgaard Data on 15<sup>th</sup> November 1994 as a replacement for Concorde Økonomi, which was released on the market in November 1986. Concorde C5 was built on Concorde XAL technology, but the user functionality was simplified to primarily target companies with up to five users. |
| Concorde C5 Light | Concorde C5 Light was a version of Concorde C5 with fewer accounts and a smaller database that ran exclusively on Microsoft Windows and was targeted at very small businesses. The product, which was to replace Concorde Light, was launched in late 1995 and was the first software product in Denmark marketed via a TV advertisement. Concorde C5 Light cost less than 400 USD and over 14,000 copies were sold via selected computer stores and wholesale markets in 1996. |
| Concorde Light | A full version of Concorde with a maximum of 150 financial accounts, 50 accounts receivable, 25 accounts payable, 150 products and a 4 MB database sold via retailers for less than 400 USD. |
| Concorde Software A/S | In 1998, Damgaard Data Distribution A/S changed its name to Concorde Software International A/S, and, a few months later, to Concorde Software A/S and, in 1999, to Damgaard A/S. |
| Concorde Tekst | Concorde Tekst was a simple word processing program accompanying Concorde. Tekst could be used to write letters to customers or suppliers, after which names and addresses from the financial management system could be merged into the text of the letter. The program was built on standard components that came with the PolyPascal development tool. Over time, Word-Perfect, and later Microsoft Word, established themselves as affordable standard word processing products. Damgaard Data didn't expend resources on offering similar facilities in subsequent products. |

| | |
|---|---|
| Concorde XAL | Concorde XAL, a financial management system for medium-sized companies, was launched in April 1991 and became Damgaard Data's third quick product success. The product was an innovation in the financial management systems' market as it was equipped with development tools that enabled resellers and customers to customise and further develop the product with new facilities and features. Concorde XAL, thus, ended up serving many more types of businesses and purposes than Damgaard Data would ever have been able to offer with its own development resources. Concorde XAL was one of the first examples of the multiplication effect a software program with development tools could achieve via resellers and customers' further development. Moreover, Concorde XAL was available on a wide range of operating systems, which also contributed to the wide spread of the product. Concorde XAL was also the product that formed the basis of Damgaard Data's internationalisation efforts. |
| Concorde Økonomi | Concorde was Damgaard Data's second product, launched at the Office & Data Fair in the Bella Center in autumn 1986. The product, which was a multi-user financial system for small businesses, earned enormous success and formed the backbone of Damgaard Data's development from a small start-up business with only a handful of employees to a company with 100 employees and a turnover of 20 million USD in 1991, when the next major product, Concorde XAL, was launched, after which Concorde was renamed Concorde Økonomi. |
| Connect A/S | Connect A/S was a partially-owned subsidiary of Damgaard Data, which was involved in the development and production of network cards for PCs. The company went bankrupt in September 1989 after which Michael Konnerup bought the activities from the bankruptcy estate. |
| Control Data | Control Data or CDC was a computer and software company based in Minneapolis, Minnesota. Since being founded in the 1950s, the company primarily developed computers for computational-heavy tasks, but when the company established itself in Denmark, it managed to win a number of large customers within administrative data processing via the establishment of a local software development department. Control Data's management misjudged both the emergence of minicomputers and PCs and suffered huge losses in the 1980s and had to lay off thousands of employees until the company was almost dissolved in the 1990s via divestments and shutdowns. From 1991 to 1997, the Danish subsidiary of Control Data became one of Damgaard Data's greatest Concorde XAL resellers in Denmark. |

| | |
|---|---|
| Country manager | The head of a foreign subsidiary; usually the most senior manager of the subsidiary in the legal sense and, thus, the job title reflects that in the country in question. For instance, the name in Denmark is administrende direktør, in Germany it is Geschäfts-führer, and in Sweden verkställande director (VD). However, internally in a group, the subsidiaries managers are mostly referred to as country managers. |
| Country Specific Engineering | Country Specific Engineering (CSE) was a division of Damgaard International, whose task was to specify and develop national versions of the products. |
| CP/M | CP/M stood for Control Program/Monitor and later Control Program for Microcomputers. It was developed by American Gary Kildall from the Digital Research, Inc. company (see also Operating System). |
| CPM-86 | CPM-86 was the successor to CP/M, which was also able to run on IBM's PC. Despite people with technical insight rating the system as better than PC-DOS from Microsoft, it was never a success due to factors such as its high price. |
| Creditor | A creditor or accounts payable is a person or organisation to which a business owes money (see also debtor). |
| CRI | Computer Resources International (CRI) was a Danish software and consulting company with activities in space and defence. The company emerged after Christian Roving's bankruptcy and employed more than 150 employees. It was owned by Unibank, BG Bank and IBM. In 1997, CRI was acquired by Terma A/S. |
| CRM | An abbreviation for Customer Relationship Management. The term covers business processes and software for optimising the relationship between a company and its customers. |
| CVR Number | The Danish Centrale Virksomhedsregister: the unique number of a business in the Danish Central Business Registry. |
| Cyber | Cyber was the name of a series of mainframe computers from Control Data Corporation (CDC), which was very popular for computational-heavy tasks in the 1970s and 1980s. |
| DACH | DACH is an abbreviation for Germany (D), Austria (A) and Switzerland (CH). |
| Damgaard Data Large Account | See Damgaard Consulting |
| Damgaard Data ServicePartner | See Damgaard Consulting. |

| | |
|---|---|
| Damgaard Distribution ApS | Damgaard Distribution ApS (CVR number 11668216) was founded on 13th January 1987 and was turned into an A/S on 28th February 1995. Until 1998, the company was responsible for all marketing activities in the Danish market. Its name changed in January 1998 to Concorde Software with the company now also running the international sales activities. The company then changed its name to Damgaard Data A/S in September 1998 and to Damgaard A/S in January 1999 and was listed on the Copenhagen Stock Market in September 1999. The company merged with Navision Software in December 2000. |
| Damgaard International A/S | The company was founded on 27th October 1986 as Damgaard Development ApS and formally obtained all rights to the products. In 1994, IBM Denmark bought half of the shares for one million USD, and the company changed its name to Damgaard International A/S. When IBM was bought out for 15 million USD in November 1998, the company changed its name to Damgaard Development A/S. The ownership of the company was transferred to Damgaard A/S prior to the stock market listing. The company merged with Navision Software in July 2001. |
| Damgaard Development [Damgaard Udvikling] | See Damgaard International A/S. |
| Damgaard, Charlotte | Preben Damgaard's wife. |
| Danmax | See Maxisoft. |
| Danmax Mini | A full version of Danmax, retailing at 1,600 USD, which was limited to 30,000 postings. After that, the user could upgrade for a further 2,000 USD to a version without limits. After the launch of Concorde, the price of the Danmax Mini was reduced to 800 USD. |
| Danmax XT | The first project name for the development project, which became Concorde in 1986, and later became Concorde Økonomi. |
| Dansk Data Elektronik | Dansk Data Elektronik (DDE) was founded in 1975 and stock market listed in 1984. The company became known for its Supermax computers, which were widely distributed in Denmark, particularly in the public sector. The company's management misjudged the market's development, sending hardware prices into free fall; instead it spread itself over a wide range of solution areas that it failed to internationalise for which it was greatly criticised. DDE went bankrupt in 2001. |

| | |
|---|---|
| Dansk System Industri | Dansk System Industri was started by Anne Grethe Pind in 1980. When Thomas Hejlsberg came aboard, and DSI-TEKST was launched in October 1984, the company's run of success began. DSI-TEKST contained a database and a report generator as well as word processing. The system formed the basis for several large IT projects in both the private and public sectors. When DSI released a new version under the name DSI SYSTEM in spring 1989, it also signed an agreement with Damgaard Data, which enabled the system to work with Concorde Økonomi. DSI never managed to do any significant business outside of Denmark, and as the foreign suppliers – in particular Microsoft – gained more and more Danish customers, DSI was outmatched. |
| Database | A database (or a database system) is a software program, whose primary task is to manage the data that a user or other software programs are to use. |
| Datacentralen | I/S, of 1959, was a partnership consisting of the Danish state, counties and municipalities (KL) with the state, represented by the Ministry of Finance, at the head of the table. The municipalities later stepped down and formed their own Kommunedata [Municipal Data] (later called KMD). At the beginning of the 1990s, Datacentralen became a limited company and, in 1996, CSC (Computer Sciences Corporation) acquired 75 per cent of the shares, changing its name to CSC Denmark. |
| Daybook | When a business has to post to the accounts, each entry is typed into a daybook first, which is subsequently checked to ensure it has been typed and entered into the accounts correctly. After that, the entries are sent to bookkeeping. This approach is widely used and helps reduce the number of typing and posting mistakes. |
| DB/2 | The name of a database system from IBM. |
| DDE | Damgaard Data Exchange was a staff newsletter started by employees in Damgaard Data in 1993. For the first few years, it was run by volunteers. DDE was also the abbreviation for Dansk Data Elektronik. |
| Debtor | A debtor is someone who owes a business money. In accounting terminology, customers and borrowers are called debtors, while suppliers and lenders are called creditors (See also accounts receivable). |
| DEC | See Digital Equipment Corporation. |

| | |
|---|---|
| Digital Equipment Corporation | Digital Equipment Corporation was launched in 1957 in Maynard, Massachusetts and, with its PDP-8 computer, it became the father of what was later called the minicomputer within the IT industry. In 1977, the company introduced the first edition of their 32-bit minicomputer named VAX. The series was widely distributed and, with over 400,000 units sold in the 1980s, DEC was the IT industry's second largest company, surpassed only by IBM. The company's management miscalculated the importance of the PC in the late 1980s and early 1990s and later also of UNIX and, therefore, had to report some mighty deficits during the same period, culminating in a loss of 3.4 billion USD in 1992. To get back on track, the company reduced its staff from 130,000 to 53,500. In 1998, DEC was acquired by the PC company, Compaq, which had half the number of employees, but twice as much turnover and significantly better earnings. |
| Digital Research | Digital Research was started in 1974 in California, and developed the first operating system for microcomputers based on Intel's 8080 or Zilog's Z-80. When IBM chose Microsoft's DOS operating system for their new 16-bit PCs with Intel processors in the early 1980s, Digital Research launched an alternative that, many believed, was a technically superior system, but it wasn't able to fight IBM's marketing muscle and was acquired by Novell in 1991. |
| Disk drive | See hard disk. |
| Distributor | For Damgaard Data, a distributor was a company that recruited and managed resellers on behalf of the producer. Distributors also carried out all tasks associated with general marketing. |
| DITEC | DITEC was the former consultancy department of the German subsidiary of the American Digital Equipment Corporation, which purchased the German IT company Mannesmann-Kienzle in 1991. In the aftermath of the major financial difficulties experienced worldwide by Digital Equipment Corporation in the 1990s, the staff in Germany had to be drastically reduced and, thus, DEC wanted to completely spin off its consultancy department, employing 1,500 employees at this time. No buyer was found for the activity and due to labour law rules in Germany it wasn't possible to layoff the 1,500 employees without having to pay large compensation sums to the individual staff members. Therefore, in October 1994, the owners of DEC offered DITEC's staff the consultant department on favourable terms. |
| DOS | DOS is an abbreviation for Disk Operating System. PC-DOS and MS-DOS from Microsoft were the most well-known. |

| | |
|---|---|
| Dotcom bubble, the. | From 1997 to 2001, coincidental circumstances evoked a quite unusual desire to invest, in particular, in newly-launched IT companies that had the internet as their strategic focal point. The companies used their internet addresses as their names – all ending in ".com" (pronounced "dot com"). The vast majority of dotcom companies weren't able to meet expectations, and as the disappointing results began to be reported, the propensity to invest fell substantially from one day to the next. The phenomenon was like a soap bubble that burst. |
| Dotted line | Large companies that operate with multiple product lines to multiple customer segments in many countries often have a matrix organisation whereby employees have a manager with whom they negotiate salary and working conditions (full line) and one or more other managers with whom they coordinate their activities (dotted line). |
| DSI | See Dansk System Industri. |
| DSI-SYSTEM | DSI-SYSTEM was a new version of DSI-TEKST, launched in early 1989. It had a greatly improved file system and improved possibilities for developing user-specific customisations. In September 1989, Damgaard Data and DSI entered into a partnership that allowed Concorde resellers to use DSI-SYSTEM to develop more comprehensive customer-specific solutions than was possible by using Concorde alone. |
| DSI-TEKST | DSI-TEKST was a word processing system with a variety of programs for data handling, printing reports and data communication. It became very popular in the 1980s and early 1990s (See also Danish System Industry). |
| Due diligence | The term refers to the thorough review of a company's finances, obligations and other important issues. |
| EDP | EDP is an abbreviation for electronic data processing (See also IT). |
| EMEA | An abbreviation for Europe, the Middle East and Africa. Many international companies gather all countries in this area into one managerial region. |
| Encryption | Encryption is a technique for reformatting information so it can't be read by anyone without authorisation. Encryption is particularly relevant when sensitive information is to be transmitted via a non-secure communication channel (e.g. email or the internet) or for data security (such as files on a computer that may be stolen or hacked). |
| Error | See bug. |

| | |
|---|---|
| ERP | During the 1990s, Enterprise Resource Planning (ERP) became the category name for software developed by Damgaard Data, SAP, Navision Software, Baan, IFS and others, and which included support for more and more business processes. ERP, also called business management software, had to contain a suite of integrated applications, which an organisation could use to collect, store, manage and interpret data from its many business activities. |
| Ethernet | Ethernet is the term for computer connecting technology in a communication network. The technology was developed by Xerox in the 1970s and gained popularity as a PC connector during the 1980s. Despite the fact that IBM invested heavily in getting its own Token Ring technology accepted on the market, it only succeeded within the company's traditional customer segments, while more and more manufacturers supported Ethernet. With better products at significantly falling prices, IBM lost its highly-gained market share during the 1990s. Today, Ethernet is the dominant standard for connecting computers. |
| File system | The file system is that part of the computer's operating system, which handles the user's data. When a user begins a task, the computer can't know how much space is to be allocated to data. Modern file systems handle this task, ensuring the user can easily store and retrieve data, although in practice it's spread across many locations on the physical media. |
| Floppy Disk Drive | Floppy disk was the term given to data-storage medium that resembled small LPs and which could be inserted into the computer via a floppy disk drive. The computer could read data from and write data to the disk via the disk drive. |
| Fourth Generations Tools | See 4GL tools. |
| FK-DATA | See FK-SOFT. |
| FK-SOFT | FK-SOFT was an activity under FK-DATA, started by Finn Kusk in 1984, which marketed Danmax under its own name. In 1986, FK-SOFT also marketed a version of Concorde Økonomi under its own name. From 1984 until the end of the partnership in March 1988, FK-SOFT was Brdr. Damgaard Data's largest reseller and distributor. |
| FK-Soft Revisor [FK-SOFT Chartered Accountant] | A version of FK DATA's version of Danmax, which was made available free of charge to chartered accountants. |
| FTP | FTP stands for File Transfer Protocol; a standard method for transferring data files between computers. |
| Gates, Bill | William Henry Gates III (1955). Founder, and until 2000, CEO of Microsoft. |

| | |
|---|---|
| Graphical user interface | Today, almost all types of computers have a graphical user interface, which means that all functions are represented by icons or menu texts that are activated by pressing or clicking on them. This wasn't the case in earlier computers, where you needed to know and enter the commands that made the computer perform tasks. Apple was the first with a commercial product – Macintosh – that could only be served via a graphical user interface. With Microsoft's launch of Windows95, the graphical user interface became the default for most types of computers and software systems. |
| Great Plains Software | Great Plains Software, based in Fargo, North Dakota, managed by Doug Burgum, launched its first financial management system under the name Dynamics in February 1993. The program was designed to run on Microsoft Windows alone. The company was purchased by Microsoft in April 2001 and became the backbone of the new Microsoft Business Solutions division, which purchased Navision in July 2002. Great Plains Software was very successful in the USA, but it had difficulty gaining a foothold in the international markets. |
| Gregersen, Morten | Software developer and the first employee at Damgaard Data. |
| Hard drive | Data can be stored on magnetic discs similar to LPs. The discs rotate and a reader similar to the needle of a record player can write to and read data from the disc. The technology was introduced by IBM in 1956 and became a regular component of major computer installations in the 1960s and 1970s. The technology developed rapidly during the 1980s, and in 1984, IBM launched its PC AT model, which contained a 10-megabyte hard drive. |
| Havidan | Havidan was a little Danish company that imported microcomputers from the Far East in the 1980s. Erik Damgaard's friend, Morten Gregersen, got a job at Havidan and was, thereby, introduced to HERA-SOFT from HERA-DATA, which he then presented to Erik Damgaard in 1984, who found it an inspiration for Danmax's development. |
| HERA-DATA | See HERA-SOFT |
| HERA-SOFT | HERA-SOFT was a financial management system for microcomputers developed by HERA-DATA, founded by carpenter Helmuth Rasmussen. The first version of the program came on the market in 1982 and it experienced some popularity in the mid-1980s. |
| High level programming | Programming languages, such as C, FORTRAN or Pascal, are high-level languages that allow a programmer to write programs, which are more or less independent of a particular type of computer. Such languages are deemed high-level languages because they are closer to human languages and further away from machine language. |

| | |
|---|---|
| Hosted services | See Hosting. |
| Hosting | Hosting refers to IT tasks being "hosted" on computers belonging to a hosting provider. Typically, in large and professionally driven data centres. Since the turn of the millennium, more and more companies have chosen to run their IT tasks at hosting providers. Today (2018), hosting is often called cloud computing. |
| IBM PC | See Personal Computer. |
| IBM Personal System/2 | IBM Personal System/2 was a new series of PCs launched by IBM in 1987 in an attempt to regain control over the PC market by introducing an advanced and copy-protected architecture. IBM's dominant market position was to ensure that the systems would sell in relatively large numbers, particularly to large companies. Others, who wanted to develop and market PS/2 compatible systems, had to pay a royalty to IBM. The major manufacturers bristled at IBM's licence terms, which demanded royalties for every machine sold, and counteracted by developing the Extended Industry Standard Architecture (EISA). Despite some of the innovations in PS/2 becoming the cornerstone of the industry, IBM failed to gain control over the PC market. |
| ICL | International Computers Limited (ICL) was a major British hardware, software and computer service provider in operation from 1968 to 2002. ICL tried to expand its product range over the years, but most of its earnings came from the company's mainframe customer base, consisting primarily of large public sector contracts in the UK. In 1989, ICL bought the Danish company, Regnecentralen, and in 2002 the company was acquired by the Japanese company, Fujitsu. |
| IDG | International Data Group Inc. (IDG) is an America-based market analysis and media company. |
| Intel 8080 | The Intel 8080 was the first 8-bit microprocessor from Intel Corporation. |
| Intel Corporation | Intel Corporation (Intel) was launched in July 1968. It primarily produced electronic components for data storage. The company's major breakthrough came when it was chosen as the supplier of the core microprocessor for IBM's PC. |
| I/S | An Interessentskab, or a Danish Incorporated Partnership, is a partnership of at least two members, individuals or companies, who are fully liable for the company's obligations. |
| ISDN | Integrated Services Digital Network (ISDN) is a set of communication standards for the simultaneous transmission of voice, video, data and other network services via the public telephone network. The key feature of ISDN was that it integrated speech and data on the same lines and added features that weren't available in the classic telephone system. ISDN has now been replaced by ADSL. |

| | |
|---|---|
| IT | An abbreviation of Information Technology. |
| Jamaica | Jamaica was the codename of a quite ambitious development project started by Navision Software prior to the merger with Damgaard. The purpose of the project was to develop a techno-logy platform on which new versions of the company's financial systems could be based. The project was immediately ceased after Microsoft acquired Navision in 2002. |
| Kontor&Data | Kontor&Data [Office&Data] at the Bella Center in Amager was the largest IT fair in Denmark during the 1980s and 1990s. As IT gradually became a part of almost every area of business and as penetration of the internet increased, the reason for general IT fairs disappeared. |
| Kusk, Finn | See FK-SOFT. |
| Learning-to-Learn | An 11-day training programme for all Damgaard Data employees, designed to enable them to carry out their tasks more indepen-dently and encourage them to regularly take initiatives to impro-ve their work. The programme was implemented in 1995-97 and cost the company approximately 2 million USD. |
| Lotus | Lotus 1-2-3 is a spreadsheet program from Lotus Software (now part of IBM). It was IBM's first major application, and its popu-larity in the mid-1980s contributed significantly to the success of IBM's PC in the professional world. |
| Lotus Ami Pro | Lotus Ami Pro was a word processing program developed by Samna Corp, Atlanta, Georgia, which was acquired by Lotus De-velopment Corporation in November 1990 for 65 million USD. |
| Lotus Approach | Lotus Approach is a database system that Lotus Development Corporation acquired the rights to in 1994. |
| Lotus Develop-ment Corporation | Lotus Software (known as Lotus Development Corporation be-fore being purchased by IBM for 3.5 billion USD in 1995) was a software company based in Massachusetts. Lotus achieved great success with the Lotus 1-2-3 spreadsheet program, launched at the same time as the emergence of the first PCs. The company later developed Lotus Notes, in association with Ray Ozzie's Iris Associates, a calendar and collaboration system that also achie-ved wide market penetration. |
| Lotus Freelance Graphics | Lotus Freelance Graphics is a software program for making pre-sentations similar to Microsoft PowerPoint. Lotus Development Corporation obtained the rights to the product when it purchased Graphic Communications Inc. in 1986. |
| Lotus Organizer | Lotus Organizer was a Personal Information Manager (PIM) that contained a calendar as well as contacts and checklists. It was originally developed by the company Threadz, which was acqui-red by Lotus Development Corporation. |

| | |
|---|---|
| Lotus SmartSuite | IBM launched SmartSuite in 1994. It included the programs Ami Pro 3.0, Lotus 1-2-3 4.0, Freelance Graphics 2.0, Approach 2.0 and Organizer 1.1. The product competed with Microsoft Office. |
| M&A | Mergers & Acquisitions. The term for the purchase, sale and merging of businesses. |
| Macintosh | Macintosh was the first computer with a graphical user interface (like Windows), which was launched by Apple Computers in January 1984. Despite Macintosh being far easier to use for the non-IT-savvy user, its high price prevented the computer from defeating the technically more complicated DOS-based IBM-compatible PCs. However, Macintosh won its followers and gained widespread popularity among users working with creative tasks. Apple shortened the name to Mac in the late 1990s, and at the beginning of the millennium, its laptop, in particular, achieved great success and – perhaps due to its still high price – also achieved a cult-like status as a symbol of freedom and individuality. In October 1991, the Danish company PPU launched the Maconomy financial system for Macintosh. The product, which had a graphical user interface, got a lot of media coverage, but Macintosh wasn't a platform for administrative computing, and with a price of 4,200 USD for a single user, Maconomy was significantly more expensive than any other product on the market. |
| Magellan project, the. | Microsoft's Magellan was a financial system for very small businesses that was to compete with the then market-dominant product Quicken from Intuit. Microsoft attempted to buy Intuit in the mid-1990s, but the initiative was stopped by the US competition authorities. Microsoft was going to try to take market share from Intuit with Magellan, which, at that time, held over 60 per cent of the US market. |
| Mainframe | The word "mainframe" comes from the quite large cabinets that the first computers on the market in the late 1950s required. Later, it became the term for large and powerful computers, which, in contrast to the later mini- and microcomputers, required special rooms with raised floors and cooling systems. Large data centres today are furnished similarly to those earlier mainframe installations, but now the cabinets contain dozens of cheap standard components. |
| Matrix printer | Numbers, letters and simple graphics were formed by a print head with pins punching through a coloured ribbon to leave marks on the paper. Matrix printers were widely used until HP launched a cheap laser printer in May 1984. |
| Maxisoft | Maxisoft was the name of Brdr. Damgaard Data's first financial management system, which they presented at the Office & Data Exhibition at the Bella Center in 1984. As the competitor HERA-DATA used the term "Maxi" for a version of its program, Maxisoft was renamed Danmax. |

| | |
|---|---|
| MB | MB is an abbreviation of megabyte, meaning a million bytes. In reality, a megabyte is often more than one million bytes (see byte). |
| Method, the. | See OnTarget. |
| Microcomputer | In the mid-1970s, "microcomputer" became the name for a small, relatively inexpensive computer, where most of the key components were placed on a single printed circuit board and where the entire system was delivered together with a screen and keyboard. In the mid-1980s, the term was replaced by "Personal Computer" or "PC". |
| Microsoft Excel | A spreadsheet program from Microsoft, launched in 1987. With Version 5, which came on the market in 1993, Excel constantly increased its market shares. |
| Microsoft Office | Microsoft Office is a series of applications sold as a single suite, typically including Word, Excel, PowerPoint, OneNote and Outlook. The package was announced by Bill Gates at the Comdex Exhibition in Las Vegas in August 1988 and was ready for delivery in November 1990. |
| Microsoft Power-Point | A program for presentations from Microsoft, launched in May 1990. |
| Microsoft SQL | A database system from Microsoft. The first edition was launched in April 1989. |
| Microsoft Windows | Microsoft Windows was Microsoft's first operating system using a graphical user interface known from Apple Computers' Macintosh (Apple Computers actually sued Microsoft for violating their rights. A settlement was reached in 1993). With Windows95, launched in August 1995, Microsoft continued its monopoly-like status in the market for PC operating systems. Windows95 was a huge step forward for Microsoft and featured a number of technical improvements that drove IBM's OS/2 out of the market. Despite Windows95 being delayed several times, the product was very much supported by software developers around the world, and an enormous marketing investment ensured the product tremendous attention prior to its launch. |
| Microsoft Word | Microsoft Word is a word processing program, launched in October 1983, which has gained market share over the years and is the most widely used today (2018). |
| Microsoft Works | Microsoft Works was a simple and cheaper (40 USD) alternative to Microsoft Office, which was launched in 1987. Due to its low price, and as it was often preinstalled on new PCs, the product was quite popular. The product was replaced by Microsoft Office Starter Edition in 1999. |
| Middleware | Middleware is a common term for that software between the operating system and the application. |

| | |
|---|---|
| Minicomputer | The term "minicomputer" was introduced with the launch of the VAX computer from Digital Equipment Corporation in 1977. By modern standards, there is nothing "mini" about the minicomputer, but, in the 1970s, when they were compared to mainframes, it was a fitting term. |
| MRK | The Marketing, Research and Communication company, where Preben Damgaard had a student job in the early 1980s. |
| MS-DOS | See DOS. |
| MSF | Microsoft Solution Framework (MSF) is a set of principles, models, disciplines, concepts and guidelines for the development and delivery of software products and services. MSF was developed by Microsoft for internal use, but was released for external use in 1993. |
| MS-SQL | See Microsoft SQL. |
| Native filesystem | The data and file management system that Damgaard Data developed for Concorde XAL was called "Native". |
| Navi-Hub | Navi-Hub was the name of a development project initiated by Navision Software prior to the merger with Damgaard, which was to enable the delivery of information services directly to users of the company's products via the internet. For example, information required for credit checking customers could be downloaded from the software whenever a user needed it. The project was continued after the merger and expanded to include all of the company's products, but was suspended after Microsoft bought the company. |
| Navigator | Navigator was the name of a financial management system developed by PC&C, which was launched in October 1987 and distributed in Denmark by IBM until December 1994. |
| Navision Attain | When Damgaard Data merged with Navision Software, all the products were renamed. Navision Financials, which was renamed Navision Solutions in a new edition, was further renamed Navision Attain after the merger with Damgaard Data. |
| Navision Financials | In 1995, PC&C changed its name to Navision Software, and launched the first global financial management system, Navision Financials, that was certified for Microsoft Windows 95. |
| Navision Solutions | Navision Financials changed its name to Navision Solutions in December 2000, shortly before the merger with Damgaard. When the merged company changed its name from NavisonDamgaard to Navision in February 2001, all products were renamed and Navision Solutions became Navision Attain. |
| NCR | Cash register manufacturer NCR Corporation (National Cash Register) was founded in 1884 in Ohio. From the 1960s and until the company was acquired by AT&T, NCR was active in almost every area of IT and even had solid representation in Denmark. |

| | |
|---|---|
| Netscape | Netscape Navigator was the most widely used web browser in the early 1990s with a market share of over 90 per cent. That position was quickly eroded when Microsoft included its free web browser, Internet Explorer, in the operating system with Windows 95. |
| Netware | Software from Novell enabled software programs on PCs to share, for instance, data and computer equipment. |
| New Line | See ACE. |
| Nixdorf | Nixdorf Computer AG was a German computer company founded by Heinz Nixdorf in 1952. In the 1980s, the company had more than 30,000 employees and was Europe's fourth largest IT producer. Nixdorf overlooked the possibilities and threats of the PC wave and, after reporting large deficits for a number of years, was acquired by Siemens Informationssysteme in 1990, which also changed its name to Siemens Nixdorf Information System (SNI). |
| Norsk Data | Norsk Data was a computer manufacturer established in Oslo, Norway, in 1967. The company was most active from the early 1970s to the end of the 1980s. At its peak in 1987, it was Norway's second largest company with more than 4,500 employees. The company had offices in several countries, including a large and quite active branch in Denmark. Norsk Data failed to respond quickly enough to the PC wave and was almost dissolved as early as 1992. |
| Novell | See Netware. |
| Object-oriented Programming | Object-Oriented Programming (OOP) is a method of separating data and program logic in such a way that you can reuse the same program logic in different contexts and divide large programs into smaller self-contained modules (objects). OOP makes developing large programs and distributing that development to separate organisational entities easier. |
| OEM | OEM stands for Original Equipment Manufacturer: the term for companies that manufacture products, which are included in other companies' products. |
| Office & Data | See Kontor&Data |
| Olivetti | Olivetti started in Ivrea, in Northern Italy, in 1909, as a producer of typewriters and became a player in the IT industry in the 1980s after several barely successful attempts in the 1960s and 1970s. The IBM-enabled PC M24, launched in 1983, formed much of the basis for the company's success. When the PC market experienced frequent product shifts and rapidly falling prices during the 1990s, Olivetti couldn't keep up and it eventually sold off its PC business in 1997. |

| | |
|---|---|
| Olivetti M24 | Olivetti M24 was launched by Italian Olivetti in 1984, making the company the third largest supplier of PCs in Europe for a short period of time. The machine was also sold on OEM contracts by AT&T and XEROX in the USA, but it didn't achieve the same popularity. When Damgaard Data introduced Concorde in 1986 and was to deliver multi-user solutions with Novell Netware, the M24 had technical problems, which could, thankfully, be solved by replacing the keyboard. |
| Online | Online refers to a user having direct access to the computer and receiving an immediate response to their input. This is how all computers work today, but in the IT industry's youth and until the introduction of minicomputers – and microcomputers, in particular – this wasn't the case. Today, the term is most frequently used in relation to accessing the internet. Someone without access to the internet is offline. |
| OnTarget | OnTarget was the name of a comprehensive program of business development tools developed by Navision Software's subsidiary in Spain, which was to be used to professionalise all aspects of their resellers' businesses. In the 1990s, both Navision Software and Damgaard Data experienced how the capacity of their reseller channels limited the growth of their market share. Therefore, both companies invested considerable resources into recruiting new resellers and helping existing resellers to expand their business. After the merger of Navision Software and Damgaard, the OnTarget project changed its name to The Method and was to be used by all the company's resellers in all countries. |
| Operating system | An operating system manages the very basic tasks, such as starting up the computer, reading the user's keyboard entries, sending signals to the screen, retrieving and sending data to be processed by the computer to and from the hard drive, floppy disks and communication ports |
| Oracle | Oracle is the name of both the company that started in 1997 in California, and its first product, which was a relational database. The Oracle database became almost an industry standard for particularly large IT installations and, in the 1990s, Damgaard Data developed Concorde XAL to be able to use it. |
| OS/2 | OS/2 was an operating system for PCs started jointly by IBM and Microsoft in 1985. The first version was released in December 1987, but didn't gain any significant market share. In 1990, Microsoft pulled out of the partnership to invest in its own Windows operating system instead, while IBM continued to invest billions in further developing OS/2. |

| | |
|---|---|
| OSF/1 | Open Systems Foundation was a partnership between a wide range of UNIX-based systems suppliers, which was to lead to a joint version of UNIX for the benefit of both customers and suppliers. The collaboration, initiated by Digital Equipment Corporation in 1988, quickly gained support from Apollo Computer, Groupe Bull, Hewlett-Packard, IBM, Nixdorf Computer and Siemens AG, while Sun and AT&T chose to stand alone. OSF ceased its activities in 1994, when several of the companies were struggling with major financial difficulties and it proved that UNIX couldn't win the battle for users, who preferred Windows from Microsoft, whose offer of cheap user software was growing steadily. |
| OUP | An abbreviation of "organisationsudviklingsprojekt" in Danish; the major organisational development project initiated by Damgaard Data in 1993. |
| Partner | See reseller. |
| Pascal | Pascal is a programming language developed by Swiss computer scientist Niklaus E. Wirth in 1968-69, first published in 1970 and named after the French mathematician and physicist Blaise Pascal (1623-1662), who was also one of the first inventors of the calculator. Damgaard Data's first two products, Danmax and Concorde, were written in Pascal. |
| Passat principle, the. | The culture of Damgaard Data gave its employees very wide scope, including the delegation to make decisions that could have major financial consequences. The slogan, guiding many decisions that couldn't immediately establish a close relationship between investment and dividends, was the "Passat principle" (with the VW Passat car as a symbol): the sensible solution that was neither cheap and flimsy nor expensive or extravagant. |
| PC Personal Computer | See IBM PC. |
| PC-DOS | See DOS. |
| PC&C | PC&C (Personal Computing and Consulting) was started by college friends, Jesper Balser, Torben Vind and Peter Bang on 2nd November 1984. It launched its first financial management system, PCPLUS, in 1985. Berendsen Computer Products distributed PCPLUS until October 1987, when PC&C entered a distribution agreement with IBM Denmark for their new product Navigator. After that, Damgaard Data took over the distribution of PCPLUS. In 1995, the company changed its name to Navision Software; in spring 1999, the company was introduced on the Copenhagen Stock Exchange, and in December 2000 they merged with Damgaard Data. |

| | |
|---|---|
| PCPLUS | PCPLUS, launched at the Office & Data Exhibition in autumn 1985, was the first financial system from the company PC&C (later Navision Software). The product was designed for the first versions of the DOS operating system from Microsoft and placed great emphasis on design and user-friendliness. Until October 1986, it was distributed by Berendsen Computer Products. When PC&C signed an agreement with IBM to distribute its new product, Navigator, Damgaard Data took over the distribution of PCPLUS. |
| PDP | Programmed Data Processor (PDP) was a series of minicomputers from Digital Equipment Corporation, which achieved great success in the period between 1957 and 1990. |
| Performance | The term "performance" is used frequently within the IT industry. Despite the performance of computer systems being doubled since the 1980s with 18-24 month intervals (a phenomenon called Moore's law) and prices simultaneously decreasing, the interaction between users' needs and the software developers' imagination has continuously managed to exploit the increased performance to the full. Therefore, we can still experience computer systems running slowly, despite the capacity available on even our mobile phones far exceeding the total capacity available to the USA when it sent the first humans to the moon and back in 1969. |
| Personal Computer | The term Personal Computer or PC was already used in the early 1970s in Xerox's Palo Alto Research Center (PARC). However, it was IBM, with the launch of its first 16-bit Personal Computer in August 1982 that took ownership of the concept. It wasn't the computer itself that started a revolution of the IT industry, but rather the business model that IBM chose to employ. Almost every component was taken from other suppliers and the operating system was developed by Microsoft. IBM didn't copyright the design and, thereby, enabled others to produce both hardware and software, which kick-started major competition that pushed prices down and demand up. This meant that first smaller companies and later private consumers could have PCs. |
| Platform | Platform is a term used in the IT industry to describe a number of related hardware and software components required for using a software application. |
| PolyData | PolyData was one of Denmark's biggest importers and distributors of hardware and software in the 1980s. |
| PolyPascal | PolyPascal was a version of the Pascal development language developed by Dane Anders Hejlsberg and marketed by PolyData. |
| PolySoft | PolySoft was a software company of the PolyData Group, which developed the financial management programs PolySoft and Albatros (see PolyData and Albatros). |

| | |
|---|---|
| Porting | Porting is the process of customising software so that it can run in a computer environment that differs from that for which it was originally designed (e.g., different CPUs or operating systems). |
| PowerPoint | Software from Microsoft for making presentations. |
| Pre-sales | Selling solutions within the IT industry often requires preparing detailed offers, demonstrating the products and answering technical questions. This work, which doesn't directly concern the commercial terms of sale, is called pre-sales. |
| Prime Computer | Prime Computer, Inc. Massachusetts, was a producer of minicomputers from 1972 to 1992. The alternative spellings "PR-1ME" and "PR1ME Computer" were used as company names or logos by the company. |
| Private label | Private label is an expression covering products marketed under a name other than that of the manufacturer. The phenomenon is widely used in all industries and is used when companies consider their own brand to be strengthened by suppressing the original producer's name. |
| Product management | Product management is the discipline (and in larger companies often an independent organisational entity) dealing with maximising the yield of a product or product line over its entire life cycle. |
| Product marketing | Product marketing is the discipline (and in larger companies often an independent organisational entity) responsible for formulating, illustrating and communicating how the company's products can create value for customers and partners in such a way that they clearly differ and appear more attractive than the competitors' products. |
| Project Dambuster | The project name for preparing Damgaard's stock market listing, which happened on 8th October 1999. |
| Project Hveen | The project name for the preparation of the merger between Damgaard and Navision Software, which happened on 21st December 2000. |
| ProjectPartner | The name of an ambitious project management method that Damgaard Data developed and introduced to the largest resellers in 1992-1995. |
| PS/2 | See Personal System/2. |
| Raikes, Jeff | During the acquisition of Navision and until 2008, Jeffrey Scott Raikes (1958) was president of Microsoft Business Division. |
| Rasmussen, Helmuth | Owner of HERA-DATA and developer of HERA-SOFT. |
| RC | See Regnecentralen. |

| | |
|---|---|
| RC-Partner | RC-Partner was Danish company Regnecentralen's replacement for the Piccolo microcomputer, which was again replaced by Piccolinen in 1984. Regnecentralen's microcomputers used the CP/M operating system and, later, as 16-bit processors gained ground, the CPM-86. The systems experienced considerable success, primarily because they had a monopoly-like position in Danish primary and secondary schools and colleges, and they even experienced some success in the private sector. When Microsoft's DOS operating system won the market, Regnecentralen failed to adjust and quickly lost its otherwise good position on the Danish market (see also Regnecentralen). |
| Regnecentralen | Regnecentralen, founded in 1955, was the first Danish computer manufacturer. Despite the company employing highly qualified technicians and developing advanced products, it had difficulty selling its products outside of Denmark. The company became too dependent on the domestic market and didn't get the production volume needed to keep up with the development. Regnecentralen was acquired by the British company ICL in 1989 (see also RC-Partner). |
| Release | Release is used in the IT industry in different contexts. It's used to indicate a version of a product with a specific purpose. Thus, a beta release is for testing purposes only, while a general release is for production purposes. It's also used to specify the time at which a product is ready for a particular purpose. |
| Reseller | In Damgaard Data's sales concept, the reseller is the company, which manages the relationship with the customers and assists them in implementing and supporting the products (see also Distributor). |
| Response time | Within IT, the response time is the time that elapses from when an IT user presses the return key until there is a response from the computer. Even today, when most computer systems have very high capacity, long response times can be a problem. Many bottlenecks can cause long response times, but often it's down to the interaction between the number of transactions, the number of concurrent users and the way in which the software is developed that causes the overall system to be unacceptably slow. |
| Riis, Jens | Jens Riis (now Svanholdt) was a software developer and employee number four in Damgaard Data. |
| Royal Oaks | See Atlanta. |
| Sabanci University | A relatively young (1995) and well-reputed private university with campuses in and around Istanbul in Turkey. |

| | |
|---|---|
| Sandbagging | Sandbagging is a well-known phenomenon in all major companies whereby budget managers battle to get their sales targets as low as possible and their cost targets as high as possible. If successful, they can reach their budget more easily and successfully, ensuring they receive their bonuses. The phenomenon also includes all managers giving their employees higher targets than they themselves have. That way managers can achieve their targets, despite their employees not reaching theirs. |
| SAP | SAP (Systeme, Anwendungen und Produkte in der Datenverarbeitung) was founded in 1970 in Germany by five system developers from IBM. Until mid-1995, the company's software ran exclusively on mainframes, after which it gradually introduced products that could run on PCs and UNIX machines. SAP, which was stock market listed in 1988, is currently the world's largest supplier of financial management systems and related products to large and medium-sized companies. |
| Senge, Peter M. | Peter M. Senge (born 1949) is an American author and founder of The Society for Organizational Learning. In 1990, he published the book *The Fifth Discipline: The Art and Practice of the Learning Organisation*. Senge introduced the term "learning organisation", which is based on the conscious development of the individual employee's ability to realise their own visions, which, thereby, create the dynamics that develop the entire company. |
| Service bureau | Service bureau was an expression that emerged in the 1960s: the majority of companies didn't have their own IT systems but rather had their IT tasks carried out by companies that owned large computer systems and executed IT tasks for many companies, which each paid for the capacity they used. Throughout the 1980s and 1990s, many companies acquired their own IT systems, and service bureaux experienced hard times. After the breakthrough of the internet and a significant improvement in data communication capacity, the service bureau concept has gone through a renaissance as cloud computing and Software-as-a-Service. |
| Silicon Graphics | Silicon Graphics (later SGI) was launched in Mountain View, California, in November 1981. The company was known for developing and producing highly powerful UNIX workstations, which were mainly used for engineering purposes – and the generation of 3D graphics in particular. During the 1990s, the company faced strong competition from PCs, which were growing ever more powerful while continuously falling in price. Many technical and graphical software programs, which had previously been used primarily on Silicon Graphics computers, were now being ported to cheaper PC systems. The company first filed for bankruptcy in May 2006, and the remains of the company were sold for next to nothing in April 2009. |

| | |
|---|---|
| Software-as-a-Service | Software-as-a-Service means subscribing to a software program. Typically, the program is run on computers installed in large data centres, which the provider organises while the user interacts with the program via their web browser. However, there is nothing to prevent all or part of the program from running on the user's own computer while data is being synchronised and stored on a central server. In 2016, Erik Damgaard launched the new Unicota financial management system, delivered as Software-as-a-Service, whereby the program is delivered to the user via a component running on their computer. This form of delivery (which doesn't use a web browser) allows for a more customised user interface, which is better suited to the task that the software is to carry out. |
| Software-fabrikken | Softwarefabrikken [the Software factory] was an activity started in 1995 under Damgaard Data ServicePartner, where resellers could purchase development capacity for smaller projects. |
| Source code | Source code is the text of a programming language written by the programmer. The source code can either be interpreted and executed directly by the computer or compiled (translated) to machine code for later use on the computer. Thus, source code can be read and understood by programmers who know the programming language in which the source code is written. To change a piece of software, you need to have the source code, which is why some software contracts require the delivery of the source code (see also compiler). |
| Sperry | Sperry Corporation (1910-1986) was an American company that, via a number of acquisitions, entered the computer industry and developed mainframes under the name UNIVAC and achieved significant success throughout the 1970s. The company merged with competitor Burroughs and changed its name to Unisys in 1986. |
| SQL | Structured Query Language: a method of handling data in a database. |
| Standard Edition | Standard Edition was a version of Axapta with limited functionality that could only run on a Microsoft SQL Server Express database. The product was intended for smaller companies that could upgrade, once they developed, to Axapta Professional Edition and from there to Enterprise Edition. After the merger with Navision Software, Standard Edition was removed from the product list as it competed directly with Navision Attain. |
| Subscription | Software products are virtual, which means that the marginal cost of producing an additional copy is close to nothing. Therefore, it's attractive for software manufacturers to provide customers with access to new versions with error corrections and new features in exchange for paying a fixed annual subscription sum, rather than paying full price each time. |

| | |
|---|---|
| Sun Microsystems | Sun Microsystems, Inc. founded on 24th February 1982 in Santa Clara, California (part of Silicon Valley), became most famous for its quite powerful UNIX (Solaris) workstations as well as for developing the Java programming language, the Solaris operating system and the NFS file system. Sun contributed significantly to the development of several key computer technologies, including UNIX, RISC processors, thin client computers and virtualised computing, but, after the dotcom bubble burst in 2001, it was severely hit by falling sales and subsequent major losses. On 27th January 2010, Oracle Corporation purchased Sun for 7.4 billion USD. |
| Support | "Support" in the IT industry refers to both helping customers use products and to the continued development of a software product. However, the word "service" typically refers to the maintenance and repair of hardware. |
| SWAT | Special Weapons And Tactics. The term is often used in business to describe a small group temporarily brought in to tackle a difficult problem. |
| System 2 | A new financial management system developed by FK-Data as a replacement for FK-Soft, based on Damgaard Data's Maxisoft. |
| System integrator | A system integrator is a company that helps its customers design and implement IT systems, which often require that sub-systems developed by different vendors interact. |
| Tatung | Tatung was a Taiwanese electronics and computer company with its development department in the UK and production in Taiwan. |
| Testimonial | Customer testimonials are quite often an important factor in companies deciding to invest heavily in new IT solutions. Crucial for the vast majority of companies is that they aren't the first to use a new technology; that they can see it operating in other companies. Therefore, suppliers of IT solutions work hard on targeting as many customers as possible to act as references. In other words, suppliers can make public the customer relationship and that customer is ready and willing to tell other (potential) customers about their experience. |
| Thy Data Center | EDB-Butikken [the EDP Shop] was founded by Egon Østergaard in Thisted, North Jutland, in 1986, as a reseller of FK-Soft. In 1991, Egon Østergaard entered into a partnership with Per Møller and after receiving an angry letter from another company by the same name, they changed their name to Thy Data Center. Within a few years, the company was one of the largest and most loyal Concorde XAL resellers in Denmark. Thy Data Center also initiated the development of independent program modules for Concorde XAL, and later Axapta, which were sold via other resellers. To support product development activities, they were separated into the independent company Dynaway. Both Thy Data Center and Dynaway were acquired by EG A/S in 2011. |

| | |
|---|---|
| Token Ring | A Token Ring is a technology for connecting computers. As products for connecting PCs emerged in the mid-1980s, most manufacturers supported the Ethernet technology developed by Xerox. So as to avoid a competitive rat race controlled by others, IBM invested heavily in developing and maturing the alternative Token Ring technology in the 1980s. On paper, Token Ring had a number of advantages, but in practice it turned out that the much cheaper Ethernet was able to handle the same tasks. IBM experienced some initial success with Token Ring with its core customers in the financial world and in the public sector, but the wide spread of Ethernet ensured rapid development and constantly falling prices that even large companies and public institutions couldn't ignore. Token Ring lost the battle to Ethernet (see also Ethernet). |
| Transactions | In an IT context "transaction" refers to the completion of a task. For example, if you buy a book via the internet, the transaction includes both ordering, delivery and payment. Only if all parts of the transaction are successful is the overall transaction successful. Dimensioning a computer system to handle a given amount of transactions within a given time frame and a given response time is by no means a trivial task. All computer system subcomponents, such as the computers, data media, network, operating system, database system, application program, network, and so on can have a decisive influence on how fast transactions can be processed. |
| TurboPascal | TurboPascal was a software development system for Pascal's programming language developed by Dane Anders Hejlsberg and originally sold through the company PolyData. Damgaard Data's first two products, Danmax and Concorde, were developed using TurboPascal |
| Ultrix | Ultrix was a variant of the UNIX operating system, which ran on minicomputers from Digital Equipment Corporation (see UNIX and Digital Equipment Corporation). |
| UNIX | UNIX is an operating system originally developed by AT&T for internal use and use on many different types of hardware. As AT&T allowed academic and public institutions to use UNIX without paying, it won enormous market penetration. Many users developed extensions for the system, thereby making it a complete operating system that could be used as an alternative to the commercial and proprietary operating systems from hardware manufacturers. |
| VAX | VAX (Virtual Address eXtension) was a series of minicomputers from Digital Equipment Corporation (DEC), launched in the mid-1970s, which achieved immense success (see also Digital Equipment Corporation). |

| | |
|---|---|
| Version | As software, unlike many other product types, can be further developed and new features continuously added, which the user can immediately utilise (but can also choose not to use for several reasons), version numbers are attached to the different editions. |
| Vice President | An American job title; a high position, which, however, isn't included in the company's top management. |
| Wang Laboratories | Wang Laboratories was founded in 1951 and until its bankruptcy in 1992 had offices in Massachusetts. In the 1980s, Wang Laboratories had an annual turnover of 3 billion USD and employed over 33,000 people. Wang became particularly known for word processing systems and what was called Desktop Publishing (DTP) in the 1980s. |
| WordPerfect | WordPerfect was a word processing program developed in the late 1970s for Data General for delivery on their minicomputers. The developers retained the rights to the program and formed Satellite Software International (SSI) to sell it under the name WordPerfect in 1980. A porting to MS-DOS followed in 1982. The program's list of functions was significantly more advanced than the main competitor WordStar, which dominated the market for microcomputers with the CP/M operating system. WordPerfect quickly replaced the majority of other systems, especially after the release of Version 4.2 in 1986. When 5.1 was released in 1989, WordPerfect became an industry standard on the DOS market. When Microsoft Windows charged forward in the mid-1990s, WordPerfect launched a number of versions that malfunctioned and were difficult to use. At the same time, Microsoft launched highly-improved versions of its own word processing system Word, including the ability to run the program with known Word-Perfect commands. Within a few years, WordPerfect completely lost its leadership position in the market for word processing systems. |
| XAL | See Concorde XAL. |
| XAL Services | XAL Services is the name of the subsidiaries established by Damgaard International to educate and support the resellers in the countries where IBM handled the distribution. |
| Zilog Inc. | Zilog Inc. was founded in 1974 by two engineers from Intel Corporation and developed the Z80 microprocessor, which was bit compatible with the Intel 8080 processor. Zilog Inc. chose to outsource the production of Z80 to various manufacturers, who then competed against each other, driving prices down and demand up. |

Hans Peter Bech

## **About the author**

Hans Peter Bech, cand. polit. (born 1951), has been working with international business development, marketing, sales and leadership for almost 40 years.

Starting out as a sales trainee for Control Data Corporation in 1980, he was promoted to sales manager in 1982. From 1986 Hans Peter worked for several start-ups, building their global marketing and sales organisations.

He joined Damgaard Data in 1997 and was responsible for their activities in the German-speaking markets. After the merger with Navision Software in 2000, he was appointed Vice President, Central Europe.

In 2001, he returned to Denmark and founded the consultancy firm TBK Consult. Since 2008, he has been blogging about international business development.

He published his first book *Management Consulting Essentials* in 2013 and, in 2015, he released *Building Successful Partner Channels*, which became an international bestseller.

Hans Peter lives with his wife, Sue, in Hillerød, Denmark. He has two children and seven grandchildren, enjoys travelling, skiing, biking, hiking and plays guitar and sings in two bands.

Made in the USA
Columbia, SC
21 April 2020